D1578301

What's the Point in Discussion?

Donald Bligh

intellect™
EXETER, ENGLAND
PORTLAND, OR, USA

First Published in Paperback in 2000 by
Intellect Books, FAE, Earl Richards Road North, Exeter EX2 6AS, UK

First Published in USA in 2000 by
Intellect Books, ISBS, 5804 N.E. Hassalo St, Portland, Oregon 97213-3644, USA

Consulting Editor:	Masoud Yazdani
Cover Illustration:	Julie Payne
Copy Editor:	Wendi Momen
Production:	Sally Ashworth

A catalogue record for this book is available from the British Library

ISBN 1-871516-69-2

Printed and bound in Great Britain by Cromwell Press, Wiltshire

Contents

Preface

This book is particularly concerned with using discussion for the promotion of thought and, to a lesser extent, the development of attitudes. Thought is central to the work of a university and crucial for democracy. I have written primarily in the context of university teaching, but the ideas are relevant for teachers at all levels and to discussions in many other contexts.

The aim of this book

My aim is to give teachers information to help them use, and diversify, their teaching by discussion. Most university teachers are, of course, highly professional as historians, physicists, lawyers, geographers, surgeons and so on. But as teachers, they cannot claim to be professional until they can claim special training and competence as teachers. (Special competence, implying a special education to acquire it, is central to nearly all definitions of 'professions' and 'professionalism'.) As teachers, most university academics do not have that special education. The special education needs to be grounded in a recognised body of knowledge. As a generalisation, university teachers do not have that knowledge. The same could be said about most education and training in industry and the professions. My working life has been largely devoted to supplying some of that knowledge whilst preserving teachers' freedom in how to apply it. This book, like its predecessors, is to serve that purpose.

The sheer quantity of knowledge required to understand what goes on in discussions is vast and complex. It includes many areas that are disciplines in their own right. I am aware that my treatment of some of these disciplines is superficial. Even so, I expect that some university teachers will find the quantity of information in this book more demanding than they would wish. I make no apology for that. University teachers and staff developers must face the need to develop the intellectual bases of their work. They expect it of lawyers, engineers and doctors. Let them apply the same rigour to themselves.

Its organisation

Partly because of its complexity, the book has been nearly 30 years in gestation. It was always planned as a sequel to *What's the Use of Lectures?* It has the same basic form. That is to say, in Part I it starts with finding out what objectives discussions can achieve and then asks what factors affect the achievement of them. To the second question, it gets two answers. The discussion group's task will influence what is achieved (Part II). So will the factors influencing how group members interact (Part III). These two sets of influences provide evidence that, both from the students' and the teachers' points of view, it is best to '*Start with simple tasks in small groups for short periods of time, and then gradually increase their respective complexity, size and duration*'. I have called this my maxim. It implies the need to use a developmental sequence of discussion methods. Look at Figure 21.1 on page 193. Part IV describes and explains that sequence.

I don't mean to imply that teachers and students must use every method earlier in the sequence before any later one. But the common practice of expecting new undergraduates to handle group tutorials and seminar techniques before they have learned basic discussion and thinking skills, is foolish.

Nor do I mean to imply that methods earlier in the sequence should be abandoned when later ones are accomplished. Quite the contrary. New methods expand a teacher's repertoire. An infinite variety makes teaching fun.

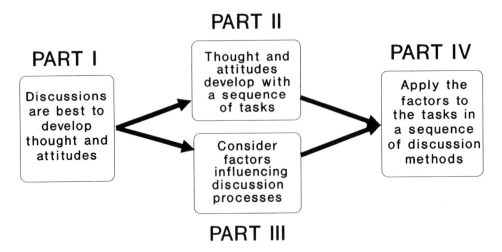

How not to read this book

It's not a novel. Don't start at page 1 and read through to the end. If you have a perfect memory, that's fine. You will then see how all the facts culminate in the sequence of methods described in Part IV. That's where it's all leading to.

The steps of the argument lead from Part I to Parts II and III, and then to Part IV. That's why they are presented in that order. But when understanding an argument it is usually best to see where it's all leading to first.

So if your memory is not perfect, turn first to Part IV and read all the major headings. Get the shape of how it develops. Then read the minor headings if you wish; or go back straight away to Part I. Turn the pages reading the headings as you go. Try to grasp the structure of how the argument in the book goes from step to step. Summaries at the end of sections and chapters should help, particularly the conclusion on pages 217 and 218 at the end of Chapter 21. As you turn the pages, if you see areas that interest you and you want to dip into the text, go ahead. Do the same with the diagrams.

Parts II and IV are sequential so it's probably best to read them that way, but you don't have to. In Parts I and III the chapters are separate items and could be read in any order. The conclusion at the end of Part I is a convenient summary of that part. Regarding Part III, I particularly recommend dipping in as points there interest you when reading other parts of the book. Treat Part III a bit like a reference book. Don't try to read it straight through. There's a lot to take in and think about all at once.

From this, you will see that parts of the book need to be read in different ways. That's true of most books because ideas connect in various ways. Readers should find their own set of connections by dipping in where they want, in the order they want.

Acknowledgements

I have several acknowledgements. I must thank the Scottish Education Department, Martin Shaw and Eva Forbes for assistance to review the literature; James Kilty, Elisabeth Dunne, Jessica Claridge, Masoud Yazdani and Barbara for reading early drafts; and David Jaques for supplying some information on delphi and pyramid groups. My thanks also go to Intellect Books for their continuing support and patience.

Part I

What can Discussion Achieve?

In this part I shall consider the questions whether small group discussion can appropriately be used to teach
1. information (Chapter 1),
2. thinking skills (Chapter 2),
3. affect – by which I mean attitudes, feelings, motivation, values and morals (Chapter 3), and
4. interpersonal skills (Chapter 4).

The quickest way to read Part I is to look at the Conclusion on page 27 at the end of Chapter 4. It gives short answers to those four questions. Then read the headings in bold print and think about each in turn before going to the next one. You will see they answer the questions by looking first at educational, and then psychological evidence.

Chapter 1
Discussion is effective, but not efficient, to teach information

A. Educational research

B. Psychological research

C. Conclusion

The need for brevity makes the title of this chapter a bit sweeping. First, it's obviously not true for every discussion that ever took place. Second, effectiveness and efficiency are relative. They're a matter of comparing one method with another. So I shall be prepared to argue, 'Discussion is *usually* as effective as other methods to teach information, but it is not always as efficient.'

On the face of it, students acquire information when presented with it by experts or authorities in lectures, on television, in films, in books, on the Internet, on audiotapes and so on. These are called presentation methods. They can be contrasted with discussion methods in which the learners contribute by talking.

From the teacher's point of view there are two anxieties about students' learning in discussion groups, particularly if the teacher is not a member of the group and can't correct students' errors:

'Will students learn misinformation?' That's a question about the *effectiveness* of group discussions.

And 'Aren't discussions too time consuming for the amount of information students need to know nowadays?' That's a question about their *efficiency*.

So the questions that arise are, 'What are the relative effectiveness and efficiency of discussion and presentation methods?'

A. Educational research

What research is there? Fortunately, there have been a number of educational studies, though few recently, of the relative effectiveness of discussion groups and other methods to teach information in classroom settings. Experimental comparisons of discussion with other teaching methods, where tests of factual information have been the criteria of effectiveness, are summarised in Table 1.1. I have separated reports of discussions in which teachers participate (tutored discussions) from those in which the teacher is not a member (tutorless discussions). For the details see Appendix 1.1.

1. Tutored discussion and presentations are equally effective to teach information

It will be seen that, overall, there is little difference between the effectiveness of presentation and discussion methods when the teacher is a discussion member. The teacher's first anxiety is not well founded. In fact, tutored discussions are slightly more effective than lectures when measured by a delayed test. This could be because individuals particularly remember facts associated with what they themselves have said.

The number of experimental comparisons of discussion with presentation methods where acquisition of information is the main criterion

Teaching Method	Discussion more effective	No significant difference	Other methods more effective
Tutored Groups	37	2	3
Tutorless Groups	15	16	6

Table 1.1. Discussions are at least equally effective as other methods to teach information

You will see from Appendix 1.1 that the most common method to be compared with discussion has been lectures. You might ask whether a comparison with other presentation methods would produce a different result. There aren't many published comparisons with teaching on the Internet yet, but the general answer is 'No'. There is a great deal of evidence that presentation methods are all equally effective in teaching information. Dubin and Taveggia (1968) summarised hundreds of comparisons of lectures, reading, discussions and other kinds of face-to-face teaching and found no difference between them. Chu and Schramm (1967) reviewed 202 comparisons of television with lectures and traditional classroom teaching at the college level and found them equally effective. Dubin and Hedley (1969) looked at 191 comparisons of television and traditional teaching and also found no difference.

2. Tutorless discussions with short simple tasks can sometimes be more effective than presentation methods

With that knowledge I expected there to be no difference between tutorless discussions and other methods. But, as you see, far from learning misinformation, on balance there is some evidence that tutorless discussions are more effective than presentation methods, not less. If I had included another 60 studies from primary schools, the imbalance would have been far stronger. That, too, is surprising. I should have expected children at primary level to be far less competent at helping each other than university students. Indeed, whilst some studies show that teachers explain better than children (eg. Power et al, 1985), several find no difference, and a few have found pupils *more* effective (eg. Greenwood, 1984 and Romer et al, 1985).

How can this be? The answer, it seems, is that peers are particularly effective at teaching each other when the process has been structured in small steps for them. That is to say, when there are a lot of simple tasks that do not take long, rather than one larger task that takes the same time in total (Tans et al, 1986; Yager et al, 1985). This illustrates an important maxim to which I shall return again and again: *Start with simple tasks in small groups for short periods of time, and then gradually increase their respective complexity, size and duration.* In Part IV I describe ways to apply it.

Why were students and children so effective? It's not because they were so clever. It's because the teachers analysed what had to be learned into short simple tasks. Conversely, there is also some indication that when discussion is very free and unstructured, whether tutors are present or not, scores on factual tests are lower than after presentation methods such as lectures. It's analysing and structuring the tasks that's important. That's why Part II describes ways to analyse tasks.

If the effectiveness of tutorless groups were on the basis of Table 1.1 alone, I should wish to be cautious about vaunting their effectiveness. The comparisons detailed in Appendix 1.1 vary in the discussion methods used, the methods they were compared with, the material taught and the criterion measures. But you will see, as you go through this book, that there are other reasons to suppose that the use of tutorless groups is an important teaching strategy.

3. Presentation methods are more efficient to teach information

What about the second anxiety with which we began – the questions about efficiency? Even if tutored discussion methods are equally effective, common sense says that, if the class sizes for discussion have to be smaller, they are not equally efficient at conveying information compared with lectures and reading. When the teacher participates in discussion groups, the cost per student will be greater.

But again, tutorless groups are not so vulnerable to this criticism. If it is possible to organise a lot of simultaneous tutorless groups with simple tasks for short periods of time in the middle of the lecture period, the cost per student need be no greater. The class size will be no less.

Of course, unsupervised reading usually has a relatively low teaching cost and is quicker, provided students are sufficiently motivated to do it and the reading material is not too expensive. For example, the cost of an Open University student is about a quarter of a traditional full-time student at other universities. So reading is probably more cost-effective to teach facts. That is to say, reading is more efficient than lectures and discussion methods. The same might be said of the Internet, audio and video presentations once the initial costs have been met, if teaching facts is all that concerns you.

4. Use discussion to teach information combined with other objectives

We shall see evidence in the remainder of Part I that discussion methods can achieve several different kinds of objectives at the same time and this is one of their major advantages. For example, Smith et al (1982) compared discussion and individual learning and found that discussion not only resulted in better retention of information and higher levels of achievement amongst a range of ability groups, but more motivation and self-esteem as well.

It is clear from the comparisons in Table 1.1, from before-and-after tests, and from comparisons with no teaching at all, that discussion methods do teach some information. So while discussion may not always be the most efficient method for teaching information alone, it might be cost-effective to use it for that purpose combined with some other objective, such as the development of thought and attitudes.

5. Summary of educational evidence
So on the basis of educational research, as a broad generalisation, we may conclude
i) tutored discussion and classroom presentation methods are equally effective to teach information and in the long run tutored discussions may be more effective,
ii) small tutorless groups meeting with simple tasks for short periods of time may sometimes be more effective to teach information than presentation methods,
iii) discussion methods are not likely to be the most efficient method if a teacher only wants to teach information,
iv) but discussion methods will be efficient if they achieve other objectives in addition to teaching information.

B. Psychological research

The fundamental difference between discussion and reading or listening to lectures is that discussion requires interaction with others in a group. Lectures and reading are relatively individual activities, even though a hundred other people in the room may be doing the same thing. So comparisons of group and individual performance have some relevance.

1. Memorising in groups seems better than memorising individually
On the whole, psychological experiments on the differences between individuals and groups in learning information appear to favour groups when there is any difference at all. For example, in a series of maze learning experiments Gurnee (1937;1939) found that groups made fewer errors and worked quicker. In the experiment by Perlmutter and de Montmollin (1952) individuals learned two syllable nonsense words on their own while sitting in groups of three. They then performed a similar task co-operatively in the triads (I then G). As an experimental control, other students undertook co-operative learning before learning individually (G then I). This gave four sets of scores. There were five trials in each condition. The results are shown in Figure 1.2. Learning in groups was superior to individual learning and equally good whether or not the students had learned individually first. (So the scores for group learning are put together.) There is clearly a strong learning effect from one trial to the next. The steepness of the curve shows that groups learned much faster than individuals. This may be the reason why those who had experienced the group task first (G then I), performed better as individuals on their first trial. They also learned faster on

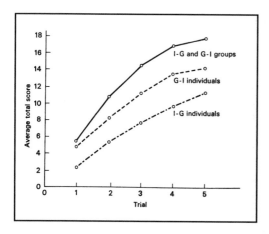

Figure 1.2.
Average learning by individuals and in groups

subsequent trials than individuals who had not experienced group work.

If this were generally true, it would have important educational implications for the value of group work upon later individual study. You may say that learning nonsense words is not the same as learning new technical terms as part of an academic discipline because the latter have meaning. (I sometimes wonder how much meaning they have for students at the time.) Anyway, you would be right that meaning aids memory, but of course that is why psychologists want to remove that variable from considering whether learning individually or in groups is better.

Superficially, other experimenters have obtained consistent results in demonstrating the superiority of groups for memory tasks. For example Yuker (1955) asked 40 groups of four to study a story, recall it first individually, then in groups and finally as individuals again. The recall scores for groups were superior to average individual recall in 38 of the 40 cases, and better than the best individual recall in 29 cases. The second individual recall was superior to the first.

2. Some reservations about groups being better

However, the superiority of groups could be an additive effect rather than indicating that individuals learn better in groups; and the last finding could simply be the result of practice, not anything to do with group interaction. So the Yuker experiment is not as convincing as Perlmutter and de Montmollin's in demonstrating the usefulness of groups for memory tasks. Gurnee's results may also have been the result of pooled knowledge rather than superior learning. Furthermore, while the Gurnee experiments appeared to test memory, they also involved some reasoning, and, as we shall see, there is a much stronger case for the superiority of groups for teaching thinking skills.

A later experiment by Perlmutter (1953) implied that a group product is partly additive and partly the result of interaction. He, again, found groups slightly, but insignificantly, superior when the task was to recall a story; but while some of what was recalled seemed to be a product of the groups, some bore the hallmarks of particular individuals. Perlmutter observed that the style of a group's product is not obviously related to the style of the individuals who compose the group. True interaction creates something new. To get the full benefit from discussion methods teachers need to ensure that there is a genuine interaction of minds leading to a joint product.

3. Discussion can aid retrieval from memory

So far we have discussed the effectiveness of presentations and discussion to teach information, as if the sole task were to get the information stored. The major problems with memory are not to do with fixing our experiences in a mental store, but in retrieving them from the store when we want them. Recent psychological evidence suggests that discussion can help people recall information when they want it for other objectives such as problem-solving and decision-making. If so, discussion may be useful when teachers have more than one type of objective.

Does organisation of the subject matter aid recall? One might think that the organisation of ideas in books, lectures and other presentations would be better than in discussion, and the ideas should be easier to retrieve. Important ideas are stated and then elaborated; and Van Dam et al (1985) have shown elaboration to be effective. But an experiment by Zimmer (1985) might imply the opposite. Students who received unstructured written material scored significantly higher on delayed multiple-choice items, generated more ideas relevant to the text, and wrote more coherent and logical essay examinations, both immediately and some time later.

A potential advantage of discussion is that it allows a given item of information to be cross-related to many others while there is a tendency in sequential presentations for connections of ideas to be more like a herringbone than a network. McDaniel (1986) has shown that where subject matter is descriptive, recall of subject matter is better when people can cross-relate it. But when memory of a sequence, such as a story or a chain of reasoning, is required, mental strategies to recall individual items (acting as signposts) are more effective. This suggests that discussion is more effective to teach a network of interconnected facts, such as descriptive material, than sequences.

One of the difficulties of research into the effectiveness of teaching methods is that one can rarely be sure that differences in effects do not partly result from strategies at the time of the test rather than the original learning. I call this the problem of temporal validity (Bligh, 1974). Adams (1985) reviewed experimental research and has suggested that people can improve retrieval from their memories by strategies such as

i) establishing landmarks or signposts amongst the material to be remembered, such as noting key words in a text or discussion,
ii) viewing the material from many points of view or in different contexts, and
iii) mentally going over the sequence of the material.

Discussion might favour someone who uses strategy (ii), while strategy (iii) is probably more appropriate to the sequence of a presentation. Strategy (i) is a technique of using cues or reminders associated with chunks of information.

One of the advantages of discussion is that the contributions of other group members give us cues so that our memory resources are well used. There is evidence that people who have good memories are good at using cues. Intons-Peterson and Smyth (1987) showed that, compared with novices, memory experts search for and repeat cues in passages to be remembered. Schacter and Worling (1987) have shown that when people feel they know something but can't quite recall it, they do in general have some knowledge about what they can't recall. What they don't have are cues or techniques to use them.

Another advantage is that memory gaps can be filled in by other group members. It seems likely that it is a decline in the ability to use cues that explains the difficulties of older people in free recall, cued recall and recognition. These tasks require conscious recollection, while tasks that require a more automatic and less conscious memory appear unaffected by age (Light and Singh, 1987). Recognition requires fewer resources than recall and these resources diminish with age (Craik and McDowd, 1987). This explains what might seem like a paradox. Elderly people learn better from discussion because cues enable the subject matter to be related to their experience. But they often feel inadequate in discussion because they cannot recall all the information they need to articulate. So they don't like the method by which they learn best.

4. Summary of psychological evidence
Psychological research still leaves a lot of questions unanswered, but some generalisations can be made if treated with caution.
i)   On the whole if individuals interact in groups, they remember material better than when working on their own,
ii) but the experimental reports leave some uncertainty about what, psychologically, went on in the groups.
iii) Discussion can aid the recall of information so that it can be used.

C. Conclusion

When the criterion of effectiveness is the ability to store information and then recall it when required, educational and psychological research agree that there is not much difference between discussion when the teacher is a group member, and presentations such as lectures and books. There is some reason to think that short tutorless discussions in carefully structured steps can be more effective than most presentations. Educational evidence leans slightly in favour of presentations insofar as they are more efficient with large classes. They may not be more efficient if a large number of small tutorless groups can be organised in a large class.

Psychological research slightly favours group co-operation using discussion. There is also psychological evidence that discussion facilitates recall so that information can be used to develop thinking or attitude change.

On balance, the two kinds of evidence point in the same direction: with the exception of multiple small short tutorless groups, discussion is not more effective than presentation methods for teaching information alone, but it has advantages when teachers want to develop thinking and attitude change as well.

Chapter 2
Discussion methods can teach thinking

A. Educational research

B. Psychological research

C. Conclusion

The conclusion from this chapter is not quite as simple as a bald heading can suggest. In this chapter I argue that discussion methods can teach thinking skills, but the right techniques will require knowledge of how these skills are learned. How do I justify this claim? As in the first chapter, there are two sources: educational research and the psychological evidence that explains it.

Most discussion groups are concerned with some kind of thinking. Committees take decisions (well sometimes!). Seminars are for constructive criticism of a presentation. De Bono claims that brainstorms can be used to generate new ideas and creative thinking. Syndicates, which I describe in Chapter 22, are intended to teach research and investigative techniques. And there is a host of small group discussion methods which purport to teach problem-solving and the mental skills that problem-solving requires – the ability to bring ideas together and see how they connect, to apply principles, to see similarities and differences, to break a problem down into simpler elements, to evaluate priorities and so on. I deal with these skills in Part II and the methods in Part IV.

A. Educational research

1. Discussion teaches thinking skills better than presentations
Can discussions teach these thinking skills better than presentation methods such as lectures? Table 2.1 (and its Appendix 2.1 on page 272) show that they can.

Admittedly the table only gives a crude comparison and there are many fewer experiments on which to base this conclusion than were available in Chapter 1. Although Appendix 2.1 gives a little more detail, it's also true that Table 2.1 does not distinguish between different discussion methods and the different types of thought mentioned in the last paragraph. Educational contexts are not sufficiently controlled to make these distinctions accurately. Moreover much of the educational research predates the revolution in cognitive psychology. The differences between different thinking skills are seen much more sharply now.

Nevertheless, the balance of the findings leaves little doubt, and if I had included all the comparisons at school level, the conclusion would be overwhelming.

Furthermore, not all the research reports showing the power of discussions to promote thought are comparisons with other teaching methods. Some are descriptive and describe the kind of thought increased in some detail. For example, Galotti (1995) used pairs of students (dyads) to describe the reasoning style of each partner in four kinds of task: geometric analogies, moral dilemmas, deduction and everyday reasoning. This task made the students more critical and creative regarding their patterns of thinking. Greeson (1988) describes students as asking more questions, sharing information and generating many more ideas after monitoring discussions focusing on students' personal goals. Geerlings (1994) interrupted students' discussions at irregular intervals to sample their thoughts at that instant. He found that students' thoughts were related to the discussion topic 75% of the time. That is very high compared with lectures (Bloom, 1953).

The number of experimental comparisons of discussion with other methods where the development of thinking skills is the criterion

Discussion more effective	No significant difference	Other methods more effective
37	2	3

Table 2.1. Discussion is more effective than other methods to promote thinking

B. Psychological research

For these differences in thinking skills we must turn to psychological research. Even now the coverage is patchy.

1. Groups solve problems better than individuals

Do groups solve problems, and perform other thinking skills, better than individuals working alone? For example, do they make better decisions? There is evidence that they do (Johnson et al 1987; Johnson 1980; Watson and Johnson 1972). In an experiment Margulis (1984) studied the effectiveness of 20 triads, 16 dyads and 10 individuals in solving data processing problems. Not only were the dyads and triads more effective in terms of the time taken, but their relative effectiveness increased with more complex problems. Much earlier, Barton found that high school pupils performed better on subsequent tests in algebra if they first worked in groups rather than individually. In another early experiment Watson (1931) gave three matched intelligence tests to postgraduates first individually, then in groups and then individually again. Six of the 15 groups performed better than their best member and 11 performed better than the average of their individuals' scores.

Goldman (1965) gave problems to pairs and Laughlin et al (1969) gave intelligence tests to groups of three varying in mixes of ability. Both found that the performance of their groups was better than that of individuals.

In a now classic experiment Marjorie Shaw (1932) gave complex problems to groups of four and to the same individuals thinking on their own. She found the groups obtained a higher proportion of correct solutions. She observed and took notes on how the groups worked. Methodologically this was an advance at the time, though it is commonplace now. She noticed that groups checked their ideas more thoroughly than individuals. Consequently they rejected incorrect lines of enquiry both more often, and sooner, that individuals.

Shaw also noticed that not all group members co-operate equally. Yet if they don't co-operate, whatever instructions they are given, they behave more like individuals. This was confirmed by Skon et al (1981) when comparing the learning of co-operative groups, competitive groups and individuals. Co-operation promoted higher achievement and better reasoning, regardless of the mix of ability.

Compared with individuals, Lorge et al (1955) and Tuckman and Lorge (1962) found groups produced better solutions to a range of problems. Barnlund (1959) reported that the decisions taken by discussion groups were better than those by individuals and by groups taking majority decisions. He partly attributed this to the greater interest in the topic that discussion aroused.

In an interesting experiment Laughlin and Doherty (1967) showed that discussion is more important to dyads in problem-solving and decision-making than the opportunity to have all the necessary information written in front of them. Laughlin and Doherty wanted to find out the relative importance of discussion and memory in solving problems to attain a concept. Pairs of women had to work out the concept from cards they were shown under various conditions including discussion vs no discussion and memory vs having paper to write on. Discussion resulted in a more economical decision paths and fewer false hypotheses, but took longer. The opportunity to write made no difference nor did the particular thinking strategies they used.

Against this, Moore and Anderson (1954) gave problems in symbolic logic to Navy recruits and did not find groups superior. One explanation is that the recruits found the tasks so difficult that there was insufficient expertise to share. An experiment by Kanekar and Rosenbaum (1972) showed four-man groups to be better than individuals at anagram tasks, but so were 'nominal groups'. That is, group scores produced by pooling the scores of other individuals working on their own. So their results were ambiguous.

2. Are individuals in groups better than individuals alone?

On the whole it is clear from these experiments that groups solve problems better than individuals. We all know that many heads are often better than one. What is not clear in all the research reports is whether the performance of individuals in groups is better than the same individuals on their own. It is clear in some. So there is some reason to suppose that groups teach thinking better than individual study.

However, there are some reservations about this. The relative merits of group discussion and individual study would be clearer if we knew why the thinking of individuals in groups is sometimes better. It could be that the group product is better because individuals can see their errors when they are pointed out to them, but that individuals don't learn to avoid them in future.

Groups might also produce better decisions and solutions to problems because the pooling of opinions compensates for the ignorance or other inadequacies of individuals. Discussion and thought might be of little importance, and learning to think even less important.

There is some evidence that the success of groups is nothing more than a statistical artefact. Knight (1921) asked students individually and without consultation to estimate the temperature of the room. Answers ranged from 60F to 80F, but the average was about correct. In other words, the mere pooling of opinion, not discussion, led to greater accuracy.

3. Group work takes more man-hours

The efficiency of groups is again an area of doubt. In an experiment by Taylor and Faust (1952), individuals, dyads and quartets played 20 Questions. While dyads and quartets were equally superior to individuals in terms of the number of questions asked, the number of failures and the time taken, individuals were superior in terms of the average 'man-minutes' (or person-minutes) per solution.

The inefficiency of groups was also shown in an experiment by Davis and Restle (1963). They compared quartets and individuals on three problems and found in all cases that the groups produced proportionately more solutions, but there was no difference in the time taken, so individuals were more efficient in terms of man-hours. Husband (1940) compared groups of two (dyads) with individuals on a number of tasks and found the dyads superior, particularly on decoding tasks and jig-saws, but their superiority on routine tasks such as arithmetic calculations was insignificant.

Indeed a theme running through much of the experimental evidence is that groups are particularly superior on tasks with a common focus, such as visual tasks. However, groups are not superior in their efficiency as measured in man hours spent to obtain a successful solution. In other words, a group has more resources and it spends them. With increasing group size, the law of diminishing returns applies, unless components of the task are spilt up and shared between group members, as in the syndicate method of doing group projects.

4. Discussion has advantages in teaching thinking

Against this, individuals maintain attention much longer in groups than when studying alone. This advantage applies to memory tasks too.

Furthermore we all know that contributions from other group members can stimulate us to think in new ways. Members challenge and test each others' ideas in a way that cannot happen on one's own. To respond to a challenge requires thought.

Discussion also allows us to use the experience of others because discussion allows it to be shared. Thorndike (1938) observed that divergent tasks, that is problems with many possible answers, were performed better by groups than by individuals, because a variety of individuals is more likely to have varied experience and opinions.

This reminds us, as in the experiment by Husband, that the advantage of groups over individuals varies with the nature of the task. Consequently, vital teaching skills lie in ensuring that:

i) the tasks designed will practise the thinking required and
ii) group interaction will permit it to be practised.

That is why Parts II and III are about designing tasks and the factors that influence group interaction, respectively.

C. Conclusion

As a generalisation, educational research suggests that discussion methods are superior to traditional teaching methods for promoting thought. This is a very important conclusion. That is why Part II is devoted to how students learn to think.

There are many kinds of thought and many kinds of discussion group. At present there is not as much evidence on the relative effectiveness of different discussion methods, nor on teaching various kinds of thought, as one might wish. So the generalisation must remain a rather bald one. Nonetheless, Part IV shows the variety of discussion methods and what they are good at teaching.

Psychological research shows that groups solve problems better than individuals, but it is less clear whether individuals in groups think better than individuals on their own. That would be clearer if we knew what it is about the way people think in groups that makes them more effective at solving problems.

Psychologists have given a number of possible explanations:
i) the sum of a group's knowledge is usually greater than the knowledge of any individual in it,
ii) groups check and reject errors,
iii) able group members have most influence,
iv) group work maintains attention better than individual work, and
v) their superiority is a statistical artefact. (See Shaw, 1981.)

Personally, I think there is another simple explanation. If you are going to say something in a discussion, you have to think, at least a little, before you speak. Consequently, little by little, discussion makes people think. But tests have to be very sensitive to show statistically significant differences between one method and another.

Chapter 3
Discussion can help develop attitudes, values and motivation

A. Educational research
B. Psychological research
C. Conclusion

The argument here is that discussion is more effective than presentation methods for developing attitudes, values and motivation because it involves participants more actively. It is most effective when participants discuss feelings from their own experience. Therefore, use methods that provide an experience followed by discussion.

The police in my area give talks to schools about drugs in the hope that children won't use them or will kick the habit if they already do. They talk in vain. Talks give information. They don't motivate unless there is a small flame of motivation to start with, that can be fanned into a fire. If their flame of motivation is to use drugs, they use the knowledge to win arguments with parents who try to discourage them!

Smokers know that smoking may kill them and secondary smoking may kill their family; but they don't stop. Knowledge alone is not enough. It has to be combined with some kind of motivation or feeling.

First, then, I must justify my assertion that discussion is more effective than presentation methods to develop attitudes, values and motivation.

A. Educational research

Admittedly the number of research studies that have been carried out is few compared with the multiplicity of variables involved. Nevertheless, where there is some consistency in the findings, a general picture can take shape even though the details cannot be added. The details may not matter. What teachers need are generalisations as the basis for decisions, not absolute certainty on every last detail.

1. Comparative studies justify the effectiveness of discussion to develop attitudes, values and motivation
Table 3.1 confirms my assertion, as a broad generalisation, mostly with reference to lectures. It is a conclusion that has been reached by other reviewers (eg. Gall and Gall, 1976; McKeachie, 1978; McKeachie and Kulik, 1975). Nor is the superiority of discussion a short-term effect during the life of an experiment. Mitnick and McGinnies

(1958) have shown that, compared with lectures, discussion is more effective in changing attitudes in the long-term.

The number of experimental comparisons of discussion with other methods where change of attitudes is the main criterion

Discussion more effective	No significant difference	Discussion less effective
20	11	4

Table 3.1. Discussion is more effective than presentation methods for developing attitudes For detail see Appendix 3.1 on pages 273 and 274

Most of the comparisons reviewed here are between discussion and the passive reception of presentations. If the important factor influencing the amount of attitude development in teaching contexts is the amount of personal involvement and activity, we should expect other active methods, such as games and role play, to be equally, if not more, effective. This seems to be confirmed by an experiment by Breckheimer and Nelson (1976) in which there were five groups of five students meeting six times. They experienced games, racial role-playing, discussions about race, discussion of non-racial issues and no activity, respectively. Afterwards, the first four groups showed less verbal prejudice. The game players increased their inter-racial behaviour, while the racial discussants and role-players chose more inter-racial partners for a project than previously. But we will see in a moment that it is not that simple.

Before that I must give other evidence in favour of discussion rather than presentations.

2. Discussion is more effective than presentation methods to generate interest in a subject

We all know that students are more likely to do well at a subject if they are interested in it. So it is crucial that the teaching methods generate that interest. Table 3.2 shows that, on balance, discussions are more inspirational than lectures. As Appendix 3.2 shows, the indications that students are interested or uninterested are quite diverse. They include attendance and dropout rates, questionnaires and purpose-designed tests of motivation.

The number of comparisons of discussion with other methods (mostly lectures) where interest in the subject is the criterion

Discussion more effective	No significant difference	Discussion less effective
7	4	1

Table 3.2. Discussion is more effective than presentation methods for developing interest in a subject For detail see Appendix 3.2 on page 275

3. The relative popularity of discussion implies it is more likely to be effective for attitude related objectives

There is another criterion of the effectiveness of discussion for motivation and attitude development and that is their relative popularity. Students are much more likely to learn a subject if they enjoy studying it. It is difficult to be motivated towards something you don't enjoy. Repeated surveys by the National Union of Students (eg. Hale Report, 1964; Saunders et al, 1969) have shown their desire for more seminars and other kinds of interactive teaching. For example, in a survey of 1052 college of education students (Stones, 1970), over half rated seminars superior to lectures for 'inspiring ideas' and 'developing standards of judgement'. McLeish (1970) also obtained ratings of teaching methods from ten colleges of education and several universities and found the same preference for seminars and tutorials, and a dislike of more individual methods.

The number of experimental comparisons of discussion with other methods (mostly lectures) where popularity is the main criterion

Discussion more popular	No significant difference	Discussion less popular
20	1	1

Table 3.3. Discussion is more popular than lectures For detail see Appendix 3.3 on page 276

Another indication of popularity is 'high persistence' or low dropout rates. House and Wohlt (1991) and Giles-Gee (1989) have both reported lower dropout rates when students are tutored. Discussions satisfy a basic human need to relate to other people. Without it, students leave.

There is evidence from most forms of vocational training, too, that active methods are preferred. Indeed, Emery (1968) has argued that learning in the workplace and in communities will not be diffused unless people enjoy it, and that participation is a prerequisite of enjoyment. It's human nature. (The most striking example is the methods of Paulo Freire [1970] who used discussion of personally relevant objects to teach literacy in the Brazilian jungle to tribes who had previously resisted it.) Motivation is the key.

There are, however, exceptions using older students. Gauvain (1968) found that medical practitioners preferred lectures though they remembered what was said in discussions better. Reid-Smith (1969) reports that librarians also preferred more formal methods.

4. Descriptive studies confirm the effectiveness of discussion to develop attitudes

Evidence in the educational research literature for the effectiveness of discussion in changing and developing attitudes is not confined to studies comparing teaching methods. I'll give two examples. The moral attitudes of young offenders on a test were markedly improved, compared with controls, after six 90-minute discussions in a 4-week period (Fleetwood and Parish, 1976). (Of course, as the investigators were quick to point out, their considered opinion in a paper and pencil test may be different from their impulsive behaviour!) Peterson and Clark (1986) have used the group discussion and decision procedure to reduce smoking amongst teenage girls. The girls also became more negative toward smoking and more aware of associated illnesses. These changes did not occur amongst a control group.

5. Discussion is particularly effective combined with methods giving new experiences

Some of the most effective teaching for attitude development involves combinations of teaching methods including discussion. But it's not easy to say why. The combinations produce so many interacting variables, it's hard to separate their influence scientifically.

However, there is an explanation. Many of the studies with the strongest changes in attitudes report methods giving students a new experience followed by discussion of the experience. The experience provides the personal involvement that lectures do not. For example, Braza and Kreuter (1975) compared the attitudes of students who were sent out to face community health problems, and students who studied the same problems vicariously in the classroom. You hardly need to be told which group showed the greater attitude change. Van Reeth and Souris (1972–3) show how the use of role play increased students' awareness of patients' emotional problems. Role play followed by discussion has been used to similar effect by Pancrazio and Cody (1967), Grabowsky (1970), Fiss (1978) and Barnard (1982), to name but a few. Indeed, debriefing a role play by discussion is a standard and essential technique.

Other ways of providing an experience depend upon the subject. Chapel and Veach (1987) show the importance of patient contact to develop attitudes in medicine. Fyfe (1979) developed more accepting feelings towards masturbation using discussion after sexually explicit films. (Actually he would have been even more thorough if he had constantly stopped the film and discussed it point by point.) Naor and Milgram (1980) provided field trips for preservice teachers to experience a variety of handicaps. Acting and free artistic expression combined with group techniques based upon students' questions, and involving a very free emotional interchange, enabled students to reduce alcohol abuse by increasing their awareness of, and respect for, the beliefs and values of others (Kunkle-Miller and Blane, 1977–8).

I am not claiming that in these studies it is the discussion alone that changes attitudes. Quite the contrary. But it does seem reasonable to believe that discussion is an essential ingredient. Why? Because without the discussion there is no opportunity for students to have considered the facts and experiences they have just obtained. Students acquire many facts and experiences every day of their lives, without changing their attitudes. It is the period of reflection upon their new experiences that is different, and that consolidates new thoughts and feelings.

We can conclude:

i) Discussion without the experience changes attitudes more effectively than the experience alone.

ii) Discussion after the experience is more effective than discussion without the experience.

I can't prove this; but it seems reasonable and it is consistent with evidence presented in Appendix 4.2.

6. Summary

Comparative studies, descriptive reports and the relative popularity of discussion methods suggest that the development of attitudes, values and motivation are appropriate objectives of discussion methods. There is some reason to think that they are particularly effective when used in combination with other methods when the other methods provide knowledge and experience to discuss.

B. Psychological research

The superiority of discussion over formal presentations for changing attitudes has been known to psychologists for over 50 years. During the Second World War when there was a need to consume alternative foods, Lewin (1943) met with groups of housewives. Half the groups were given a compelling talk on the nutritiousness and economy of meats they mostly ignored, together with recipes for their use. The others took part in discussions during which the same information was imparted and which concluded with a show of hands by those intending to try the new diet. Later it was found that 32% of the discussion groups had tried the new foods compared with only 3% of the lecture groups. A similar experiment – to persuade mothers who had just had their first child to give their babies orange juice and cod liver oil – was conducted before they left hospital. Again, discussion with a group decision proved far more effective by two and four weeks later. The analogy of tutors persuading students to do a piece of work, or adopt a certain professional practice, is not hard to make.

The Lewin experiments stimulated a lot of research because it was disputed whether the differences were due to:

i) the discussion process,

ii) participants' feeling of involvement in it (compared with a lecture),

iii) the process of taking a decision,

iv) a feeling of commitment,

v) group pressure because their decision and commitment was public, or

vi) group pressure because of what other people said, that is, group consensus.

Which of these factors motivate? Supposing you want to persuade medical or business students to adopt a certain professional practice. What technique will be effective? Pelz (1958) concluded that the discussion process and perceived group consensus are important, but taking a decision and public commitment to it are not.

Bennett (1955) also tried to sort out whether the discussion, the public commitment, or the combination of the two was an influential factor. When he asked students to volunteer as subjects for experiments in the psychology department, some had a lecture, some discussion groups which made no decision, some made decisions with varying degrees of anonymity, while others served as controls. He concluded that the crucial factor was not participation in discussion, but the extent of group consensus perceived by the individual when making his or her personal decision.

However, Bennett's conclusion that discussion itself is unimportant has been challenged by other researchers. Pennington et al (1958) emphasised the importance of both group interaction and the taking of a group decision, while Bennett's students took individual decisions. Changes of opinion were greatest when there was both discussion and a group decision, as in case discussion. There seems little doubt that group pressure is powerful, whether by individuals perceiving group opinion, or by their feeling committed to a decision publicly made. But that does not mean that discussion alone is ineffective.

Levine and Butler (1952) found that discussion with group decisions was more effective than a lecture as a method to induce 29 supervisors to make less biased performance ratings of 395 factory workers. They drew a more general conclusion: that discussion is better at overcoming resistance to change. A natural explanation is that people are more active in discussion. Active learning is more effective than passive reception. Skinner's rats learned quicker than Pavlov's dogs because they had to do something to get their food; Pavlov's dogs stood, strapped in, and waited for it.

Yet surely it is possible to listen actively. Stiff (1986) has argued that there is a direct linear relationship between measures of how actively involved the recipient of a communication is, and the effect the communication has on attitudes. He also reported a curvilinear relationship between involvement and how far the credibility of the communicator affected attitudes. Perhaps if lecture audiences could listen as actively as those in discussion, they would think and develop their values, opinions and attitudes just as much. But the fact is that in general they don't.

Because discussion increases understanding, it often results in empathy and a softening of attitudes. Judgements were made by 24 men and 24 women before and after discussion of guilt and sentencing in a rape case. There was ambiguity both in the evidence and in the instructions by the judge, and discussion resulted in a shift towards leniency (Rumsey and Rumsey, 1977).

It would be quite wrong to suppose from these research studies that discussion methods, or any other methods can achieve great changes in attitudes in a short span of time. Indeed it might be alarming if they could. Festinger has shown that attitudes will not change at all if individuals are asked to change more than a little at a time. Wright (1986) even found that students' attitudes shifted negatively when presented with a threatening essay supporting a point of view with which they had previously completely agreed. Beem and Brugman (1986) tried to measure the effect of 10 one-hour 'value development' lessons given to 850 10–15 years olds. Contributions in class were observed. Although, compared with controls, the pupils came to like school a bit more, there were no significant differences or changes in their relationships with other pupils or their sense of inner well-being. (These points are applied in Chapter 11.)

C. Conclusion

On the weight of evidence there is no doubt that discussion is more effective than presentations in developing attitudes and values. All six of the factors (i–vi) listed on page 18 probably contribute to this effect. Which is the more powerful, and in what circumstances, is still a disputed issue. Nevertheless the general implication for teachers is clear.

There is reason to think that role play, games and similar methods with high activity and personal involvement may be equally, or even more, effective than discussion, but as yet there is insufficient evidence to say which. If that is true, once again, there is an argument for mixing discussion with other teaching methods. The most effective and natural combination is for participants in high activity methods to reflect upon and discuss their experiences and perceptions afterwards.

Chapter 4
Specific methods teach interpersonal skills

A. Discussion can help us to see ourselves in new ways

B. What interpersonal skills can discussion teach?

C. Summary

D. Conclusion

The message in this chapter is that
- specific discussion methods can teach perception, including self-perception,
- to learn interpersonal skills, it is necessary to simulate the skills and use discussion to reflect upon the experience.

This means that discussion has a dual role. It practises some interpersonal skills. It provides an opportunity to consider other interpersonal activities rationally.

A. Discussion can help us to see ourselves in new ways

1. Free Group Discussion develops perception, self perception and mature attitudes

The educational importance of perceptual preconceptions has been demonstrated in a now classic piece of research by Abercrombie (1969). She gave medical students pictures and objects to observe. The ensuing discussion was free and associative in the sense that it was unstructured and the tutor intervened only occasionally to steer the discussion forward, to clarify a point, restate the aims of the discussion or make an observation about the process of the discussion. On differences in perception and judgement becoming evident, students began to discover many of their assumptions, the ambiguity of evidence, the uncertainty and personal nature of their knowledge, and the importance of their previous experience. They realised that their preconceptions were not shared by others. Quite simple objects were perceived differently. They were not so simple after all.

   These discoveries also led to developments in self perception. For example, one of the pictures shown was of a baby. Its eyes were closed and its features perfectly relaxed. The students discussed what they saw for some time, but it occurred to none of them that it was a dead baby. Their past experience was that babies are very much alive, and when they sleep they are perfectly relaxed. Emotionally, death was a possibility the students rejected, though they all knew that the incidence of infant mortality, even in western societies, is quite high compared with most other age groups. The discussion that followed was a step towards maturity. It broadened their understanding of medical work; they saw mortality statistics with more humanity; and it facilitated personal adjustment toward their chosen career. Other perceptual tasks included the comparison of two X-ray plates, a discussion of the concept of 'classification', and the interpretation of an experiment.

Discussion helped the students understand themselves and others. Similarly Burke (1977) has shown how dialogue between black and white students can help them to appreciate each other's views.

What do we need to learn before we can understand ourselves? What do we need to understand about ourselves before we can learn? And what can we learn when we have some understanding of ourselves. Roncelli (1980) says that students can only communicate about, and use, imagery in literature if they have first been induced to describe themselves in words and actions in the classroom. He believes that direct experience of one's own appearance, voice, smell, taste and feelings is a prerequisite to appreciate indirect imagery in literature. Pitts (1975) on the other hand, has argued the opposite, namely that discussion of literary works helps students to gain more self-awareness about their own belief systems. Both views are plausible, but it is also arguable that literature provides a distorting mirror of society and ourselves.

2. The Johari Awareness Model

The best known perceptual model of human relations learning is the Johari Window (see Figure 4.1) (Luft, 1984). In discussion, individuals may learn things about themselves from what others say. In other words, aspects of individuals to which they were 'blind' (Q2), become 'open'. When discussants first meet, they are open (Q1) about very little. Gradually as trust and confidence develop, hidden (Q3) aspects of their lives and personalities become more open. Luft makes the important point that those things which one hides (Q3) are an indication of where one is blind (Q2). So when Joe discloses to Mary behaviour, thoughts and feelings he had previously hidden, he not only increases the area that is open between them, but enables Mary to use what is newly open to interpret more accurately things of which Joe is blind. The new interpretation enables facts that were unknown (Q4) to enter Q2. These, in time, she may reveal to Joe so that both unknown and blind areas decrease as open areas expand. Similarly, these revelations may enable Joe to remember facts about his early life that he had not known.

	Known to Self	Not known to Self
Known to Others	**Q1.** Open	**Q2.** Blind
Not known to Others	**Q3.** Hidden	**Q4.** Unknown

Figure 4.1. The Johari Window

The Johari Awareness Model is attractive for a number of reasons. It can be applied to any human interaction, including all the interactions in a discussion group. It is content-free. It is simple yet represents the total person in relation to other persons. It distinguishes between consciousness which is intrapersonal and awareness which is interpersonal. It recognises that interaction in groups has more to do with what is subjective, qualitative and emotional, than with what is objective, quantitative and rational. It also recognises that we all have limited knowledge of the causes of our own behaviour and directs attention to the changing processes of interaction, rather than anything fixed. It can also be applied, not just to individuals, but to the relationships between groups. For example, the relationships between unions and employers may gradually become more open in negotiations. It's a matter of trust.

The Johari Awareness Model does not prove that small group discussion can teach self awareness, awareness of others and interpersonal skills, but it makes it easier to see how those objectives might be achieved. Like any other interpersonal situation in life, discussion groups require the use of some interpersonal skills. They provide feedback on members' use of those skills. Group members may choose whether to respond to the feedback or to ignore it. Even to ignore it is, in a sense, a response. In this way groups, like any other personal interaction, influence behaviour. Groups provide an environment in which emotions can be expressed and experienced. Members can practise accepting, supporting and helping each other together with a thousand other interpersonal skills.

It's more than that. In groups and everyday life, we are under constant pressure to adjust our behaviour towards others as a result of information we receive about that behaviour. Similarly we provide others with information about them. These are socialising, and culture forming, processes.

3. There is empirical evidence that T-Groups can teach self-awareness

If information from others about oneself fosters self-awareness, why not devise a discussion method to provide information to do that? A T-Group is designed for that purpose. In a T-Group, members discuss their 'here and now' experiences. Group members are instructed to share their experiences and perceptions of each other openly. That is their task. (See Chapter 23.) In other words, a lot of Q2 becomes Q1. The 'T' stands for training. I shall regard T-Groups as the same thing as 'sensitivity groups' or 'encounter groups'. What evidence is there that T-Groups work?

There have been a very large number of studies of their effectiveness. There's no need for me to produce tables. Peter Smith (1975) reviewed 100 publications, confining his survey to comparative investigations where there were control groups, repeated measures and at least 20 hours of group work. In 78 of these studies T-Groups were more effective than controls. In particular, these groups appear to result in improved personal relations, a more favourable self-esteem and a reduced prejudice. Cooper and Mangham (1971) also reviewed research into T-Groups and concluded that individuals in these groups showed improved interpersonal perception and communication skills compared with matched pairs or with other teaching groups. I have not found substantial evidence that other discussion methods can teach with the same intensity those interpersonal skills that are practised in discussion itself, but common sense suggests that others will to some extent.

Sitting in a group designed to let everyone say exactly what they think of you (and you of them) may seem daunting. Certainly some people have criticised T-Groups for being over stressful, but Lubin and Lubin (1971) have argued that they are no worse than many other situations in life and are much less stressful than college examinations! They don't have to be threatening; they can be supportive.

On the other hand, T-Groups require skilful handling to deal with perceived threat. The trainers themselves need training in the method and training should include experience of the method in a non-leadership role. Don't use the method if you've not had that experience. Only use it if you have been trained to do so, have been trained in psychotherapy or group counselling, or have used free group discussion extensively. (See Abercrombie on page 21, and FGD in Chapter 23.)

B. What interpersonal skills can discussion teach?

1. Discussion can teach interpersonal skills practised in the discussion itself

The claims made for T-Groups are more than teaching a perceptual skill – self-awareness. It is said that T-Groups develop interpersonal behaviour. Presumably one argument is that in T-Groups you learn by practice, interpersonal skills regarding how you express your opinions of others. That requires sensitivity and tact. Those are important skills.

2. Discussion can promote personal and social adjustment

Another argument is that if you see yourself differently, you will behave differently. Behind this argument lie theories of interpersonal behaviour. The argument is that if we are not well adjusted, for example if we have excessively low or high self-esteem, this will show in how we behave towards other people. If discussion can give us an accurate perception of ourselves, our behaviour towards others will be based upon reality.

Much counselling and psychotherapy is underpinned by such theories. They employ special discussion techniques, but there is every reason to believe that the confrontation of perceptions in other forms of discussion can also make perceptions of oneself and others realistic, thereby promoting personal and social adjustment.

Table 4.2 compares discussions with presentation methods (mostly lectures) where change in some form of personal or social adjustment is the criterion of effectiveness. The balance of the studies I have been able to find suggests that discussion is relatively effective for this purpose.

3. To teach interpersonal skills, simulate and practise them with a discussion debrief

However, whilst personal and social adjustment, such as levels of anxiety, may influence interpersonal skills, that is not the same as teaching the skills directly by

Comparisons showing discussion more effective

1. Diflorio (1996)	Co-op learning v. L-D	Interview: student relationships
2. Cabral-Pini (1995)	Co-op learning v. L	Decreasing math anxiety, inter-racial relations
3. Courtney et al (1994)	D (Co-op learning) v. L	Reduced anxiety
4. Heverin (1993)	Communication and Problem-solving v. L	Marital adjustment (Premarital relationships)
5. Klein (1983)	Experiential learning v. L	Self efficacy; conflict management
6. Camp et al (1994)	PBL v. L	Zung Self-Rating Depression Scale
7. Asch M.J. (1951)	FGD v. Ls	Minnesota Multiphasic Personality Inventory (MMPI)
8. Wieder (1954)	FGD v L-D	Covert prejudice on California E-F Scales, measures of 'conventionality' and 'authoritarian-aggression'
9. Abraham et al (1982)	T-Gp v. Sem v Auditoriaum gp	Attitude toward self
10. Yorde & Witmer (1988)	D+L v. Relaxation by EMG biofeedback	STAI and SSS – stress reduction
11. Erlich (1979)	D v. L	Defensiveness

Comparisons showing no significant difference

1. Bechtel (1963)	Small gp D v. L	Allport Vernon Lindzey Study of Values Bill's Index of adjustment
2. Ruja (1954)	D v. L	Emotional Stability
3. Brooks (1993)	Co-op learn v.Private study v. L	Health/alcohol locus of control
4. Wieder (1954)	FGD v. L-Demo	MMPI and Bill's Index of Adjustment
5. Timmel (1954)	Gp Project v. No teaching v. L	MMPI

Comparisons showing discussion less effective

1. Erlich (1979)	D v. L	General and test anxiety reduction
2. Wanlass (1983)	D v. L	Decreased sexual guilt

Table 4.2. Discussion is more effective than presentation methods to promote personal and social adjustment For the Key to Abbreviations, see Appendix page 267

practising them. The criteria in Table 4.2 are perceptual. They are in the mind. Anxiety, for example, is all about perceptions of the future. They are internal to the perceiver. The criteria in Table 4.3 are to do with practical and professional behaviour. They show contrasting results.

Discussions on their own are no better at changing skills and other behaviour than lectures. Neither discussion nor lectures practise the required behaviour, they just allow talk about it. Simulated practice of the skills themselves is effective, for example in role play, because all the required skills are inter-related through behaviour. No doubt the role play is maximally effective when it is followed up by discussion of the experience. Follow up discussion ('pooling the experience') will consolidate memory of the experience, make students think about it, and register aspects that need correction next time. But discussion without the experience to discuss is ineffective.

Comparisons showing discussion more effective

Discussion on its own

1. Williams et al (1983)	4hr. small gp D v. Placebo control	Assertiveness
2. Itskowitz et al (1989)	Structure D v. L+Unstructured D	Gains in sensitivity (empathy)
3. Heverin (1993)	Communication,	Non-verbal skills
	Problem-solving v. L	(Premarital relationships)

Simulated activity (probably with follow up discussion)

1. Saunders et al (1975)	Microteaching v. L+D	Questioning skills
2. Teevan & Gabel (1978)	Role play v. L	Counselling skills
3. Willis & Gueldenpfenning (1981)	Skills Practice v. L	Tutoring skills
4. Evans et al (1989)	Workshop practice v. L	Interview skills
5. Falvo et al (1991)	Role-modelling v. L	Simulated patient interaction, communication
6. Flanagan et al (1979)	Role play v. L	Parents' time-out procedure
7. Hale & Camplese (1974)	Mastery method v. L+D	Student talk, teaching skills
8. King K. (1980)	Modelling v. L+D	Teaching skills, eg. praising, paraphrasing
9. Adams et al (1980)	Role Play v. L	Behaviour modification techniques
10. Bookman & Iwanicki (1983)	Practice problems v. L+D	Problem-solving
11. Costanzo (1992)	Practice v. L	Interpreting cues.

Comparisons showing no significant difference

Discussion on its own

1. Heverin (1993)	Communication, Problem Solving v. L	Verbal skills (Premarital relationships)

Simulated activity (probably with follow up discussion)

1. Walker (1985)	Role play v. T-Gps v. L-D	Verbal rhetorical sensitivity
2. McGuire (1984)	Role play v. Video v. L	Items interview elicited Number.of words spoken by patient
3. Tait (1993)	Role playing (modelling) v. L	Analogue coding grief facilitation
4. Talbert et al (1975)	Modelling v. L+Modelling v. L	Teaching techniques
5. Austin & Grant (1981)	L+self video with and without feedback v. L	Interview skills
6. Tomm & Leahey (1980)	L+Demo v.Make your own Demo	Interview skills

Discussion less effective

Discussion on its own

1. Powell (1988)	D v. L	Assertiveness
2. Powell (1987)	D v. L	No change in self concept behaviour
3. Connolly (1992)	D v. L+D	2/3 groups' involvement in pre-retirement education, behaviour change
4. Cook et al (1974)	D v. Film Demo+D D v. Didactic+D	Skills of psychiatric aides
5. Diflorio (1996)	Co-operative learning v. L-D	Interpersonal skills
6. Bennett (1955)	Consensus + Individual decisions in D v. L	Acted on willingness to volunteer

Simulated activity (probably with follow up discussion)

1. Kaplan (1988)	Group field tasks v. Tuts	Social work skills

Table 4.3. Comparisons of discussion and other methods for teaching interpersonal skills. For the Key to Abbreviations, see Appendix page 267.

C. Summary

Discussion can create awareness of oneself and provides an opportunity to learn those interpersonal skills that are used in teaching itself. It can promote personal and social adjustment, and has a debriefing role when teaching interpersonal skills by simulated activity.

D. Conclusion

1. Discussion can be used to teach information but it is not very cost-effective for this purpose, unless either it is used to achieve other objectives at the same time, or a large number of tutorless groups are organised simultaneously.
2. Discussion can be, and commonly is, used to teach thinking skills. But it will only do so if the tasks are designed to make students practise the thought process that is required.
3. Discussion is more effective than presentation methods in developing attitudes and values, but it is probably most effectively used in combination with role play and other active methods.
4. All teaching includes developing perception. Discussion, possibly in conjunction with other methods, has a particular role to teach self-awareness and awareness of others. Discussion can teach interpersonal skills practised in the discussion itself, and can promote personal and social adjustment. To teach interpersonal skills, simulate and practise them with a discussion debrief.

From this summary, it is clear that discussion has a role in all these aspects of education, but that role is subtly different according to what you want to teach. It offers an unrivalled opportunity for the promotion of thought. Accordingly, that is the major focus in this book and why Part II concentrates upon the design of thought-promoting tasks. Nonetheless, I shall not entirely neglect the development of attitudes, perceptual skills and interpersonal skills.

Part II

What Discussion Tasks Develop Thought and Attitudes?

Part II is concerned with the psychology of task design. That's a neglected area in the study of education. I hope it will become a science. The tasks suggested in Part II are a beginning.

If we want to teach students to think, we must devise tasks that make them practise the kind of thought required. If we want participants to develop feelings and attitudes towards something rationally, they must first express their current feelings and attitudes so that they, and others, may think about them in a rational manner. The kind of thinking and feeling they learn will greatly depend upon the kind they practise. So part of the art of teaching is to understand the skills of thinking and feeling that different tasks require.

It is obvious that, to take part in discussion:
i) Participants must attend and listen to what others say (Chapter 5).
ii) They must understand what is said from the language used; and they must be able to use (possibly a technical or special) language to say what they think (Chapter 6).
iii) Their thinking should use the canons of reason; that is to say, they should be able to analyse and relate what has been said according to logical and rational principles (Chapter 7).

In a way, all tasks can be regarded as problems.
iv) Some problems demand only one, or a precisely restricted number of answers. These are sometimes described as requiring 'convergent thinking' (Chapter 8).
v) Other problems require much more creative and 'divergent thinking'. They allow a wide range of possible answers (Chapter 9).
vi) Next, decision-making tasks require creativity to set out the options, values to select which should be acted upon, and convergent thinking to apply principles (Chapter 10).
vii) Finally, we must consider how to encourage expressions of values, personal feelings and attitudes in a rational manner, and how discussion can result in their development (Chapter 11).

University students and children of school age already possess all these skills at some level. The aim is to develop them further. We have seen in Part I that they develop through the use of discussion methods. You can't force participants to think or feel in particular ways and you probably wouldn't want to, but, where appropriate, Part II will suggest teaching tasks that may assist students' self-development.

The seven groups of tasks I've listed imply a developmental sequence of skills; but because participants already possess them at some level, the sequence is not absolutely binding. Because different discussion methods are suitable for different tasks, the sequence of tasks implies a developmental sequence of discussion methods described in Part IV. (See Figure 21.1.) Again, I mean in broad outline. I am not arguing that the sequence of discussion methods should be rigid, every method being practised before the next. Furthermore, the sequence is cumulative. That is to say the methods used at the beginning should continue to be used in combination with later ones. In this way teachers constantly increase their repertoire of methods and techniques, using them flexibly as they judge appropriate.

Chapter 5
Listening and attending

A. Recognising the words

B. The background to poor listening skills

C. Recognising the feelings

D. The problem of distractions and divided attention

E. How can leaders help serial processors?

F. Conclusion

A. Recognising the words

It might seem logical to suppose that the process of listening to a discussion is a sequential one – what might be called serial processing. In this view, the sounds arrive at the ear and are transmitted as neural impulses to the brain. The brain's first task is to analyse the sounds into units which might then be recognised as familiar words by matching them with a lexical memory – a store of words in one's memory. Next their meanings must be identified. (Those words which have meaning for an individual, educationalists call the individual's 'passive vocabulary'.) Then by relating the meanings of words in a sentence, the meaning of the sentence can be understood.

That's an over simplification. Words are not spoken as distinct units. There is evidence that the brain simultaneously uses lexical, syntactic and contextual information it already possesses to identify the words another participant has spoken (Haskell, 1991). They help you deal with accents. The brain also uses these factors to interpret the meaning of what is said.

Thus the brain uses what you might call 'parallel processing'. It may be necessary when the same word is spoken in different ways or with different accents and dialects. Furthermore, spectographic analysis of speech sounds shows that speech sounds are more continuous than you might expect. The sounds of words run into one another and their pronunciation is influenced by the pronunciation of those either side of them. Hence the pronunciation of the same word is not always the same. When it has to, the brain sorts this out by simultaneously using all the evidence available to it, not by using one bit at a time in sequence. At an unconscious level, the brain can use serial or parallel processing according to what it needs.

B. The background to poor listening skills

1. *Listening is not taught*

The art of listening has been neglected. Communication has three elements: the sender, the medium and the receiver. It is curious that so far as the written medium is concerned, our educational system spends a great deal of effort on writing (sending) and on reading (receiving). But when it comes to spoken or 'oral' communication, though there is considerable effort to teach the skills of talking and speaking (sending), very little effort is devoted to the art of listening (receiving). In this chapter I am principally concerned with listening by students.

2. *Reasons for ineffective listening by students*

There are several reasons for poor listening by students. Focus on a recent discussion. Which of the following might be true of whom?

i) 'Message overload' such that, even with parallel processing, it is not possible to attend to everything. When a subject is new, there is a lot to take in. When tutors are very familiar with a subject, they can easily overlook students' difficulty. Tutors have well established neural pathways to deal with it.

ii) 'Message underload' when the students' mind is insufficiently occupied and wanders. This is more likely to occur with quick thinkers.

iii) The students' preoccupation with their own concerns. Tutors need to be sensitive to the possibility that inattention by students results from personal stress. So much student stress is hidden. Inattention is one of the few available signs that a personal tutorial is necessary. (See Figure 23.5 on page 263.)

iv) Universities and colleges are international communities. Students may be inexperienced at interpreting the wide variety of accents and dialects.

v) Similarly, students learning in a second or subsequent language may have difficulty with the speed and vernacular of speech. These too require teacher vigilance.

3. *Consequent listening habits*

These factors result in bad listening habits:

i) Overload and underload can both result in 'pseudo-listening'. The students appear to give responsive non-verbals, while in practice their mind is wandering.

ii) Others fail to pick up non-verbal communication and are unable to interpret the words and feelings that are expressed. This is a particular difficulty for foreign students and when others listen to foreign students. Their non-verbal signals are not necessarily the same. Sensitive listening is an art. It needs constant practice and no one ever reaches perfection.

iii) When human beings cannot remember everything they are told, they invent information to complete the picture. This is a normal and essential perceptual process, but it leads to distortion.

iv) 'Ambushing' is listening in order to attack what is said. This is unconstructive. It is common in political debate and occurs in college seminars too. It's not aimed at seeking the truth. (It's at its worst as cross examination in the law courts.)

4. Exercises to teach listening

At the beginning of Chapter 23, you will find skills under the headings reflecting back, summarising, information relating, interpretation, note-taking, responding to feeling and feedback. They all practise listening skills. Divide your class into pairs (dyads). Let one student speak while the other practises the skill you nominate.

C. Recognising the feelings

Listening is also about acknowledging others' feelings. It is an active process of welcoming what others have said, of recognising and accepting the feelings being expressed, and of supporting participants' rights to have feelings and to express them.

Reflecting back feelings is an important technique. (See page 244.) This can be done by calmly repeating a contributor's emotive word with the intonation of a question. For example, 'Irritating?' The reflecting back of feeling will invite the contributor to enlarge upon their feeling of irritation and get it into the open. The feeling must then be accepted as 'acceptable'.

Recognising feelings involves an attitude of mind. Feelings are not only acknowledged with simple concise language (eg. 'That made you anxious'), but by a relaxed, friendly and interested facial expression, and by body language such as leaning forward, nods of understanding and frequent eye contact without it being continuous and drilling.

It is a matter of respecting the speaker as someone of value, particularly when they are foolish or angry. It includes asking open questions, not interrupting and not putting words into others' mouths. Particularly with students from another culture, it is worth giving tasks in pairs to practise bidding farewell, apologising, disagreeing, praising, thanking, suggesting, self disclosure and so on.

D. The problem of distractions and divided attention

1. Require participants to summarise what's been said

A particular feature of group discussions is that participants have to listen with divided attention. It demands parallel processing. This is demanded in two ways.

First, there can be a conflict between attending to (internal) thoughts and (external) contributions – participants have to listen to others at the same time as thinking about what is said and how they, themselves, might respond. Allow silence for thinking. Don't feel you have to fill it or you'll over-dominate.

Second, there can be a conflict between two external sets of stimuli – it often happens in discussion that two or more people talk at once. If listeners use only serial processing they must either block out all but one contribution, or switch to and fro, tuning in to each contributor in the hopes of grasping all that is said.

In practice, most younger people switch so frequently that they can recall the unattended voice while it is still 'echoing' round their nervous system. They hardly realise they are switching at all and their brains then deal with the messages in parallel. Older people do not switch so easily and are more likely to process information serially.

There has been almost no research into conflicts of the first kind – the competition between internal thoughts and external speech – although it is an almost normal circumstance in discussion and ordinary conversation. This is because experimental psychologists can't easily know or control what their subjects think, but they can control external stimuli.

One way to make students concentrate is to give tasks that summarise what others have said. You will see on pages 201–203, when describing pyramid groups, I suggest that when a class first meets, participants should listen to a partner and then introduce him/her to another pair.

Another device in group tutorials, seminars and debates is to establish a convention that each contributor begins with 'I understand you to say that…', before going on to make a fresh point. This technique is known as a 'perceptual check'. I describe it in more detail on pages 241 and 244. It's a bit formal and might discourage contributions before confidence is fully developed, but it develops accurate listening and acknowledges respect for each other.

2. Ask 'what is the question at issue?'

How do discussants cope with receiving two contributions at once? Particularly in the 1960s there was quite a bit of research to answer this question. Not all of it need concern us; but most people cope by breaking the messages into chunks and switching attention backwards and forwards between the various sources. There's evidence that if you don't switch every couple of seconds, you will not be able to retrieve from your immediate memory what was said by the unattended source. If two people talking at once have similar voices, switching is more difficult, listeners spend more time and mental energy distinguishing them and this leaves less to deal with their meaning.

As you might expect, research shows that there is much less interpretation of the meaning of unattended stimuli; but that is not to say there is none at all. When two people talk at once and you attend to only one of them, part of the meaning of the other one will often get through. That suggests there is at least some parallel processing. An alternative interpretation is that blocking, or 'filtering', out in the serial process is only completed after some of the meaning has been apprehended.

An important filtering device is to teach students to ask themselves 'What is the issue being discussed?', 'What is the question?' Early in their student careers, get students to write down the question individually. They can then briefly share their perception of the issue in a short buzz group with their neighbour. (See page 204.) If they have to make a summary or take notes, they should then be filtering out anything irrelevant. Filtering reduces the information load when having to attend to two contributions at once and makes the other task – giving a summary – more feasible.

E. How can leaders help serial processors?

Some participants can't cope with listening to two people at once or listening and thinking at the same time. (Most of us get like this as we get older and we're not so quick at switching to and fro either.) Amongst students, they are likely to be the silent ones or those with less confidence. If you have blocked out what some people say, you are likely to be less confident about how a contribution of your own will fit into the conversation. There will be anxieties such as, 'Has my point already been rebutted?' And if you have taken some time out to think about a point, the right time to make it may have passed by. On the other hand, if you listen to others you will have little time to collect your thoughts together and you will soon be wondering why everyone else seems so much more articulate and clever than you. It is the responsibility of the teacher or group leader to prevent these feelings developing.

1. Take stock of discussion periodically
In a group tutorial, a seminar, a committee, or in other discussions with a leader, such as a teacher, the leader can, and should, help by taking stock of the discussion from time to time. This should fill in any major gaps that divided attention caused some participants to miss. If they can feel encouraged to contribute before more gaps occur, they will develop more confidence.

2. Maintain a record of the discussion
Everyone's attention wanders for brief moments. They are called 'microsleeps'. If the important points in a discussion are recorded in some way, participants can catch up. How this is done depends upon the discussion method used. In plenary discussions teachers often record major points on a flip chart, blackboard or overhead transparency. Increasingly computer projection is used. In tutorless groups which have a listing task, the list serves as a record. On page 247 I describe how to take notes in a discussion and students can be taught this technique.

F. Conclusion

Maintaining attention in boring lectures is a problem well understood. Maintaining attention in discussions is less of a problem because students are relatively active, but almost because of that, inattention between contributions can easily go unnoticed.

Don't be afraid to give listening tasks in pairs or triads using your subject matter. Listening to others has the spin-off benefit of learning to respect others. That's priceless.

Chapter 6
Tasks to help group members understand and talk

A. Tasks for understanding unfamiliar words
B. Tasks to help students say what they think
C. Conclusion

It's obvious that to take part in discussion, group members must understand what is said by others and be able to express themselves coherently. They must be able to understand language and to use it. So helping group members to talk has these two aspects.

A. Tasks for understanding unfamiliar words

By 'understanding' in discussion, I mean the process of relating what is said to ideas an individual already possesses. That is to say, understanding is a process of building relationships between ideas. Consider the concept of a 'regional centre' in geography. At one level students can understand what this is if they know what a region and a centre are. But as the students continue to study various economic activities, administrative boundaries, geological conditions and so on, the words 'regional centre' take on new associations. The meaning develops by more associations in various contexts. That's where discussion is valuable. The students' understanding may eventually become close to what the teacher meant in the first place, though it is unlikely ever to be the same.

Note three points. First, the teacher and the student usually cannot mean the same thing by the key words in your discipline. Second, words like 'region' may seem clear to the student at first, before discovering that it is extremely vague and uncertain. Deeper clarity takes time. Third, to derive the meaning of what is said is a process of construction. It helps when the words are familiar, that is, when they are part of the individual's passive vocabulary.

A problem arises when a new word is used – possibly a technical term – which is not part of the individual's lexical memory, and certainly not one for which they know the meaning. For students, this happens all the time. Half the battle when studying a subject is to understand its specialist language. What the students have to do is to construct links between the new word and concepts they already possess

To some extent students can use syntactic and contextual factors to construct these links, but that leaves too much to chance. Teachers need to devise tasks (that is, to devise contexts) that will not only help their students to relate technical terms to ideas they already possess – their 'passive vocabulary' – but to make the new terms become part of their students' 'active vocabulary'. This demands devising tasks that require the students to use the words, preferably in a variety of contexts.

Notice that for this purpose the discussion groups should be small like dyads or buzz groups (see page 204 *ff*), otherwise not every student will have a chance to use the words in several ways. That's another reason for part of my maxim: *Start with simple tasks in small groups for short periods of time, and then gradually increase their respective complexity, size and duration.*

1. Why discussion is effective

The way to learn a language is to use it. Almost all academic learning includes learning the specialist language of a subject. A language is not learned passively, and even reading it is not as effective as using it.

Buzz groups are valuable for practising the language of a subject in another very important way. Let us imagine three levels of language. There are those terms that are in everyday use in ordinary language at the first level. At the second level there are technical terms defined in terms of level one. Then there is a third level of technical terms defined in terms of level two. For example, in psychology a concept such as 'conditioning' can be explained in ordinary language using words such as 'rat', 'lever', 'reward' and so on. But the concepts of 'extinction' and 'higher order conditioning' can only be understood if the term 'conditioning' is understood first. Experimentally I have found that if these terms are introduced in a lecture, 80% of the students will know the meaning of the word 'conditioning' immediately after the lecture, but only 20% will know the meaning of 'extinction' and 'higher order conditioning'. In other words, there is a considerable fall-off in level three comprehension. However, if there is a buzz group after the word 'conditioning' has been taught, but before the terms 'extinction' and 'higher order conditioning' are presented, post-test scores for the latter are very much improved. Indeed they are over 60% and approach the 80% figure for level 2 terms. What has happened? One explanation is to say that by use of the level 2 term 'conditioning' in discussion, it has moved from level 2 to level 1, so that the level 3 terms that depend upon it have also moved downward, in this case from level 3 to level 2.

Discussion makes technical terms part of students' ordinary language. It makes what they have learned part of themselves, not a detached body of knowledge, filed away for occasional use. It makes them educated as distinct from knowledgeable.

There are four types of discussion task that can contribute to this understanding and use of new terms. I do not say that any one is sufficient.

2. Ask members to discuss classic and counter examples

One way to teach students to understand a concept is to ask them in small groups to identify the characteristics of a classic example or 'paradigm case'. Indeed this technique can be used with familiar words such as 'crime' or 'mammal' when students do not know their precise meaning. The teacher might say 'Write down the characteristics of "murder" that make it a crime.' or 'Contrast cows and hens and say why cows are "mammals", whilst hens are not.' Notice that the 'contrast' task requires some negative thinking (to consider characteristics the hen does not possess). Most people have difficulty manipulating negatives.

Tasks of these forms are quite good for teaching the skills of analysis – something often not well taught but, on their own, classic examples are not always sufficient to teach a concept. Firstly, they are not always typical. For example, the relationship of murder to manslaughter (unintentional killing) does not have its counterpart in most other crimes. Secondly, classic examples, though typical, may leave out consideration of atypical examples. They may make the concept too narrow. For example, a group might not derive the concept of a 'mammal' from classic examples such as cows, cats, dogs, pigs and other animals that have four legs, a body and a head with two eyes, a nose and a mouth. Humans, whales and dolphins might be excluded, and crocodiles included.

3. Ask them to consider a range of different examples

What is needed in this case is for the group to consider which of cows, humans, whales and crocodiles are mammals and why; in other words, to consider a range of possible examples including pertinent negative cases (eg. crocodiles) and positive examples that are not classic cases.

With this kind of task the group should identify the definitive characteristic (eg. the female's possession of a mammary gland to feed its young); but it might also identify other characteristics that are not definitive (eg. features of child rearing behaviour).

4. Get them to agree upon a formal definition

To agree a formal definition, group members must go through the mental tasks of analysis and discrimination required in B. They must also decide which characteristic(s) are definitive and then incorporate them into a form of words.

5. Give tasks that relate the word to its theoretical context

The formal definition begs the question of why some characteristics are regarded as definitive and not others. It is not a question of these characteristics being in common. As in my example, there could be characteristics in common between all mammals which are not possessed by non-mammals, but which, nonetheless, are not definitive characteristics.

The choice of definitive characteristics depends upon a theory. Concepts and their definitions depend upon a context of theory and they cannot be fully understood except in that context. Although the definition of a mammal existed before Darwin published his *Origin of Species*, the concept cannot now be fully understood outside the theoretical context of evolution. The contexts of concepts develop over time.

Essentially, students cannot be said to understand a concept unless they can relate it to others. As I said, it is a matter of making relationships. The kind of relationship will depend upon the sort of concept that it is. That is why using it in context is so

important. To teach students how to use a concept, X, within its theoretical contexts, dyads or buzz groups might be asked to discuss one question like the following:
How is X related to …?
What effect does X have on … ?
What conditions are necessary for X to occur?
What principle is applied to X when … ?
What might be the moral justification for X?
What is assumed by the concept of X?
What is the purpose of X?

Teachers teach concepts every working day. Yet I hope the foregoing shows that this is a more subtle business than might at first appear. To acquire a concept requires the student to undertake a sequence of mental tasks. The teacher has to work out the elements of that sequence and design tasks that employ those elements. These then need to be incorporated into the lesson plan with estimates of the time required, plan how feedback is to be obtained and given, and decide the physical provision (eg. arrangement of chairs and overhead projector) necessary.

B. Tasks to help students say what they think

The most important reason why students don't contribute to discussions is lack of confidence. It's fear. I will consider this again under 'motivation' in Part III. Here I will consider two aspects.

1. Let members prepare individually first, then share thoughts in pairs
There may be lack of confidence that what they say will be accepted. Particularly when the remarks have wide exposure, the teacher and group members need to accept them if possible, and if not, be very sure to support the speaker as a person – that is accepting the person as an individual worthy of respect. Often this can be done by showing appreciation and understanding of why he said what he did (even though it was wrong) and, perhaps, that he is in good company, many people having thought the same.

However, particularly at the beginning of a course, it is best to avoid wide exposure until confidence is built up. That is why I shall recommend in Part IV starting with individual work, then work in pairs and pairing with various partners, followed by gradually enlarging the group size to buzz groups of 3 or 4, and only later using larger groups, eventually including the most fearsome person of all, the teacher. (See Figure 21.1 on page 193.) This recommendation I call my maxim, namely, *Start with simple tasks in small groups for short periods of time, and then gradually increase their respective complexity, size and duration.* I shall constantly argue for it. Nearly all the tasks suggested here in Part II could be given individually and then in pairs or small buzz groups.

2. Give practice in using new terms immediately after they're introduced
A second reason for students' lack of confidence is the fear that once they have started talking, they won't be able to say what they want to mean. That is, they won't express

The time which elapses between the onset of the stimulus and the onset of the response is called the latency. Thus the time between tap and kick is the _____ of the knee-jerk reflex.
The weakest stimulus sufficient to elicit a response marks the threshold of the reflex. A tap on the knee will not elicit a kick if it is below the _____.
If you blink when something brushes your eye, the _____ is a response.
A puff of air striking the eye will elicit a blink only if the force exerted by the air exceeds the _____ value.
The fraction of a second which elapses between the 'brushing of the eye' and 'blink' is the _____of the reflex.

Figure 6.1. An extract from Skinner's programmed text, 'The Analysis of Behavior'

their thoughts accurately or won't be able to express them at all. We have all had the experience of not being able to find the words we want – or of words being on 'the tip of the tongue'. This problem is a semantic one. We know the meaning, but we can't find the words to fit it. The words are not sufficiently active in our vocabulary.

However it may not be only semantic. It seems we don't only store our vocabulary according to the meaning of words, but according to their sounds. Burke et al (1991) gives an example of someone constantly saying 'charity' instead of 'chastity'. They suggest that some moral associations in meaning, combined with the similar rhythm and sounds of the words, increased the probability of the wrong word coming to mind. The trouble is, the more this happens, the more likely it is to happen in the future. It's as if the neural pathways for the wrong word get more firmly established than for the right one.

There's a similar effect that, when a word has been used recently, it is more likely to be used again. That fact gives the teacher a chance to reinforce the right neural pathways by making students use new terms as soon as possible after they have been introduced in reading or a lecture. The extract from Skinner's programmed text shows how he uses the principles of recency and follow-up activity immediately after new terms are introduced. Of course, the activity is not discussion and for that reason it does not provoke much thinking. Nonetheless, the emphasis is upon using the language, not just understanding it.

More active and more thought provoking would be to give a task that involves writing a sentence or two using the new language, followed by discussion in pairs or buzz groups.

A different kind of accuracy is that which has to be learned by trainees for all those professions using interviewing and other interpersonal skills. It is concerned with accuracy of feelings as well as facts. The same principle applies. In the above example, a counsellor has to give an immediate response to what the single mother has said, probably using some of the same words.

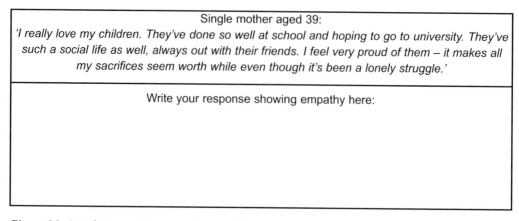

Figure 6.2. A task to practise accurate empathy

3. Give word recognition tasks with discussion to associate the context

In addition to their meaning and sound, we also seem to classify words according to their initial sound or letter. I'm no good at crosswords. I can't seem to search my brain for the right word even when I know it; but when I know the first letter rather than any of the others, my chances of success are much improved. The initial letter helps me to recognise the correct word when I can't recall it. The difference between recognition and recall is crucial. You recognise a person's face, but you can't remember their name. Recognition is easier. Why? Because information given through seeing the face limits the options on who it can be. But you must recall a name from all the names you've ever heard.

Recognition tasks can build an accurate vocabulary provided the words are given the right associations in the students' minds by follow-up activity. Consider the medical student who has so many names to learn that he cannot remember which is the tibia and which the fibula, which is the radius and which the ulna, which are the metatarsals and which the metacarpals, and which are bones in the arm and which in the leg. A task to label the bones in the arm may help students remember which is which, provided there is a follow-up discussion of why the 'U — is longer than the — ' – a discussion that forces them to distinguish the ulna from the radius. This task involves recall aided by minimal recognition followed by active discussion.

These examples show that finding the right words to say in discussion is no simple matter and we should empathise with nervous and hesitant students.

4. Use listing tasks in students' early development

The problem of finding the right words is different from a syntactic difficulty. If you try to produce the script of a recorded discussion, you may be surprised at first to discover that for much of the time people don't talk in sentences. It seems as if the rules of syntax are too difficult to obey when concentrating on the meaning. The brain uses syntactic rules on at least two levels. One is deciding the main structure of the utterance – what the subject of the sentence might be, where the main verb will go, and so on. Then there are minor rules to do with prepositions (by, with, from, etc.), definite and indefinite articles (the, an, a) and verb endings (ed, s, es, etc.).

From an educational point of view it doesn't matter whether students talk in sentences in our discussions. We know they can in other contexts. What matters is to develop their powers of thought. So there's no need to inhibit their thought by requiring them to contribute in perfectly formed sentences. As we shall see, it is possible to give listing tasks that are intellectually quite demanding and which don't require any syntax. Language should be our servant, not our master.

C. Conclusion

As you know, the maxim I'm principally trying to get across is *Start with simple tasks in small groups for short periods of time, and then gradually increase their respective complexity, size and duration*. Part of my argument for this maxim is that students need to acquire the basic skills for discussion before you plunge them into searching tasks that really stretch them intellectually. They need to learn how to attend and listen closely, to understand and to use language accurately, and then to reason logically.

This chapter has been concerned with tasks to teach understanding and accurate use of language. It's concerned with ensuring that students literally know what they're talking about! Stop and think whether I could, and should, have suggested some other tasks. Of course, I've not been subject specific. So jot down some tasks to teach these skills in your subject area.

Chapter 7
The use of reason

A. Learn, and teach, how to analyse rational discussion
B. Tasks to teach the skills of reasoning
C. Common errors of reasoning in discussion
D. Conclusion

Having listened and understood what has been said in discussion, we expect our students to think and reason about it. They have to learn how to do so. To quote Johnson-Laird and Byrne (1991), what they have understood and remembered are propositions to be manipulated *'in order to*

formulate plans;
evaluate alternative actions;
determine the consequences of assumptions and hypotheses;
interpret and formulate instructions, rules and general principles;
pursue arguments and negotiations;
weigh evidence and assess data;
decide between competing theories; and
solve problems.

A world without deduction would be a world without science, technology, laws, social conventions and culture.' All these are tasks you might give a discussion group. They all require reasoning. My maxim is *Start with simple tasks in small groups for short periods of time, and then gradually increase their respective complexity, size and duration.*

The topic of this chapter is enormous. Whole courses are given and books written about both the logic and the psychology of reasoning. To place them in the context of discussion is a yet further complication. I shall first suggest a way to analyse reasoning in discussion; then look at some types of reasoning; and finally alert you to some common errors in discussion.

A. Learn, and teach, how to analyse rational discussion

What is said in discussion is a series of propositions. If the discussion is reasoned, the propositions are of seven kinds and bear certain relations to each other. (See Figure 7.2.) Consider the short extract from a biological discussion about turtle migrations.

> *Tutor*: To lay their eggs, the females find their way back to the beach where they themselves hatched maybe 20 years earlier. Why do they do that?
>
> *John*: I reckon they're like pigeons. They've got some in built mechanism that detects the earth's magnetic field. How else could they find their way from Brazil to Ascension Island right in the middle of the Atlantic Ocean?
>
> *Sue*: That couldn't be the only reason why they go to Ascension Island.
>
> *Dave to John*: How could you test your theory? It's much more likely that they're guided by the taste of the water.

Figure 7.1. Short extract from a discussion on biology

1. Be clear about what question is being discussed

The first analytical skill is to be very clear about what issue is being discussed. It is a good idea to formulate it consciously as a question whether in your mind, on paper or as a contribution to clarify the discussion. Without this skill you cannot monitor a discussion, take stock of it, or summarise it. (See Chapter 23, Group tutorial.)

Notice that the tutor asks the question 'Why?' and John tries to answer the question 'How?' Sue adds to the confusion by using the word 'why' while what she means is that John's mechanism alone could not explain *how* the turtles find Ascension Island.

However, it may also be educationally profitable to consider the question about how the turtles find the island; so a wise tutor will let the discussion run. There will be plenty of time to draw attention to the two questions being different. To jump in to correct John's response would be excessively controlling, could be perceived as a 'put down', and might therefore discourage participation. That is a very common teaching error.

When teaching several groups simultaneously such as buzz groups, horseshoe groups and other tutorless groups (see Chapter 21), I recommend presenting the task on paper, the blackboard or the screen to ensure that the task is clear and time is not wasted. In tutorials it is quite a good idea to stop occasionally and ask the group to write down what they think the question under discussion is. You may be surprised at their varied answers and the inability of some students to do so. But it soon teaches students to concentrate on what is said in your discussions.

2. Select what is relevant for reasoning

Once the question is clear, one of the first tasks tutors must learn, if they didn't learn it in their student days, is to constantly analyse a discussion to select what is relevant and reasoned. Students must do the same. Without this skill there is mental overload.

What about the other utterances in discussion that are irrelevant to the reasoning? They may reflect participants' thoughts on other matters and for counsellors those may be worth following up; but for teachers concerned with teaching a subject, they are likely to be discarded. They may have non-cognitive significance. That is to say, they may indicate how participants are feeling and in that case they may affect how the group interacts and how the teacher manages the group. (We will consider these group dynamics in Part III.)

Reasoning in discussion has seven kinds of statement that are relevant before the conclusion is reached. (See Figure 7.2.) That requires identifying the seven types and how the relations between them operate. At the speed of some discussions, that is a heavy demand.

3. Identify and check any claim

Once the question and the relevant facts have been identified and clarified, it is necessary to focus on assertions that claim to answer it. We call them 'claims'. Any one of the seven propositions in Figure 7.2 could be regarded as a claim. Of course, if no student is prepared to answer there will be no claim. In that case, any discussion will not be well focused. It is likely to consist of information that might be used or discussion about how the group should proceed.

There are two things to check with any claim. Is it true? And does it answer the question? We have already seen in the example above that John doesn't answer the question asked, but refocuses the discussion onto another question. If we accept that the question now being considered is 'How do turtles find where to lay their eggs?', not the question the tutor actually asked, John's claim (after pruning out non-essential information) is 'Turtles use the earth's magnetic field (to find where to lay their eggs)'.

4. Identify reasons to support the claim

Claims are supported by '*generalisations*' combined with specific '*instances*' or examples of the generalisations. (See Figure 7.2.) The generalisations may be rules, principles or theories. They are not necessarily universal; they could be statistical. To support the claims, not only must the stated generalisations and instances be true, they must combine in such a way that the claim logically follows. This process is central to most discussions.

In the case we've been considering there is a logical difficulty and it is a common difficulty in science. Science strives to find generalisations such as 'All turtles use the earth's magnetic field'. The trouble is that John seeks to justify a claim about all turtles from a limited sample. He's trying to generalise from one instance. That's bad logic. It looks as if John is assuming that: if *some* turtles use the earth's magnetic field then all turtles use the earth's magnetic field, and *some* turtles (namely those finding Ascension Island) do use the earth's magnetic field. Therefore *all* turtles use the earth's magnetic field.

We must return to study these logical difficulties in detail in a moment because teaching students to reason is a fundamental aim of most discussion methods, yet it is not easy.

5. Check the backing of generalisations and the particular facts

If the truth of generalisations or particular facts are challenged, they will, as the new focus of discussion, become claims with their own supporting facts and generalisations. Generalisations and their particular instances are in turn backed up using background knowledge of more basic principles including paradigms of enquiry,

Reasoning in discussion

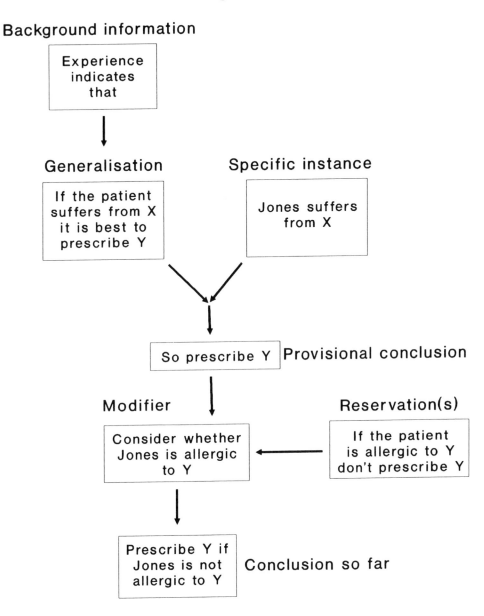

Figure 7.2. Seven propositions in reasoning (After Toulmin et al, 1979)

methods of obtaining information and fundamental laws. This background information has been called '*backing*'. (See Figure 7.2.)

John's backing for the assertion that turtles finding their way to Ascension Island use the earth's magnetic field is that they are like pigeons. If this is treated as a claim, it has two underlying premises: that pigeons use the earth's magnetic field and that turtles are like pigeons in this respect. To justify these premises requires delving ever backward into the 'background information'. Dave's question on how John could test his opinion (not a theory) is therefore pertinent. (In fact an experiment has been devised using satellite tracking and attaching magnets which fall off the turtles after several days, to see whether they then change direction.)

6. Consider, and watch out for, modifiers

Claims, generalisations and assertions of particular facts may need to be modified because they don't always apply, because they are subject to certain conditions or because they are not certain. So some contributions in discussion are '*modifiers*' or '*qualifiers*'. (See Figure 7.2.) Sue has already qualified John's opinion because, on its own, detection of the earth's magnetic field would not guarantee that the turtles arrive at Ascension Island. The turtles would have to have some measure of distance, another co-ordinate, or some other information as well.

7. Listen to, and evaluate, reservations

Next, there are reservations such as '*objections*' and '*counterclaims*'. As we have seen, the objections can be of two kinds. There are objections that claims, generalisations and specific assertions are not true. And there are objections to the reasoning, namely that the claims are not logically supported by the particular instances or their generalisations – in other words, that the premises do not justify their conclusions. Counterclaims are claims in their own right and need to be supported by their own generalisations and particular instances, but they are also objections if they are incompatible with the alternative claim. However, that incompatibility is something that every discussant should check. Indeed, seeking the compatibility of opinions is a useful mental device and an important skill for chairpersons and negotiators.

It is remarkably common for heated debate to be reconcilable because both claims and counterclaims are true, yet for no one to notice that there is no conflict. Dave's counterclaim is reconcilable in this way. There is no reason why turtles should not use both the taste of the water and the earth's magnetic field. Indeed, memory of the taste might provide the extra information that Sue thought was necessary.

8. Conclusion

Notice that even a small extract from a discussion raises a large number of taxing questions. Never suppose that teaching students to think in discussion is a soft option. Done properly, it is extremely demanding for the teacher and students alike. It is so demanding that we must now, as promised, consider reasoning in more detail.

B. Tasks to teach the skills of reasoning

1. Give tasks to decide the truth of statements containing logical operators

Discussions consist of, and decide upon, propositions. Therefore a reasoned discussion will use propositional logic. It relates propositions using logical operators such as 'and', 'or', 'not' and 'if ... then'. For example, deductions using 'if ... then' have the form shown in Figure 7.3. We saw just now, that John seemed to assume a logical form of this kind. This deduction is called *modus ponens*. P is called the 'antecedent' and Q the 'consequent'.

Notice if the pavements are not wet, then it is not raining. That is 'if not-Q then not-P'. This valid inference is called *modus tollens* or 'denying the consequent'. But if the pavements are wet (Q), it does not follow that it is raining (P). They might be wet because of a burst water main or for many other reasons. This fallacy is called 'affirming the consequent' and it is remarkably common. So is the fallacy of 'denying the antecedent' – it does not follow that if it is not raining (not-P), that the pavements are not wet (not-Q). (See Table 7.4.)

Premises If it is raining then the pavements are wet It is raining	Premises If P then Q P
Conclusion The pavements are wet	Conclusion Q

Table 7.3. Modus ponens

Validity	Name	1st Premise	2nd Premise	Conclusion
Valid	Modus Ponens Modus Tollens	If P then Q If P then Q	P not-Q	∴Q ∴not-P
Invalid	Affirming the Consequent Denying the Antecedent	If P then Q If P then Q	Q not-P	∴P ∴not-Q

Table 7.4. Valid and invalid implications

Now if teachers are to stop students from using these logical fallacies, it would be helpful to know why they make them. Rumain et al (1984) thought these errors occur because people mistakenly assume that 'if P then Q' implies 'if not-P then not-Q'. This seems plausible because in many everyday situations it is true, even though it is not logically valid. For example, the terms of any purchase are something like, 'If you give me the money, then I will give you the goods, but if you don't give me the money, then

I won't give you the goods'. Statements giving permission also have this logical form. For example, 'If you are a member, you can enter free of charge' is also usually assumed to mean 'If you are not a member then you can't'. In other words 'if P then Q' is misinterpreted as 'if P then Q and if not-P then not-Q'. That is the same error as claiming that 'If P then Q' means 'if, and only if P, then Q'. (For example, 'if and only if it is raining, then the pavements are wet'.) These could be construed as errors learned as a result of many situations when someone saying 'if' meant 'if and only if'. ('If, and only if,' is sometimes written as 'iff'.)

In other words these errors have been learned by practice in situations where the false assumption has been correct. The teacher's solution is to provide decision tasks where that assumption is incorrect.

Another cause of the error is that students do not notice the ambiguous meaning of the word 'is' when the subject matter is unfamiliar. In 'Paris is the French capital', 'is' means 'is identical to' and the sentence can be reversed without a change in meaning (ie. 'The French capital is Paris'). In 'Paris is beautiful', 'is' means 'has the characteristic of being'. 'Beautiful' is an adjective describing Paris, not something identical to it. Errors arise from sentences like 'The elephant is the largest Indian mammal' where the meaning of 'is' is not so clear. Is it a definition or a description? Both are common in academic discussions.

2. Give tasks to list reasons applicable in their subject

Another possible reason why people affirm the consequent is that they think that P is the only cause of Q. It's as if they think the pavements are only wet when it is raining. The example may seem trivial, but this error of logic could be very serious when committed by medical students if they concluded that the only cause of sore throats, headaches and feeling poorly is influenza, when meningitis has the same initial symptoms.

The error disappears when other possible antecedents are introduced. For example, if people are told:

If P then Q	If it is raining	then the pavements are wet
If R then Q	If it is snowing	then the pavements are wet
If S then Q	If a water pipe has burst	then the pavements are wet
And then they are told		
Q	The pavements are wet	

People are then much more cautious before assuming the cause of Q is P rather than R or S. Likewise, medical students need to be taught that meningitis and other diseases could cause those symptoms, not assume that the only possible cause is influenza.

This implies that students need to be given tasks to list as many reasons, causes or antecedents of Q as possible. If they already know that there could be many possible reasons for Q, they are less likely to assume that one of them is the only one.

This goes some way to explain a phenomenon that once mystified psychologists and educational researchers: students' logical reasoning is subject specific. It had been thought that if you teach students the rules of logic, they will be able to apply them to any subject matter – in short, that there would be transfer of training to other contexts. Courses and textbooks full of exercises were written on general subjects. But they didn't work. Professors of logic don't apply logic to unfamiliar subjects very much better than lay people. The skills don't transfer as much as might be expected. Academics who are rigorously logical in their discipline can be quite irrational on university committees.

So the strategy with students is to give tasks to list, or even brainstorm, reasons for something within the subject matter being taught. The aim is to develop in the students an automatic tendency to seek many reasons, and many causes, for a phenomenon, not just one. It is part of getting students to see the broader picture. It is part of open-mindedness. People who are willing to consider many causes of a disaster are less likely to blame one. Such richer understanding brings greater tolerance. So greater rationality affects attitudes too.

3. Give hypotheses to be tested

Affirming the consequent is also a common error amongst students doing standard scientific experiments. They mistakenly reason, 'If the hypothesis is true, I should get that result. Oh, I have got that result. So the hypothesis must be true'. They seek to verify the hypothesis, not to test it. To test it they should try to deny the consequent, not affirm it. That is, they should try to disprove a hypothesis by using *modus tollens,* not confirm its truth.

If they fail to falsify it, their belief in the hypothesis can be strengthened. They should reason, 'If I don't get that result, the hypothesis is false. Oh, I have got that result. So I've failed to show that the hypothesis is false. So, although I can never be certain, I can have increased confidence that the hypothesis is true' (cf Popper, 1968).

E	K	4	7
P	not-P	Q	not-Q

	P	not-P	Q	not-Q
% Choosing	89%	16%	62%	25%

Figure 7.5. Wason's four card trick

The prevalence of trying to confirm hypotheses, rather than test them, has been shown by Wason (1966) in a widely replicated experiment. He presented four cards as shown in Figure 7.5. Subjects were told that each card had a letter on one side and a number on the other. They were asked to test the hypothesis that 'If there is a vowel on one side, there is an even number on the other' by turning over only the necessary card or cards. E and 7 are the correct answers, but, as you see, 62% chose 4 and only 25% chose 7. (Oaksford and Chater, 1994.)

One explanation is that people naively select the cards mentioned in the hypothesis. If that is the case and if students are repeatedly given a hypothesis of this kind in groups, they get wise to it. They learn to test hypotheses, not to confirm them.

4. Give concrete examples at first

Another reason for students' poor performance with Wason's selection task is that letters and numbers may seem to be abstract. When concrete examples have been used, students have been much more successful. But then it was found that the concrete examples needed to be within the students' experience. They did not perform well when considering unfamiliar situations, even when they were practical and concrete.

5. Give false hypotheses to test

In particular, they scored much higher if, on some occasion(s) they had experienced a mistaken hypothesis. This gives us a clue how to teach students to avoid this logical error.

6. Start with familiar concrete hypotheses; then widen their context

The teacher's strategy should be first to teach the principle by using simple hypotheses concerning familiar subject matter, and then gradually to contextualise them by giving practical examples taken from the less familiar scientific literature that is also part of the students' curriculum. The teacher gives the hypotheses; the students have to devise experiments to test them. Let the situations described in the early practical examples contain some broad hints about the facts to be used to test the hypothesis. Then gradually require more initiative and inventiveness from the students in designing (thought) experiments. That way you gradually build up research skills in your department and that can only be good for everyone.

I have been assuming that there isn't time, or it's not feasible, for students to carry out the experiments they design. They have to be thought experiments designed by small tutorless groups in lectures, or by tutorial groups possibly with some guidance and prompting from the tutor. But of course, where possible, it is a very good teaching practice to use small group discussions to design experiments that students then carry out in the laboratory. Most teachers do not integrate their teaching methods enough.

7. Give tasks to reason with negatives

Another explanation for this common error is that people are reluctant to choose the negatives not-P and not-Q, even when 'If not-Q then not-P' is the right answer. People shy away from reasoning that is difficult and there is a great deal of evidence that reasoning with negatives is difficult. Mental tasks with negatives take longer. (Compare $9 + 4 = ?$, $9 - 4 = ?$, $13 - 4 = ?$, and $13 + 4 = ?$) Using True, False, Don't Know tests with matched pairs of true and false statements related to statements made in lectures, I have found that students make more errors with false negative statements than true negative ones (Bligh, 1974). Understanding that a negative statement is not true involves understanding a double negative.

But as we have seen, the testing of scientific hypotheses involves negative reasoning. If it's difficult we must make it come more easily by practice. So giving tasks to reason with negatives is a useful strategy. Particularly effective are plausible but false hypotheses. They demand reasoning with negatives and possibly double negatives. Students are instructed to design experiments to show they are false.

Reasoning with negatives is also very important in law. For example, 'except' operates like a negative in exception clauses (eg. in house insurance contracts), but 'notwithstanding' often operates as a positive. Law students must learn to be fluent when handling several words of this kind in one sentence. Small group discussions involving false claims and negative statements in legal documents can help to develop these skills.

8. Practise estimating probabilities

Most discussions consider whether something is true. That is, whether a proposition is true or false. That is why, so far, we have considered reasoning using propositional logic. But sometimes we can't know whether something is true; we can only consider probabilities. Discussions involving estimates of probabilities are quite common in decision-making tasks such as those in business studies and medicine.

Let's consider again the patients who report to their doctor with `flu-like symptoms which might be meningitis. Let's suppose that for every person who gets meningitis there are a million who get `flu. That's to say, with those symptoms, the probability *prior* to seeing the doctor is one in a million that they have meningitis. However, when doctors confront the *evidence*, in 95% of cases when a patient has meningitis doctors think they might have it; and doctors think they might have it in 1% of cases when they have only got `flu.

If your doctor thinks you might have meningitis, what are the chances that (s)he's right? Most people would think (s)he's probably right. Actually the chances are 10,526 to 1 against. For every million people who report to their doctor with 'flu-like symptoms, there are 10,000 (1% of 1,000,000) where the doctor thinks they might have meningitis when they have not. This compares with 0.95 (ie. 95% of 1) cases where the doctor thinks they might have meningitis and they have. So the ratio is 10,000 to 0.95. That is 10,526 to 1.

How is it that most people's estimates of probability can be so wildly wrong? It seems they underestimate the importance of prior probabilities, and are more impressed by probabilities based on evidence. It's partly that they look for causes and don't see prior probabilities as having any causal influence on why the doctor's opinion might be right or wrong (Tversky and Kahneman, 1980).

Estimates of probability are also influenced by the *availability* of relevant experience, particularly recent experience. If you had a friend whose doctor recently thought he had meningitis and he had, your confidence in doctors' opinions would be all the greater. If he had not, it would be weakened. This error is known as the 'availability heuristic'.

Tversky and Kahneman (1974) also describe a 'representative heuristic'. Steve is *…very shy and withdrawn, invariably helpful, but with little interest in people, or the world of reality. A meek tidy soul, he has a need for order and structure and a passion for detail…*When asked the probability that Steve is a farmer, doctor, librarian or pilot, most people say 'librarian' because the description represent their stereotype of a librarian. But the prior probability would not justify that decision. There are many more farmers and doctors than there are librarians.

How can students be taught to be more rational and statistically literate? I don't see any option except to explain the arithmetic (of Bayes's Theorem) in more detail than space allows here and to give practice in estimating probabilities. I shall mention these difficulties in decision-making again at the end of Chapter 10.

C. Common errors of reasoning in discussion

We all make errors in reasoning, not least in the heat of discussion, but we might make fewer if we knew the most common ones. Furthermore, they are easier to correct when participants know their names. Most people know names such as 'false analogy' and 'begging the question', but there are many more. So I will briefly introduce some of them here.

1. Hasty generalisations
These are of two kinds: drawing conclusions from too few instances and generalisations from atypical examples. Generalisations about ethnic or national groups are particularly prone to these errors.

2. Overlooking exceptions
In this case, the generalisations are perfectly sound as generalisations, but the speaker does not recognise that they are not absolute rules. He or she has failed to check that the generalisation applies in this particular instance. For example, in Figure 7.2 a reservation would apply if Jones was allergic to Y such as penicillin.

3. False cause
This error is made in three ways: confusing correlation with causation, by a false inference from temporal succession, and resulting from mistaken belief.

Over the past 50 years the sale of refrigerators correlates positively with the increase in crime, but no one would suppose that one is the cause of the other. Why? Because we cannot see any mechanism by which one could affect the other. It is also true that in the same period the increase in reported crime correlates positively with the growing number of telephones, and while we would not think one is the cause of the other, we may be aware of a common factor, namely, that people are much more likely to report a crime when they have a telephone with which to do so.

These two examples draw attention to two mental checks that discussants should carry out when cause and effect is claimed. Is there a mechanism by which the claimed cause has the claimed effect? Is there a common factor, or even a common cause, underlying the correlation?

It has been observed that crime in the UK has decreased since the building of new prisons was introduced. To claim cause and effect is to make a false inference from temporal succession. Yet crime also fell in countries where there was no prison building programme. This fallacy would be more evident if the claimant had checked whether there were counter examples. That is to say, check for instances when crime has increased following the introduction of prison building.

The history of science is full of examples of mistaken beliefs about cause and effect. The fact that astrology – the belief that the position of stars influences human affairs – is not yet dead shows the importance in discussion of sometimes asking the question, 'How could we test whether that is true?'

4. Self-fulfilling prophecy
If you tell a football team during their tactical discussion that they will lose on Saturday, they are more likely to do so. Most managers know that.

5. Poisoning the wells of knowledge
This fallacy occurs when participants will not accept knowledge from any source that contradicts their chosen belief. Fundamentalists who believe that every word in the Bible or Quran is true because it is God's spoken revelation, will not accept counter evidence. They reason that if there is a conflict between, say, scientific evidence and God's word, God's word must take precedence. In effect they declare that knowledge from any other source is poisonous to the purity of their source.

6. Analogies and false analogies
Good analogies explain, but they don't justify. Yet it is not uncommon for discussants to think they have justified their belief when they have only explained what it is.

The other trouble with analogies in discussion is that participants need thinking time to analyse and match each component to the case being discussed. Discussions usually proceed too fast to do so. Vigilance is required.

7. Circular arguments and begging the question
Begging the question is a kind of circular argument. The speaker assumes what he is trying to prove as a premise to 'prove' it. The circle is easily overlooked in discussion if the circular chain of argument is long, if it is disguised by using different words with equivalent meanings, and when different speakers contribute to the chain.

A particular form of question begging occurs in the habitual use of certain adjectives with pejorative or favourable effects. Phrases such as 'high spending councils', 'naive optimist' and 'extreme left wing radicals' can easily go unchallenged when the speaker's major point seems more central to the discussion. Yet they have a drip, drip, drip effect that may unconsciously persuade the unwary.

Questions of the 'Have you stopped beating your wife?' kind notoriously beg the question of whether you ever beat your wife. Yet it is not unusual for discussants (particularly some television interviewers) to demand 'yes' or 'no' answers.

8. Evading the question
Politicians are renowned for evading the question often because it would be wrong to

answer it. (Consider, for example, the effects of hinting at changes in economic policies.) But in academic discussions such consequences are unlikely. As I said at the beginning of this chapter, an imperative when listening to discussion is always to be clear what the issue is.

9. Appeals to authority

There are some circumstances when the opinions of authorities can reasonably support an argument in discussion. But that does not mean that an authority's opinion should not be challenged and justified. The danger occurs when appeals to authority become a substitute for thinking and observing for oneself. The advancement of science was held up for hundreds of years when medieval scholars trusted the word of Aristotle rather than observing and reasoning for themselves (cf. Galileo's fate).

10. Remarks against the claimant

The converse of appeals to authority are dismissive remarks about another group member or an authority he or she cites. 'He would say that wouldn't he?' is a fallacy attempting to dismiss what someone says – his claim – on the grounds of (real or imaginary) facts about that person. The truth or falsity of what someone says in discussion has nothing to do with the characteristics of whoever says it (except rarely in T-Groups, when those characteristics are the topic of discussion). NB. Teachers use put-downs more often than students, but productive and harmonious groups are those where the teacher values, and encourages others to value, every other member and what they say.

Dismissive remarks against a claimant often consist of labelling what allegiance or what group a person belongs to, such as 'He's a communist' or 'He's a racist'. They use the fallacy of 'guilt by association'. Using 'hasty generalisation' they assume all communists etc. are the same. At worst they are name calling. The uncomfortable fact – admit it – is that we tend to be more convinced by these dishonest tactics when they favour our point of view.

Labels may help to *explain* why the person makes their claim by suggesting what background information the person believes to support their claim; but the claim itself should still be *justified or rejected* on the facts of the case, not on facts about its claimant. The difference between explaining and justifying is often blurred in discussion and in lectures too. Justifications explain; but not all explanations justify.

11. Appeal for unity

In effect, an 'appeal for unity' consists of saying 'You ought to believe (or 'do') this because everyone else does'. Appeals to nationalism or ethnic identity are of this kind. So are advertisers' claims that more people use their product than any other. These appeals are blatant.

In group discussions the appeal is more subtle and normally unspoken. It is group pressure – the power of group conformity. We consider this in Part III.

D. Conclusion

If you listen closely with a clear mind to reasoning in discussion, you will see that participants virtually never fully spell out their reasoning. They always assume background knowledge, or that others will accept unstated premises as obvious, or that conclusions can be drawn from a single fact, and so on.

In section A of this chapter I tried to give you a structure in Figure 7.2 indicating various elements of reasoning in discussion. The types of reasoning might include deduction, hypothesis testing and inferences on the basis of probability. In discussions, reasoning of these types come thick and fast. Examples of each were given in section B.

Tutors have to be vigilant regarding the reasoning used. They must then exercise considerable judgement about what reasoning expressed by participants to encourage the group to consider further. This is easier if, when preparing the tasks to be set, they work out the types of reasoning involved. Even so, with all the other things that have to be monitored in discussion, the vigilance and rapidity of judgement required is extremely demanding.

In section C we looked at errors of reasoning common in discussion. Knowing names for them makes them easier to spot. Then there is skill required in judging how to respond to them with tact and gentleness, or whether to do so at all.

Chapter 8
Problem-solving

A. Psychological descriptions of problem-solving
B. Precepts for teachers
C. Conclusion

The tasks teachers give small discussion groups can almost invariably be conceived as problem-solving tasks. In this chapter I am primarily concerned with factors that help students solve problems with one answer, or at least a limited number of specifiable answers. Creative tasks (Chapter 9) and decision-making are problems of a kind. By their nature creative tasks usually have a multitude of possible answers. Decisions (Chapter 10) often have to be taken when there is uncertainty and no right answers.

Problems with specifiable answers are particularly characteristic of science and engineering subjects, but they are also common in other subjects. These problems pose a particular difficulty for teachers. They require students to think, but it often seems as if either the students can solve them or they can't. If they can, they can do the required thinking and there is nothing left to teach or discuss. If they can't, the students think they have nothing to contribute and all the teacher can do is to tell them how to solve it. Because 'telling' does not get the students to do the thinking (it only gives information), it seems as if teachers have a dilemma.

Many are the group tutorials in science and engineering that never overcome this dilemma. Partly because there seems to be no room for personal opinions, the tutor asks questions that have a right answer. If the students know the answer, they give it and the obligation to talk seems to be back with the teacher again. The teacher then asks the next question and so on. The result is a quizzing that tests knowledge, not a discussion that promotes thought. When students don't know the answers, the tutor 'tells', and the result is a mini (or not so mini) lecture.

To resolve this dilemma teachers need to know how students might solve problems. Only if teachers know what strategies or mental processes students might use, can they knowingly give tasks to develop them. Therefore this chapter aims to unravel what those processes might be and to suggest corresponding teaching techniques.

A. Psychological descriptions of problem-solving

1. Gestalt theory's account of problem-solving
The clearest account of problem-solving processes was given by the Gestalt psychologists over 60 years ago. They are clearest because the problems were simple

and they were simple because they studied problem-solving by animals. Modern research into problem-solving adds remarkably little. Some of the classic studies were on monkeys by Wolfgang Kohler. Let's consider an example.

In one experiment a monkey was in a cage with two sticks which could be fitted end to end like the extension to a snooker cue. Outside was a banana that the monkey could reach through the bars with one of the sticks, but not with his arm alone. With successive trials the monkey became quite skilled at retrieving the bananas. Then a banana was placed further away so that it could not be reached using only one stick. After vain attempts to retrieve it with one stick, the monkey appeared to give up, retreated into the cage and sulked or sometimes played with the sticks in an apparently irrelevant way. Then after a period of apparent inactivity, the monkey leapt up, fitted the two sticks together, and retrieved the banana.

This account of problem-solving involves ten stages:

i) First, the monkey had some prior knowledge. He knew what bananas are and that they taste good.

ii) He had already acquired and practised some relevant skills. He knew how to unzip a banana and, so far as the main problem is concerned, he had practised retrieving the banana with one stick (though how to do that must have been a problem at first). He knew the rules and procedures of solving the problem with one stick, but not with two.

iii) The monkey had, or was given, a goal and motivation to achieve it, namely eating the banana.

iv) The monkey not only recognised that there was a problem, he knew what it was. He had an initial conception of the problem even though it was inadequate to solve it. His conception was based upon his previous experience and skills, but they were insufficient for the new problem. He needed an additional concept and skill.

v) He became familiar with the elements of the problem such as the concepts involved and/or the equipment to be used.

vi) During play, he almost randomly reorganised elements of the problem (the sticks) in new ways to form new relationships.

vii) There was a period of irrelevant activity or overt inactivity.

viii) He appeared to have a sudden flash of insight into how to solve the problem. The insight was, for him, a new concept, namely the concept that the sticks could be attached end to end.

ix) There was a period of work applying previous knowledge and procedures to the insight that had been gained. In this case he had to work screwing, or attaching, the two sticks together.

x) The new skills of putting the sticks together and then using them, could now be practised every time the monkey was presented with a problem of the same type.

If we look at this carefully we can see that the monkey progressively adds one skill to another to form a long chain. (Recognising a banana, knowing how to pick it up and unzip it, retrieving it with his arm through the bars of the cage, retrieving it with his arm and one stick, joining two sticks together, and retrieving with two sticks.) Indeed, Newell and Simon have pointed out that if some mud clogged up the screw fitting of the two sticks, the monkey would have to tack on a new skill, namely how to clean the attachment. New skills are added to old ones to produce a chain of goal-directed behaviour.

This is exactly what we expect of our students. To solve ever more complex problems, students build one skill upon another. If you consider how students started in primary school, this is particularly obvious in the case of mathematics, computing skills and essay writing, but it applies in all disciplines and, as we shall see, discussion is an important part of the building process.

In effect, the ten stages on page 57 are sub-tasks of the main problem-solving task. When students can't solve the whole of a problem, the skilled teacher is able to break it down into its sub-tasks.

1. You have to understand the problem
What is the unknown?
What are the data?
What is the condition(s) set by the problem
Is it possible to satisfy the condition(s)?
Is the condition sufficient to determine the unknown?
Or is it insufficient? Or redundant? Or contradictory?
Draw a figure
Introduce a suitable notation
Separate the various parts of the condition
Can you write them down?

2. Find the connection between the data and the unknown.   **Consider auxiliary problems. Devise a plan of the solution**
Have you seen it before?
Or have you seen the same problem in a slightly different form?
Do you know a related problem?
Do you know a theorem that could be useful?
Look at the unknown
Try to think of a similar problem having the same of a similar unknown
Here is a problem related to yours and solved before. Could you use it? Could you use its result? Or its method?
Could you introduce some auxiliary element to make its use possible?
Could you restate the problem? Could you restate it still differently again?
Go back to definitions
If you can't solve the problem, first try to solve a related problem
Could you imagine a more accessible related problem?
A more general problem? A more special problem? An analogous problem?
Keep only part of the conditions set by the problem. How far is the unknown then determined? How can it vary?
Can you derive something useful from the data?
Can you think of other data appropriate to determine the unknown?
Could you change the unknown or the data, or both if necessary, so that the new unknown and the new data are nearer to each other?
Did you use all the data? Did you use the whole condition?
Have you taken into account all the notions involved in the problem?

3. Carry out your plan
When carrying out your plan of the solution, check each step
Can you see that the step is clearly correct? Can you prove it is correct?

4. Looking Back – Examine the solution obtained
Can you check the result? Can you check the argument?
Can you derive the result differently?
Can you see it at a glance?
Can you use the result, or the method, for some other problem?

Table 8.1. Polya's guidance on 'How to solve it'

I do not wish to claim here that there is a single universal set of processes for solving every conceivable problem. If there was, many problems would not be problems at all. But the Gestalt analysis is a very useful one, particularly for science and engineering teachers when faced with the dilemma I described above.

The weakness in using the Gestalt account is some vagueness in steps (vii) and (viii), a period of irrelevance or inactivity followed by (a seemingly inexplicable) insight. Gestalt psychologists explain insight as a new association of the elements of the problem. If that is so, can students do better than inactivity and irrelevance to achieve it?

The essence of a problem is that the way to solve it has to be found. To be a problem, some aspect of the task must be unfamiliar. Solving it involves fitting it into a framework of thinking that is more familiar and where you can apply familiar rules.

2. Polya's 'How to solve it'

It is at this point that Polya's checklist in 'How to solve it' might be helpful, particularly in science. He conceives of problem-solving in four stages. It is the second that fills the gap in the Gestalt account. It consists of questions and instructions. You couldn't give all of them to a problem-solving group at the same time and they aren't all appropriate to every problem. Nonetheless, the checklist is a useful reminder of the sort of questions a problem-solving group should ask itself. (See Table 8.1.)

3. Newell and Simon's information processing theory

Newell and Simon think of problem-solving rather like finding your way in a maze. You start at a definite given point or 'space'. You then meet a succession of choice points (spaces) at which you apply an operation (turn right, turn left, etc.), each choice being determined by the sequence of operations previously applied. Thus there is a whole branching structure of possible paths called the 'problem space', but you can only take one at a time. Your goal is to reach the middle (the solution) and you may have a series of sub-goals on the way. You use certain strategies (called heuristics) such as means-ends analysis, to determine the operations (choices) you make. problem-solving operations are limited by the individual's cognitive system and the conditions laid down by the problem.

Newell and Simon have programmed computers to solve puzzles where there is a fixed goal with sub-goals, and specific operators within a defined 'problem space'. Like Polya's rules of thumb, it works best in science subjects where the relevant information and operations (eg. in maths) are restricted. But the information required to answer questions in the arts and social sciences are far from restricted. Puzzles, and to a large extent problems in maths, science and engineering, usually tell you what operations are legitimate; social problems are not like that.

So, whilst Newell and Simon's approach deserves a mention because it has been influential in cognitive science for over 30 years, I have reservations about its application to education at the present time.

Despite its vagueness in places, I still find Gestalt theory most applicable to problem-solving in group discussions. It is therefore Gestalt theory I mostly have in mind when suggesting the following precepts for teachers designing discussion tasks.

B. Precepts for teachers

1. Ensure students have the necessary prior knowledge and skills

In practical terms this means either selecting students who have the necessary prior knowledge and skills, or teaching them. The latter involves designing the sequence of tasks in the students' curriculum and those tasks must be matched with appropriate teaching or learning methods. We have seen in Chapter 1 that knowledge can be imparted by any presentation method such as offering lectures, reading, films, video and computer assisted learning. The skills need to be taught through practice, perhaps by first setting simpler problems in much the same way that the monkey practised with one stick first. This accounts for stages (i) and (ii).

2. Set the task clearly

When setting a task or problem a teacher sets a goal. That is, what would count as achieving or solving it. It is always worth explaining why you have set it because, assuming there is a good reason, the explanation will enhance motivation.

It is quite common for students to misunderstand the task that has been set. This is not surprising because, owing to its nature, some of the subject matter is likely to be unfamiliar. For that reason it is always advisable to display the task either in a handout or on the blackboard or screen. This is particularly advisable when the task has two or more parts. To use only speech is lazy and creates avoidable misunderstandings.

3. Assist representation of the problem

Firstly, students need to recognise that there is a problem. They need to conceive of it in some way. But in what way? In what terms do they represent the problem? If the monkey had conceived of the problem as, 'How can I get out of this cage?' he would probably never have solved it. 'How can I stretch further?' was also abortive. If he had conceived it as, 'How can I make this stick longer?' he would have been on the right lines.

The representation of a problem is a fundamental step in science. In chemistry, physics, maths and many branches of engineering there are diagrams and formulae. The diagrams and formulae may be different in the different disciplines, but in all cases they are an attempt to represent the problem. Equally in the arts and social sciences, the concepts in which a question is presented control where one looks for an answer.

Almost inevitably when they first perceive a problem, students will conceive of it in terms that are familiar to them. They will try to use concepts and mental processes that they are accustomed to. In the same way, the monkey tried to stretch with one stick. That's how he knew he'd got a problem. The usual procedures did not achieve the goal. The very nature of a problem situation is that the usual way of thinking about it is unsatisfactory. The usual rules and procedures won't give the result you want. Consider for example a physics student who thinks in Newtonian rather than quantum mechanics, or when a client in marriage counselling thinks in legal terms, rather than in interpersonal or moral terms.

So, having understood how students see the problem, the next question for teachers is 'How can I get my students to think about this problem in a new way?' Good problem-solvers spend proportionately more time than novices building new representations of the problem and they spend more time modifying them. They constantly adapt their 'schemata', that is, their frameworks of thinking.

As we saw at the beginning of Chapter 4, one of the functions of discussion is to get participants to think of problems in different ways (that is, with different schemata). I have noticed that teachers who have difficulty in explaining something, often have that difficulty because they, themselves, can only think of representing it in one way. They can only see it in one context. That is why discussion methods often help teachers, too, to see their subject in new ways. A natural mistake by teachers is to assume that students can see a problem the same way that they do.

If students are having difficulty in representing a problem *in any way at all*, there could be a number of reasons. One is that they cannot see the total picture. In which case the teacher can encourage them to represent what they do know – that is, to depict those relationships that they do understand in the way they understand them – and then try to build upon that. Offering encouragement to students who cannot even see that there is a problem, let alone how to solve it, requires a lot of gentle praise and patience. It requires some of the teacher's greatest skills.

Novices tend to try to solve problems in one step. In physics, for example, they try to think of a single equation that will take them directly to a solution. In management they think of ends (goals) and then search for a direct means of achieving them. That's why the monkey tried at first to solve his problem directly with a one-step process using one stick. The solution required a two-step process, joining the sticks and then using them.

Novices also tend to conceive of problems in terms of their peripheral characteristics, such as the equipment that might need to be used, while experts tend to classify problems according to the principles their solutions might apply (Chi, Feltovich and Glaser, 1981). For this reason a common and important teaching tactic is to try to get students to look at underlying principles. They are often in the form of assumptions. So teachers ask, '*What (principles) are you assuming when you analyse (or represent) the problem in that way?*'

How can teachers get students to represent or conceive of a problem in a new way? As with the monkey, it is necessary to become familiar with the elements of the problem.

4. Analyse the problem into its elements

The representation of a problem normally involves analysing the problem into its parts and depicting its elements showing their relationships. To represent a problem situation in a new way, students need to break it down into its elements and mentally put them together in a new way. That is, analysis followed by synthesis.

I have noticed that many students have great difficulty with analytical thinking because it has never been taught. University entrance qualifications require the writing of essays. That is synthesis. The exams don't demand analysis, and students can get adequate grades if they put down enough memorised facts one after another. Sometimes one discovers that any analytical thought displayed was done by their teacher. The students merely remembered the product.

So analytical thought has to be taught. The essence of analytic tasks is to identify the characteristic(s) of something. So questions of the type '*How is X different from Y?*'

and '*In what ways is X the same as Y?*' develop this facility. Thus if you try to say '*How are books different from newspapers?*' you will find you are forced to analyse their characteristics. If you use a comparative task of this kind, insist that the students present the dimension of comparison as shown in the first column of Figure 8.2 (what is called the 'analysans') as well as the characteristics in columns 2 and 3 (the 'analysanda'; singular = 'analysandum'). This obliges the students to think at the appropriate level of abstraction. If you doubt that this will make the students think, try completing the rest of Figure 8.2. You have known what books and newspapers are for years, but I think you will agree that this apparently simple task can be quite stretching.

Analysans	Characteristics of Books	Characteristics of Newspapers
Differences 1. Binding 2. Publication 3. 4. etc.	1. Bound 2. Occasional 3. 4. etc.	1. Not bound 2. Regular 3. 4. etc.
Similarities 1. Medium 2. 3. etc.	2. 2. 3. etc.	Printed paper

Table 8.2. Format of comparative task to teach analytical thought

That's the sign of a good task:
i) Clear and easily understood.
ii) Quick and easy to set.
iii) Everyone can achieve at least part of it (bear achievement motivation in mind).
iv) Achieves the educational objective (in this case further develops analytical thinking).
v) Yet is demanding for the most able students.
vi) Not excessively time-consuming.
vii) The teacher can observe how much students have written from a distance (feedback to teacher).
viii) Follow-up pooling of answers can be crisp (feedback both ways).

Using the same type of chart as shown in Table 8.2, jot down the differences and similarities between: oil extraction and coal mining,
electricity and water,
an arm and a leg,
animals and plants.

Remember, identifying the analysans in the left hand column is what assists conceptual development.

Analysing the characteristics of a problem situation is not always so straight forward. The task doesn't necessarily have to be comparative. Essentially, the preliminary task is to set students individually, or in tutorless groups, to write a list of the characteristics of the problem situation. For example, *'List the factors involved in ...'* (why some people don't take holidays in Spain, yesterday's fall in share prices, the causes of an historical event, the flight of a queen bee, etc.). The factors given will tell the teacher a lot about how the students see the problem. It will reveal which factors they ignore or undervalue compared with those the teacher's solution uses or emphasises. (NB. Many tutors feel reluctant to use buzz groups or individual work in the middle of a seminar or group tutorial. Teaching analytical skills exemplifies occasions when they should do so.)

Sometimes, when students have a list of characteristics or factors, a further analytical task is to ask them to discriminate between items on their list. For example, which of the reasons against taking holidays in Spain are climatic, which financial, which are matters of inconvenience and so on. This analytical task also includes classification, a process that requires some synthesis. That is to say, associating some elements according to an analysans.

5. *Let discussion build memory patterns*

Having elicited the characteristics of, or the factors in, the problem situation, a creative task is to list factors, or combinations of factors, that might be different if the problem was solved. In the case of the monkey these might include the cage door being open or someone helpful outside the cage as well as the stick being longer. This range of possibilities is sometimes called 'the problem space'. Likewise with the problem of marketing Spanish tourism, a brainstorming or horseshoe group might be asked, *'What factors would have to be different for more tourists to go to Spain?'*

To answer this the students would have to imagine (ie. represent) some of the factors in different relationships. For example, perhaps tourism to Spain could only expand at a different time of year when the climate is different and the transport cheaper. It is quite common for the range of possibilities that come to mind to be restricted or blocked by previous experience. This can happen when students have so over-learned the rules to earlier problems that they automatically and perhaps unknowingly misapply them to the current problem. What discussion does is to throw ideas together so that they become familiar and so that new relationships of facts become apparent and not blocked or restricted. Ideas are not thrown together completely at random, nevertheless discussion is analogous to the monkeys' play at stage (vi).

What such representations do is to show new inter-relationships of the various elements of the problem – their re-synthesis. Successful problem-solvers have the ability to analyse and inter-relate repeatedly until they find new relationships that achieve their goal. Several experimenters (eg. Larkin et al, 1980; Simon and Simon, 1978) have shown that the first representations by successful problem-solvers are more complete and accurate than those who are less successful. In other words, they have been able to link together many elements of the problem into a single idea which is then easier to handle.

The ability to handle patterns, or 'chunks', of information as a single unit overcomes a difficulty. One of the difficulties people have in solving problems is that the problems require them to process more information at once than they can handle. In a famous paper, Miller argued that the maximum number of items most people can hold in their mind at once is 7 plus or minus 2. But it is clear that the requirements of many problems greatly exceed that number and that some people solve them successfully. How do they do it?

If ideas can be grouped together, they can be remembered as one item, not several. For example, both de Groot (1966) and Chase and Simon (1973) have shown that, compared with non-experts, expert chess players can take in much more information from observing a chessboard of pieces for a short period of time. The reason seems to be that experts can either recognise or construct (probably both) patterns amongst the pieces. They have a large repertoire of patterns. They also have patterns of move sequences. They don't have to think through every possible move in a sequence individually. Non-experts do.

However, the patterns are specifically about chess. Many researchers have shown the importance of specific contexts and subject matter when solving problems. Memory patterns may explain their importance. It is inferred that if students can build up memory patterns in their subject, they will become better problem-solvers in that subject. Therefore building students' memory patterns should be an important feature of a teacher's technique. Indeed it is an important aspect of all education and training. It is essentially a matter of practice. You can imagine a doctor first analysing what a patient says into symptoms and then linking them together as a diagnosis, before going on to other sub-problems such as how to treat it, how to make arrangements for the treatment, and so on, some of which may have become fairly routine as a result of practice.

6. Make the problem familiar and assist insights by discussion

If having memory patterns closely related to the subject matter of the problem eases the load on a student's memory, it is a short step to assert that problems in familiar subject matter will be easier than those where the example is strange.

It might be concluded that if teachers can make the subject matter familiar, they can help students to solve problems. Even when students are not actively or overtly taking part in a discussion, when they hear the subject matter related, 'patterned' or 'chunked' in new ways, insights to solve the problem become more likely (stages vii and viii).

There is little doubt that discussion will help students to solve a particular problem. It is much less certain that that success will be transferred to other problems. What is difficult is transfer. Presumably the closer the original problem is to subsequent problems, the more likely the skills of one will transfer to the others. But closer in what respect? In subject matter? I think 'Yes', but what is generally meant is transfer to problems with different subject matter, but with a similar form or pattern of reasoning. It is learning forms of reasoning that is important. Discussion teaches this because it is the context in which students have to understand and articulate patterns of reasoning.

What students generally find difficult to learn is the form, the pattern of reasoning, rather than the subject matter. Learning to reason normally takes longer than remembering the relationship between particular facts. There is an important exception, namely when the information load associated with unfamiliar (unpatterned) subject matter is greater than the load associated with forms of reasoning. For example, Kotovsky, Hayes and Simon (1985) have shown that while two problems may have a very similar form, one may be much more difficult for students to picture in their mind's eye.

You won't be surprised that the notion of 'insight' has been subject to criticism. It seems a bit too much like 'divine intervention'. Yet most of us would admit that we have had an 'aha experience' in which, after struggling with a problem or to understand what someone is saying, we suddenly see how the facts fit together and we say, in effect, 'now I understand'. What teachers are trying to do is to help students see how the facts fit together. That is what an explanation consists of. Furthermore, research shows that in practice, human problem-solving is not as logical as algorithms assume.

More recent research has shown differences between novices and experts in how they conceive of the facts they fit together. Undergraduate physics students will try to solve a problem by juggling formulae, whilst the experts are more inclined to conceive of the problem as one of a type such as thermodynamics or Newton's laws of gravitation. Expert chess players think more in terms of general strategy, whilst lesser players work out specific sequences of moves. To put this another way, beginners think in terms of specific rules and procedures to solve problems, whilst those more experienced look at the wider structure of problems or a menu of possible structures. They draw on their experience, in effect saying, 'I've had a problem structured like this before. What did I do to solve it?' In reasoning about problem structures the specific concepts or content of the problem takes a back seat for the moment. Gick and McGarry (1992) point out that they also use analogies with problems they have failed to solve before. So they reason with analogies that are not available to the beginner. They may be using idealised representations of the problem.

You might think that beginners attend to detail and that, by taking a broad strategic approach, the experts overlook the details. The opposite is the case. Beginners do work on details, but most human problems have too many for them to attend to, whilst nearly all the details fit into the broad strategies adopted by the experts. Indeed, whilst the beginners apply specific rules and procedures, the experts have a whole 'package of procedures' at their command (Holyoak and Spellman, 1993).

What then, should be the teacher's strategy to help their students become more like experts? Encourage students to represent problems visually and in as many ways as possible. Do the same yourself. Let them build up their breadth of experience and 'package of procedures' by giving a lot of easy problems either before, or rather than, giving more difficult ones. In lectures and tutorials give, and encourage the use of, analogies. Gick and Holyoak imply that if a teacher can present two analogies for a problem, students will more certainly grasp its structure at an abstract level. The greater the degree of abstraction, the more detail is omitted. The optimum level of abstraction is that in which the similarities of the analogies are maximised and the differences are minimised.

So an important function of discussion is to make familiar what has been strange. This takes time, so it is a mistake for tutors to hurry on to the next topic too quickly.

When students have had the insight and at one level understand how the problem is solved (stage viii on page 57) they nonetheless then need time to work upon those insights to check upon the solution. I learned this when working with student teachers returning from teaching practice. Some of their discussions didn't seem to me to be getting anywhere but to them they were learning to relate, contextualise and reason about their experiences. They reported how beneficial the discussions were.

The form or 'structure' of a problem is not the same as how it is 'represented' or perceived. The structure may be quite abstract, for example, most problems have rules or boundaries that set the limits of the problem. Such rules may be abstract even when the problem can be represented graphically or in some other physical form. Rules for long division, for example, may be abstract, but a long division problem can be represented pictorially. Many children can understand the picture, but can't operate the rules.

7. Practise applying the principle

Having learned how to solve a particular kind of problem, students need to practise working with that solution to similar problems so that the pattern of reasoning becomes familiar and fluent. Then it can be the basis of further learning and more difficult problems. This is how skills in mathematics, English, computing, speaking a foreign language and so on, are built up. This principle is totally consistent with my contention that tasks and teaching methods need to be in a developmental sequence.

The teacher does not have to be present during these periods of practice, hence the importance of setting follow-up tasks after a group tutorial. (NB. This is the opposite of what many tutors do. They set work to be done before a tutorial, to be submitted at that time, and possibly read to the class.)

The type of problem I have considered so far is the kind where the student (and the monkey) have to discover a principle before applying it. Only the last stage (stage [x]) is concerned with the application of the principle discovered.

In many, if not most, problems we give to students, they have been given the principle in lectures or textbooks; they don't have to discover it, they only have to apply it. Task 2 in Figure 8.3 is typical of those given to first year law students. (Admittedly Task 1 is an analytical task to distinguish 6 sub-rules of the main rule, but it is quite likely that a lecturer will have done that for them.)

So what is involved in the application of principles? What is the pattern of reasoning the students have to learn? As we have seen, principles and generalisations have the form 'if x then y'. To apply such principles requires:

i) storing knowledge of the principle or generalisation that if x then y (in this case having the definition of theft in one's memory),

ii) being able to retrieve that knowledge; that is search one's memory to find it (eg. being able to recall the definition of theft),

iii) recognising that x^1 is an instance of x. In other words there has to be a matching process between one of the principles a person knows and the problem information he perceives (in the example in Table 8.3 this means checking that there is an instance in the scenario, of each of the six elements in the definition), and

iv) infer from that recognition that y^1 is true.

We have seen in Chapter 1 that the storing of knowledge can be achieved by presentation methods of teaching. So (i) can be achieved by those methods. Steps (ii), (iii) and (iv) are well taught by discussion about x^1 partly because discussion will build up memory patterns and partly because discussants will see x^1 from different points of view. They will have different conceptual schemata. And placing x^1 in many different frameworks of thought increases its familiarity. If the students can't do (ii) and (iii), the tutor will have to use the techniques mentioned in sections 3 and 4 above to help them represent and analyse the problem.

Rule:	Theft is dishonestly appropriating property belonging to another with the intention of permanently depriving him of it.
Task 1	Analyse the rule into six elements that must be satisfied before someone can be found guilty of theft.
Example	Adam is going to the races. Brian gives him £50 to place a bet on a horse in the 2 o'clock and Adam fully intended to do so, but owing to a train delay Adam only arrived at 2.15pm, was told the horse had lost. He kept the money without telling Brian.
Task 2	Apply the six elements to decide whether Adam was guilty of theft.

Table 8.3. A problem to be solved by analysis + application of principles

In Task 2 there is a right answer and if students apply each of the six elements correctly they will obtain it. That is, in effect, an *algorithm*. That is to say a set of problem-solving procedures which, if followed correctly, will guarantee a correct answer. The rules of arithmetic are examples of algorithms; so are the rules for calculating your tax code. Algorithms are usually set out in a series of steps with 'Yes' or 'No' answers as in Figure 10.2 on page 85.

In well defined problems there is:
i)   information about an initial state of affairs,
ii) a specified goal or solution to be reached,
iii) rules governing what you are allowed to do to solve the problem (legal operators), and
iv) rules that restrict the use of the legal operators (operator restrictions).
The trouble is, not all problems have yes or no answers or clear rules and certainly not all have a series of well-defined steps. These are almost normal in the arts and social sciences. Consider 'Was Hamlet mad?' It might seem like a yes or no question, but the answer is probably 'It all depends on what you mean by ... ' As Kahney (1993) put it '...an ill-defined problem is how to pass an examination in psychology'!

8. Use general heuristic procedures
Consequently what is needed in arts and many social studies disciplines are rules of thumb rather than well-defined steps. These rules of thumb are called *heuristics*. But how do you obtain them?

Problem-solving consists of information processing, so we should expect recent developments in information theory, artificial intelligence and computing facilities to offer some insights into how to help students learn to solve problems.

In practical educational terms, progress so far has been disappointing. This is because computers often want yes/no questions and cannot solve other problems unless you first tell them how to do so. In particular, any computer program will assume a particular way of representing the problem. But if you already know how to represent the problem in order to get the solution, it seems you already know the solution by some other means. So what new do the computers tell you?

The most useful developments have been by Newell and Simon (1972). They looked at how problems were solved and tried to describe the processes in terms of information processing. Having done so, they argued that if their description was correct, it should be possible to write a computer program to simulate the process. If the program didn't work, there must be something wrong with their simulation and they should change it until it worked a lot better. In this way, that is by simulation, computers were used to test theoretical problem-solving procedures. In others words, they detected gaps between theory and practice and then modified the theories underpinning their computer programs until they worked in practice. The general program they developed was called the General Problem Solver (GPS).

The gaps between theory and practice showed the inadequacies of human problem-solvers. It would be helpful to teachers if Newell and Simon were able to say what the most common inadequacies are. This they have not done, no doubt because the approach is still in its early stages and only a limited range of problems have been used.

However they have described the 'heuristics' most successfully used. These are:
i)   an analysis of means and ends,
ii) the creation of sub-goals,
iii) working forward using the information given, and
iv) working backward from the desired solution.

These are strategies that teachers could ask small groups to practise. Each is stock in trade in business studies and they might be a useful strategy for science students to try when they get stuck. Means-ends analysis involves breaking the task down into sub-goals and working out the steps to reach the end-goal. The creation of sub-goals is also necessary to write a clearly structured essay and, as I suggested before, demands analytical skills that many university entrants lack.

C. Conclusion

The theme of this chapter and running through the whole book is that students need to learn to think by a developmental sequence of cognitive tasks *beginning with simple easy tasks in small groups for short periods of time, and then gradually increase their respective complexity, difficulty, size and duration.* Therefore an essential preliminary skill for teachers is to be able to break tasks into smaller ones, before gradually grouping them into larger ones. It's not easy. This chapter tries to give hints on how to do so.

Chapter 9
Teaching creativity

A. Its importance

B. Opinions on what creativity is

C. Creativity as diverse abilities for teachers to cultivate

D. Unusual association of ideas as necessary, but not sufficient, for creativity

E. Creativity as an attitude

F. Creativity as cognitive strategies

G. Conclusion

A. Its importance

It's the job of universities to produce new ideas. They do research. Creativity is their business. Advances in work, social understanding and leisure are strongly influenced by, if not dependent upon, creativity in science, the social sciences and the arts. Yet very few university teachers make it their business to teach creativity. They teach what is known and teach students to think in traditional ways in their disciplines. (The very notion of a 'discipline' seems to suggest a rigidity – a way of thinking that has to be learned.)

Nearly 50 years ago Carl Rogers inveighed against our culture by making the following points:

1. In education we tend to turn out conformists, stereotypes, individuals whose education is 'completed', rather than turn out freely creative original thinkers.
2. In our leisure-time passive entertainment is predominant, whereas creative activities are much less in evidence.
3. The sciences supply technicians, but they supply few who can creatively formulate fruitful hypotheses and theories.
4. In industry creation is reserved for the few – the manager, the designer, the head of the research department. For many, life is devoid of original or creative endeavour.
5. In individual and family life the same holds true. In the clothes we wear, the food we eat, the books we read and the ideas we hold, there is a strong tendency toward conformity. To be original or different is felt to be dangerous.

B. Opinions on what creativity is

The choice of tasks to teach creativity depends on what it is. Yet one of the difficulties in talking about creativity is to say exactly what it is. I shall regard it as a general name for a number of different abilities. So when suggesting possible tasks to teach it, in each case I shall first outline the ability to be taught.

Creativity is sometimes discussed as if there was something mystical about it. Perhaps that is why the most popular recent British and American textbooks on undergraduate cognitive psychology don't even mention the word, let alone consider the subject (for example, Eysenck and Keane, 1990; Anderson, 1995; Smyth et al, 1994). Another reason is that, being a general name for several different abilities, *scientific* methods should define and treat the psychological abilities separately. Nonetheless, *educational* methods to produce originality have something in common.

Newell and Simon, who tried to program a computer to be creative, said there are four characteristics that any theory of creativity must include:
i)   a creative product or process has novelty value.
ii) it involves unconventional thinking,
iii) it requires high motivation and persistence, and
iv) the problem to be solved is usually vague.

Irving Taylor said there are five levels of creativity which vary in depth and scope, but are not fundamentally different processes.
i)   At the 'expressive' level, skill is unimportant. Examples include young children's drawing that express feeling rather than accuracy of observation.
ii) At the 'productive' level there is more realism and representation; consequently free play of the imagination is more restricted.
iii) The 'inventive' level displays more new conceptions and involves an element of discovery.
iv) Few people reach the 'innovative' level because this requires challenging or modifying the foundations of a science or art. For example, the cubists and quantum physicists challenged basic assumptions in their fields.
v) The final level is called 'emergentive' because it results in a new principle at an abstract or fundamental level.
The products of levels 1 and 2 are new for those who produce them, but not for society as a whole. Most university students operate at level 2, whilst their teachers hope that at least a few will reach level 3. So this chapter is primarily concerned with ways to move students from the productive, to the inventive level.

There is general agreement that creativity is a process that produces something original, whether for the individual or the wider society, but there is little agreement on what the process is. I shall contend that it may be several of many different processes which, for convenience I shall classify into four:
    C   A complex of innate or maturing abilities
    D   Novel association of ideas

E   The application of certain attitudes

F   Unusual cognitive processes

Clearly, the tasks to teach creativity will depend on which of these you emphasise. Insofar as there is general agreement that it can be taught, there is also general agreement that small group discussion is one of the methods that might be used to teach it. And, in my opinion, discussion should always be used with other methods in preparation for, or in follow-up consolidation of, the experiences the other methods provide.

C. Creativity as diverse abilities for teachers to cultivate

In the past there has been a debate as to how far creativity can be taught at all. In an extreme view, creativity and intelligence are kinds of innate potential ability. You're either born with the potential or you're not. For those that have them, the seed is there to germinate and grow. They develop with maturation, but education and the environment have very little part to play in developing them. In its stark form this elitist 'no hope' view is almost certainly false. Everyone can develop some of the characteristics of creativity. Fortner (1986) has even improved the creativity of 'learning-disabled' 7–11 year-olds, compared with controls. After 27 sessions of non-judgemental brainstorming they showed increased 'thought units', use of subordinate clauses and 'thematic maturity' in spontaneous story writing.

In a less extreme view, creativity will be a potential ability, like intelligence, which requires activity in a suitable environment to bring it to fruition. It is the teacher's job to provide the tasks and the environment.

In fact, there has been quite a bit of work comparing intelligence and creativity and investigating how far they are the same thing, or how far they are different things, but related. In the former view, creativity is an aspect of general intelligence, labelled 'g' by Spearman. In recent times this view has been associated with Arthur Jensen (1984) who sees intelligence and creativity as the product of an efficient and discriminating nervous system. If that were so, one would expect a high correlation between measures of intelligence and creativity. The problem with this is that creativity itself is not something quantifiable (though indicators of it might be), so almost any kind of correlation is open to challenge. However, Torrance (1966, 1972a, 1972b, 1981) and others (eg. Crockenberg, 1972 and Yamamoto, 1965) have concluded that creativity and intelligence are correlated more highly for people of average and rather below average intelligence than for those who score more highly. To reach this conclusion they not only looked at biographical data and other people's estimates of the individuals' creativity, but a series of tests of creative thinking that Torrance devised in 1966, which are still used today. These results suggest that creativity is made possible by intelligence, but they are not the same thing. In this interpretation, intelligence facilitates creativity, but you can be very intelligent without being creative. A stronger view is that intelligence doesn't just make creativity possible, it positively promotes it.

Gardner (1983) has suggested that there are several different intelligences each with a different neurological base: linguistic, logico-mathematical, spatial, musical, bodily-kinesthetic, intrapersonal and interpersonal. Gardner believes most activities require contributions from more than one of these domains. But if that is true of intelligence, it is even more likely to be true of creativity. There should be different creativities based upon different combinations of traits or intelligences.

1. Persistently use a wide variety of tasks combining disparate abilities

The implication of this is that teachers should give a wide variety of tasks requiring links between these different abilities. Whatever the activity, it needs to be debriefed using discussion because understanding the discussion obliges participants to use the different intellectual abilities.

The Williams-Stockmyer programme to teach creativity places particular emphasis upon 'switching' between use of the left and right cerebral hemispheres. So they required students to perform specific mental tasks – selecting the key concepts of a problem, representing the concepts in pictures, analysing them into 'fragments', reconstructing them with explicit 'organising tools' or rules, and completing puzzles. This sequence is verbal-visual-analysis-synthesis combination. Williams and Stockmyer (1984) found that students trained in this way solved problems with greater validity, distinctiveness, diversity and abstraction than students trained to question assumptions, to withhold judgement and to brainstorm (see page 219).

McGuire (1985) even claims that creativity can be taught with an authoritarian teaching style, provided 'holistic' teaching strategies are used. These included 'opportunities to brainstorm, assigning open-ended tasks, encouraging guessing, solving problems by any method students prefer, and encouraging drawing, tactile manipulation and mental imagery'. Certainly these methods use a variety of mental abilities, but they don't seem very authoritarian to me.

Ziolkowska (1977) emphasised that developing creativity requires a long-term strategy. She found that students systematically and consistently required to propound new hypotheses and formulate appropriate questions were better at these two elements of creativity than controls and students who were only given the tasks sporadically. This may seem like nothing more than saying students learn what you teach them, but it gives the lie to claims that creative skills cannot be taught.

2. Recognise creative talent

Give emotional support a little but often. Remarks such as 'That's a good idea', 'I hadn't thought of that', 'I liked your ...' and so on are quite natural and need not arouse other students' feelings of favouritism.

3. Be a sponsor or a patron

For fear of those feelings, this kind of support is best given more discreetly outside the discussion circle. It is more than recognising what the student has done. It is encouragement towards the next creative output. It is forward looking and provides practical help.

4. Provide refuge from attacks

Creative ideas often seem unconventional, ridiculous or threatening at first. Students and parents may offer destructive criticism. The creative student may need help to understand parents' and other students' hidden feelings. Creative individuals are often censured or attacked because they are perceived as unconventional and 'not one of us'. They can sometimes be ostracised, marginalised or ignored by other students. They therefore need emotional support.

5. Help creative students to understand and accept their divergence
It's not that creative students are superior beings, but 'All people are different. We each have different talents that are worth developing. You are good at …'

6. Help others to understand and appreciate the value of creative talent
This does not necessarily need to refer to anyone they know. Sadly, history is littered with examples of creative individuals who were only valued after their death.

7. Let creative individuals express and communicate their ideas and individuality
Use dyads at first, because in dyads they will get a fair hearing and won't be out-numbered. By constantly changing the pairings, the creative individual will gradually develop accepting relationships in the wider group.

These precepts are ways teachers can provide some support, but they are not a substitute for being accepted by one's peers.

D. Unusual association of ideas as necessary, but not sufficient, for creativity

1. Give tasks to generate associations. Select the original and appropriate ones
Originality results from associating ideas that would not normally be associated. The history of science has many examples. So give tasks that try to relate apparently uncon-nected ideas. Edison, perhaps the world's most successful inventor, had a deliberate policy to try to relate his current problem to apparently unconnected ideas. A physicist was reported as keeping a bowl containing slips of paper, each stating a physical fact. Periodically he would take out two with the hope of finding a serendipitous relationship. Discussion, too, is a context in which ideas are presented next to each other facilitating new associations for the prepared mind. Whatever the technique, the vast majority of associations will be wasted as irrelevant or ridiculous. In this view, creativity is essentially a process of generate and select – generate associations and select those that are both original and appropriate.

2. Test students for varied ideas on a topic
Sometimes creativity consists of producing very varied answers to a problem. This is known as 'divergent thinking'. It is the production of divergent ideas that makes unusual associations more likely and hence the production of creative work. So to foster creativity teachers need to teach the ability to make unusual associations of ideas.

This view of creativity has the advantage that divergent thinking is relatively easy for teachers to practise and test. A typical test of divergent thinking is to give subjects a concept and ask for as many associated concepts as possible (Guilford and Hoepfner, 1971; and Wallach, 1970). Hudson (1966) showed a correlation between his test of divergent thinking and ability in arts, as distinct from science subjects; but he failed to demonstrate a correlation with other manifestations of creativity. The Wallach and Kogan Creative Battery (Wallach and Kogan 1965b), seeks original responses to a variety of problems but later work (Wallach, 1976) showed that this test was unable to predict who was creative in other ways. So it looks as if the ability to make diverse associations of ideas is a distinct ability. It may be necessary for creativity, and therefore needs to be taught, but it is not sufficient.

3. Associations are relatively topic specific

The Torrance Tests of Creative Thinking produce correlations as high as 0.5 between test scores and measures of creativity (Torrance, 1972a, 1981). The Torrance test includes a number of sub-tests and, for each sub-test, scores are obtained for fluency, flexibility, originality and elaboration; but when results were factor analysed by Plass, Michael and Michael (1974), the sub-tests came out as stronger factors than the traits that Torrance supposed he was measuring.

Similarly, there seems to be little relationship between the ability to produce a lot of ideas and the production of other kinds of creative work. Mansfield and Busse (1981) found a poor relationship between 5 tests of ideas and originality, with supervisor ratings and other manifestations of creativity. Mednick (1962) thought creativity consists of the ability to relate ideas that in most people's minds are only remotely associated. He devised a Remote Associates Test (RAT) in which subjects had to find a word associated with three other words which were remote from each other. However, correlations between other criteria of creative achievement and scores on the RAT have been unconvincing (Mansfield and Busse, 1981; Mendelsohn, 1976). Furthermore, people taking the RAT said that they did not allow themselves to associate words freely, but speculated upon hypotheses and tested them. In any case, the association test is the wrong way round. To analyse three words for a common link is, self-evidently, an analytical task; while associating three words with a given single concept is a process of synthesis. An analytical task may have only one answer; a creative problem allows many possible answers.

There is good reason to think that people who are creative in one subject area are not creative in others. For example, creativity is said to favour the prepared mind, but what this means in effect is that particular problems and facts have to be prominently in mind for them to be creatively associated with some new idea. In other words, some subject specialisation favours creativity in that subject. If that is so, we should not assume that creativity is a general trait. In which case the strategy for teaching it is quite different. It is no longer a matter of developing a dormant mental facility. Rather, there should be concentration on learning the basics of a subject, its interconnections and its outstanding problems that require original solutions. In short, develop prepared minds. This requires perspiration as well as inspiration. It requires students to sit down and learn the facts as well as the teacher to organise speculative discussions. It supposes that creativity is more learned than inborn.

On the basis of prepared minds, the way to foster creativity is to give tasks to make students associate ideas that others would not normally associate.

4. Require subsidiary subjects too

From the point of view of teachers, the fact that the ability to associate ideas seems subject specific simplifies their task. The creative tasks they set can be specific to their subject. On the other hand, they need to encourage students to study subsidiary subjects because that will benefit their own. Over-specialisation is the path to dull minds and a dull department. For example, concepts from biology and cybernetics can enhance the understanding of economics and mechanical engineering and vice versa, but you might not consider them kindred disciplines.

So the question now is 'What task designs can teachers use to make students associate diverse ideas to their subject?'

5. Use 'forced association' tasks

One kind of task is 'forced association', but you will need to explain why you are setting it or students will think it is irrelevant, not worth doing and you've gone crazy. It is a matter of mentally loosening habitual categories of thinking. You ask questions like, 'What's the connection between Buddhism and the British Coal Industry?' You will get different answers if the students are studying economics, geology, theology, sociology, fine art or politics; and the differences could be instructive about the terms in which they think.

If students can't get started on a forced association task, give a short list of stimulus words. The subjects mentioned in the last paragraph could be one list. Another might consist of words like 'growth', 'past', 'place', 'effects' and 'value'. This list hints at attributes of Buddhism and the British Coal Industry that can then be compared or contrasted.

6. Teach 'attribute listing'

A technique students can be taught to use without needing a list of hints is to analyse and list the attributes of the concepts they are trying to associate. I recommend doing this in three columns in the same way as we saw in Table 8.2. Once they are set out in this way, it is easier to make associations between the concepts.

Notice that these are *open-ended tasks*. There is virtually no limit to the number of possible attributes. In general, it is open-ended tasks that encourage divergent thinking and creative responses. So it's worth checking through the tasks you give students to see how many are open and how many are closed.

7. Try morphological synthesis

Morphological synthesis is a rather more closed task. Essentially, it consists of making associations by completing a chart of the kind shown in Figure 9.1. It is unknown how some bodily reactions take place so quickly. The researcher must speculate a hypothesis by considering how and through what medium of communication the reactions take place so fast. Each cell in the chart represents some association of medium and method. Additional methods and media can be added. Most options can be dismissed straight away, but the chart might produce an association that has previously been overlooked and that might be worth testing. Warren and Davis (1969) found that groups using morphological synthesis and short attribute lists produced more, and better quality, ideas than controls and a group with long attribute lists. Morphological synthesis produced them quicker. It has mostly been used with gifted children (eg. Subotnik, 1984 and Laney, 1984) and that suggests it could be used at university level. Obviously it requires some preparation and its creative purpose needs to be carefully and persuasively explained.

In some patients, sugar touching their foot unknown and unseen, has visceral reactions in other parts of the body, including the brain, quicker than any known method of bodily communication. Speculate upon the method and the medium.							
Method of Communication	**Medium of Communication**						
	Bones	Skin	Nerves	Artery	Veins	Lymph	Others?
Convection Radiation Heat conduction Electricity Chemical chain reaction Transport of substance Suggest others							

Figure 9.1. A chart to show relationships to form a morphological synthesis

8. Conceptual mapping
One creative task almost every student has at some time is to write an essay. The essay structure reflects the student's association of ideas. But how do you teach students to structure their essays? The simplest device is to use small groups (i) to jot down the key concepts and ideas for an essay all over a sheet of paper, (ii) then draw lines or arrows between those most closely associated, and (iii) plan a connected route to cover the points. But this is open to two serious criticisms.

One problem with this method is that different arrows will mean different things and the resulting essay structure will seem confused. For example, Reynolds and Hart (1990) classified the arrows as 'is a type of', 'is part of', 'is characteristic of', 'defines', 'is an example of', 'influences', or 'leads to'. A more serious criticism is that it only produces a linear descriptive essay, not one focusing on a central argument that interprets all the facts.

The solution to this is to insert a vital step between (i) and (ii). Instruct the students to look at all the facts and concepts noted, and try to identify the central fact or interpretation that can act as the focus for an argument. This vital step is to associate all, or nearly all, the facts, ideas and concepts in one synthesis. It is an associative task, but it requires a process more like the Gestalt psychologists' flash of insight than association by conditioning. There may be a period of group silence or irrelevant activity before a group member hits upon a unifying idea, followed by a period of work applying it.

The need for this step is well worth teaching. Unfortunately, at school and later, the time pressures of examinations militate against teaching students that a period of seemingly irrelevant activity might be productive.

9. Association of ideas on the Internet
Siau (1995) claims that brainstorming over the Internet does not have some of the disadvantages of face-to-face brainstorming groups. There are no 'passengers' ('free-riding' members) in the group because you can only be a member of the group by taking part; and one contributor's participation does not block the immediate thoughts of another.

E. Creativity as an attitude

From another point of view, creativity is more a matter of attitudes of mind, motivation and values, than some special kind of potential ability or unusual association of ideas (Amabile, 1983).

1. Encourage intensive work and associated values
Firstly it is clear that most creative people have periods of very intensive work. Secondly, and more importantly, any area of creativity has associated values. These are fairly explicit in the arts and art criticism (Getzels and Csikszentmihalyi, 1976). Several researchers have also shown that scientists also have distinctive values, particularly those scientists who may be judged creative (Roe, 1952; Mansfield and Busse, 1981). Scientific explanations are judged to be more creative if they are:
i)   consistent with most known facts,
ii) conceptually parsimonious,
iii) fundamental,
iv) have general application, and
v) are highly predictive.
Roe (1963) has noticed that creative scientists are tolerant of ambiguity yet strive to resolve ambiguities. Getzels and Csikszentmihalyi have found that professional artists and laymen agree upon what works of art are original, but laymen were less tolerant of artistic innovation.

These researches suggest that certain values are associated with creativity. They do not show that that is all that creativity is. However, from the point of view of trying to teach people to be creative, they show that the teacher's task will involve the same skills as teaching other kinds of values. These teaching skills are different from those required to teach cognition. (See Chapter 11 and Free Group Discussion on page 256.)

2. Build self-esteem, confidence, security and verbal fluency in groups
It is partly a matter of building self-esteem, confidence, verbal fluency and security in experimenting with new ideas. Jablin and Sussman (1978) analysed the contributions of 96 undergraduates to brainstorming groups. They concluded that students who produced most ideas perceived fewer status differences amongst the group, regarded

members as having a high status, and had less anxiety about voicing suggestions than those who produced few ideas. In fact, the level of creativity of 75% of the students could be directly predicted from these attitudes.

F. Creativity as cognitive strategies

However, there is a fourth approach to creativity which regards it as neither potential abilities, the association of ideas, nor a particular set of values, but the adoption of certain cognitive strategies. Commonly this view regards creative people as having a wide range of strategies, as having a variety of cognitive frameworks or schema and as choosing unusual schema to conceptualise problems. In other words by looking at the problems in a variety of ways, some of which are unusual, they produce original solutions.

Again, if this is what creativity is, it has definite implications for teaching. Firstly it is clear that creativity can be taught, particularly by discussion, because it is possible to teach people to think about problems in new ways and to involve them in using those ways in discussion. Indeed, a great deal of teaching consists of widening students' repertoire of concepts. If students have a wide repertoire of concepts in one subject but not in another, this could explain why creativity can be subject specific. Secondly, it explains why people who have more than one discipline, or who exchange ideas with people from other disciplines, are more likely to produce creative solutions to problems.

1. Encourage the use of analogies
The implication is that creative people solve problems by analogy. The strategy of searching for analogies is one of the techniques recommended by Gordon (1961) in his work on synectics. However, Perkin (1983) has argued that the use of analogies has been over-rated and is rarely used in practice.

2. Brainstorming groups
The brainstorming technique originally devised by Osborn (1953) required participants to suspend their judgement and to associate ideas freely. The technique has been sufficiently used in industry and elsewhere for the name to become part of the language, but the term is usually used inaccurately. (For details of the precise technique see pages 219–221.)

3. Use checklists
I earlier mentioned 'attribute listing'. Checklists have also been recommended by Warren and Davis (1969) to stimulate creativity in other ways. Suppose you need to teach student occupational therapists to redesign a doorknob for a housebound disabled or handicapped woman. No doubt the design should depend upon what she can do, but students may be invited to consider adding or subtracting something to the existing doorknob, changing its colour, materials, shape, style and size, and rearranging its parts. Thus there is a checklist of elements to consider in creative redesign. The list will vary with the nature of the creative task, though Osborn (1953) posed 73 general purpose questions under the six headings 'What can you magnify,

minimise, substitute, rearrange, reverse and combine?' that he thought should stimulate creative responses to any kind of problem. For example, these six questions could be applied to setting next year's budget or deciding policies to reduce crime.

4. *Try thinking the opposite*

Rothenberg (1979) noticed that creative people often include in their repertoire of strategies a tendency to challenge habitual patterns of thought by deliberately thinking of the opposite and testing whether the negation of customary beliefs is plausible. Indeed, Rothenberg defined creativity as a set-breaking set. In other words, a disposition to contradict traditional dispositions. That is not a very adequate definition, but it does provide a testing strategy that could produce original conclusions in discussion.

Regrettably, some university teachers find creative students threatening when they challenge orthodoxy or what the teacher is saying. For these teachers it takes courage to say, 'That's a good idea. I hadn't thought of that.' If you want to teach creativity you must discard any authoritarian tendencies and make sure your open-mindedness is displayed.

5. *Think of a relevant problem*

Getzels and Csikszentmihalyi (1976) persuaded art students to talk about their thought processes in their studios. They also obtained records or assessments of students' creativity and checked them against their professional careers some time later. What they found was very interesting. Creative people were constantly open minded in the sense that they were always willing to explore new approaches before deciding on one of them, and even then they were always ready to consider new ideas. They described this as a problem-finding behaviour. They say that creative people positively search for problems. Again, that is a task that teachers can give either to individuals or to discussion groups which, if Getzels and Csikszentmihalyi are correct, should produce creative ideas.

Sternberg (1985) has argued that creativity is a combination of some of these strategies. In particular creative behaviour involves the selective encoding, combination and composing of information relevant to a problem. These three processes are each part of creativity.

G. Conclusion

From this review it seems that creativity is probably not (C) an inborn ability, though there may be inborn characteristics which could enable it to develop. It seems more likely that creativity requires (D) free association of ideas, (E) affective characteristics such as enthusiasm, persistence, and values specific to the subject, as well as (F) having a wide repertoire of cognitive strategies which enable a person to perceive problems from a variety of view points. Creativity involves a combination of these four things. While discussion methods may not be sufficient to teach them, and they may each require different discussion techniques, discussion is nonetheless necessary to develop all four.

Chapter 10
Decision-making and judgement

A. Tasks for each step in decision-making

B. Difficulties in decision-making

C. Issues when teaching decision-making

D. Conclusion

Decision-making brings together all the aspects of thinking that we have so far considered. Businessmen, managers and administrators sit on committees. Doctors, social workers and others typically plan a case conference. As a teaching method this is usually called 'case discussion' (see Chapter 22). Case conferences and discussion are used for complex decisions. The maxim *'Start with simple tasks in small groups for short periods of time, and then gradually increase their respective complexity, size and duration'* applies here too. Start with small decisions individually or in buzz groups. (Turn to Chapter 21 and see the variety of methods you could use.) In a medical context, let students take a patient's notes and her presenting symptoms, diagnose, and decide what to do. In other contexts devise, or remember from your own experience, a critical incident and ask students what they would do.

Let us look at the steps in a more complex decision-making process. Each step has to be taught, and could be taught using teaching methods simpler than case discussion. For this reason I suggest the kind of task a group might be given for each one. There is an argument for saying they are best taught cumulatively in reverse order and I will consider this at the end of the chapter.

A. Tasks for each step in decision-making

1. Ask yourself, 'What is the students' background knowledge?'
In any decision, its maker is likely to bring to bear a vast background general knowledge, sets of assumptions, theories and general principles. These include relevant concepts, language and experience of life. Students of law, business administration, education, engineering and medicine are essentially trained to take decisions, but most of their training consists of learning the facts, theories and general principles. These facts and theories are usually acquired from lectures and reading, not by discussion methods. But the rest of the decision-making process is best learned by discussion.

2. The decision question – What has to be decided?

As an individual task or in small tutorless groups, ask the students 'What has to be decided?' Students must learn to recognise when a decision is necessary (and when it is not) even if they don't know what it should be. The weakness of laissez faire managers is that they don't. The recognition assumes there is an aim or goal and a situation consisting of specific facts. In that context the task for the student is to identify the real issue – what is important and what is urgent. What is important and what is urgent are not, of course, necessarily the same thing. It's a matter of asking the right question(s) the decision must answer, given the specific facts. I shall call this the 'decision question'. Consider the situation described in Figure 10.1 as a case for student discussion.

What do they think is (are) the real issue(s) that requires a decision(s). What is (are) their goal(s) and what subordinate goals must they achieve to attain it?

3. Require explicit criteria for an acceptable decision

Require your groups to state the criteria for an acceptable decision. A decision is always the answer to a question. What would count as a satisfactory answer? Discourage over-simplification. Encourage the group(s) to make their assumptions explicit. Important amongst those assumptions will be restrictions on what answers to the question are allowed. If the question in a case study is 'How can we increase our profits?' there will be all sorts of limitations on what answers are acceptable. You must increase profits without lowering employees' morale, without sacrificing long-term goals, without annoying shareholders, without making a sub-standard product ...etc. There will be other practical limitations whatever the decision.

Put another way, these limitations are criteria for what is an acceptable decision, an acceptable answer to the question. In effect, a decision question always has a number of subordinate questions. The discussion group must tease them out. If you're teaching your students to think, don't let the discussion stop after superficial answers. Probe deeper. It's a matter of professional and academic standards.

Notice that, even at this early stage, the criteria are set for evaluating the eventual decision and how it is implemented. If they are made explicit, they can't be fudged later.

4. Set tasks to represent the facts and goals

How do you conceive of the situation described in Figure 10.1? How do you represent the facts in your mind? Your conception, your representation, will entail a body of theory such as a model of how certain facts are related. The body of theory will be a context to which you relate the facts. This kind of task can be given to buzz groups or horseshoe groups.

Your conception will involve giving greater weight to some facts than to others. For example, you might see the hierarchy of the departmental *structure* with four sections each with a head, or leader, and each with several support staff including secretaries. Alternatively you might think of the management of this department in terms of the

You are a fairly new head of a department containing four sections. Section heads Tony, Ian and David had all applied for your job and been rejected. You applied when it was advertised again. The local culture is more authoritarian than you are used to. You are a caring person with quietly held, liberal attitudes, but your leadership role does not allow your natural shyness to show, nor the depth of your compassion for others. For example, you believe that crime and many of the macho local attitudes could be softened and more caring attitudes developed, if mothers and fathers bonded more closely with their children by cuddling them more. Local research shows that very few mothers breast feed their children, so bonding opportunities are missed.

The sections headed by Ian and Tony are concerned with the marketing and sales of two different products. Tony has been in the department a long time as heir apparent. He is aggrieved that your arrival resulted in more responsibilities for him, for which he has extra support staff, but not promotion. You hope the extra responsibilities will earn that promotion. He had been one of six candidates shortlisted by another company; but the list was cut to three on receipt of references. Tony mistakenly blames you: but you know from Tony's confidential file that his other referee, his former head of department, has secretly never supported him.

Ian is enthusiastic, ambitious and independent, but not sufficiently organised to lead a team. Moira was appointed to get his section better organised, which she has done, but Moira wants to be your pet and the power behind the throne. In her last job she tried to suck up to the boss, but when he refused to treat her as his favourite, she tried to persuade the secretaries to complain about him sexually. They refused, supported him and ganged up on her. Thence she applied to your department where she has done exactly the same thing, though this time more successfully. Your public advocacy of cuddling and breastfeeding has allowed your compassion to be misrepresented as 'comments about breasts'. Like water dripping on a stone Moira makes constant confidential complaints about you to the company's Personnel Office who feed them to your superior. To Moira, Cath was a popular, successful and highly qualified rival in Ian's team, who had earned your confidence, but Moira marginalised her by working on Ian before team meetings. Frustrated, Cath soon resigned. Moira's scheme is to get you demoted or sacked, and replaced by Ian.

In this she is supported by Mike, a successful leader of a flagship project you initiated. He is part-time from another department. He has been a consultant for the arbitration service, ACAS, and tends to see problems, offences and mismanagement, like reds under the bed, where there are none. Like Tony, having added 2+2 and got 5, he wrongly suspects you of not supporting his promotion and mistakenly feels trapped whilst you are there.

A previous Managing Director had tried to close down the training section, but failed to convince the Board after David, its leader, did some last minute lobbying. This has made David cynical about those with power and has tried to stir dissent amongst secretarial staff. His protégé is Angela who lives 60 miles from the office and stays in company accommodation when on late turn. Her husband dropped out of teaching and joined the police where, frustrated and perhaps humiliated, he feels the masons have barred his promotion. You have received masons' handshakes when running projects for the police and feel very compassionate towards him. Conscious that police work involves unsocial hours, you worry that Angela's late turn exacerbates the situation and you ask how he is getting on. To you, the caring nature of your enquiry is obvious. You are totally aghast some time later to discover that Angela complained of harassment because you 'used your power to find out about her husband'.

Figure 10.1. Identify the real issue(s) – What is important? What is urgent? Represent them

aims and *motives* of its members. Or you may classify the kind of *problems* you, as head of department, are facing. There could be many ways of thinking about the situation in the department. They usually have a central concept like the structure, motives or problems I have highlighted.

5. Present alternative representations of facts and goals

At first, tasks of this kind are quite difficult for students to understand if they cannot think of the overall situation in more than one way. So it may need the creative process of a brainstorming group. To consider models and methods of representation requires a higher level of thinking and abstraction.

Because of the high level of abstraction, to explain this task to students it may be best to give some examples. That's what I've just tried to do in section 4 above. Here's another example. When considering back pain I have noticed that chiropractors think first about bones; they take X-rays and manipulate my spine. Physiotherapists attend to muscles and give me exercises to strengthen them. Neurologists first consider the possibility that I've pinched a nerve. Others want to change my posture and lifestyle. So far I've not consulted a psychiatrist. We might call them differing points of view. I'm sure all their perspectives have some merit, but they clearly reach different decisions about the best treatment.

Many of us take wrong decisions because we fail to think about a situation from every point of view, so it is wise for decision-makers to try to represent their situations in as many ways as possible. That is the purpose of this step. Brainstorming discussion or the Nominal Group Technique could be used. (See pages 197 and 219.)

When the facts of the case are represented in new ways, it is not unusual for the group to have to go back and redefine the decision question.

6. Search for relevant areas of ignorance

In practice we have to take decisions without knowing all the relevant facts. To anticipate where errors might result, decision-makers must ask themselves, 'What don't I know that might affect the wisdom of my decision?' So student decision makers should practise answering this question. The search to answer this question requires some divergent thinking – creativity. The number of answers is not limited to one or two. Buzz groups are therefore a bit small. Horseshoe groups with 6 to 8 members are best for this task. (See pages 212–214.)

Having got a list of areas of ignorance, ask the group to divide it in three:
i)   areas where it is impossible in principle to obtain the relevant facts (for example, what is in your competitor's mind),
ii) facts that they could in principle obtain, but could not in practice owing to lack of time, money or other resources, and
iii) areas where information can be obtained.

7. Obtain additional facts

If, in answer to (iii) above, there are additional facts that could be obtained to produce a better decision, then it's common sense to obtain them. The group should first say how and estimate the cost in time and money. It might involve looking the facts up in a book or report, carrying out some research, or something in between. Syndicate method (see page 227) could permit an extended inquiry. A case conference (see page 223) may want more immediate answers.

The next thing is to obtain them. This could result in reorganising and representing known facts in new ways from a new perspective. Remember, in Gestalt psychology this is often how problems are solved (see Chapter 8).

8. The Gestalt period of apparent inactivity

If we think of decision-making as a problem-solving task following the sequence described by Gestalt psychologists, the next step would be a period of apparent irrelevance or inactivity. Much depends upon the time frame in which you are teaching, but if suitable, this could be the time to take a break. In some circumstances that would not be suitable. In some it would be an occasion for students to stand up and stretch their legs for two minutes. In others it would be an afternoon tea break. In yet others the group might continue when they meet next week.

Rather than take a break, this could be a suitable time to hold a 'quiet meeting' (see page 232). I normally use that method at the end of a period of teaching, but there is every reason to use it in the middle when the work has been intensive.

Whether you take a break or not, or whether you use a quiet meeting, steps 2 to 8 are all about how the decision-making task is conceived. It is about conceptions and perceptions of information. Steps 9 to 11 are about thinking about the information and then choosing.

9. Set out the alternatives

The next and crucial step is for the group to set out alternative courses of action. This could be done individually followed by the first stage in brainstorming sitting in horseshoe formation. You will see in Chapter 22 that the group should resist rushing on to step 10 and immediately passing judgement on fellow students' suggestions however stupid they may seem. Half of the fun is being able to make ridiculous proposals!

Notice that thinking of alternatives is a creative act.

10. Identify the consequences of each alternative

It may be that some proposals from step 9 can be dismissed fairly quickly. With the more plausible proposals it might be wise to remind group members of the criteria they made explicit at step 3 and the various ways of representing the facts that they considered in step 5.

Of course, in many situations decision-makers cannot predict with certainty the consequences of any decision they take. They can only make predictions based on informed subjective estimates. For example, economic predictions tend to reflect the way economists represent their information. They represent people's economic behaviour as rational and assume that only their values and the available information vary.

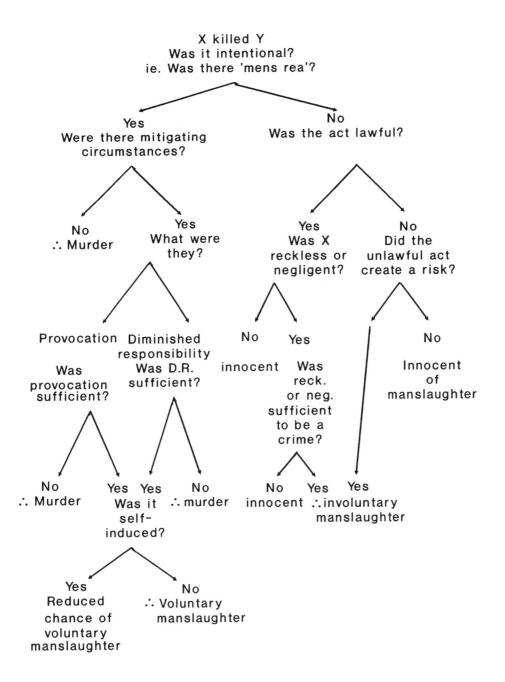

Figure 10.2. A decision tree to decide on murder, manslaughter or innocence

A typical economic model:

i) lists all the possible consequences of an economic decision,

ii) gives numerical scores for each consequence according to how far it is desired (valued),

iii) gives numerical scores to each possible consequence according to a *subjective* estimate of the probability of its occurrence,

iv) multiplies the two scores together, and

(v) adds the products for all possible consequences. The decision which gives the highest result is the best bet.

This kind of model depends upon the desirability (usefulness or '*utility*') of a consequence and a *subjective expectation* of how likely it is to occur. It has therefore been called the 'Subjective Expected Utility' theory (SEU). This kind of model has been applied in a wide range of disciplines. It is not necessarily quantitative as in economics. Although it may not show *how* people take decisions, it seems to predict the decisions they take pretty well. It predicts their preferences.

It often happens that the consequence of one decision leads to another decision that has to be taken. That in turn may lead to another and so on. If all the possibilities are laid out graphically as in Figure 10.2, you get a branching structure known as a decision tree. Asking students to set out a decision tree can be quite a thorough test of their understanding. Depending on the subject, each branch could have an estimate of probability.

11. Weigh the consequences and choose

This is the point of decision. It is the point when values are applied. If you want your students to really thrash out their values and moral principles, make sure the options are evenly balanced or that the decision involves a dilemma of different kinds of values that cannot easily be reconciled (eg. aesthetic, happiness, justice). Otherwise it might seem that if participants are rational, this step is straight forward, the real work being done at step 10 when working out all the consequences. In that case all participants would have to do is choose the most beneficial, or least harmful, consequence.

In practice it's not that simple. We all make bad decisions sometimes; so we'll consider some of the difficulties in a moment.

12. Implement the decision

The process of implementing of a group's decision is not likely to be another discussion. So it is not my concern in this book. I mention it here only for completeness.

13. Evaluation of the decision and its implementation

Again, the process of evaluation is not necessarily another discussion, though it might be. If so, it might well be another group of decision tasks, namely, 'Did we take the right decision?', 'If so, how could its implementation be improved?' 'If not, what should we do about it now? What can we learn from our mistake(s)? Why did we have difficulty?'

B. Difficulties in decision-making

What are the common difficulties that teachers should look out for at steps 10 and 11?

1. Irrational behaviour
I said step 11 seems straight forward, if participants are rational. In practice decision-makers are not rational. For example, studies show that even experienced decision-makers may choose the same decision for different reasons, for the wrong reasons, and even when they would attach different scores to the values and probabilities of the consequences. Dawes (1971) showed that members of a selection committee selected the same candidates for different reasons. Different criteria correlated highly. Furthermore, although the selectors claimed they considered a large number of factors, a mathematical model of their behaviour showed that only three were of any significance, though a different three for each selector.

2. Information overload
What could be the explanation for this behaviour? Maybe the selectors were fooling themselves or the mathematical model was wrong; but the more usual explanation is the difficulty of information overload. Selection tasks, like many other decisions, often require holding more information in one's head than most people can manage. So decision-makers simplify and ignore information without knowing it – probably because they don't have an adequate way of representing it.

3. Poor self awareness
Notice that the accuracy of decision-makers' self reports is open to question. Decision-makers don't always know why they took the decision they did. They rationalise. There is evidence that 'people tend to confuse what they did with what they intended to do and with what they believe is generally done' (Ericsson and Simon, 1980; Herrmann, 1982; Nisbett and Wilson, 1977; Smith and Miller, 1978). But it is also true that, when several criteria correlate highly, statistical techniques may attribute great weight to a criterion which was not influential, but which correlated highly with one that was. In this respect the statistical models may be almost too clever at simplifying complex judgements.

4. The risky shift phenomenon
A curious finding has been observed when students are first asked to take a decision on their own before taking it after a period of discussion, and then a third time individually. Compared with decisions first taken individually, decisions taken by the discussion group, and then individually, showed less caution. It seems students were prepared to take a more risky decision after they had discussed the matter with colleagues.

Several explanations for this shift of opinion have been offered. The original experiments (Wallach et al, 1962) used mature, confident, ambitious, male students of industrial management from the Harvard. Critics thought they would be exceptionally prone to take risks, but the phenomenon is just as evident with female liberal arts students. It has also been suggested that western culture, and American culture in particular, values risk as entrepreneurial and 'go-getting', and that a vocal risk-taker in a small group acquires a high status or leadership that others will follow. Cautious individuals may feel more secure and confident when responsibility for the decision is diffused throughout the group and the vocal risk-taker will take most of the blame.

Of these explanations, the confidence of group support and the leadership hypothesis seem the most important. The risky shift can also be influenced by how the decision task is worded and is increased when there is an initial disparity of opinions. (See also Wallach and Kogan, 1965a.)

5. Uncertain facts or values
Decisions and judgements are difficult when decision-makers are uncertain about the facts (such as uncertainty about the present situation or what would happen if they did X) or uncertain about their values (such their priorities).

How do people react when they are uncertain? One answer is that, lacking information or priorities, people rely on simple rules of thumb, called heuristics. Tversky and Kahneman (1973) suggested that when people lack the necessary information they retrieve from their memory or elsewhere, whatever information is readily available. They then give it undue weight. We saw in Chapter 7 that this is called the 'availability heuristic'.

6. Over-weighting the recent and insignificant
One set of information that is readily available is the decision-maker's recent experience. Consequently many decision-makers give it undue weight. When designing experiments on heuristics, psychologists have wanted decision tasks which are repeatable and quantifiable, and in which they can control the true probabilities, the subjects' beliefs and their incentives. For this reason they have given students tasks to decide what colour ball they would be most likely to pick out of a bag. Such tasks may not seem typical of the decisions teachers give their students, but one interesting discovery is that, although the colour of the latest ball to be taken out of a bag may be insignificant, subjects strenuously try to see meaning in it. In management styles, such managers are those whose decisions react to events, rather than planning and controlling them.

7. Illusory correlation
The same happens in case discussion when students are given irrelevant information. They try to make it relevant somehow. Similarly Chapman and Chapman (1971) have shown that therapists insisted on seeing correlations between clinical symptoms and patients' drawings when research had shown there weren't any. For example, they perceived patients with a particular illness as drawing eyes close together. This has been called 'illusory correlation'. It has other possible explanations such as the

clinicians seeing what they expected to see, or selectively remembering patients for whom there was a relationship.

8. Underestimating prior probabilities
There is also a tendency to avoid the effects of sample size. Students were told that there were two hospitals in a town, a large one and a small one. The two hospitals issued statistics of how many boys and girls were born each week. Asked which hospital would more often show over 60% boys, over half the students thought there would be no difference and the remainder were equally divided. Since random variation would be more likely to even out with a large sample, the statistics of the larger hospital should show less extreme variation.

9. Reluctance to use or interpret quantitative methods
A related finding is that people tend to exaggerate the probability and consequences of events that have a very low probability of occurring (for example, less than one in 100), but underestimate the probability of events that normally occur, say, 80% of the time (Poulton, 1968, 1982). (See my example of the doctor and meningitis in Chapter 7.) This comes from a reluctance to calculate probabilities, perhaps resulting in turn from a lack of confidence in quantitative techniques and how they were taught.

10. The gambler's fallacy
Another heuristic is known as 'the gambler's fallacy'. If a horse has never won a race you might think it unwise to place a bet on it. On the other hand, some people risk a bet on it supposing that it must win some day. They act as if success must even out in the long run and therefore past failures increase the probability of future success! A business studies student or personnel manager who adopts this heuristic will make some bad decisions – but it happens.

11. Stereotyping and preconceived ideas
Even when people have relevant information, prejudice, preconceived ideas or biases may distort their perception and hence their decisions. Kahneman and Tversky (1973) gave students a description of another student from an undisclosed part of the university. Students classified him as a computer scientist on the basis of their stereotype of computer scientists. Even though the proportion of computer scientists on campus at that time was very low, students felt very certain in spite of the unrealistic odds. When presented with other information there is a tendency to ignore statistical information about probabilities.

12. Conclusion
All these heuristics result in distortions. They are caused by selective perceptions and selective memories. In everyday life both our perceptions and our memories are necessarily selective. There is no way our brains can handle the amount of available information otherwise. In fact, such processes of selection are essential for our survival, so we should not be surprised that inappropriate heuristics get used when there

doesn't seem to be an appropriate one. The teacher's task is to make participants aware of these pitfalls and to give ample practice in taking decisions. Experience counts. Decision-making is not an area where there are short cuts to be learned.

C. Issues when teaching decision-making

1. The use of 'mathetics'

As I said at the beginning of this chapter, there is an argument for teaching decision-making skills backwards. This method has been called 'mathetics'. That is to say, the first skill you teach is number 11. You give students all the available facts (steps 2 to 7); you tell them the options (step 9) and the consequences of each (step 10). The task is to choose the best option on the basis of the consequences given. It's primarily a task clarifying values and avoiding some of the difficulties I've raised in Section B.

After that you give them a task involving steps 10 and 11. You give them the basic facts (steps 2 to 7) and the choices that confront them (step 9) and require the students to consider or work out the consequences (10) and decide their priorities (11).

The third stage is to make all the facts available (2 to 7) and to give students the thinking tasks (9 to 11). Subsequent tasks will include more and more of the decision-making process until students can do it all. Of course, with more competent students or with easier decision-making tasks, you don't have to teach one step at a time. For example, you might go straight away to what I've here called the third stage; or you might chunk the steps together in other ways.

The point is, when you want to teach students to deal with complex decision tasks, you don't have to keep preparing a lot of complex cases in every detail with all the sources of information that might imply. You'll need some, though.

The educational argument for a mathetics approach is to do with motivation when there are large complex decisions. It is thought that coming to a decision gives a sense of achievement and completion (a bit like job satisfaction). On the other hand, starting at the beginning, setting oneself rather daunting decision criteria and recognising that there is relevant information one does not know and cannot know, is not so inspiring.

Mathetics is also about learning by repetition through using 'backward chaining'. You romp through the already learned last steps and connect the chain. Otherwise there are too many steps to understand all at once, each having their own rationale and style.

If you read the Preface, you will know that I recommended reading Part IV of this book first. A complex argument is easier to understand when you see where it's leading.

2. Doubts about a step-by-step approach

Against the whole approach I have adopted in this chapter, evidence is inconsistent and ambiguous whether a step-by-step procedure is effective in decision-making tasks (Pavitt, 1993). There are more questions than I can answer here. Do formal discussion procedures result in decisions of better quality? What is important? Is it the fact that each step is considered, or that they are considered in a rational order? How far does the benefit of systematic procedures vary with the decision-maker using them?

These questions open up an old debate about whole or part learning. That is, whether it is best to learn all elements of a skill together or whether it is better to learn one element at a time. The usual compromise is to say, if it is too complex for the students to perceive all aspects of the decision as a unity, then split it up into small steps; otherwise give the whole task at one go. I agree with this and accept that most teachers do not set decision tasks so complex as to require a teacher to separate each step. Nonetheless, group awareness that their task requires these steps is crucial.

3. Tell group members to share information

In areas of employment such as medicine, penal practice, architecture, environmental planning, engineering, social work and all manner of other social services, case conferences to take decisions are usually inter-professional. The whole idea of having a discussion is that various kinds of knowledge and points of view are shared. It is a mind-broadening process and that is certainly part of the educational aim of using discussion methods.

Imagine then, the dismay at discovering that student groups often only discuss information that they all possess. Individuals with relevant knowledge not possessed by others often fail to share it with their group.

The solution to this problem is simple. Make sure to tell students to share what they know, particularly what others may not know. Indeed, the solution to many teaching problems consists of making students aware of how one is trying to help them. Too often teachers proceed as if their techniques should be secret, as if in fear that students will refuse to be helped!

D. Conclusion

From the point of view of handling information – that is a cognitive view point – decision-making could be seen as the most difficult task. Certainly we pay the highest salaries to complex decision-makers. Yet, at some cognitive level, we all take hundreds of decisions every day. So the teacher's task is to build complex decision skills upon the simpler and more familiar ones. Much of the teacher's skill therefore lies in the design of the tasks. I describe a procedure for this when considering the preparation of case discussions on pages 224 and 225.

I have tried to show that elements of decision-making can be developed using teaching methods other than case discussion. In fact, they use all the methods more preliminary to case discussion. (See Chapter 21.) They are all methods without a tutor as a group member and, given horizontally floored rooms, they are all methods in which the teacher can manage several groups at once. Accordingly, they can be used in average sized classes. That is up to 40 with 10 buzz groups of four members or five brainstorming, horseshoe, syndicate or case discussion groups of eight members. The secret lies in a planned sequence of task designs – that is to say, in applying my maxim.

Chapter 11
Developing 'affect'

A. Theories of attitude change

B. Seven responses in discussion

C. Factors influencing the development of affect in discussions

D. Conclusion

By developing 'affect' I mean developing values, personal feelings, motives and motivation, emotions and attitudes. But rather than use this unfamiliar word, in places I shall lump them all together and call them 'attitudes' or 'values'.

Consider the following introductions to a period of teaching:
A. 'Today I aim to develop your powers of reasoning.'
B. 'Today I aim to develop your problem-solving skills.'
C. 'Today I aim to develop your attitudes.'
D. 'Today I aim to change your attitudes.'

Maybe you would never say any of these things. My point is that A and B are at least tolerable. C and D would be disastrous. Developing affect is not the same as developing cognitions. It is altogether more subtle. It requires much more maturity, sensitivity and skill from the teacher. Why?

Attitudes are part of our persona. We can admit to not knowing something, or not being able to solve a problem, much more happily than to admit that our attitudes are inadequate. You can't force someone to change their attitudes. That is something individuals have to do for themselves.

What you can do is be aware of the processes involved and help students to exercise their own freedom to change. Consequently, this chapter aims to help that awareness by giving an understanding of the theories and processes of attitude change and to be aware of the factors influencing attitudes in discussions.

A second consequence is that attitude teaching, unlike cognitive teaching, does not often consist of presenting specific tasks, though it can do. More often, conflicting attitudes emerge in a discussion of another kind of task. One skill of the perceptive teacher is to sense when a discussion revealing attitudes could be helpful, and to postpone the achievement of the original task and let the discussion resolve the attitudinal conflicts. It may seem like letting a discussion drift away from the original task and it is. The teacher is seizing the opportunity to let affect develop when it arises.

It is a matter of using the emotional energy of the moment, observing the discussion, and occasionally steering it in a direction where you think it would be useful to go. (See free group discussion in Chapter 23, pages 256 *ff.*)

It's not easy. That is why I say that teaching methods and techniques to develop affect should normally be learned and used only when competence has been developed by the teacher and the students using other methods. Furthermore, methods such as counselling and T-Groups can be damaging if used insensitively and teachers need specialist training before using them. In this chapter the methods I chiefly have in mind are tutorials, such as free group discussion (FGD), and case discussions.

I said attitude teaching could involve presenting a specific task. In particular, all decision tasks apply values and attitudes, so discussion of values easily arises in decision contexts. For this reason, value questions commonly arise during case discussion. (See Chapter 22.)

Attitudes are dispositions to respond in certain ways. In this chapter I am mostly concerned with *responses* to what is said in discussion, or perhaps *responses* in discussion to some observation or experience such as a role play. These are responses to *cognitive stimuli*, namely perceptions, interacting with either *cognitive*, or *affective* predispositions, or both. Thus the *responses* to the *stimuli* are modified by our *predispositions* which could be *physical, cognitive* (such as beliefs and perceptions), or *affective*. The responses may likewise be *physical behaviour, cognitions, affect* or a combination of all three.

The permutations could be pretty complicated, but I'm primarily concerned with changes in affect. So I'm concerned with processes that start with cognitive stimuli in discussions and finish with new affective dispositions. The main routeways for consideration in this chapter are shown in Figure 11.1 below.

Stimuli	Predispositions	Responses	New dispositions
physical	physical (eg. posture)	physical behaviour	physical
cognitive (what another said)	cognitive (beliefs)	cognitive (thought)	cognitive (new knowledge/beliefs)
affective (feelings etc.)	affective (values motives/feelings etc.)	affective expression	affective (attitudes values etc.)

Figure 11.1. Probable factors leading to attitude change in discussion

A. Theories of attitude change

Essentially there is a four stage process in developing values and attitudes in discussion:

i) Elicitation of an individual's current attitudes and values regarding some object or issue under discussion.

ii) Open recognition of those attitudes and values by the group and respect for the individuals who hold them.

iii) Rational consideration of (conflicting) attitudes and values in discussion.

iv) A willingness to develop or 'change' one's attitudes and values.

Understanding this sequence is fundamental to free group discussion, T-Groups and counselling.

If you are a tutor monitoring attitude development, awareness of this process is very useful to interpret the stages individual group members have reached. As a tutor, your role in developing attitudes and values is to observe and monitor this process in discussion and occasionally to intervene to steer the discussion to issues being overlooked or ignored. It requires patience. It is not unusual for relatively silent members to have deeply-held values and it may be particularly necessary to help them at stages (i) and (ii).

The other thing you need is some knowledge of theories of attitude change by which to interpret what you observe. Psychologists' theories of attitude change are controversial and none is wholly satisfactory. They each tend to focus on selected parts of this process. They need not be seen as always in conflict. So when interpreting how my students develop from week to week, I shamelessly use bits from all the theories at various stages.

1. Selective association with existing feelings

Let us be clear from the start that you cannot teach someone to have certain attitudes and values without using and developing attitudes and values they already have. If I wanted to turn you into a racist, no doubt I could select and present all manner of *facts* about other ethnic groups that might disgust you, and focus on all the features of your own race and culture that might make you think well of it. I would then hope you would *generalise* from my biased and carefully selected facts. But facts alone do not change values. I should still be relying on, and building upon, your initial *feelings* of disgust or approval towards certain things and I would need to know in advance what those particular feelings are. I should also be relying on your feelings of *trust* in me to accept my facts as a true and fair account, and on your *willingness* to make or accept the generalisation. Disgust, approval, trust and willingness are all predisposed feelings that my propaganda would try to exploit.

In essence, what I have described is a process of conditioning. I'm calling it an associationist's account. It's a process of selectively reinforcing an association between certain ideas (cognitions) and attitudes using feelings that you already have. It's not so very different from Pavlov's hungry dogs associating food they value with the sound of a bell, or conversely, coming to associate a neutral object with something they dislike.

(This raises questions beyond the scope of this book about propaganda, indoctrination and the professional values of teachers. Suffice to say that by conviction I take a liberal view of morals and perhaps an even more liberal stance than most teachers.) My conception here is that teaching attitudes and values should consist of giving students the opportunity to discover and develop their own, rather than conforming to mine. Part of the point in discussion is that, more than didactic methods; it allows students to hear a variety of opinions and to test their own against them.

That said, I do accept that many professional values are selectively reinforced by didactic methods. If a nurse tutor instructs a trainee nurse to do X in order to make the patient comfortable, assuming the trainee is motivated to value the instruction, the tutor reinforces the trainee's value for the patient's comfort.

This process of selective reinforcement of existing feelings primarily takes place at stage (iii). Yet, as we shall see in a moment, a theory with a different perspective is needed when there are conflicting values expressed at stage (iii). Clearly, conflicting values do not reinforce existing values.

2. Psychoanalytically derived approaches

In everyday conversation our attitudes, values and moral principles are often hidden. Freud was frequently concerned to elicit hidden sexual attitudes, but the same applies to attitudes of other kinds. They may be implied, but not explicit. The explicit elicitation of values at stage (i) is therefore difficult for teachers to achieve. I briefly mention the technique of 'reflecting feelings' in Chapter 5 and I describe it in more detail in Chapter 23.

Elicitation of feelings involves trying to get individual students to recognise for themselves the values implied by what they have said. It's a process of self exposure. That needs courage. To facilitate courage, an element of trust and mutual support in the group is required. Hence the teacher's techniques are called 'facilitation' (though over-use of that term has widened its meaning in recent years). In the same way, psychoanalysts and counsellors have to work hard to establish the trust of their clients, and it takes time. Indeed, I regard psychoanalysis and counselling as methods of teaching.

Because public recognition and exposure of one's values requires courage, as we shall see in Part IV, full open recognition of students' values in discussions is only achieved after participants have developed confidence and trust in each other, not least in the teacher. For that reason methods to develop attitudes, namely free group discussion, counselling and T-Groups, are best introduced only after skills and confidence have been developed using group methods which are more cognitively based. (See Figure 11.1.) In origin, these teaching methods were influenced by psychoanalytic methods. Hence my use of the phrase 'psychoanalytically derived'. But I do not mean to suggest that they are used as a therapy.

You might ask 'Shouldn't the mutual respect and trust of stage (ii) really come before stage (i)?' Yes, to some extent, but elicitation and trust develop together like this. When students express a previously hidden attitude or feeling, they take a risk. If they are then respected and accepted as persons of value in themselves (regardless of whether their attitude is acceptable), trust is developed. Willingness to take a further risk is encouraged. Little risks are taken first. With support, bigger ones can be taken later. It is not too difficult to imagine the risk taken by a clergyman in some company saying he is homosexual. It is more difficult for teachers to recognise how hard it is for some students to express an academic opinion or attitude.

In an academic context, psychoanalytic approaches are much less clear what happens at stages (iii) and (iv). In practice, what happens is that step (iii) reveals conflicting values. It is the conflict that is discussed and needs to be recognised whilst maintaining respect for the individuals whose values are considered.

Then what happens in step (iv) is that a discussant recognises that one value must take precedence over another. Priorities are decided. For example, Smith may have feelings of patriotism and compassion. In deciding to give to international aid charities, rather than to charities for less needy people nearer home, he gives greater priority to compassion. In this way his value for compassion is developed. He may nonetheless continue to hold some patriotic values. In other words one set of values or attitudes is developed and strengthened.

Where one set of attitudes and values are given wider application at the expense of another, the other's values may change. For example, if, as result of his priority for compassion, Smith became an international charity worker, he might in time say, '*All people are of equal value. They all have feelings. The fact that I was born and brought up in one country is no reason to give priority to that country. Patriotism is wrong. It's an irrational prejudice. I shall embrace internationalism and justice for* all *peoples.*' In the same way discussion of two conflicting attitudes can lead to the rejection of one of them. However, that is not the only way of interpreting what happens when conflicting attitudes are discussed in groups.

3. Dissonance theories

Dissonance theories are inclined to explain all attitude change as attempts to resolve such conflicts, not by total rejection of one leaving the other victorious, but by gradual shifts and modifications of the dispositions. Festinger's original thesis (1957) was apparently simple. It can be summarised as follows:

i) *Awareness of holding inconsistent beliefs creates a feeling of discomfort (dissonance).*
In practice we all have some inconsistent beliefs and attitudes, but, as psychoanalysts remind us, we are generally not aware of them. Discussion methods are particularly effective in eliciting inconsistencies because other group members submit one's ideas to the test of consistency. Festinger called the feeling of discomfort 'cognitive dissonance'.

ii) *The discomfort motivates the individual to reduce or avoid it by changing attitudes.*
We reduce the discomfort by changing our attitudes, values and beliefs. Clearly, discussion is a particular context in which one might feel discomfort and group pressure to modify one's attitudes if they are blatantly inconsistent either with other attitudes or with the facts being discussed. But dissonance doesn't depend on other people. Festinger thought we are motivated to eliminate the discomfort regardless of whether others knew about it. Indeed, to change one's attitudes freely is crucial.

iii) *The strength of the motive varies with the total discomfort experienced.*
Festinger was tempted to give a quantitative account of dissonance. Discomfort is greater when conflicting beliefs or attitudes are important and when they are far apart. Trivial and slight differences are not so troublesome.

iv) *The total of discomfort is obtained from the relationships of all relevant beliefs.*
Dissonance theorists recognise that you don't usually have just two attitudes or beliefs

in conflict. We have clusters of associated attitudes and beliefs. Indeed a cluster is itself the product of a partial dissonance reduction process. So the discussion process is usually trying to iron out inconsistencies between clusters of beliefs and values. So when beliefs P, Q, R, S and T are inconsistent with cluster W, X, Y and Z, the discussion has not only to resolve the differences between P and W, but all the other relationships as well. So the total discomfort is the addition of all these conflicts.

Furthermore, since no one is wholly consistent, it is likely that members in group discussion will hold various combinations of beliefs and attitudes from both sides of the inconsistency.

The tutor's role is not to point out the inconsistencies, but to let students discover them for themselves. When developing affect the teacher's role is mostly to listen and occasionally to give a steer with open questions when certain issues are being avoided. For example, *'What is your view of Z?'*, said to someone who believes P, Q and R.

v) *When there is discomfort, individuals try to avoid situations that might increase it.* One way to avoid cognitive dissonance is to refuse to face evidence contrary to one's opinions. We all do it. If you listen to party political broadcasts, which do you listen to most often: those from your preferred party or the party most opposed to your point of view? Contrary to scientific method when you try to disconfirm an hypothesis, we prefer to have our attitudes and beliefs confirmed rather than tested. (See Chapter 7.) I look at sport on television much longer when my favourite team is winning. When they are losing I switch off sooner because I don't like to face that uncomfortable fact. (For some sports fans, the discomfort results in aggression.) It's a refusal to face the truth. In many walks of life, that's serious.

Dissonance theories have been subject to criticism, but for our purposes they survive it quite well. Much of Festinger's original research and subsequent criticism of it concerns attitude change following forced compliance (either with or without incentives) to behave contrary to one's values and beliefs. But forced compliance should not be relevant to academic discussion. After a review of research, Wicker (1969) concluded that changes in attitudes did not change how people physically behave; but changes in outward behaviour do change inner attitudes. This seemed to challenge the definition of an attitude as a disposition to behave in some way, rather than any particular theory. Petty and Cacioppo (1986) thought attitude change depends on how much the recipient of a communication thinks about, and elaborates, it. Bem (1967) thought attitudes change through self perception rather than feeling cognitive dissonance. But as I explained at the beginning, you need some kind of motivation to change attitudes. Elaborated thoughts and self perceptions are only cognitions. Dissonance theories provide a mechanism for how cognitions influence motives. *If you aim to help students develop their attitudes and values, it is their motivation you must monitor during discussion, not just their thoughts.*

4. Sherif and Sherif's latitudes of acceptance and rejection of attitudes

Rather than supposing that differing opinions in discussion always create a feeling of discomfort, Sherif and Sherif (1967) emphasise the amount of tolerance individuals have towards others holding a different attitude or opinion. This seems very relevant to academic discussion. Individuals' degrees of tolerance differ widely and such tolerance is related to standard personality measures such as tolerance of ambiguity, dogmatism and authoritarianism.

i) Sherif and Sherif say that on any issue being discussed, each participant is likely to have a *central position*. If another person's central position overlaps, they will agree.

ii) But how far you agree could be a matter of degree. Imagine we are visiting an art gallery together and I say to you, 'That's a beautiful picture'. You may be prepared to acknowledge that it is beautiful without the picture really being one that conforms to your central idea of a beautiful picture. You can stretch a point and agree that 'it is beautiful' without any dissonance. My statement is tolerable. It is within your *latitude of acceptance*.

iii) If I say, 'That picture is amongst the top 10% in this gallery', you may feel *neutral, uncertain* and *non-committal* about that. You couldn't really agree. It's taking the admiration a bit too far. You haven't counted which are more beautiful and which less, even if you could. On the other hand, you don't feel sufficiently strongly to disagree.

iv) However, you would *reject* my opinion entirely if I went further and said 'It's the most beautiful picture in the gallery'. That's beyond your limits of being non-committal.

Therefore in this model, for any proposition in discussion, each participant's attitude may occupy one of four possible areas: a central position, an area of tolerable acceptance, an area of uncertainty or indifference, or an area of rejection. Figure 11.2 below shows how two participants' attitudes might relate to each other. In that figure, there is only a small area of agreement. In others it could be larger or smaller. Obviously, with three or more participants the relationships become more complex.

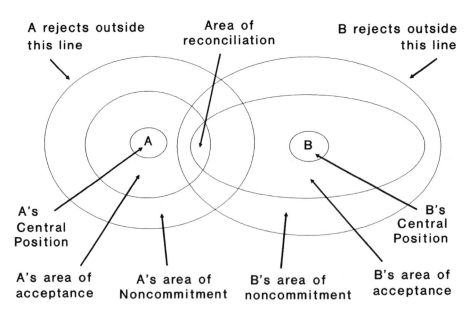

Figure 11.2. The mutual limits of acceptance and rejection of attitudes (*After Sherif and Sherif, 1967*)

B. Seven responses in discussion

We have seen that attitudes develop when resolving differences in discussion. These four theories take different perspectives on how this is done. Whilst their details may conflict, broadly speaking they are compatible, but none of their accounts are sufficient on their own. I cannot claim that what follows is a synthesis. It provides another framework of ideas for teachers to contextualise what they observe.

When someone expresses an attitude in discussion, there are at least seven ways another person may respond. There may be others.

1. They may agree

Supposing you are an examiner and you are attending the meeting of the examining board. Suppose you gave one candidate 30% when your central position, in Sherif and Sherif's terms, was that his script was worth in the region 28% to 32%. Suppose another examiner awarded 32%, believing it was worth in the region of 30% to 35%. Very likely you would agree on a score of 31%. There's little difficulty in resolving the initial disagreement because your central positions overlap. Your attitudes to the candidate's answers are roughly the same.

2. They can change their attitude or opinion

If the other examiner awarded a bare pass at 40%, very likely you would be prepared to compromise your opinion and award 35% because, although 35% is not in your central position, it is within your 'latitude of tolerance'. That figure is still a fail mark and you think the candidate should fail. But for the other examiner who thinks the candidate should just pass, the compromise crosses a boundary. In effect the compromise for him means a significant change of opinion. In Festinger's terms, 35% is more uncomfortable (dissonant) for him than it is for you.

3. They may try to persuade the other person to change theirs

If he awarded 50% and you awarded 30% you will both experience quite a bit of dissonance. The mid position is the borderline pass/fail. You might try to persuade him to adopt your point of view. If so, you will try to associate your opinion with selected values you know he holds. You will point out the candidate's lack of reasoning and the facts he didn't seem to know. Conversely, he may draw your attention to all the candidate's virtues in the belief that you consider them to be virtues. You will both be using the associationists' approach.

4. They may further justify or explain their own attitude or opinion

Suppose he awarded 60%. Now the gap is looking irreconcilable. When the disagreement is irreconcilable, in effect you are saying, *'I can compromise some distance, but 45% is too much. I can't go that far.'* Up to a point you are prepared to balance his opinion and yours as having equal weight, but there is a limit to your tolerance. You've given up trying to persuade him to your point of view. You are more concerned to convince yourself than to convince him.

5. They might seek support from others in the group

You appeal to other members of the exam board. Why and how? The answer to 'why' varies with the psychological theory. Associationists might say the other examiner will value the opinion of the group and you are trying to associate your views with theirs. The psychoanalysts say you want the security of the group's support. For example, Berne (1964) might say you are acting the role of a child seeking parental protection. Festinger would say that group support would decrease the dissonance you feel.

How will you get the group's support? By *explaining* why you believe what you do. But more than that, you will essentially *justify* your own attitude. This may seem similar to trying to persuade the other examiner if the values appealed to are the same as his. But they could be very different. Your intention now is to defend yourself against criticism and to be accepted by the group.

6. They can agree to disagree

So far as the beauty of a picture is concerned, it is possible to agree to disagree. That is not so possible in a decision-making group like an exam board where unanimity is preferred, but it can happen. Someone might say, *'I don't agree, but I accept the decision of the Board.'* In academic discussion, on the other hand, agreement to disagree is very acceptable because we want to encourage independent minds.

7. They may derogate (slag off) the other person

If the other examiner awarded 100% or even only 70% you might say, *'He's crazy! No way is that worth 100%. I'm sticking with my opinion. That's only worth 30%.'* Saying 'He's crazy' is not to deal with the facts and the disagreement. It is to derogate or insult the other person. Psychoanalysts will say it relieves feelings of frustration. To derogate is not a rational response. The truth or value of what someone says is regardless of who says it or their characteristics. In my opinion, it is never acceptable in discussion. It demeans those who insult as well as the insulted. Very obviously it lowers the tone of the discussion. Derogation is also not very plausible when the other person has high prestige or credibility, although in the long-term it does tend to undermine their credibility. Irrationally we are more inclined to accept derogation when we hold the same attitude, value or opinion as he who derogates. (Consider your attitude to insults thrown at political parties other than the one you favour.)

Notice, there seems to be a curvilinear relationship. With increasing dissonance (if you are like most people) at first you are prepared to shift your opinion a bit, but if there is too much dissonance, at first you'll say *'I'll move this far and no further.'* After that you may be less willing to change your judgement until eventually at the derogation stage, you won't budge your opinion at all. That's not to say that the amount of discomfort does not increase the greater your disagreement. But there must be a point of dissonance in between which produces the maximum shift of response.

That's the point advertisers, politicians and other persuaders would dearly like to know.

The same goes for value judgements that are not numerical. If you have a slightly different political opinion from a friend regarding how much government intervention in social affairs is desirable, or how severely criminals should be punished, you may change your opinion a bit, but you won't make a radical change all in an instant.

The same applies in discussion groups. Most people are prepared to shift their opinions a little way in response to the opinions of others, but there comes a point where the change demanded is so great that they're not prepared to change at all. Of course, depending on the size of the discussion group and how vocal its members are, there won't be just two opinions. There will be a number of opinions each tugging at the others in various directions.

C. Factors influencing the development of affect in discussions

We might like to think that attitudes and values are developed as a result of rational discussion. Indeed, we have already seen in Chapter 7 that one purpose of discussion is to develop the powers of reason. But, by their nature, attitudes and values have emotive elements that may seem to over-power the desire to reason. So it is worth looking at the rational, and not so rational, considerations influencing discussions at stage (iii).

1. The order of points in discussion
There is some evidence to suggest that attitudes expressed earlier in a discussion are more influential than those expressed later. This is not only because leaders and other articulate members are likely to speak first, nor only because at that stage their opinions are presented unopposed. It is that early opinions and attitudes set a perspective, an agenda and ways of thinking.

However, it is not always as simple as that. For example, if there is a long delay before counter arguments are given and before others have to make up their minds, the most recent contributions will be influential. Earlier arguments can be forgotten. (Consider election campaigns.)

In general, it pays to present your strongest arguments first, but if the group is not particularly attentive or interested, unimportant arguments presented later can seem a bit of an anticlimax. In that case working up to a climax that clinches the argument can be better.

2. Points made in discussion
When arguing in discussion a lot of people only state facts. They don't state their values, attitudes or moral principles. That's why stages (i) and (ii) are necessary. Furthermore, they don't explicitly state their conclusions based upon those facts and values. They leave it to other members of the discussion to draw the conclusion for

themselves. If other members do so, this strategy would indeed be effective, but many don't. So in general, it is better to give facts, values and draw the conclusion explicitly.

Contributions giving both sides of an argument are more persuasive with participants opposed to your point of view. It's as if they think, *'At least he's considered my point of view even though, on balance, he's rejected it. I can't reply until I've understood why.'* This obliges the opposition to consider one's own arguments rather than only reasserting their own. It therefore ensures that conflicting ideas are confronted rather than each being asserted without their reasons being examined or contested.

If you present one-sided arguments, those who agree with you will have their opinions reinforced by association with their values. On the other hand, participants of the same opinion as your own may entertain doubts if you give arguments opposed to your agreed position. Conversely, with group members initially opposed to your position, failure to consider well-known objections and counter arguments weakens one's persuasiveness; but, perhaps surprisingly, introducing new unfamiliar objections and counter arguments also weakens one's persuasiveness.

People who have heard both sides of an argument are less likely than those who have only heard one side to change their minds later when subjected to counter arguments they have not heard before. This is described as 'inoculation' against counter influence.

What sort of appeal in discussion will arouse feelings that develop motives, values and attitudes? Obviously it depends a great deal on the particular feelings. One approach has been to say, if someone argues against your attitudes or opinions, it constitutes a threat. There is dissonance. It may be a threat to one's self-esteem or customary ways of thinking and behaving. Being required to change one's mind or habits is often threatening. The natural reaction is to defend oneself against the threat, either by justifying one's own position, or by attacking the other's. That in turn will threaten the other person.

One way to be more persuasive is to reduce the threat (dissonance) by giving assurance or suggesting ways that reduce the threat. A typical strategy for reconciliation is to emphasise common values so as to suggest that the change of mind or behaviour is not so great.

Interestingly, when threats are too horrible to contemplate, they are ignored, whilst lesser threats are not. This is known as 'the defence against anxiety'. It can result in inattentiveness or, by contrast, aggressiveness against the 'messenger' giving bad news. For example, not only do smokers ignore the consequences of their habit, they are more willing than non-smokers to believe contributions that discount the evidence.

Personality factors influence these responses and to these we must now turn.

3. The characteristics of group members

Some people change their attitudes in discussion more easily than others. We say they are persuadable. Others are more rigid. High persuadability is related to several factors that leave a lot for teachers to observe and interpret:

i) *Authoritarianism.* People who are obedient to authority and admire toughness, power and aggression are more likely to follow group leaders' opinions. I was particularly struck by this when teaching police to be sensitive, caring, compassionate and gentle. Since, more than most cultures, they admire toughness, power and aggression, I thought I had a difficult job. It was quite the opposite. I was presented as an authority. I said they should be more liberal in their values and be more sensitive to others' feelings, and they were! They obeyed!

If you want group members to make up their own minds by discussion of pros and cons, rather than be excessively influenced by one or two participants, it is best to use leaderless groups of four, five or six members. That is a group large enough to contain a variety of opinions, yet small enough for a fairly even distribution of contributions.

ii) *Perceptual dependence.* There is experimental evidence that people who are responsive to their environment, rather than being driven by their innermost thoughts, are most likely to be persuaded by other group members. Those group members are, of course, part of the individual's environment.

iii) *Social dependence.* Some people, more than others, need the support of those others. Consequently they are more likely to be persuaded by other group members, at least in the short-term. They may seem fickle if, some time later, they meet a strong minded person with a contrary opinion.

iv) *Gender differences.* In many cultures women are more dependent and acquiescent than men.

v) *Low self-esteem.* High persuadability is related to low self-esteem. On the other hand, group members with high self-esteem are more easily persuaded by contributions that further enhance it. It seems that group members with an outwardly high opinion of themselves are most easily persuaded by flattery, although, as we shall see in a moment, outward opinions may hide contrary inner ones.

vi) *Fertile imaginations.* Members with a tendency to fantasise are more able to imagine what others are saying and that is the necessary first step to accepting it.

vii) *Member's credibility.* One of the strongest influences upon participants' attitudes in discussion is the credibility of a contributor. Important factors contributing to credibility include expertness, trustworthiness and impartiality. Both relevant and irrelevant aspects of credibility influence changes in attitude. For example, where member A agrees with B on one issue, there is a tendency for B to have high credibility with A on another unconnected issue. Similarly, appearance, dress, manner of speech, non-verbal signals, age and sex are just a few of many irrelevant influences upon members' credibility in discussion.

viii) *Cognitive clarity.* The fact that group members will not be converted to ideas and attitudes that they don't understand has several consequences. One is that contributors who can express their feelings clearly will be most influential.

Another is that some people *need* cognitive clarity more than others. Others can tolerate ambiguities and inconsistencies more contentedly. The effect of this varies with the individual's cognitive *style* and leads to contrasting behaviour in discussions.

When people described as 'levellers' are motivated to achieve cognitive clarity, they tend to over simplify. They may adopt simple, possibly sweeping, attitudes and not face the complexities of real life. They ignore contrary examples and may twist ideas to fit their sweeping generalisations. In that case, it is important to let the discussion continue to give time for complexities, such as exceptions to simple rules, to be raised.

In contrast, 'sharpeners' wanting clarity try to achieve it by analysing the details of ambiguities, complexities and exceptions to rules. To do so, far from trying to ignore inconvenient facts, they hunt for clues that might resolve the ambiguities and explain the exceptions. They listen more intently.

This means that sharpeners are more likely to change their attitudes when motivated to sort out their ideas. But there is evidence to suggest that levellers change more when motivation is weak (Baron, 1963).

One might expect that intelligent and educated people will understand others' contributions more clearly and that they will therefore be more open to changing their opinions and attitudes. On the other hand, they might also subject what is said to more searching criticisms. People with more education are less likely to be convinced by one-sided contributions.

ix) *Defence mechanisms.* According to psychoanalytic theory, when individuals have two or more incompatible motives they experience a conflict, perhaps at an unconscious level. Defence mechanisms are attempts, not to resolve the conflict, but to avoid facing it. These are usually unconscious. Indeed *repression* is a mechanism to avoid being conscious of the conflict so that certain feelings, attitudes and values are not expressed in discussion – at least not directly. *Projection, displacement* and *reaction formation* exemplify indirect expressions of defence mechanisms that teachers may observe.

Projection occurs when the individual perceives another person as having a motive or attitude, such as a racist attitude, that they unconsciously have themselves.

Displacement occurs in discussion when a member misapplies an attitude, motive or value towards some other object than the one to which he really feels it. For example, someone might disapprove of viewing pornography on the Internet when what they really disapprove of is any exploitation in producing it or what they believe to be the consequences of seeing it.

Reaction formation operates when a group member asserts the opposite of his own unacceptable feelings (cp Shakespeare's 'Methinks the lady doth protest too much'). I always remember one police officer's emphatic, but irrelevant, assertion that he had never had homosexual feelings.

D. Conclusion

Unlike the other chapters in Part II, this chapter has been more concerned with the task of the teacher or group leader than with the tasks the discussion group might be set. It is concerned with observing attitudes and the processes of attitude change in discussion. This is because attitude change and development itself is not a task that can be imposed on group members. It has to come from within each one of them. It has to build upon affect that members already have.

To make sense of those observations I have described their theoretical contexts and influences.

Part III

What Factors Affect Interaction in Discussion Groups?

If you want to improve your teaching by discussion you will need to interpret what goes on in your groups. To do that you will need to know the factors that influence behaviour in discussion. You will need to use the language and concepts of group dynamics. Part III aims to give you the language and concepts.

When reading Part III constantly try to think of discussions in your experience that illustrate the factors described. Discussions vary; so don't expect that everything will fit your experience. But take what does fit and try to deepen your understanding of what happened. There are a lot of facts in Part III. Only you can apply them to your experience, so you may have to work at it a bit, because the information is rather dense.

When looking at people in groups, a very natural question to ask is, 'Why did he or she do that?' For example, we might ask 'Why did she react like that?' or 'Why didn't they say anything?' or 'Why was he able to achieve that objective?'

You can usually answer questions like these by considering some combination of nine factors. The trouble with writing about them is that they all interact so much that when describing one, I find I am writing about the others. They cannot be considered in isolation. To understand the dynamics of your discussion groups is to appreciate how each of the nine factors influence, and are influenced by, each other. The factors are:

1. The motivation of group members
This includes emotions, feelings and all affective factors. They are all forms of psychological energy. The crucial question is not, as in Chapter 11, 'How can I develop affect?', but 'What motives and emotions are important influences upon group members?'

2. The tasks, goals or objectives to be achieved
Tasks vary, but in what way do the variations result in different kinds of discussion? For example, how does the difficulty of a task vary with group size?

3. Group norms, conformity and nonconformists
These are the 'rules' that hold a group together as a group. They are mostly not explicit, yet tutors expect certain behaviour and surely ought to make it clear. What

norms do you want in your groups? These expectations impose powerful group pressures towards conformity; but how? And how do nonconformists influence their groups and how can they be encouraged?

4. Group composition
This factor might be called 'group membership'. It is concerned with the characteristics of group members. We considered some in the last chapter. It is obvious to any teacher that the abilities, knowledge, experience, personalities, ages and sexes of group members influence how they behave and how they interact in a group.

5. Group size
Obviously group size is a matter of how many people are in the group. So size affects group composition. But how does the size of a group affect the way members' characteristics interact? And how does that affect your choice of teaching methods?

6. Group structure including the roles adopted by individual members
The structure concerns the relationships between group members. For example, in most teaching groups, the teacher has a different role from other group members. His relationships will be different from those between other group members. But what are the important dimensions of members' relationships? Authority? Knowledge? Esteem? All relationships in a group are unique, so what factors determine the group structure?

7. Group history and experience
Any of the other seven factors may change, so the time dimension is a factor that may affect what group members do. Early experience may influence later behaviour so you must think about it in advance. A group may take a little while to overcome a bad experience early in its life. In this way it may be useful to think of groups, like an organism, having a life and a sequence of development. If so, a teacher will need to appreciate what a typical sequence of development might be, otherwise he might expect too much too soon. Are there developmental phases or critical periods as in human development?

8. The group environment
This can be divided into the physical, social, psychological and possibly some other kinds of environment. I'm chiefly concerned with the physical environment here – others are mostly covered by the other factors. Of particular interest is where people sit in a group. What are the distances between group members? What other physical factors influence discussion?

9. The interaction of group members
In a way this ninth factor need not be mentioned, because it can be explained by the interplay of all the other factors. In practice there are some aspects of interaction in group discussions that are best considered separately. The most important of these are aspects of communication. Of course, how people communicate is a matter of convention. It is part of group norms. How far they co-operate or conflict may be a matter of motivation, group size, the group's experience, composition and so on.

Chapter 12
What motives and emotions affect group members?

A. Fear as the dominant emotion in discussion groups

B. The effect of feedback on identity, anxiety and performance

C. The effect of others in the group

D. Co-operation in groups is better than competition

E. Use the desire for friendly interaction

F. Task motives: To achieve, or avoid failure?

G. The pitfalls of groupthink

H. Conclusion

Some student motives are helpful; others are a hindrance. The art of teaching, as in any other form of management, is to use the helpful ones and to reduce the effect of the others. To do that, teachers need to identify which are which.

A. Fear as the dominant emotion in discussion groups

1. The causes of fear
The motive that dominates discussion, particularly in large groups, is fear. Why should this be? It is crucially important to understand:
i)   that groups are the source of understanding one's social identity, and
ii) that younger university students are at a stage of life, leaving home, where they seek an answer to the questions 'Who and what am I?'
iii) that the answers to these questions are obtained by comparing oneself with others.
     Students, particularly older students, are anxious that they will say something foolish, something everyone else will disagree with, or that they cannot defend.
Common anxieties include:
'Will I be accepted by the group?'
'Will I be able to understand what others say?'

'How will I know what to do?' and
'Will I be able to do what is expected of me?'

These anxieties are wholly natural. Indeed, many tutors have similar fears: 'What will I do if I'm asked a question I can't answer?'

Babad and Kuriloff (1986) showed that the fear is of participation. In a controlled experiment observers' and participants' perceptions and learning were similar except that participants felt anxiety about personal disclosure, the trainer's authority, and their responsibility. I once recorded the heart rates of experienced students in a university tutorial with a very experienced teacher. The heart rate for some students rose from 80 beats per minute to over 160 when they spoke, yet they were outwardly calm. For others who were visibly nervous the rise was only 30 or 40 beats. When someone spoke, their neighbours' heart rates also rose 10 beats per minute.

2. The effects of fear

Leary and Atherton (1986) demonstrated that people become inhibited when they are socially anxious. The anxiety is related to low expectations which are, in turn, associated with a poor self image. Clabby and Belz (1985) describe barriers to learning amongst adults as including ambivalence about their success, fear of risk-taking, over-dependence on authority figures, tension, defensive dominance and intrusive memories of poor learning experiences.

The problem for the teacher is not only that fear inhibits participation in groups, it inhibits thought as well. If students are worried about what others will think of them and what they say, they will not be using all the facts at their disposal to solve a problem or perform some other group task. They will wish to conform to others' opinions. They will use facts selectively, thereby distorting their own perceptions. They will use mental energy to block uncomfortable facts. In short, they will not face reality. They will not think independently. Their powers of thought will not be fully used and some of those powers will be used to prevent certain thoughts coming to consciousness. So there is a process of self-deception, a process of defensiveness.

Therefore, if thought is a major educational objective, fear reduction is a major teaching strategy. Anxiety inhibits thought and thereby inhibits education.

3. What teachers must do to reduce fear

Students' anxieties are to do with what other people will think of them and what they will come to think of themselves. That is their sense of their own identity. Anxieties are to do with esteem, particularly self-esteem. Like all anxieties, they are about the future because the future is uncertain.

So a primary duty of teachers is to build students' confidence and self-esteem. For this, supportive understanding and judicious praise are vital. Feedback about oneself or one's past performance could give that confidence.

Anxiety caused by uncertainty can be reduced by confident expectations and information about the future. Hence there is an important link between students' motivation and the information they have about themselves.

Fears are heightened by the presence of an audience. So keep groups small, that is, not larger than four, until some confidence and self-esteem are developed. Dyads and buzz group methods are therefore crucial to effective teaching in the early stages.

Figure 12.1 shows that if you want your students to risk being creative, or if you want them to respond to the challenge of a difficult task, they need high support as well. Intellectual challenge and emotional support must go together. One without the other won't do. But the task must be achievable. A sense of achievement increases confidence. So design small tasks that have some challenge, but are achievable. A small group is more likely to be supportive, familiar, attractive, like oneself and increase self-esteem. A competitive group will be less supportive than a co-operative one. So tutors will need to think about the size and composition of groups.

	High Risk/Challenge		
High support	Stimulating Sense of achievement Rewarding	Fear Conflict Anxiety	**Low support**
	Socialising Cosy Complacent	Apathy Boring Absenteeism	
	Unchallenging		

Figure 12.1. Combine high support with high, but achieveable, challenges

Here, then, is a whole nexus of factors that generate motivation towards a group's task and feelings towards its members: self-esteem, self-confidence, feedback, a sense of achievement, and the supportiveness, co-operation, familiarity and attractiveness of group members.

In the primary schools of England one can see children learning to think with uninhibited joy at exploration. Yet, to my observation, a great deal of the process of secondary education, particularly in Scotland, is a process of threats and punishments, of humiliation and conformity and where independence of mind is squashed in the name of discipline. It creates an ethos of defensiveness. While that ethos remains, the methods of post-secondary education must counter its legacy. There is no way to preserve the clarity of one's thinking and at the same time be committed to preserve one's self-esteem by not facing facts.

B. The effect of feedback on identity, anxiety and performance

1. Feedback answers the questions 'Who and what am I?'
Feedback on performance from the teacher and other discussants gives information. It is information that the individual can use to answer questions of social identity. It helps to answer questions such as 'What did I do well?', 'How can I improve?', 'What am I like?', 'What am I good at?' and even 'What career should I undertake?'

2. *Give feedback to reduce anxiety*

Giving feedback is a process of reducing uncertainty and consequently it reduces anxiety. Unfortunately, high levels of anxiety can block out incoming communication (Wang, 1985) so people who suffer from high anxiety may block out encouraging feedback that could reduce it. For this reason high social anxiety is associated with how people listen and how they communicate. Schlenker and Leary (1985) point out that if what is being communicated is important and the listener has low expectations of his achievement, there is an interaction which produces high anxiety. This has a negative effect which can produce physical or psychological withdrawal from the situation, possibly leading to a rather introverted preoccupation with one's limitations. Consider, for example, if a tutor is giving instructions and emphasising that the task is very important, students with low self esteem or high social anxiety will have greater difficulty in hearing and understanding what is being said. So they handicap themselves from the start.

All this emphasises the importance of reducing anxiety in discussion groups as soon as possible. To participate in small groups is less fearsome than in large groups. Achievable tasks also reduce anxiety. Hence, again, my maxim is *Start with simple tasks in small groups for short periods of time, and then gradually increase their respective complexity, size and duration.*

3. *Give feedback for confidence and self-esteem*

If verbal feedback is the more effective, what should tutors say? Reeve et al (1986) found that students' belief in themselves and their own competence was more important than feedback on their performance. Harackiewicz and Larson (1986) showed that the influence of a supervisor on a subordinate's self-perceived competence significantly affected their enjoyment, particularly when the feedback was given in a 'controlled manner'. Sansone (1986) also compared feedback given to students on their performance at a specific task, with supportive feedback about their personal competence. Both enhanced students' interest in what they were doing, but personal feedback had a greater effect upon their self-esteem. In a further experiment it became clear that self-esteem and the students' perception of their own competence are different factors both promoting the students' interest in what they were doing. However, perceived competence enhanced enjoyment only when the manipulation of self-esteem included valuing the quality of their performance.

This suggests that tutors can increase students' motivation and interest by general expressions of confidence in their ability, and can also direct their interest to specific projects if they relate their general expressions of confidence and esteem to the specific tasks required.

Butler and Nisan (1986) experimented with giving various kinds of feedback and concluded that motivation intrinsic to the specific task depended on the degree to which the task continued to be perceived as challenging and as providing satisfying information about one's competence.

4. Feedback enhances performance

There is plenty of evidence in the psychological and management literature that feedback information enhances performance. It is also obvious that in discussions participants get verbal and non-verbal feedback on their ideas, feelings, attitudes, perceptions and inter-personal behaviour. The question is 'What kind of feedback enhances performance the most?' Tripathi and Agarwal (1985) found that students receiving verbal feedback spent longer and performed better at problem-solving tasks than those with tangible rewards or no rewards at all.

However, anxiety can create a vicious circle by overloading the students' neural system. We all know of cases where someone is so worried that he cannot take in what feedback is being given. It is not difficult to imagine lesser cases of anxiety having a lesser, but nonetheless significant, effect. There are well-attested neuro-physiological reasons for this (Wang, 1985). Tobias (1985) points out that high anxiety can also block out retrieval of information from one's memory. How can the vicious circle be broken? Tobias believes that this effect can be reduced by acquiring study skills and test-taking skills, either because practice reduces the cognitive capacity demanded by learning and taking tests, or because retrieval of required information is facilitated.

C. The effect of others in the group

There is reason to think that people perform better in the presence of other people, even if they do not overtly interact with them. There are two possible explanations for this: audience effects and coaction effects.

1. Audience effects

In the theatre they often say at rehearsals, 'It will be all right on the night'. Somehow the presence of the audience brings out the best from the actors. Presumably the audience is responsive and thereby gives feedback. The effect of the crowd at a football match is the same, particularly when the team is playing at home.

Work by Cottrell (1972), Good (1973), and Martens and Landers (1972) interprets audience effects in terms of expectancy theory. They suggest that it is not the mere presence of other people that is arousing, but the belief that others present will pass judgement on one's performance.

Cottrell believed that social facilitation effects are the result of expectations that feedback will be good or bad. These expectations are learned. Using a word association test with 32 women, Good showed that those who would be evaluated and were told they would do well, performed significantly better than those who were either led to expect that they would do poorly, or that their performance would not be known to the experimenter. Thus Good demonstrated what any good tutor knows: that the expectation of encouraging feedback improves performance.

The experiment by Martens and Landers was interesting because it compared people working on a manual task, either alone or in twos, threes or fours under three conditions: one in which their performance could be directly observed, one in which the results could be indirectly known and a third in which no evaluation was possible. The expectation that those who were more directly observed would perform worse was confirmed. Presumably under Cottrell's hypothesis, if they had been encouraged to believe that they would do well, they would have done.

2. Coaction

These audience effects can be contrasted with coaction effects. Coaction occurs when performance at a task is apparently improved by the knowledge that others present are doing the same thing. For example, though I know of no empirical confirmation, students in an exam room with others probably do better than students taking the exam in isolation. As long ago as 1897, Triplett showed that cyclists at time trials rode slower on their own than when they knew (though probably could not see) there was someone else on the other half of the track.

In educational group work audience and coaction effects cannot always be disentangled. In Chapter 21 I suggest that an important technique in small group work is to give students a task to perform individually before forming them into groups (coaction). In this way they bring some ideas they have already thought about to the group, and the groups get off to a good start. If, when working individually in this way, students know that they will need to contribute their thoughts to a group, they usually work harder than if they were working alone and unpaced. In other words, they use time more efficiently.

3. Which is better – coaction in groups or unpaced study alone?

The efficient use of time is a sensitive issue. Time in class may be used more efficiently than time spent in unpaced study at home, but it is precious. And there are incentives at the present time for distance learning, and open learning techniques in which the students are alone and unpaced, particularly for those using the Internet. The educational justification for this approach lies in evidence accumulated since the 1960s with reference to independent learning such as presentations by the Open University. Yet we saw in Chapter 2 that group work is important to get students to think.

Thus there appears to be a conflict between research into independent learning which says that students learn better when they work unpaced alone, and small group research which suggests students learn more efficiently when paced by the knowledge that others in the same room are engaged on the same task. Two points should be made. First, the research evidence in both camps is ambiguous, suggesting there are underlying factors of which neither is taking account. Secondly, some suggestions have been made as to what those underlying factors are which reconcile the apparent conflicts.

The first reconciliation is to say that there isn't a conflict at all because the independent learning research suggests that students learn more thoroughly, while the group research suggests they learn more efficiently per unit of time. It may well be that independent learning is not so efficient or intensive as individual learning in the presence of other people doing the same thing. That may not worry the government, and others who encourage independent learning because it only wastes the resources of the private individual – his own time. And in any case that waste has to be weighed against the travel time to meet the rest of the group.

The second reconciliation emerges from work by Zajonc (1965). Zajonc reviewed social facilitation studies, and concluded that the presence of others is arousing. That is, the presence of other students produces or releases motivating energy. According to arousal theory, performance should improve with increasing arousing audience effects up to an optimum point, but thereafter, over-arousal will lead to a deterioration of performance. Consider, for example, introverts who cannot perform in front of an audience but who can do very well on their own. Kelley and Thibaut (1969) have shown that arousal and motivation are greater in the presence of other people. Activity by others results in greater speed and emotional excitement than is experienced when working alone. Secondly, even after students have become fairly fed up with problem-solving on their own, the presence of others can re-invigorate them to work on the same or similar tasks. Students who were not interested in a task showed more interest when there was an audience. Kelley and Thibaut also believed that the variations in performance by individuals are greater in social conditions than in isolation, and this can best be explained by the arousal theory.

What are the implications of this when getting students to prepare for group work? Should teachers set work in advance for students to bring to class to share in a group, with the expectation that they will do well? Or should they set work to be done individually in class in the presence of others, in the belief that coaction will have a positive effect? In practice the size of the task and the spontaneity required may well influence this decision.

We have seen that individuals work more quickly when others are present, but leaving that factor aside, what evidence is there that coaction results in superior performance? That is to say, what evidence is there that individual work before a group task is better than preparation at home? As long ago as 1920, Allport conducted a series of experiments on coaction. Typically subjects were asked in a limited period to list as many words as they could unconnected with a given word. Subjects alternated between working on their own and working whilst others engaged on the same task were in the same room. In another experiment subjects were asked to write down arguments against short presented texts. In general Allport found that people working in the same room, but not communicating with each other performed better than those working alone. This implies that the use of individual work in small groups, as suggested in Chapter 21, is at least sometimes a good idea. Tutors may feel that it does not use the presence of other group members, but in fact it does.

D. Co-operation in groups is better than competition

On the whole, group members obtain more satisfaction from cohesive and harmonious groups than those displaying discord. This may seem to be obvious in that students seek friendship, esteem and a sense of achievement from participation groups.

1. The adversarial tradition

Yet, academic staff sometimes think their purposes can best be served by creating debates and conflicts of opinion in small group discussion. Their belief that sound judgements can be made if conflicting points of view are contested is part of a long adversarial tradition in parliaments, the law courts and academic criticism. But in practice it convinces people of their own point of view and narrows their minds. (In the law courts the objective is different. It is not to educate participants, the learned counsel, but to permit independent minds, the judge and jury, to reach a decision.) In general, discord produces frustration, not learning.

2. Motivation compared in co-operative and competitive groups

There has been a great deal of research into the relative merits of individual work, co-operation and competition in groups. Johnson and Johnson (1987) reviewed 321 research studies. They believe that the pattern of interaction in co-operative and competitive groups is quite different because they have different objectives. They outline three contrasting chains of cause and effect, shown in Table 12.2. Co-operative groups have a positive interdependence leading to an interaction that promotes acceptance, support and trust. This in turn encourages exchange of information, mutual influence and an effective use of resources. The consequent motivation is intrinsic, with high expectations of success, an interest in mutual benefit and a high commitment to learning. Because interaction is rewarding, there is a high emotional involvement in learning from each other. In contrast, the negative interdependence in competitive groups creates a style of interaction that leads to distrust and mutual rejection. Consequently there is little, or misleading, communication.

It is possible that coaction is an important motivating factor in the superior performance of co-operative groups. In a study by Brown and Abrams, children took a reasoning test. Some were told that they were in a project co-operating with another school and some that they were in competition. Those who believed they were co-operating scored two more out of 32 than those who believed their performance was competitive.

The evidence with regard to the individuals who compose the group is not so clear cut. Some individuals perform better in a competitive climate. Hence, a distinction needs to be drawn between the achievement of the group and the achievement of the individuals that compose it.

3. On balance participants prefer co-operative relationships

Reviewing 35 studies in which participants' preferences were considered, 19 preferred co-operative groups, 12 had no preference either way, and the remaining 4 preferred competition. Looking at the relative effectiveness of co-operation and competition in 66 comparative studies, Johnson and Johnson concluded that the average person in a co-operative group performed at the same level or better than 79% of a typical competitive group. From this there seems little doubt that co-operative groups are more effective than competitive ones.

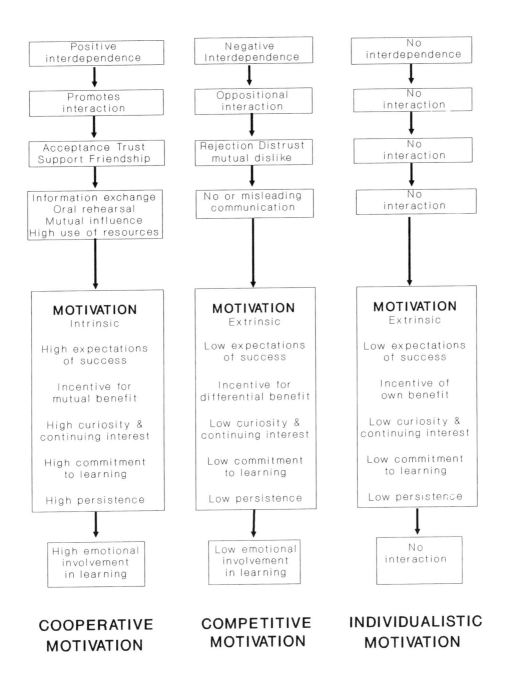

Table 12.2. Motivation when members are co-operative, competitive or individualist

But that is not all. Johnson and Johnson found considerable evidence that, compared with competitive groups, co-operative groups 'result in more positive relationships among the members, relationships characterised by mutual liking, positive attitudes towards each other, mutual concern, friendliness, attentiveness, feelings of obligation towards each other, and the desire to win each other's respect. These results hold even when group members are from both sexes and different cultures, social classes and ability groups'. They found 180 studies, with a total of 1140 separate findings. 69% of participants preferred co-operation to competition, 27% had no preference and 4% favoured competition.

Interestingly, they reported that co-operative groups encouraged more favourable attitudes towards supervisors and superiors. They found them more supportive and accepting. This is important in many contexts because the group will be motivated to follow his leadership and to accept his norms of behaviour.

Johnson and Johnson also found that in co-operative groups self esteem was higher, there was more critical thinking, deeper thinking and greater increases in social skills, such as decision-making, leadership and communication. In short, the groups were more effective in achieving their tasks.

Kelley and Stahelski (1970) wanted to see if a competitive individual entering a co-operative group tried to dominate it. First of all, co-operative members began behaving competitively, breaking trust, withholding information, and reducing communication. Consequently, the competitive individual saw the group as having always been competitive and remained unaware of his influence on the group. On the other hand, the previously co-operative group members were very well aware of his impact. Here lies a difficulty for teachers. A co-operative climate is easier to destroy than to build.

4. Students prefer groups to independent work

Johnson and Johnson obtained similar results from their meta-analysis comparing co-operative groups with individual work. Of the students, 55% preferred co-operative groups, 39% showed no preference and 6% preferred individual work. The average co-operative group student performed better than 78% of students working by independent study.

Perhaps surprisingly, competitive groups were preferred to independent study by 31% to 17% and the average student in them performed better than 57% of those who studied independently. This, of course, does not deny the value of independent study to obtain facts followed by co-operative groups for other objectives and their tasks as described in Part II.

E. Use the desire for friendly interaction

Human beings are social animals. It is natural for people, particularly young people, to talk. Teachers should use that fact. Repression of this natural desire in lectures is unnatural. That is why the use of buzz groups in lectures (see pages 204–211) is so successful. It uses the natural desire to release tensions in a constructive way.

One reason why co-operative groups are successful is that they use a natural desire for friendship. Psychologists call this 'affiliation'. People will normally join a group, not for the sake of the group, but to satisfy their own needs. In education and employment, as in all walks of life, groups form spontaneously.

Other factors favouring group formation are mutual attraction, common needs, personalities, similar social, racial and economic status and the perception group members have of each other's abilities. Admittedly, teachers cannot easily use these factors to generate learning or group harmony. When students arrive there is not much teachers can do about their physical attractiveness, economic background or racial origins. Nor, in the short-term, is there much they can do about students' personalities and abilities. These variables affecting interpersonal attraction are not those that can easily be managed or manipulated. So don't try. Use the resources available.

Use affiliation, the desire to talk and the wish to belong to create a group climate in which there is friendship and a sense of group identity. All people have a need for friendship and a sense of belonging to a group. Management of the proximity, contact and interaction of students can provide the opportunity for individuals to obtain satisfying friendships through feeling that they are accepted by other members of the group. These management techniques are the techniques of teaching. The discussion methods considered in this book vary primarily in the way the tasks, size, composition, structure and environment of different groups are managed. These things affect student motivation.

Although a teacher cannot do much about the attractiveness of individuals, there are three characteristics of groups which people find attractive and which the teacher can try to cultivate. Students will find small group teaching attractive if it is rewarding, if they share the values and goals of the group, or if they see the group as helping to achieve external goals, such as career success. For these reasons teachers should ensure
i)   that small group teaching is enjoyable,
ii) that students are able to recognise their own achievements in it,
iii) that they will see the contribution of group work to examination success and other
        goals, and
iv) that the groups enhance the individual's confidence and self-esteem.

F. Task motives: To achieve or avoid failure?

There is an important difference in the desire to achieve as much success as possible and the desire to avoid failure. They result in different strategies and attitudes to work. Students who only desire to avoid failure may do the minimum necessary work and may have a poor attendance record at group tutorials. Those who wish to achieve as much as possible will be more highly motivated and won't want to miss any teaching that is offered.

This distinction applies to the achievement of both groups and individuals and is related to the tasks they choose. Those who wish to avoid failure are more likely to choose to do essays or other assignments at the extremes of difficulty because it is possible to achieve very easy tasks, and failure to achieve very difficult ones does not bring blame or criticism. On the other hand, students who want to achieve as much as they can will choose feasible tasks which will stretch them a little, but not so much as to risk failure.

G. The pitfalls of groupthink

A committee is a decision-making discussion group. Janis (1972, 1982) has shown that there is a complex of motivations that can tempt a group of decision-makers to avoid taking responsibility. Decision-makers are often subject to pressures, conflicts, doubts, personal struggles, hostilities and friendships, which tug them in conflicting directions. One way to avoid conflicts is to avoid taking any decisions at all. Janis has called this 'Groupthink'.

1. What is 'Groupthink'?

Groupthink is defined as a collective pattern of defensive avoidance resulting in a deterioration of mental efficiency, reality testing and moral judgement. Many of Janis's examples are political. There are eight characteristics:

i) *Rationalisation.* A group invents justifications for the decisions they have taken or have failed to take in order to avoid the doubts and a need to reconsider the decisions.

ii) *An illusion of unanimity.* Members in the group who have doubts perceive that they are the only one and that everyone else is in agreement. Silence implies consent. Consequently, there is a tacit agreement by a silent majority, who are covertly opposed to the proposal.

iii) *Pressure to conform.* Those who do express their dissent are made to feel a group pressure that is not really there.

iv) *Self censorship.* These pressures make individuals convince themselves that they should overcome their doubts.

v) *'Mindguards'.* Some group members actively prevent expression of dissent.

vi) *An illusion of power.* Because there is an illusion that the rest of the group support the proposal, there is commonly excessive optimism and risk-taking. This may be accompanied by an illusion of invulnerability and a belief that the group is beyond reproach.

vii) *A belief in their own morality.* Members convince themselves that their action is moral, and ignore consequences or principles which, to others, would seem immoral.

viii) *Belittlement and stereotyping.* Group members do not seriously consider opposition outside the group. Such opposition is 'them', not 'us'. It is regarded as too wicked, foolish or impotent to justify serious consideration or negotiation.

2. How to avoid groupthink

To avoid groupthink, Janis and Mann (1977) recommend four strategies. For any decision a group should consider:

i) the gains and losses for the group,

ii) the gains and losses for others,

iii) how far the group's self-esteem would be raised or lowered by the decision, and

iv) how far the group's esteem would be raised or lowered in the eyes of others.

3. How to make good decisions

To prevent groupthink, and to ensure high quality decisions, Mann and Janis (1983) recommend:

i) that the teachers or leaders do not give their own opinion at the beginning. This removes some pressure for conformity and permits a more honest enquiry,

ii) that every group member should be required to express objections and doubts, at least on a particular aspect of the decision,

iii) that one or more members should play devil's advocate,

iv) that the group should meet a second time to reconsider the decision, and

v) that external consultants are used.

H. Conclusion

In this chapter I've not been concerned with using discussion to motivate students towards their subject of study. That was the purpose of Chapter 11 on developing affect. I've been concerned here with how motivation influences the discussion process, not how the discussion process influences motivation.

What we have found is that the social experience of group discussion creates fear for some students and opportunities for enjoyment, co-operation and achievement for others. Obviously teachers must think how to create the opportunities, not the fear.

Chapter 13
How is a group influenced by its tasks?

A. Different tasks require different styles of discussion

B. The influence of tasks upon group dynamics

C. Factors affecting task difficulty

D. Setting own tasks

E. Steiner's theory of task achievement

F. Conclusion

It seems obvious that the way a group behaves will depend upon the task it has to perform. The problem for teachers is to how to anticipate the effect of the tasks upon the subsequent discussion process. How is the influence of the task to be distinguished from all the other influences considered in Part III?

A. Different tasks require different styles of discussion

We might expect that a group working step by step through calculations to solve a convergent problem-solving task will interact differently from a creative brainstorm, and differently again from a group with the supportive climate a teacher aims to produce for attitude development. The procedures are different. Certainly that is one consideration.

It is an approach that assumes that discussion focuses, or ought to focus, upon a goal which is the achievement of a task; and the task is specified by the agenda, the teacher or some other authority. But first, is this the reality? It might be said that group members have their own, and hidden, agendas. Goals may also be conscious or unconscious.

Second, it is natural to think that every task should have a goal or some way of knowing whether it has been achieved. But this is controversial. One school of thought (eg. Stenhouse, 1969) argues that the processes of discussion are important, not its end products. There should be no end product predetermined in advance. In this view students should be on an unending journey of discovery, including self-discovery. They should be striving for unattainable goals and discussion is precisely the context in which they should do so.

I don't need to argue with this. Perhaps there can be times and places for discussions with specified objectives, hidden objectives or no objectives. All I need to claim here is that the styles of discussion and group interaction will be influenced in each case. The influence is relatively direct.

B. The influence of tasks upon group dynamics

Yet tasks primarily influence group dynamics indirectly through their effect on the other factors I listed at the beginning of Part III. For example, any teacher knows that the work a group is given will influence their morale, which member has most expertise, the most appropriate group size, and so on. We've already seen in the last chapter that there are contrasting effects upon motivation when the task is co-operative, competitive or individualistic.

1. Observe task tensions and group maintenance
What Bales showed as long ago as the 1950s is that, whatever the task, tensions arise that threaten the stability of the group. Members may disagree about the way to proceed. There may be conflicting values. Or there may be external pressures such as imposed urgency.

Whatever the tension, group members must take time out from discussing the task to deal with the tension and maintain the group as a group. Contributions are made to maintain group harmony and its sense of purpose. Benne and Sheats (1948) went further and showed that there are three general types of goals – task achievement, group maintenance and the satisfaction of personal needs that are irrelevant to the task. The motives behind each are usually different. Table 13.1 shows the kind of contributions to discussion associated with task achievement and group maintenance. I am not suggesting that the lists are by any means complete. Far from it. (I deal with personal needs and the kind of discussion contributions typically associated with them in Chapter 15. See also Table 17.1.)

The distinction between task oriented contributions and group maintenance is of major importance. That is not to deny that some contributions are both (eg. consensus-taking and facilitating communication). They are two major functions of a group. We will see later that groups often have two leaders, one for each of these two functions.

2. Encourage group maintenance and tell the students why
There's a paradox. Contrary to what you might think, groups that spend longer on group maintenance achieve more. That is to say, discussions about group processes accelerate achievements on content. Why? Because groups that don't maintain themselves spend much longer disagreeing. Taking time out from discussing the topic to examine how you are discussing it, pays dividends. Managers in industry keep rediscovering this – get harmony on the shop floor and production increases.

So how can you encourage contributions to group maintenance? The simplest way is to describe its positive effects, and why. This is an example of a teaching technique grossly underused by teachers, namely describing teaching strategies and why they work. In other words, explaining to students how you wish to help them. Either because teachers themselves do not know enough about teaching techniques, or because they mistakenly think their professional techniques should be trade secrets, there is a reluctance to talk about education with the people they are trying to educate. Education should be a joint enterprise. Surely students are mature enough to take part in their own education by understanding what they are doing, why they are doing it, and how.

The second way is not only to make your own contributions to group maintenance, but to let discussions on group processes by other group members continue even when you can't see what they are achieving. (Sometimes teachers unconsciously feel threatened that such contributions manage the group and that that is their province alone.) Very often such discussions deal with blocks, hang ups and hidden agendas that are not evident to the teacher. They will dry up and run out of energy when the problem is cleared. These 'process discussions' demand maturity and complete calm from the teacher. From them, teachers can learn a great deal about their students that they could never learn another way.

Task oriented contributions

Initiating: Stating or defining the group task, stating goals, proposing action, making plans, suggesting ideas to achieve the task, giving ways to use the group's resources.
Giving information: Stating facts, providing relevant data.
Stating opinions: Saying whether procedures will work, expressing judgements, speculations.
Asking for information: Identifying information needed, asking for ideas and suggestions.
Asking for opinions: Seeking expressions of feelings about ideas, procedures and proposals.
Clarifying: Restating ideas in own terms, interpreting, questioning proposals.
Elaborating: Building on ideas of others, restating own ideas in more detail.
Consensus testing: Stating conclusion or decision and asking for group commitment, vote or decision.
Orienting: Moving to, or keeping to, a topic, either relevantly or irrelevantly.
Summarising: Restating discussion content, combining it into fewer points.
Evaluating: Judging the merit of ideas and proposals.

Contributions that maintain the group

Recognition and support: Address others by name, value good ideas, proposals and actions.
Acceptance: Friendliness, warmth, smiles, nods, showing presence is valued.
Harmonising: Helping members to understand disagreements and each other, reconciling, helping members to see others' viewpoints.
Compromising: Combining ideas into agreeable form, giving way, provisional consent to experimental try-out.
Norm testing: Trying out ideas and procedures to see whether acceptable to the group.
Facilitating communication: Helping participation, exploring feelings acceptably, explaining group processes, voicing what the group is feeling.
Tension release: Acceptable release of anger or frustration, typically by humour.

Table 13.1. Examples of task and group maintenance contributions

C. Factors affecting task difficulty

The difficulty of a task is normally defined in terms of the number of people who can do it. This raises a number of questions for teachers. 'How can I design a task to ensure that it is achievable?' 'Will a group need to behave differently for difficult tasks than for simple ones and if so how does that affect how I should organise the groups?' 'With mixed ability classes, some tasks will be too difficult for some students and too easy for others. What will be the effects of this?'

Unfortunately, research to give direct answers to these questions is unsystematic and patchy. Consequently it is difficult to make generalisations that will be directly helpful. My approach must be indirect by considering factors that influence task difficulty.

1. Assess the information to be processed and the motivation required

Perhaps one generalisation we can make is that, other things being equal, task difficulty will increase linearly as the amount of information to be processed is increased. There is evidence for this from the heyday of information theory in the 1950s. For example, Lanzetta and Roby (1956 and 1957) gave instrument reading tasks to triads and found that the number of errors increased linearly with the amount of information that had to be communicated.

So teachers need some skill in estimating the amount of information that tasks require and how easily it is available to the group. The information processing here includes what goes on in the students' minds and the processes of communication between them.

But, of course, other things are not equal. In particular, task difficulty affects motivation and its effects seem to be curvilinear. For example, if a task is very difficult students may give up. If it is very easy, they may not bother. But if it is somewhere in between, there may be sufficient challenge to give a sense of satisfaction when it is achieved. The same curvilinear relationships seem to apply to confidence, the wish to conform and other motivational, emotional or affective factors.

2. Ensure clarity of purpose and procedure

A task can be made easier if its goal and the path to achieve it are clear. This has been shown for individuals (Cohen, 1959), but I know of no direct confirmation with group tasks. Raven and Rietsema (1957) showed that groups with a very clear task were more likely to do it, showed less tension irrelevant to it, were more committed to the group and conformed more closely to group expectations than members of groups with unclear tasks.

In most working conditions the motivation of a group is directly related to the clarity with which its task, and the way to achieve it, are specified. Similarly, the number of errors and time taken to achieve a task are lessened when the task and the method to achieve it are clear. Clarifying a task, and saying how it has to be carried out, reduces the information that has to be processed. Clarification may consist of focusing on particular information that is relevant; but in academic work, discovery of the path is often part of the task because teachers want to teach students how to analyse problems, not just perform the mechanics of their solution.

3. What are the channels, patterns and ease of communication?

It is possible that tasks of contrasting difficulty require different patterns of communication. This may affect how groups need to be organised. Bass et al (1958) have shown that there are fewer bids for leadership in five-person groups when the task is easier. Presumably, when a task is easier, there is less information to manage and less necessity for someone to organise it.

Shaw (1954) showed that when communication in groups of three (triads) had to go through one individual, the group was quicker at simple problems than when communication was unrestricted. But with complex problems, unrestricted groups were quicker. This suggests that with simple tasks there was more redundant communication in unrestricted groups. (As an extreme example, if the central person could do the task on their own, no communication at all would be necessary.) But with difficult tasks the communication conveyed necessary information. (For example, if a difficult task required the full experience and knowledge resources of a group, that experience and knowledge would have to be communicated. That would take time and would take longer if it all had to be passed on by the central individual.)

This study could be reinterpreted in the light of a later one (Shaw and Briscoe, 1966) which distinguished between the co-ordination requirements of a task. They had two tasks of equal difficulty requiring different amounts of co-operation and gave them to groups of 3, 4 and 5 members. Contrary to their expectation, the groups were equally successful at doing the tasks, but groups requiring more co-operation took longer. The moral for teachers is 'don't have larger groups than the difficulty of the task requires, or you will waste time on group co-ordination rather than learning'. Once again, there is evidence favouring the use of smaller groups than many teachers use. In this case use threes rather than fives.

4. Difficulty, conformity and confidence

What is the relationship between task difficulty and confidence? One might think that students low in confidence and low in self-esteem will conform more to group opinion than those whose confidence is high. Similarly, the more difficult the task, the greater will be their conformity because they will be less certain of the correct answer. However the relationships between difficulty, conformity and confidence do not seem to be linear. In an experiment by Gergen and Bauer (1967) students with medium esteem showed the greatest conformity; and there was more conformity on tasks of medium difficulty than on tasks judged to be easier or more difficult. I find this experiment difficult to interpret, which is a pity because task difficulty, independence of mind and confidence are important factors when teaching.

D. Setting own tasks

With the development of student-centred teaching it is becoming increasingly common for groups to select their own tasks and even for students to design their own curricula. For example, student groups may choose their own project work.

1. What factors influence the choice?

If a group sets its own tasks, what are the factors that influence its decision? There are several ways of looking at this question.

i) *Combined goals of group members.* One is to regard the group's choice as a balanced synthesis of the goals of its individual members; but this theory does not explain how the synthesis takes place (Cartwright and Zander, 1968).

ii) *Motives of individual members.* Another view is to see the chosen task as the product of an interaction of the motives of group members. Again, this is not very clear, but no doubt sensitivity to the feelings of group members is an important skill when tasks are being decided. Teachers sometimes talk about their groups being, or not being, motivated. I don't think there is any such thing as the motivation of a group. Admittedly, individual members of a group have motives, it makes sense to talk about the 'achievement' of the group, and members may set down common aims, purposes or goals, but there is nothing in reality corresponding to a group motive.

iii) *Tasks as incentives, not goals.* A third conception regards the task as an incentive rather than a goal, but this does not explain how the tasks are decided and that is the crucial question for group facilitators.

iv) *Individual preferences negotiated for group acceptance.* A fourth approach is to see the tasks adopted by a group as the choices of individual members which are then accepted by others, perhaps with modifications. This seems to be the most satisfactory explanation and it allows us to think that changes in the aspiration levels of groups will be responsive to the same factors as those of individuals.

Zander (1980) reported several reasons why an individual might choose a task reflecting the wishes of other group members: his liking for other members, the extent to which member's wishes are overlapping, the importance of having the same goal, and whether the task is moderately challenging as distinct from difficult.

2. How does task difficulty affect choice?

If teachers are worried that groups will set their standard too low, we must ask what level of difficulty groups are likely to select.

If we take the fourth approach above, the answer is that the aspiration levels of groups roughly correspond to that of individuals. When a group has been successful it is more likely to choose a difficult task, but if it has previously failed it is more likely to select something easier. In an experiment by Matsui et al (1987) individuals and groups set their own goals. Feedback resulted in improved performance only for those individuals and groups who had previously performed below their aspiration level. If a group is told that its performance is better than the average for groups like theirs, they are less likely to strive to their maximum capacity. This results in what is sometimes called 'social loafing' – some individuals in the group not trying hard enough and relying on others to do the work. On the other hand, if a group is told that its performance is worse than the average, it will raise the level of difficulty of the next task they select, but it will not go on doing so if discouragement sets in. Like individuals, groups that are anxious to succeed choose neither very easy nor very difficult tasks. They choose tasks to ensure a respectable level of achievement. If, however, the group fears failure, rather than wanting some measure of achievement, it is more likely to choose either very easy tasks where success is certain, or very difficult tasks where failure is excusable.

3. How teachers can encourage selection of realistic tasks

Because an averagely challenging goal is more beneficial than a very difficult or very easy one, students and teachers should ensure that a group chooses a task of this kind. Zander (1982) recommends a number of practices to encourage the selection of realistic tasks. Teachers should:

i)   periodically report to members how well their group is doing,
ii) clearly define the group's purposes,
iii) make sure members can match the purposes of specific tasks to these general purposes of the group,
iv) encourage the desire for group success amongst members,
v)   play down the fear of failure,
vi) encourage members to compare the performance of their group with that of others,
vii) try to have outsiders place realistic demands upon the group and
viii) improve the group's procedures so that they are as efficient as possible and that members work to maintain that efficiency.

Zander gives three reasons why groups chose unrealistic goals:

i)   Members prefer a hard task because they get more satisfaction if they achieve it and less dissatisfaction if they fail.
ii) External pressures on a group are more often towards a difficult task than an easy one.
iii) Choosing an extremely hard goal avoids the embarrassment of failure.

4. Tasks that motivate students

What, then, is the best strategy for teachers who want to get the best out of their students? The answer must be to set and encourage aspirations to succeed rather than fear of failure. And when students succeed they should receive praise to encourage them to set their aspirations yet higher. Webb (1980a, 1980b) found that the amount of off-task behaviour was negatively, though insignificantly, related to achievement, while passive behaviour, defined as lack of any discernible involvement in the group task, was also negatively related. Thus active participation is important for achievement. Mere presence in a group is not enough. This may impose constraints upon group size.

Tasks promoting intellectual development probably have the following characteristics:

i)   Tasks are designed to draw upon the learners' existing knowledge, competence and experience.
ii) The learner recognises the task is relevant and transferable outside the immediate context.
iii) The tasks have some element of open-endedness and challenge, thereby offering opportunities for discovery, creativity and insight.
iv) The teachers offer formative guidance and opportunities for self-conscious reflection to apply what has been learned (FEU, 1987).

E. Steiner's theory of task achievement

By 'task' I don't necessarily mean anything big like a seminar topic. To answer a tutor's question in a seminar is also a task, though perhaps a small one.

The classification of tasks produced by Steiner (1972) are interesting because they have practical implications both in education and in groups in employment. He developed a theory in which he said that the achievement of a group, its productivity, depends upon the demands of the task, the group resources and group processes.

He classified tasks according to what is logically necessary in order to achieve them and then showed that some are much more difficult for a group to achieve than others. The difficulty varies with group size. Steiner's theory provides teachers with a perspective on why one group discussion went well and another struggled to make progress. It also prompts teachers to think in a new way about the questions they ask.

1. What resources and group processes do you assume?

Steiner's ideas are based upon knowing the probability of any individual being able to perform a task and upon the assumption that the performance of any group will not be able to exceed the total performance of all its members acting individually. The extent to which a group performance falls short of that total is a measure of faulty group processes. He said preparing a task is like planning to build a house. Architects not only need to have an image of the final product, they must check that the necessary materials and tools are available, and they must plan the sequence of activities to achieve the goal. In other words, the plan implies resources, and the processes that use them. In group work the resources include all the abilities, knowledge, skills, experience and attitudes possessed by group members. The task determines the resources required. The process variables include all the interactive factors that we are considering in Part III.

Steiner believed that the actual productivity of a group is normally less than its potential productivity because of inefficiency in a group's processes. He assumed:

Actual productivity = Potential productivity - losses from inefficient group processes

For example, if one member of a group stays silent, the group is not using its knowledge to the maximum. It is inefficient. For any tutor who struggles to persuade silent students to open their mouths, this assumption may seem plausible. It represents the teacher's task as a managerial one, namely to reduce the inefficiency of group processes. That is to 'facilitate' group processes and to maximise the use of the group's resources. Steiner assumed the maximum productivity of a group is limited to the sum of the resources of its individual members. Therefore, he argued, the potential productivity of a group is the sum of the productivity of all the group members acting individually.

However, Steiner saw that the potential of a group varies dramatically with the demands of its task.

2. Ask yourself, 'What kind of task am I setting?'

Steiner made important distinctions between tasks that are 'disjunctive', 'conjunctive', 'additive' and 'discretionary'. Disjunctive tasks are those where there is a choice, as for example, in a multiple-choice question. If only one member can do it, the whole group can do it. That member will tell the rest what the right answer is. 'Disjunction' implies 'or'. So even if only one of Smith *or* Brown *or* Jones *or* n can solve the equation, their whole group can give the right answer. Disjunctive tasks are good for sharing knowledge, but they are not much good for getting the rest of the group to think. The rest of the group don't have to work out the answer.

'Conjunctive' tasks on the other hand require every member of a group to perform the tasks as, for example, when every member has to agree to something. 'Conjunction' implies 'and'. A group with these tasks is much less likely to be successful because they require Smith *and* Brown *and* Jones *and* n to be able to do something. So conjunctive tasks are more demanding, but if achieved successfully, more learning takes place.

There are other tasks that are 'additive' in the sense that the more group members there are that can produce something, the more will be produced. In practice there are diminishing returns. To some extent, a group will produce more creative ideas, the more people there are in the group. But a group of eight will not produce double the number produced by a group of four. That's because some members will have the same ideas.

Finally, there are some tasks that allow group members to combine their resources in ways they may choose. These are called discretionary tasks.

3. Take syndicate method as an example

Let us consider the syndicate method: that is, a group of around six members engaged on a joint project. (See page 227 for a more detailed account of the method.) Assuming the teacher sets the task, the first sub-task of a group is to understand what they have to do – what the goal of the project is. Everyone needs to understand this; so the sub-task is conjunctive. It is difficult for a teacher to get everyone to understand. Conjunctive tasks require skilled teaching. In practice in this case, a group will survive if a task has been treated disjunctively, so long as one group member has understood what they have to do and can explain it (better than the teacher) to the rest of the group. In that case, the member is left with the conjunctive task when the teacher only achieved a disjunctive one.

In the syndicate method the group is required to carry out an investigation. In the Engineering Department of my university small groups of final-year students have to carry out a project such as building a car from scratch. Normally the investigation is 'divisible' into sub-tasks and it is not necessary that every group member carries out every sub-task. The sub-tasks are disjunctive. Usually the first sub-task is not to find out as much information as possible (maximising) but to exercise judgement as to what will be particularly relevant to the overall task. It is 'optimising'. Choosing who will do what is a discretionary sub-task. When the group reunites to pool the knowledge they have acquired, the sub-task is additive.

The essential feature of the syndicate method is that the group must not only understand the information that has been pooled, but all must agree upon some recommendations based upon it. (In the case of our engineering students, they must implement their recommendations too – another disjunctive sub-task.) The necessity of a common understanding and universal agreement on the recommendations makes that sub-task unitary and conjunctive. So is agreement on what their final report says. As mentioned in Chapter 22, the weakness of the syndicate method is that the group pursues the write-up in a disjunctive, not a conjunctive, way.

When you appreciate the contrasting basic arithmetic governing the relative difficulty of conjunctive and disjunctive tasks, you will realise why teachers need to concentrate much more effort helping students on conjunctive tasks. Let's look at that arithmetic now.

4. Monitor performance closely on conjunctive tasks

Conjunctive tasks are much more difficult than disjunctive ones. Where Steiner's work is fascinating is his attempt to quantify the proportion of groups that will complete a task successfully when working on disjunctive and conjunctive tasks. This explains why the success rate for conjunctive tasks is so low and suggests why or how the success rate can be improved.

% OF INDIVIDUALS WHO CAN	GROUP SIZE									
	2	3	4	5	6	7	8	10	12	20
10	1	0								
20	4	1	0							
30	9	3	1	0						
40	16	6	3	1	0	0				
50	25	13	6	3	2	1	0	0		
60	36	22	13	8	5	3	2	1	0	
70	49	34	24	17	12	8	6	3	1	0
80	64	51	41	33	26	21	17	11	7	1
90	81	73	66	59	53	48	43	35	28	12
100	100	100	100	100	100	100	100	100	100	100

Table 13.2. Percentage of groups that can do a conjunctive task according to Steiner's theory

Let us suppose that a teacher requires every member of a class to learn a particular technique; and that the technique requires knowledge, experience or other resources that only one person in ten would be likely to possess. The likelihood of any individual being successful is 0.1. If two people form a group, the chances that they will both have the required knowledge and experience is not one in ten, but one in one hundred. That is to say 0.01 or $1/10^2$. The chances of all members of a triad processing the required knowledge or experience is 1 in 1000; that is $1/10^3$. We can generalise this to say that the probability that every member of a group will be able to perform a task (that is, the probability that a group will be successful at a conjunctive task) is P^n where P is the proportion of the population that has the required knowledge, experience or other resources and 'n' is the size of the group. The results of this formula appear in Table 13.2.

If you tell a class something and then test them on what you have told them, an average mark of 60% would not be unusual. So perhaps we should not be surprised if the probability of students understanding the instructions given to a syndicate is 0.6. Supposing syndicate groups of 6 are then formed, you will see that in less than 5% of the groups will everyone understand what they have to do ($0.6^6 = 0.0467$). This explains why clarification of the task is nearly always necessary when any group first meets. It also shows that teachers must be very thorough when teaching conjunctive tasks. Consider safety procedures, for example.

5. Don't let disjunctive tasks lull you into a false sense of achievement

Let us now consider a disjunctive task. Group tutorials such as student seminars are usually of this kind. When a tutor asks a question, the larger the group, the more likely it is that it will contain at least one group member who has the necessary knowledge, experience or other resources to answer it. Consequently, as Table 13.3 shows, the probability of group success increases with group size. Table 13.3 shows the percentage of randomly formed groups of size 'n' with at least one person who can do the task. It is calculated from the formula $100(1 - Q^n)$ where Q is the proportion of persons in the population who *cannot* perform the task and 'n' is the number of people in the group. From this you will see that if 60% of a class understood the instructions and the teacher divides them into groups of 6, in 99.6% of all groups (that is $100[1 - 0.4^6]$) there would be someone who understood what they had to do.

% OF INDIVIDUALS WHO CAN	GROUP SIZE										
	2	3	4	5	6	7	8	10	12	20
10	19	27	34	42	47	52	57	65	72	88
20	36	48	59	67	74	79	83	89	93	99
30	51	66	76	83	88	92	94	97	99	100
40	64	78	87	92	95	97	98	99	100	
50	75	88	93	97	98	99	100	100		
60	84	94	97	99	100	100				
70	91	97	99	100						
80	96	97	100							
90	99	99								
100	100	100								

Table 13.3. Percentage of groups that can do a disjunctive task according to Steiner's theory

The trouble with disjunctive tasks is that they lead teachers into a false sense of achievement. Imagine a group tutorial. The teacher asks the occasional question and there is always someone who knows the answer. The discussion continues with each member displaying the particular bits of knowledge that they possess. The additive effect fools the teacher into thinking that most of the group possess the knowledge that was displayed, whilst in fact the knowledge was spread more thinly.

The first step to avoiding this false sense of achievement is to analyse the performance of individuals in a group separately. Don't let a general impression of the whole group wash over you. One way to do this is to have a notebook and write a few lines about individual students and your teaching effectiveness after each group tutorial. Such notes are also useful when it comes to writing employers' references after the students have left.

6. Give conjunctive tasks to small cross-over groups

All these ideas of Steiner's are theoretical. They are based upon simple logic and arithmetic. Steiner decided to test them out in practice.

Now we have already seen in Part I that there are many studies that have compared the performance of individuals acting on their own with the same individuals acting in a group. So there was a lot of data already published which Steiner could use. When Steiner made this comparison he was surprised to find that the difference between a group's actual productivity and its potential productivity was not very great. According to Steiner's expected interpretation this means that the groups were pretty efficient. In fact, they were so efficient that we really need to look for another explanation.

It seems likely that when individuals act alone they do not use their full resources as Steiner had supposed. For example, they may have information which they do not use or cannot recall. But when placed in a group they are stimulated to remember it. Other members act as a catalyst. So it seems that although groups may be inefficient in some respects, they can also reach parts of the mind that individuals cannot reach.

In that case the managerial question for teachers remains, 'How can I maximally facilitate the use of the group's abilities for the good of all?' Since large groups inhibit the contribution of some, the answer is to give small groups conjunctive tasks and to use the cross-over technique (see Chapter 21) to maximise interpersonal contacts.

This technique would greatly improve the efficiency of committees as well as learning groups, but I have yet to meet a chairperson with the courage to use it. In this way, although his computations were not fully confirmed, Steiner opens up a new way of looking at group tasks, their difficulty, group size and group productivity.

F. Conclusion

Throughout this chapter we have seen that task achievement is particularly affected by two factors: the amount of information that has to be processed, and motivation. We have paid less attention to a third factor: the nature of the skills to be achieved. That was the purpose of Part II. Available evidence suggests it is these three factors that teachers should consider most closely when designing and evaluating task achievement.

Chapter 14
Norms, conformity and deviants

A. The nature of norms

B. Conformity – the power of group norms

C. Why do people conform?

D. Variables affecting conformity to norms

E. The influence of nonconformists

F. Conclusion – strategies for teachers

A. The nature of norms

1. What are norms?
The norms of a group are rules or generalisations about the behaviour of members of a group. Norms can be seen as implicit rules. They are not necessarily explicit. Indeed, most of the time people are unaware of the norms to which they are conforming. Nonetheless, in order to know how to behave in a group, students quickly try to find out what is expected of them. Thus, norms describe expected behaviour. Once known, they reduce uncertainty and ambiguity about what students should do. Because norms are about what should be done, they have a moral or evaluative component and they may be prescriptive. They are mostly formed early in the life of a group as a result of perceived interaction.

Notice that norms are necessarily present in a group. If there was no regularity or consistency in the way group members behaved, if members behaved quite randomly, they would not be together in any way. But being together in some way, is the essence of a group. It follows that it is part of the teacher's job to establish norms to create and maintain a group.

Norms can be seen as implicit rules. They are not necessarily explicit. Indeed, most of the time people are unaware of the norms to which they are conforming. Do your students conform to norms you wish they wouldn't? Or not conform when you wish they would?

2. Their characteristics
Norms may vary according to five characteristics:

   i) *Importance*. As I've just implied, a group is not a 'group' at all, if it doesn't have norms. They control what a group does and is. New norms are formed only with respect to things that have some relevance for the group. But there could be many imported from other group experiences, that are irrelevant, and possibly even a hindrance.

ii) *Application.* Norms may apply to every member of a group, or only to certain members. For example, some norms do not apply to the teacher, whilst others apply to the leadership role of the teacher, but not to the students. Norms may also vary in their application on different occasions. For example, on the last meeting before Christmas a tutor may serve alcoholic drinks in a way that he would not earlier in the course.

iii) *Acceptance.* Norms vary in how far they are accepted by the group.

iv) *Deviation.* Norms vary in the extent to which group members can deviate from them. When a group member does deviate, it is very common for some sanction to be brought to bear, even if it is only disapproval.

v) Norms can also vary in their *origins*. That is, in the way they are acquired or accepted.

3. *Their origins*

Johnson and Johnson (1987) say there are four ways that norms can be started in a group. Look at the four headings below. Think of a norm in your discussions and ask yourself, 'What are its origins?'

i) *Imported.* Norms will be imported from other groups. People bring previous experiences to the group, and they have learned a multitude of cultural norms about how one should behave in the presence of other people. Most of these norms (for example, that you sit on chairs rather than stand on them or throw them) are so much taken for granted that it seems banal to draw attention to them. Nonetheless, students do bring expectations from school and from other teachers in your college or university. If you want something different, you must be clear what it is and tell them (enunciate it) when you first meet.

ii) *Enunciated.* A member can propose them directly, and either tell or ask other members to accept them. For example, it is very likely that a teacher will say at the beginning of a course what he expects from his students during it. He might say, 'Attendance at seminars is optional except on those weeks when it's your turn to start the discussion'. Others include the time and duration of the meeting.

In Part IV I describe a range of discussion methods. In effect, what I am doing is describing the norms of each method. Teachers will enunciate them as they give instructions. Particularly when you use a method you or your students have not used before, think through the instructions you need to give very clearly. Group work, by definition, involves some loss of control. If you have to re-take control because students don't know precisely what to do, you can easily lose the respect of your class.

iii) *Learned.* Norms can also be learned by modelling other group members. This is particularly likely at the beginning of a course. When students first arrive, they will feel uncertain of how they should behave; they will observe other people and copy them. They will feel there is safety in numbers, whilst being different is embarrassing.

iv) *Negotiated.* Group norms can be established by discussion. Johnson and Johnson believe this is the most effective way because members will be aware that the norms exist. Because they are known and understood, they will be immediately reinforced; and there will be a sense of group ownership for norms which members have helped to establish.

4. Their advantages and disadvantages

Group norms have one disadvantage that is so serious that we must consider it separately in a moment. That is their power to make students conform intellectually – indoctrination, albeit unwitting indoctrination. This is alarming. It is a threat to academic honesty and independence of mind. Conformity threatens the creativity and originality that is fundamental to what a university is for.

That said, there are hidden values associated with the word 'conformity'. For some people conformity is like discipline, which they see as a good thing.

From an organisational point of view the development of group norms has both advantages and disadvantages. The development of group norms has the advantage that teachers do not constantly have to tell students what is expected of them. On the other hand, the expectations may become so fixed that innovation and variety of teaching methods become difficult. Indeed, one of the aims of this book is to loosen the stranglehold that so many norms have upon small group teaching. For example, the emphasis upon tutorless groups tries to remove the remarkably common expectation that all learning groups should have tutors.

The establishment of group norms has advantages for both weaker and stronger members of a group. For stronger members they establish regularity and control into a group's interpersonal relationships without the exertion of power. On the other hand, they protect weaker members against the inconsistent and abusive use of power by influential members.

B. Conformity – the power of group norms

A major feature of group norms which many teachers underestimate is their tremendous power to make students conform. Particularly in arts and social studies, tutors want their students to develop independence of mind, yet the pressures of conformity frequently overflow from the expected behaviour of group members to the views and opinions they express. Tutors want conformity in the former, but independence in the latter.

Conformity to group norms cannot be discussed without mentioning the work of Solomon Asch (1956). He repeatedly asked subjects to say which of three lines was nearest in length to a standard line. There was an obvious correct answer in each case, but all but one of the group were confederates of the experimenter, primed to give unanimous incorrect answers on certain trial numbers. Thus an individual was faced with a conflict between his own judgement and the unanimous group pressure of people he believed to be his fellow-students. 32% of subjects conformed to majority opinion, at least on some trials. More importantly, some subjects convinced themselves that what they said was the right answer. The question teachers have to ask is 'If group pressure can produce conformity to contradict what is obvious, how far can students genuinely think for themselves on matters that are not obvious, on issues necessarily new to them, and where they are working near to the limits of their ability?' Yet critical thinking is a major objective of higher and continuing education.

Guerin (1986) considered whether the mere presence of another person creates pressure to conform to norms. He concluded that it does
i)   if there is some uncertainty in the behaviour of the person present, and
ii) if there is some evidence that the other person himself shows some conformity to norms or public standards.

C. Why do people conform?

If norms have this extraordinary power to make people conform in a group, they will certainly have that power in discussion, at least with some students, if not all. But why do people conform? Hollander and Willis (1967) have accused psychologists of describing what happens without explaining why.

Several explanations have been offered. They are not mutually exclusive.

1. Cognitive dissonance

We have already seen in Festinger's theory of cognitive dissonance (Chapter 11) that people feel uncomfortable when their opinions differ from others in their group and this imposes a pressure towards uniformity. The pressure is greater in ambiguous situations where there is no objective means of verifying what is said. Where opinions are subjective, reality is socially constructed, not least by the context, assumptions, language and culture of the group.

2. Common group goals

Conformity is greater when there is a common group goal, particularly if its achievement is advanced by each member making a contribution. That is to say, an additive group task (see Chapter 13). If unanimity is required (a conjunctive group task), the pressure is all the greater.

3. The threat of isolation and ridicule

Students may easily feel foolish and open to ridicule if they express deviant opinions even when there is no such feeling amongst other group members. The teacher's support and respect for all opinions is vital if students are to have confidence. Rosenbaum (1986) has shown experimentally, if you didn't know already, that we like people who agree with us more than those whose opinions conflict with ours. Those who disagree potentially threaten our self-esteem, because we might have to accept that we were wrong and we might have to change ourselves in some way.

Deutsch and Gerard (1955) showed that when students could respond to questions anonymously there was less conformity, though still some. The same is true when students write down the answer to a question, even when they know they will shortly have to express their opinion in a small tutorless group. When the group is large, of even a whole class with a teacher present, conformity is more prevalent. Confidence can only be built slowly. Hence my maxim, *Start with simple tasks in small groups for short periods of time, and then gradually increase their respective size, complexity and duration.*

4. *The power of social identity*

People classify themselves as belonging to a particular group and adopt its norms – or at least what they perceive to be its norms. Turner (1987) called this 'self-stereotyping'. Disputes, atrocities and wars the world over show religious, ethnic and national identities to be alarmingly powerful.

Perceptions of social identity also develop with inexplicable speed. For example, if you divide your class into groups one week, and then the next week, ask the class whether they want to form new groups or stay in the old ones, the vast majority will not want to make any new friends. This can be educationally limiting, so use the cross-over or 'square root' technique early in a course so as to build up multiple relationships. (See page 214.) Hence my maxim *Start with simple tasks in small groups for short periods of time, and then gradually increase their respective complexity, size and duration.*

5. *Group pressure*

The previous four factors are all self induced, but there are situations in which the majority bring pressure to bear on those who disagree (deviates). Discussions amongst jurors, politicians and in committees can be of this kind. Using students, Schachter (1951) has shown that deviates in discussion are spoken to more often than conformists, but not because they are popular. On the contrary, they are more disliked.

D. Variables affecting conformity to norms

These five answers to the question 'Why do people conform?' must each be modified by several factors.

1. *Individual differences*

Firstly, individuals differ in their degree of conformity. The more people conform, the less tolerance, participation, responsibility, leadership and intelligence they tend to display.

Conversely, intelligent people are less likely to conform. Amongst children there is a peak of conformity around the ages of 11 to 13 but, as far as I know, age differences have not been investigated amongst adults. People who tend to blame themselves, and people with authoritarian personalities, tend to conform more than those who are self-assured and non-authoritarian. Women are also more inclined to conform than men.

2. *Group size*

Up to a certain size of group, an individual will increasingly conform to the behaviour of a unanimous group, but after that point, increases in size have no effect; in fact, conformity may even decrease a little. Above what size of group does the pressure to conform not increase? For many years following the work of Asch (1951), group pressure upon an individual was thought not to increase above the unanimity of three others in a group of four. More recent studies have shown increases in conformity above this size.

Nonetheless, the need to form groups of only two or three to encourage the expression of independent thought should not pass unnoticed. Most tutors convene groups much larger than this.

The conforming effects of group size can be subtle. For example, Hogg (1985) showed that both men and women, but particularly women, were more likely to conform to the speech patterns of the other sex in groups of three or more. This effect does not apply to discussion in pairs (dyads).

3. Degree of unanimity

Conformity is much greater when other members of the group are unanimous. It only takes one other member of the group to dissent, or even to be non-committal, for the pressure of conformity to be dramatically reduced. (Asch, 1956; Shaw, Rothchild and Strictland, 1957). Consider also group interaction in a jury. The effect of a 'supporter' is greater if the deviant feels the supporter has a similar social identity. It is weaker if the supporter is from a different ethnic group.

Notice, therefore, the need to support and integrate students from minority cultures and ethnic groups even when these factors seem totally irrelevant.

4. Certainty – uncertainty paradox

In the early experiments on conformity (Asch, 1951; Sherif and Sherif, 1956), judgements showed greater conformity when the thing being judged was more ambiguous. Uncertainty seemed to lead to conformity of judgement. (Considered rationally, you might think the opposite – that uncertainty would allow greater diversity of opinion.) The experiments used relatively simple stimuli. In academic discussions, the judgements required from students are complex, uncertain and ambiguous. Asch and the Sherifs showed we should expect conformity to be all the greater. That unanimity is likely to bolster greater feelings of certainty.

This leads to a paradox. The less certainty is justified, the more certain people may become. Nowhere is this more evident than in discussions of religious or social issues.

How then, are teachers to encourage more open-mindedness and reservation of judgement. One task is to *list on a sheet of paper the reasons you would give for the opposite opinion to the one you hold.*

5. Perceived group competence

The influence of this variable needs to be added to the fact that conformity increases with the perceived competence of the majority, compared with the individual's confidence in his own ability. Of course, this factor also leads to conformity with the views of the teacher whose competence is normally more highly esteemed than the competence of students. Hence, it is very easy for the views of a teacher to become the norm for his tutorial groups. I think this is something to guard against in most academic subjects. Yet it is understandable that most teachers believe it is right to persuade their students of the truth of their opinions.

6. Peer influence

However, conformity to one's peers is normally stronger than conformity to authority, even when authority is coercive. Consequently, although this principle is one that many governments fail to learn, in the long run, conformity to the will of those in authority is dependent upon the persuasion and compliance of the majority. Similarly, sanctions by other students in a group are more powerful than sanctions from the teacher because they can lead to social rejection by those people the individual values and with whom he needs to identify himself. The studies of changes in attitudes to various foods by Lewin et al (see Chapter 3) can also be seen in this context.

But peer pressure is not just a matter of sanctions. Khoury (1985) has shown that the humour of undergraduates converges in a group, and that the degree of this growth in conformity is related to the individual's daily social relations.

Within the normal range of conformity, the effects of these influences upon conformity are additive rather than interactive.

There may be a conflict between individual or personal goals and the goals of the group. So whenever an individual enters a group he/she has to make compromises. Some personal goals can be best achieved, or only achieved, in the group, perhaps because of the expertise available, because groups are more efficient, or possibly because the personal motives and goals are to do with being socially accepted. In this way a group exerts pressures towards conformity. Compromise is towards conformity or group norms.

E. The influence of nonconformists

The power of conformity is so great that the study of nonconformity in small groups has been neglected. Yet it must be remembered that in Asch's experiment nearly two-thirds of the subjects did not conform. In other controlled observations, too, there have been a small but recognisable minority who did not conform.

1. Minorities make students think; so encourage them
In some, non-conformists actually persuaded the majority round to their point of view. Nearly 300 groups of children across seven European countries were tasked to choose and build a model aeroplane (Schachter et al, 1954). It was assumed that motor driven models were the most attractive choice, but planted in each group was a deviant stooge who argued that they should build a glider. In 68% of the groups the unanimity of the group was maintained against an unpopular deviant as Asch, Festinger and others would have predicted. However, in 23% the unanimity was broken; and in 9% the deviants actually persuaded the group to choose the glider. Clearly, in 32% of the groups, the deviant had some influence and it seems reasonable to think that some thought and attitude development took place in those groups, and possibly also in those where uniformity was maintained.

In the context of learning by discussion, this is significant and encouraging. The picture of one-way pressures from an all-powerful majority to a passive minority is too simple. Minorities exert influence too. Since the 1970s there have been other studies that confirm this. Wolf (1979) simulated a jury in a compensation case. The majority view that the plaintiff should be awarded $20–30,000 was reduced by $3,500 after one juror argued consistently for an award of only $3,000.

It also seems that deviants can have some covert influence. In a series of studies,

Moscovici primed stooge deviants to say that a blue colour was green on selected trials. About 8% of the majority were persuaded to agree with them. What was particularly interesting was that when group pressure was removed and students were able to respond anonymously, a significant number who voted blue in public, voted green in private.

The difference between public and private judgements is important and in later studies Moscovici and Personnaz (1986) were able to show that the effect of the nonconformists was quite unconscious. This encourages the belief that small group teaching has even more effect than sometimes appears. Seeds of doubt are sown that provoke thought.

2. How do nonconformists persuade?

This raises the question 'What is it about the arguments of nonconformists that carries conviction and outweighs all the factors I gave as to why people conform' (section C above).

i) *Consistency.* If the minority is more than one person they will be more convincing if they say the same thing. Their agreement seems to suggest that their opinions are not the idiosyncratic and ill-considered caprice of an individual. To be consistent gives a superficial appearance of rationality because the converse is true: namely, when divisions occur their message is less clear and at least one viewpoint is vulnerable to criticism.

ii) *Persistence.* If a nonconformist makes his point once and only briefly, it can be ignored. If repeated and explained, it is more likely to be seen as a serious viewpoint that must be considered. Although, of course, over-persistence can cause an anti-reaction.

iii) *Confidence.* Other group members are less likely to consider a minority view if its advocates do not seem very sure of it themselves. Once again, the teacher's role in encouraging serious consideration of unconventional opinions is important.

iv) *Tangible commitment.* Where nonconformists are seen as having made personal sacrifices for their point of view, they are heard with greater respect and more serious consideration.

v) *Principled.* Unpopular opinions are more likely to be considered if they are seen to be based upon recognised principles. Conversely, they are more likely to be dismissed if perceived to be based upon self interest. If the nonconformist does not state his principles, the teacher or the group should try to elicit them so that the discussion moves towards its fundamentals.

vi) *Open-mindedness.* This may appear to conflict with consistency and persistence, but it is possible to appear reasonable, considering objections with fair-mindedness, whilst at the same time maintaining one's position.

3. Are conformity and persuasion the same?

When the question is put like that, it is hard to think that the processes in forming an opinion are the same when conforming to a group's majority opinion, as when persuaded by the considerations raised by a minority. Conforming seems like an emotional process even if mostly self-induced. Being persuaded by considerations seems like the exercise of reason rather than emotion – but is it?

Latane and Wolf (1981) believe that the processes are the same. They say social influence in discussion is simply additive. The more people you have advocating a point of view, the more persuasive they will be with negative accelerating power. That's a bit like the law of diminishing returns. If one person advocates an opinion he will have a big effect. If two people advocate it, they will have a bigger effect but not double the effect. And so on. As more people support a viewpoint their impact is added, but in ever decreasing amounts.

Latane and Wolf reviewed a large number of studies and showed that influence conformed to this pattern, but it doesn't seem to me that their conclusion follows. The fact that results *correlate* with that sort of curve does not tell us anything about the *cause*. Nemeth and Wachtler (1983) gave discussion groups a multiple choice task and concluded that deviants stimulate group members to think more creatively and consequently their groups obtained more correct answers. They argued that where the influence of the majority was pervasive, there was more unthinking compliance. The thought processes were different.

F. Conclusion – strategies for teachers

Discussion groups need norms; they don't need conformity.

1. Prepare

When establishing groups teachers have an obligation to set out clearly what is expected. In other words, the norms of the method. That may seem obvious, but it is often neglected because teachers do not think through the procedures when preparing.

A partial exception to this in, for example, the free group discussion method (see Chapter 23) is when the group's norms are negotiated, but that itself is a norm decided by the teacher.

2. Observe and interpret

If teachers are to be sensitive to group processes, they need to observe the processes that create conformity, their power, and the variables that affect them. They will not do so if they don't know what they are.

3. Create an environment for nonconformity

Nonconformists display originality and independence of mind. These are important values in a university education. Pressures towards conformity create silent students. Teachers therefore need to create environments in which nonconformity is encouraged. This includes:

i) respect for deviants as well as other students,

ii) acknowledging the deviant's position, not ignoring it,

iii) ensuring the group recognises where it has merits,

iv) seeking elaboration of it, possibly from other students, and

v) starting with tasks in small groups so that there is no large majority to conform to and then, when there has been an opportunity to express a deviant opinion, to find the right words for it and to build some confidence, increase the group size.

This last point is, of course, part of the maxim that has been a key message running through most of this book: *Start with simple tasks in small groups for short periods of time, and then gradually increase their respective complexity, size and duration.*

Chapter 15
Which characteristics of group members make a difference?

A. Which personality factors are most influential?

B. Do men and women behave differently in groups?

C. How do age factors make a difference?

D. The abilities of group members

E. Should teachers put similar or contrasting students together?

F. Conclusion

Some discussions go well; others don't. Sometimes the only explanation seems to lie with the personal characteristics of group members. But what characteristics?

It is obvious that one could consider an infinite number of variables that might have some influence. Unfortunately, the study of compositional effects upon group performance is still in its infancy. Many variables remain unconsidered and it is always difficult to disentangle how far the presence of certain attributes influences a group directly and how far their influence is dependent upon interaction with other characteristics of group members.

A. Which personality factors are most influential?

It is almost a truism to say that the elements of personality are important factors in the way group members interact. That's because personality is usually defined in terms of predispositions to respond to others in particular ways. The pertinent question is 'What particular ways are influential in students' discussions?' The number is obviously prodigious and their interactions astronomic. So rather than trying to get your mind round all the possibilities, when reading this section, think of personalities you've known and ask yourself 'What were their personal needs?'

It is also important to recognise that the researchers in this field proceed from very different assumptions. The largest studies have been carried out by Schutz (1958) and Bales (1970). Schutz's view is that each person's behaviour and feelings towards others in a group result from *needs* which have developed from experiences during and since childhood. To say this, is a very different emphasis from thinking that behaviour in discussion is purely influenced by a desire to perform the task. Schutz had a psychoanalytic background, whilst Bales used questionnaires and detailed observations of students' discussions, monitoring who said what to whom and relating it to background information about them.

These two researchers each derived at three factors which, curiously, have some similarities, although they gave them different names. They are not all factors I should have expected. Schutz believed that three factors – control, inclusion and affection – are necessary and sufficient to explain group behaviour. Bales called them wanting to *dominate* a group, *liking* most group members and feeling themselves *allied* with others.

1. Dominance

I use the term 'dominance' here more widely than is customary, to include behaviour that is prominent, authoritarian, assertive and ascendant. For Schutz, control is a *dimension* relating to who takes decisions. At one extreme it is a desire to dominate and have power over others; at the other, a need to be compliant and submissive. Although men appear more dominating than women, the difference is not as great as commonly supposed. (See Fodor and Smith, 1982.)

For Bales, the wish to dominate may display itself in various ways depending on the individual's other characteristics. It is essentially the *interaction* of an individual's characteristics that makes their personality. There are many ways of dominating others. A dominant member is likely to be someone who receives a lot of attention from the group, values material and social success, may assume responsibility for task leadership, may speak like an authority or might think of himself as entertaining. They could dominate by rugged selfishness or by offering support and warmth.

A person who is low on dominance may well trust the goodness of others, value subjective experience or self-sacrifice for what is right, denigrate themselves and their opinions and may be reluctant to contribute in discussion.

More generally, people who wish to assert themselves in a group, influence its decisions, conform to group norms, are popular, are frequently dissatisfied with the leader, attempt to become its leader themselves and often do so (Borg, 1960). Paradoxically, they can be both rigid and creative.

Authoritarian personalities use their power when they are in a position to do so. When they are not, they expect others to do so. For example, you might expect that dogmatic and strong-minded individuals will be less able than others to change their beliefs, particularly once they have openly committed themselves in discussion. But Ehrlich and Lee (1969) remind us that this depends on the authority for the new beliefs, how novel or distant they are from the individual's current beliefs, and how central they are to their self-image. As mentioned earlier, when I taught police officers from a tough macho authoritarian culture and told them to be meek, compassionate, non-authoritarian, and considerate of others' feelings, they dutifully complied!

How can you manage the over dominant group member? Well, first, remember that it is most likely to be you! Research repeatedly shows that tutors talk 60 to 75% of the time in group tutorials, but perceive themselves as talking about 20% of the time.

However, if one student tends to do all the talking (apart from you), one tip is to sit next to him (or her). If the group is sitting in a circle, it is natural to look across the circle rather than twist your neck and speak in a voice that all can hear to someone three feet away. With eye contact inviting others, rather than your neighbour, others may contribute instead.

2. Social acceptance

Social acceptance has two aspects. They both promote the social cohesion of a discussion group. What Schutz calls 'inclusion' refers to the need to associate with others and be accepted by them. It may show itself in various ways, for example, the need to attract the attention and interest of others, the desire for prominence and recognition, or the wish to be friendly, amiable and deferent, and even the urge to punish friends when they are friendly to others. It emphasises the desire to be liked *by* others.

Bales emphasises the individual's feelings *for* others. This is sometimes called social sensitivity. Social sensitivity is the extent to which someone perceives and responds to the personal needs, emotions, and personal thoughts of other individuals. So it is necessarily pertinent in group work. In general, socially sensitive people enhance the effectiveness of a group and, consequently, social sensitivity is a major factor and a major asset in a teacher and any other group member. Shaw (1981) remarks, 'Empathy, social insight, social judgement, and similar characteristics are positively correlated with leadership attempts and success, acceptance in the group, amount of participation, and group effectiveness.'

Social sensitivity is strongly related to group morale. It is here that group trust is so important in promoting social interaction, co-operation and group cohesion. In this way socially sensitive people enhance the effectiveness of a teaching group.

Interestingly, the supportive atmosphere created by a socially sensitive teacher is more likely than the presence of an unconventional group member, to result in the independence of mind and free thinking that universities should encourage. Unconventional members will inhibit freedom of interaction if they are unpredictable. As a result, free thinking will be reduced and, paradoxically, the overall effect of an unconventional group member can be greater conformity in the group as a whole.

This is related to the fact that anxiety inhibits the security, social interaction and cohesiveness of a group, and inhibits work to achieve its task. Conversely, self-adjustment contributes to task achievement. Hence, it is important for the teacher to work at reducing anxiety amongst student groups. Yet, the manner, and particularly the questioning style, of many teachers creates anxiety and is counter-productive.

For some teachers, the implication that their role is to be socially supportive, empathetic, to reduce student anxiety and generally to foster group harmony, is contrary to their conception of their role. They see their role as teaching a body of knowledge, as opposed to fostering the welfare and adjustment of their students. A tutor has both these roles and it is wrong to see them as opposites. His skill in group management is a necessary, but not a sufficient, condition for the promotion of learning. It is in the achievement of this necessary condition that many tutors are weak, but if they solely concentrate on personal welfare to the neglect of their subject, students will not learn very much.

To say this is not wholly to deny a conflict. When tutors first meet a group they must spend a great deal of time creating the group as a group, rather than a set of individuals, and they will do this within the context of the subject matter. But having done so over a period of several meetings, their emphasis will gradually shift towards being more subject-centred, and they will place less of their energies into being student-centred. It is a matter of a shift in emphasis, not a change of direction.

3. Individual alliances as a defence against anxiety

What Schutz called "affection" refers to the personal and emotional feelings between two people. It could vary from love to hate, or from love to indifference. Insofar as it involves feelings for others, it has some aspects of Bales's 'liking for others', but only directed to one individual. So it is not necessarily socially cohesive. Indeed, it could be divisive.

The personality trait Bales identified to do with individual relationships is more cognitive than affective. A student high on this factor values mutual support in the task, the use of logic and the credibility of authority. He or she may be shy, introspective and serious. Obviously a student low on this factor would display the opposite.

Though these personality characteristics may seem to contrast in some respects, what they have in common is a defence against anxiety. In view of the importance of anxiety in groups described in Chapter 12, it will hardly be surprising that this aspect of personality has been one of those most studied. There are many different types of anxiety – depression, achievement anxiety, test anxiety, neuroticism, and emotional instability. For our purposes they have a similar effect upon small group discussion.

You can imagine that if someone is anxious, they will not want to add to their anxiety by challenging authority or the teacher in particular. So conservatism and compliance with authority and traditional values often result.

Anxious individuals usually feel inadequate either in their relations with others or in their ability to contribute to the task. Consider their feelings when giving a presentation to a seminar or when submitting their contribution for criticism to a syndicate. They commonly have lower aspirations for the group, are slower in their responses, do not contribute when they might, conform more readily to group opinion, and are better satisfied with the discussion than non-anxious individuals (Shaw, 1981).

From a university teacher's perspective, students with anxiety can pose a problem. Clearly they need support, but that does not mean dependence on the teacher. My maxim is an attempt to gradually build the confidence these students need.

4. Conclusion on personality

The interaction of personalities in discussion groups is so complex, I find it difficult to say anything in a few pages that could be helpful. Bales's suggestion is like mine at the beginning of Part III. Sit and think after a discussion class and ask yourself 'Why did that go well, or badly?' Choose a critical incident and ask yourself 'Whose behaviour was pivotal in what happened?' It might have been your own. 'Why did he/she behave like that?' If there are unanswered questions of this kind, ask yourself 'What are the personal needs of that student?' in terms of a combination of these three factors. Remember that these factors are scales that go to opposite extremes. I have not described all the opposites.

B. Do men and women behave differently in groups?

If women are more socially sensitive than men, and we have seen there is some evidence for this, we should expect the sex composition of groups to make a difference. It has been observed, for example, that women in small groups tend to be less assertive and less competitive than men. We might conclude that, since co-operation and mutual support normally strongly facilitate group learning, where possible it is best to include women in learning groups.

Wood (1987) carried out a review of laboratory research on the sex composition of groups and their productivity. She concluded that two broad factors could account for the major difference: task factors or situational factors favouring one sex more than the other; and interaction factors, such as the tendency of men to offer more opinions and suggestions than women and the tendency of women to be sociable, friendly, and agree with others. Overall, all-male groups were found to perform better than all-female ones, but Wood believed that this was because the tasks and situations favoured men's interests and abilities compared with women's. On the whole, men's interaction style slightly favoured task-oriented behaviour, while women's interaction style facilitated social cohesion.

It is not certain how far these differences are socially induced. Boys are not more task-oriented at primary school level (Nelson-le-Gall and de Cooke, 1987) even though there is some evidence that girls like being helped in their work by boys more than the other way round.

Women conform more, at least overtly, but this could be the result of the kind of task used in the study of group dynamics, or the sex of the teacher, or cultural expectations. It is possible that women are just as independently minded in private. If the latter is true, the teacher will have to use techniques to draw out covert independence and create a more permissive cultural climate within a teaching group. Women use eye contact more than men, but it is difficult for a teacher to use this for selective encouragement without risk of misinterpretation!

Conformity in same-sex and mixed-sex groups has been studied by several researchers, but since women tend to be more conformist, the results are difficult to interpret. Overall, men and women tend to conform more in mixed-sex groups than when all members of a group are of the same sex.

Similarly, Hoffman and Maier (1961) found that mixed-sex groups performed better in case discussions, problem-solving groups and role-playing than same-sex groups. This may be because a mix of sexes provides a mix of task-centred and process-oriented students, and it is known that both task and process need attention if a group is to be fully successful. Another explanation is that same-sex pairs are more individualistic than mixed-sex pairs so that the full advantages of interaction and co-operation are not taken in same-sex groups (Wyer and Malinowski, 1972). Kent and McGrath (1969) noticed that same-sex groups were more original, optimistic, and action-oriented than mixed-sex groups, but there is no obvious explanation for this.

There is some evidence that in mixed-sex pairs, women have lower expectations than men, perform worse, reward themselves less, and are more likely than men to attribute their poor performance to a lack of ability (Lanoue and Curtis, 1985). When the women worked alone or with another woman, neither their expectations nor their actual performance were inferior to men's. Cota and Dion (1986) found that the differences between the performances of men and women in the same group are greater than when they work with others of the same sex.

It is sometimes said that women prefer to let men dominate, but it may be that men wish to do so. For example, Deutsch et al (1971) showed that when pairs were given a bargaining task, men were more competitive when paired with a woman than when paired with a man.

Whether men strive for dominance or women let them do so, it is very common in mixed groups to assign the leadership role to men, but Kushell and Newton (1986) found that the sex of a group leader was not significantly related to the satisfaction of group members of either sex, except that women subordinates were more dissatisfied than men in autocratically-led groups.

Mabry (1985) thought the gender composition of groups would interact with the nature of their task, but he found no difference between the sexes, except that men tended to give more suggestions, particularly when the task was highly structured. When the task was unstructured, men were significantly less dominant. There are well-known differences between the sexes with regard to the tasks they like doing. For example, only recently Daly et al (1987) found that women had much less favourable attitudes towards mathematics and science than men. Nor is this a purely British phenomenon. In Sweden, Ekehammar (1985) reported that women students showed less self-confidence about studying and work than men, and they had particularly negative attitudes towards technology. Of course, maths, science and technology are fairly structured subjects and it may be that they do not give the same opportunities for women's more social dispositions to be expressed.

C. How do age factors make a difference?

With the expansion of continuing education, there will be a growing number of older students in discussion groups. What difference will they make? Furst and Steele (1986) asked 78 students over retiring age why they enrolled on college courses and factor analysed their questionnaire responses. Amongst the most common answers were desires for fulfilment, stimulation, practical achievement and self-understanding. Smithers and Griffin (1986) used questionnaire and interview methods with 2159 applicants between the ages of 19 and 71 years and found that mature students did as well as others: 90% graduated successfully, and 86% regarded their time at university as worthwhile. Their average age of leaving school was 16.4 years, and while 84% had taken some form of further education, only 37% had the normal entry requirements.

– *Which characteristics of group members make a difference?* –

There has been a growing body of research recently on the educational needs of mature students, and there has long been a prodigious literature comparing adults of different ages psychologically. However, very little of either of these bodies of literature is concerned directly with adults learning in small discussion groups. When that topic is discussed, it is usually by inference from the general literature.

1. Changing abilities
Knox (1986) gives a useful review. He emphasises the changing learning styles of adults. As they get older, they develop abilities benefiting from accumulated experience, such as increased vocabulary and fluency in dealing with ideas. On the other hand, learning tasks such as rote memory, discovering spatial and mathematical relations and inductive inference gradually decline in facility. (Claxton and Ralston, 1978; Cross, 1981; Holtzclaw, 1985).

2. Changes in thinking style
Knox says, 'Adults tend to evolve from unquestioning conformity to recognition of multiple viewpoints, to deliberate commitment, to application of universal principles and appreciation of relationships, both human and cognitive.' There may be a shift from an analytical, impersonal approach to problem-solving, towards a more global, social orientation. Another shift is from cognitive simplicity and concreteness towards cognitive complexity and abstraction. Thirdly, there is a shift from impulsiveness towards reflectiveness and thinking of several alternatives before taking decisions.

It should be noticed that each of these shifts in thinking style are consistent with the development of thinking advocated in Part II, and with using the developmental sequence of teaching methods I recommend in Part IV. Buzz groups are suitable for fairly quick answers to relatively simple and concrete problems, while the quiet meeting, free group discussion and personal tutorials are better for reflection, for considering complex and abstract problems, and for a more global and socially-oriented perspective (Steitz, 1985). My maxim uses natural developmental processes.

3. Consider the social needs of older students
Gerson (1985) compared the feelings of 124 mature women students who were also housewives with one or more children under the age of 19, with 44 women who were housewives and had no other role. The students got greater satisfaction from their dual roles than the housewives, but also reported significantly more strain. In both groups, women who felt the roles to be stressful were less involved in leisure and volunteer activities. Interestingly, widows with a feminist ideology appeared to live more satisfying lives. Gerson concludes that strain is not a universal outcome of being both a student and a housewife: it depends a lot upon institutional arrangements.

The same conclusion was reached by Holliday (1985) when discussing the life-span development of women returning to college and their reasons for doing so. She argues that institutions need to be keenly aware of the special needs of returning women, and to offer a variety of support services to meet these specific needs.

Conformity has been said to increase up to the age of 12 and decrease thereafter, but so far as adult students are concerned, cultural influences are probably stronger than age differences.

Social participation increases with age and the leaders tend to be older. This is partly because the rules of social interaction are exceedingly complex and take many years to learn. Consequently, the older person is often more sensitive to the needs of others and is therefore more popular and more highly esteemed.

D. The abilities of group members

How does the presence of an 'expert' or an 'incompetent bungler' influence a discussion group compared with the experimenter's 'control confederate'? Russ and Gold (1975) found that both the task expert and the bungler reduced the amount of group communication and centralised communication around one or two key individuals. In addition, both the expert and the bungler received defensive communications: the expert receiving personal attacks and the bungler receiving criticism of what he said.

Mann (1959) reviewed the relationship between personality variables and performance in small groups. He selected 350 variables from over 500 in the literature and concluded that the best predictors of an individual's performance in groups are intelligence, adjustment and extraversion, in that order; all three are positively related to popularity, leadership and their total activity rate.

Triandis et al (1963) found that the creativity of pairs of students could be predicted by adding measures of their abilities, not by measures of their interaction. This may suggest that dyads are too small for creative tasks, or that members of dyads do not interact very well. These interpretations seem reasonable because the creativity of dominant individuals correlated more highly with the score for dyads than the scores for less dominant individuals.

We have seen the importance of self-esteem. There is reason to think that it is strongly influenced by the individual's perception of the abilities of other group members. Felson and Reed (1986) identified three interacting types of influence upon self-esteem: their appraisal of their ability in relation to a specific task, their group, and the population as a whole.

There is also a tendency for leaders to be more intelligent and physically superior. Intelligent people tend to be more active in groups, they are usually more popular, more influential and less conformist than those with lower intelligence test scores.

E. Should teachers put similar or contrasting students together?

A question which is often asked is whether one should put similar or different students together in the same group. Ten years ago I boldly answered this question by suggesting that in general like kinds should be put together with reference to the skills that were relevant to achieve the task, but that there were exceptions. Now, if anything, I should be inclined to take the opposite point of view.

1. Able students 'teach' the others

Laughlin et al (1969) are among few experimenters to study the effects of homogeneous and heterogeneous ability groupings on performance. They classified 528 students into high, medium and low intelligence groups and divided them into triads with all the possible combinations of ability. Not surprisingly, homogeneous high ability groups did better on problem-solving tasks than homogeneous middle ability groups, who in turn did better than triads where all three members were of low ability. What is interesting is that groups of mixed ability with one high, one middle and one low ability student performed better than all other groups except those of uniformly high ability.

When students in pairs are working with someone above their level of ability, they improve significantly more than with partners below their ability level (Goldman, 1965). The extent to which partners differ in ability doesn't seem to matter. Students working with partners at the same level of ability don't improve any more than when working with someone below their ability. These studies suggest that the member of higher ability teaches the partner.

2. Ability matters, but compatible motivation matters more

In truth, the question of homogenous versus heterogeneous groups is probably not the most pertinent question to ask. Firstly, there are considerable limitations in attempting to isolate a single characteristic as important when the essence of small groups is the interaction between individuals with many differing characteristics.

Secondly, so far as personality characteristics are concerned, it is compatibility rather than homogeneity or heterogeneity that is important because, as we have seen, cohesion and group harmony are major influences upon group productivity and learning.

With regard to academic achievement the question of streaming has long been a contentious one, but it is only recently that small group methods have been used sufficiently to build a picture for our present purposes. In general, it must be concluded at school level that academic achievement in heterogeneous groups is greater, but the motivational and personality side effects are probably more important, though they remain ambiguous. There is reason to think that children are more creative in homogeneous than in heterogeneous small groups, but that the differences are small compared with their performance, whether in large groups or alone.

From an educational point of view, the work of Harvey et al (1961), comparing the performance of homogeneous and heterogeneous groups with reference to their patterns of thinking is important, but it has not stimulated as much research as it deserves. They classified students at four levels according to their powers of abstract thought and synthesis. They compared students whose thinking was fairly concrete, simple and at a low level of abstraction, with students whose thinking was more abstract and complex. It was to be expected that the concrete low-level thinkers would find uncertainty and ambiguity threatening, and would be more likely to look for authoritative answers and to accept normative standards than the latter group, which had several ways of conceiving of problems. Results confirmed that the most important variable was the cognitive ability of the students, not the homogeneity or heterogeneity of the groups. But this difference was only significant when the task was an unstructured and abstract one. In general, homogeneous groups performed better than mixed-ability groups, particularly when the problem was concrete or abstract, according to their preferred style. However, the number of group members able to deal with abstractness and complexity was an important factor in group performance, particularly where the problems were unstructured. No differences were observed when the task was complex and structured. With similar tasks Stager (1967) has observed that groups with more able students exhibited greater role flexibility, and were more evaluative, but they did not generate more ideas. It seems, from this work, that the compatibility of individuals' preferred thinking styles to the tasks set may be an important and under-researched factor in group performance.

It is to be expected that the problems requiring varied experience will be solved better by heterogeneous groups. Using a personality profile Hoffmann found that heterogeneous groups produced more high quality solutions to problems. But the experience has to be specific and relevant, otherwise the benefits are not great (Triandis, 1965).

In higher education, students are highly selected so that their differences in academic ability are small. Consequently, it is easy to emphasise differences too much. Because students are not usually selected for their group skills, they display a wide range in these abilities. So differences in the skills of group management, particularly those in the construction and presentation of tasks, and the creation of a supportive group climate, are far more influential in group work than the differences in ability between students selected through the fairly fine-grained net of formal entry qualifications and institutional preference.

This discussion neglects the students' point of view. What is their perception of their homogeneity and what happens when teachers let them form their own groups? It seems that identification with one's group takes place very quickly. Allen and Wilder (1979) observed that individuals believed that members of other groups had beliefs more dissimilar to theirs than members of their own group, even when allocation to the groups was manifestly arbitrary. Bryant (1975) has shown that people are more likely to sign a petition when the petitioner is dressed in a similar way to themselves. This seems to suggest that some identification is made quickly on the basis of appearances. It may stretch the evidence beyond what is plausible, but if teachers leave students to form their own groups, mutual attractiveness may produce groups with homogeneity on factors of this kind.

F. Conclusion

Whether students differ in personality, age or abilities, it is the effect of their motivation that matters most in the management of discussion methods. The task for teachers is to recognise the characteristics of their students and then consider how best they can be managed in the light of research. These judgements need to be made as part of planning the next lesson and that means making time to sit down and think about it.

Chapter 16
Factors related to group size

A. Large groups: more resources, less learning
B. The effect of greater size upon group processes
C. Conclusion – group effectiveness

Teachers who divide a class into small groups will need to consider how large those groups should be. To do this they will need to know what factors in small group behaviour are related to group size, and whether there are any particular group sizes that have special characteristics worth considering.

Several factors affecting group performance and interaction are related to group size.

A. Large groups: more resources, less learning

As the size of a group increases, so do its human resources. But can they be used? Whether that matters depends upon the task – the objective.

1. For a single product, large groups are better
It is fairly obvious that as the size of a group increases the total knowledge, skills and abilities available to it increase. The group has more potential. This is an advantage in groups requiring a creative product. There will be a greater variety of ideas. Novel associations of these ideas become more likely. Therefore creativity is fostered. Similarly, in decision-making, many heads may be better than few.

Even so, there is a law of diminishing returns when additional members can contribute few new ideas. A corollary of this is that adding a new member to a small group will have more impact than adding an additional member to a large group. (It is said that the British Cabinet ceases to exchange information effectively when it is larger than 23.)

2. For learning by all, small groups are better
But what's the point in discussion? Large size is no advantage if what you want is not a single product from the group, but learning by every member. Learning in groups is fostered by participation and opportunities for participation are decreased in larger groups. If the average member is having less opportunity to express and test his ideas in the arena of discussion, he will be learning less.

That is because, although larger groups have more resources at their disposal, they cannot use them efficiently. It is clear that if, in larger groups, some members are making fewer contributions than they would in a smaller group, it is unlikely that their full knowledge and experience is being made available to the group.

The best way over this problem is to make sure everyone has an opportunity to test their ideas is by starting with small groups for a short period of time and then gradually increasing the group size and the time available. When there's a larger group more time is needed for everyone to have their say. Smaller groups make better use of two scarce resources – time and the members' abilities. Hence my maxim, *Start with simple tasks in small groups for short periods of time, and then gradually increase their respective complexity, size and duration.*

3. Larger groups are more difficult to manage

It is also true that as groups increase in size, the range of knowledge, skills and abilities increases. So does the variety of attitudes. This may make them more difficult to handle. It is more difficult to bring every student to the same level. A diversity of attitudes may make consensus more difficult. Again, the answer is to start with smaller groups. Because their discussions are more intensive, they manage themselves and each member's needs are more likely to be attended to.

4. With larger groups contributions per member decrease

With increases in group size the average number of contributions per member decreases. This is obvious unless several members talk at the same time. What is less obvious are the discoveries of Bales et al (1951), shown in the graphs in Figure 16.1. They gave a decision-making task to a large number of groups of different sizes. It will be seen that when there are 8, 7, 6 and even, to some extent, 5 people in a group, one person tended to dominate. (See the personality factor described in the last chapter.)

Another way of putting this is to say that with increasing group size not only does the average contribution per member decrease, but the variations in participation become greater. In several groups of 7 and 8 some members did not contribute at all before the decision was taken but, of course, taken overall, the average length of time taken by the least vocal member is more than zero. Bales's attempt to fit a J-shaped curve to all these graphs seems fallacious to me. If we exclude the most talkative member from groups of 5, 6, 7 and 8, the curves are little different from a straight line.

However, the significant point is that the contributions in groups of 3 or 4 are relatively even. They perhaps approximate to a straight line, not a J-shaped curve. The domination by one member is not visible. Now, there are many situations when the teacher wants to make sure that every student has done some work and has taken part. *For this reason, groups of 3 and 4, or smaller, are of major importance in teaching. In short, dyads and buzz groups should be the staple teaching method, not lectures or larger groups. They are the methods most likely to make students active and therefore the methods most likely to make students learn. They are fundamental to the maxim.*

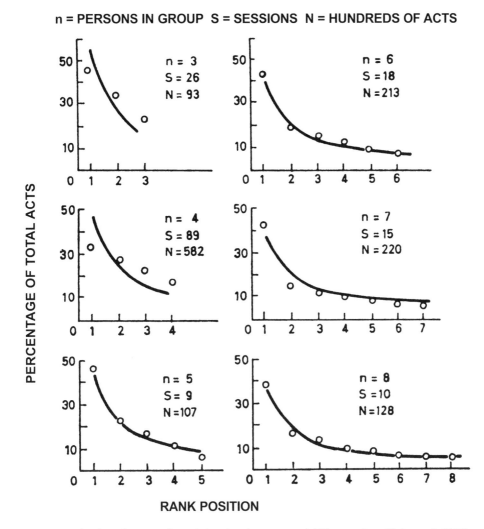

n = PERSONS IN GROUP S = SESSIONS N = HUNDREDS OF ACTS

Figure 16.1. The distribution of participation in groups of different sizes (Bales et al, 1951)

B. The effect of greater size upon group processes

1. The need for more structure

The lower participation per group member means that larger groups require more organisation and structure. The task may need to be divided into sub-tasks – an agenda. Leaders are more necessary and are more likely to emerge. In a smaller group each member will fulfil several functions; but in a larger one they are more likely to take on specialist roles.

An increase in group size also means that more of the groups' energy must be devoted towards its own group processes and proportionately less time should be taken with its tasks. That is why, with larger groups, you are more likely to have two leaders, one who is task-oriented and one who is more concerned with personal relationships and their effect upon group processes. The person who can combine both leadership roles is rare, but that is often what is demanded of tutors in group tutorials. Universities suppose that they can be task-master as well as counsellor. At times that is an impossible combination and a wise tutor will let others take on one or other role. There is no permanent loss of control because the tutor always has reserve powers and the students know it.

The larger the group, the number of relationships increases exponentially. Therefore more time needs to be spent maintaining group cohesion and harmony. Zimet and Schneider (1969) observed student discussion groups varying from 2 to 5 members. As group size decreased, average verbal interaction increased. Students' behaviour in dyads was uniquely different from larger groups and showed more mutual support and less aggression.

2. Less favourable evaluations

Larger groups are less favourably evaluated by group members. When groups are large, individuals cannot get the rewards of participation because they are less able to contribute, less notice is taken of their thoughts and feelings. Consequently, most individuals get less recognition, have less sense of achievement and less self-esteem. In a study by Patterson and Schaeffer (1977), students' ratings of the pleasantness of the group discussion, feeling at ease, and feeling a part of the group all decreased significantly with increased group size. Favourable ratings increased with the number of comments per person and restricted individual participation in larger groups resulted in decreased satisfaction. Hackman and Vidmar (1970) found the same thing: dyads are unique and satisfaction in groups with 2 to 7 members decreased in an almost linear fashion with increasing group size. The type of task made no difference.

These factors interact with a greater anxiety about contributing at all. In larger groups, people feel more nervous and more threatened.

3. The likely effect upon relationships

In larger groups, individuals are more likely to find someone they like and someone they dislike. The chances are greater that they will find someone who is friendly, who agrees with them and whose company is rewarding. Because there are also more likely to be individuals they find less rewarding, subgroups are more likely to form in larger groups than in smaller ones. To some extent divisions into subgroups also results from the fact that it is not possible to interact evenly with all members in a larger group. There are bound to be some members you talk to more than others. Perhaps individuals will be more likely to talk to their neighbours than to someone across the room.

4. Conflicts are more likely

Conflicts are more likely with increasing group size. Again, this follows from the previous section. If there are subgroups whose members like each other more than those in another subgroup, it is natural that conflicts may appear between the subgroups. Even without the formation of subgroups, a larger group is more likely to have individuals with incompatible opinions or attitudes. This makes the cohesion, harmony and organisation of large groups more difficult.

5. The effect upon conformity

The relationship between conformity and group size is not clear. In the early studies by Asch (1951) a naive subject distorted his judgements to conform with majority opinion. The size of the majority varied from 0 in a two-person group, to 15 in a 17 person group. Conformity to majority opinion increased in groups of 2, 3, and 4 respectively, but not much thereafter. Rosenberg (1961) broadly confirms this result, but Gerard, Wilhelny and Conolley (1968) found a linear relationship between group size and conformity. Mullen (1983) even reports increasing conformity to standards of behaviour as the size of groups was decreased.

In spite of Mullen's result, conformity is a bit different from consensus. As Hare (1952) found, there is likely to be less consensus amongst larger discussion groups, while, if there is any change at all, conformity normally increases with size.

C. Conclusion – group effectiveness

How far increasing the size of a group affects its performance of a task depends upon the task. Thus we have seen two conflicting sets of factors will operate with increasing sizes of group. First, a larger group will have more resources in the form of participants' knowledge and abilities. This should enable larger groups to perform better than smaller ones. On the other hand, larger groups do not bring out the best in their members because fewer can contribute, conflicts are more likely, they are less popular and social loafing is more frequent. The effectiveness of a group is the balance between the factors we have considered.

Where the task requires some combination of the knowledge and skills of participants, a larger group is more likely to be successful. These tasks are said to be 'additive'.

Where a task requires only this member, or that member, or the other member to have the relevant knowledge, abilities or experience, the tasks are said to be 'disjunctive'. Again, as group size increases, the chances also increase that one member will have the required resources. So, as with additive tasks, group performance on disjunctive tasks should improve with group size.

In industry and commerce most decision-making tasks are of one of these two kinds. Committees meet to pool their experience and to consult the opinions of experts. But in education the tasks are often neither additive nor disjunctive. They are conjunctive. That is to say they require every member of a group to achieve the same level of performance such as learning something. If every member of a group has to perform to a certain standard before the group can proceed, it will proceed at the speed of the slowest. It is evident that with conjunctive tasks the larger the group, the slower it will proceed. Indeed, the probability that it fails to complete the task at all will be greater.

This fact is of enormous significance for teaching. There are many circumstances in which teachers want an even contribution from their students. They may want to elicit ideas from all their students, they may want everyone to give an opinion, they may want every student to use the language of the subject and they may want the involvement of all their class. Groups larger than 4 are less likely to obtain the opinions, experience and commitment of all students.

Bales's work was with postgraduate students of management. There was not a tutor present in the group. Several studies (eg. Powell, 1974) have shown that tutors tend to talk between 50% and 75% of the time, not 40%. Thus the dominance of one individual is increased when a leadership role is assigned, when one individual is perceived to be more knowledgeable, older or physically superior, or when, in some other way, a leader appears evident.

Chapter 17
Group structure and leadership

A. Group structure and roles
B. Leadership

A. Group structure and roles

The structure of a group is the pattern of relationships amongst group members. It is based upon members having different roles and functions. These may be imposed or they may develop more naturally from the abilities and customary behaviour of group members. STOP. Consider a discussion group you know. Who takes what roles and why?

1. Imposed roles
It may seem obvious that a teacher has a special role and is specially appointed to perform it. It follows that the teacher is part of the group structure. Yet it is remarkably common for teachers to think that they teach a group and are not themselves part of it. Because they talk about 'teaching a group of students' they mentally detach themselves from its group membership.

Structure is important in differentiating discussion methods described in Part IV of this book. In buzz groups there are no leaders. In brainstorming and syndicates members take on specialist roles. In group tutorials the teacher is the leader and may exert some power. In seminars the presenters have a special role and status because the group acknowledges and values what they present sufficiently to discuss it. In T-groups and counselling the teachers try not to exert power, but they have authority in the sense that they influence the group climate. Similar, though more subtle, differences apply to other group members in these group methods. Differences in behaviour lead to different patterns of interaction.

2. In teaching contexts some, structures are unnatural
Yet it seems to me that some of these roles are quite artificial. They are imposed. In undergraduate seminars in which a different student reads an essay each week, the presenters are pushed to act the role of an expert when they are not an expert and when, furthermore, there is a greater expert, the teacher, present. Most undergraduates cannot carry the aura of authority that the required behaviour presupposes.

In most groups outside the teaching context people with different roles are expected to do and achieve different things, but when different roles are imposed within learning groups, members are expected to achieve roughly the same thing. When the roles are then chopped and changed week after week, it is hardly surprising that relationships within the group cannot evolve in accordance with the natural dispositions of it members. The teaching method is consequently difficult to manage, not least because most university teachers don't know enough about group dynamics to understand what they have been doing.

I am not saying that it is necessarily bad for students to be encouraged to take a role to which they are unaccustomed. If they don't do that sometimes they will not develop new skills. One argument for constantly varying the teaching method is to break up minor group structures so that students do not over practise particular patterns of thought to the exclusion of others. This is a challenge to many teachers who do not vary their teaching methods precisely because they, too, have over practised one particular teaching role.

But teachers need to be perceptive about what they are doing. They need to assess the qualities of their group members and work out the best method to achieve the course objectives. Like decisions in many other walks of life, it is necessary to consider the resources available and then, using that information, decide the best method.

If the teacher asks what factors they must consider, the answer includes the nine factors described in Part III (motives, norms, group history, etc.).

3. Voluntary roles satisfy a personal need, but with what potential value?

In less artificial groups in which individual characteristics are allowed more free play, individuals will be able to develop their own roles. In this way a structure will develop. For example, in a tutorless group one student may be more knowledgeable and become the task leader while another, being more socially sensitive, may emerge as the socio-emotional leader.

Whatever role a student takes, he takes it to satisfy a personal need. (See, for example, Bales's personality characteristics described in Chapter 15.) When reviewing

Name/Role	Behaviour	Need	Potential Value
Dictator	Dominates. Doesn't listen. Fast loud talk.	To be seen as leader.	Initiates. Takes a viewpoint.
Fighter	Argues. Criticises.	Excitement. Challenge.	Provokes group response.
Playboy or Wisecracker	Jokes. Mocks serious contributions.	Cover own anxiety.	Relieves tension.
Creep	Supports those with power.	To be accepted.	Talks for leader. Stops leader over talking.
Nit Picker	Contests everything. Agrees with nothing.	To be seen as clever and thoughtful.	Devil's advocate.
Observer	Silent. Contributions short.	Avoid showing inadequacy.	Group cohesion to involve him/her.
Sulk	Withdraws after ideas are challenged or ignored.	To be appreciated.	Challenges group to be more sensitive.

Table 17.1. Some individuals' needs, roles, behaviour and potential value

how a lesson went, it is worth asking oneself what the needs are that led to the kinds of behaviour displayed. Table 17.1 gives some popular, though perhaps not so well researched, examples.

Either by choice or imputation one person may become the group joker, another may specialise in asking questions, a third in challenging assumptions and so on. Compared with other members of a group, those with influence like being a member of a group and are themselves liked by members of it. They are the object of deference and their approval is sought more than other members', and when given power they are more likely to use it than the other members. In each case they do so to satisfy a personal need that may, or may not, be constructive for the group as a whole.

B. Leadership

1. Task- and socio-emotional leaders

Much of the early research on leadership assumed that there are certain qualities of leadership, and given these qualities, a person will emerge as a leader in no matter what situation they are placed. In the evolution of classroom groups there are often two kinds of leaders: those concerned with the task and those who are influential in social and emotional relationships. There is some evidence that where the task is either very easy or very difficult, the task-leader is more effective, but with tasks of intermediate difficulty the socio-emotional leader is more effective in terms of task achievement. Most teachers devise tasks that are of intermediate difficulty, so that their skill in management of relationships is often more important than their knowledge of their subject.

Evidence of this kind is also important in another respect. It is part of the growing evidence that different qualities of leadership are required in different situations. (The old assumption that there are certain people, and even certain classes of society, who are natural leaders is increasingly contradicted.)

2. Aspects of leadership

Following a literature review, Carter (1953) identified five different aspects of leadership:

i) The leader is often at the *centre of interaction*. He is often the focus or centre of attention, the person to whom most contributions are directed. However, this is not necessarily so. At the other extreme a person who is hostile to other group members may well be the focus of attention, but could hardly be called a leader.

ii) The person who most strongly *influences* a group towards achieving its task. Most people would agree that this is a characteristic of task leadership, but not socio-emotional leadership. Carter rejected it because many groups do not have clear tasks.

iii) The person implicitly or explicitly *chosen* by other group members. Though this is a salient aspect of leadership, it doesn't tell us anything about the qualities of leadership, or what leadership consists of. The qualities students look for change as the group matures. At first they are likely to choose a task leader. Later they prefer a socio-emotional leader. Trust in a socio-emotional leader takes time. So, be warned, don't have student elections too soon. If you are appointing a group leader, a task leader is OK before relationships have developed, but is often a disaster later.

iv) The person who most *changes the level* of group performance. This includes leaders who lead their groups astray, though insofar as group performance is the product of all the group members, it may be difficult to disentangle who has the greatest influence.

v) The person who engages in leadership *behaviour*. As a definition, this is obviously circular, but it is a pragmatic, operational definition for researchers who want to define leadership in their own terms.

There are two other aspects of leadership that Carter did not mention:

vi) A person who holds a particular position, for example, a teacher or a discussion leader may be *appointed* to hold that position and

vii) Psychologically, a leader may be seen as a person who *supports* other group members.

There have been three broad classes of leadership theories: Trait theories, Style theories and Situational or Contingency theories.

3. Trait Theories of Leadership

Be honest. As a teacher, what are your qualities of leadership? At one time, leaders were regarded as people who had particular characteristics. For example, Stogdill (1974) noticed that leaders were:

i) Often superior in *abilities* such as intelligence, insight, scholarship, ability to communicate, adaptability and incisiveness.

ii) More *sociable*. For example, they were more dependable, responsible, active, co-operative and popular.

iii) More *motivated*. For example, they showed initiative, persistence and high task-orientation.

These characteristics seem to differentiate good teachers from poor teachers, leaders from non-leaders, effective from ineffective leaders and leaders at the bottom of the hierarchy from those at the top.

Warren Bennis has argued that there are five qualities of a great leader. They describe the inspirational teacher as being an individual with:

i) *Passion*, love and an intensity of focus directed at the job in hand.

ii) The capacity to generate and maintain *trust*. This involves, confidence, constancy, care for others, candidness and genuineness.

iii) A sense of *perspective* including balanced judgement, discernment and anticipation.

iv) *Vision* with sufficient resonance that it infects others.

v) The *confident* expectation of success.

Although, when taken together, these characteristics have some value, trait theories are open to several criticisms. To possess all these characteristics would be impossible, while individual characteristics have little diagnostic or predictive significance. The best predictor of leadership is previous success in a leadership capacity (Stogdill, 1974). The theory of traits ignores how these characteristics interact with particular situations. Many of the traits are so imprecise as to be practically useless, and it always seems possible to think of good leaders who do not possess these characteristics.

Having said that, there are probably four factors that help to make someone a good discussion leader: a balanced and overall knowledge of the subject under discussion, above-average intelligence particularly verbal ability, some initiative, and self-assurance. In addition, emergent leaders display better listening skills (Johnson and Bechler, 1998).

4. Style Theories of Leadership

The classic studies of leadership style were those of Lewin, Lippitt and White (1939). They observed groups of 10-year-old boys experiencing *autocratic,* laissez faire *and democratic* adult leadership in different orders in different groups. Four adult leaders were trained to adopt each of the three styles. Hostility was 30 times as great in the autocratic than in the democratic groups, and aggression was 8 times as great. 19 of the 20 boys preferred the democratic approach to the autocratic, and 7 out of 10 preferred the *laissez faire* style to the autocratic. There was no difference in the productivity of the groups under the different styles, though the quality of work under the democratic leadership was judged to be better.

Though this work was with children, not adults, it has formed the basis of a lot of research at the adult level, both in educational and other employment contexts, with broadly similar results. In his review, Stogdill (1974) concluded:

i) Supportive, person-orientated or democratic styles of leadership are not consistently related to productivity.

ii) These leadership styles consistently result in group cohesiveness and harmony only when leaders provide opportunities in decision-making and show concern for members' welfare.

iii) With democratic leadership, satisfaction is highest in small person-oriented groups, while autocratic leadership is more favoured in large task-oriented groups.

iv) Democratic and person-oriented leadership styles result in more satisfaction than autocratic and task-oriented styles; though there is greater satisfaction with task-orientation if the task is well structured.

Like trait theories, stylistic theories take little account of the context in which leadership is being displayed. In particular, Stogdill controlled for the characteristics of those being led. So this variable was eliminated and not considered. Yet, surely, it is important. Because leadership is defined in terms of the influence of one person upon others, the influence of others upon the leader has been under-researched. A particularly important factor is that some subordinates prefer tasks that are highly structured such that authoritarian leadership is appropriate, whilst in other contexts consensus-taking is much more important.

These are situational variables and it is interesting that they have become more recognised in psychology at the same time as contextual factors have become more recognised in educational research.

Vroom has said there are five styles of leadership. He had industrial management in mind, but they can be applied to tutorials. As a teacher, which are you?

i) The leader solves the problem himself, using the information available at the time
ii) The leader obtains the necessary information from other group members and then makes a judgement himself.
iii) The leader shares a problem with group members *individually*, collects their solutions and comments and then gives the answer himself. The Nominal Group Technique is a bit like that. (See page 197.)
iv) The leader shares the problem with group members in a group and then decides the best answer himself.
v) The leader discusses the problem with group members in the group and takes consensus.

Vroom also says that the leader's task can be answered by 7 questions forming a decision tree:

● Is one decision likely to be better than another? If not, do (i).
● Does the leader know enough to take the decision on his own? If not, avoid (i).
● Is the problem clear? If not, try (iv) or (v).
● Do group members have to agree to the decision? If not, (i) and (ii) are possible.
● Would they agree to the leader's decision? If not, (v) is preferable.
● Do group members have the same objectives as the leader? If not, (v) is risky.
● Are group members likely to disagree with each other? If so, (iv) is preferable.

5. Situational Theories of Leadership

Situational theories are sometimes called contingency theories because what happens in a group is contingent upon the situation. Three situational theories deserve attention.

The Distributed-Actions Theory of Leadership has two basic ideas:

i) Any member of a group may become leader by helping the group accomplish its task whilst maintaining effective relationships.
ii) Any leadership activity may be carried out by any member.

Leadership involves a set of skills which can be learned by anyone, and that is why the activities may be distributed among the group members. The theory emphasises that in different situations the same action may or may not be leadership. Leadership is defined as the performance of acts that help the group complete its task and maintain effective working relationships amongst its members. Thus task orientation and group maintenance are essential ingredients.

The same two ingredients are prominent in Fiedler's Situational Theory. Although Fiedler defines a leader's effectiveness in terms of a group's performance in accomplishing its tasks, he divides leaders into those who are task-oriented and those who are maintenance-oriented. One is not more effective than the other because the effectiveness of task and maintenance orientations depends upon the situation. Fiedler (1967) believed that a leader's style of interacting with his group is affected by the extent to which he can exert power and influence over them. This was influenced by three factors:

i)   Leader-member relations, in particular, emotional factors such as trust.
ii) The task structure, that is to say, how far the task is clearly defined by the leader and constrained by external demands.
iii) Position power, that is, the amount of power vested in the leader's position.

Hersey and Blanchard's Theory of Situational Leadership (1977) also assumes the distinction between task-oriented and relationship-oriented behaviour. Any leader may be strong or weak on either of these two dimensions. Blake and Mouton (1964) have described situations where the leader is low in both as 'Impoverished Management'. The group will be ineffective and mature relationships will be difficult to establish. Where a leader is high on both, task and personal needs go together and Blake and Mouton call that 'Team Management'. They say that a leader who has a low task-orientation but a considerable concern for people is like a club manager. On the other hand, someone who is not concerned about people but is strongly concerned about the task is a task manager. Hersey and Blanchard call these four types 'delegating', 'selling', 'participating' and 'telling' respectively. Hersey and Blanchard's theory is situational because they believe the leader should adapt his style to complement that of group members. For example, if group members are very task-oriented but have poor mutual relations, the leader should concentrate on the relationships and not worry too much about the task.

Throughout this discussion I have used the term 'leader' because I have assumed that this person might be either the teacher or a student, depending on which of the teaching methods described in Part IV is adopted. For example, in syndicates, horseshoe groups and case discussions where there is no teacher continuously present and the group size may be six or more, a student leader is likely to emerge. In free group discussion and sensitivity groups (T-groups) where leadership is distributed, some students will exercise more leadership than others.

Chapter 18
The history and previous experience of the group

A. What norms do students assume?

B. Patterns of development in tutorless groups

C. Patterns of development in subject-centred groups

D. Patterns of development in student-centred groups

E. Conclusion

How might a teacher expect student groups to change and develop? Research suggests that the answer depends on the norms they bring to the group and the kind of group itself – its size, membership and task. For this purpose we will consider:

A. The expectations and norms students are likely to bring to a lesson and then consider three kinds of group.

B. Small tutorless problem-based groups such as buzz groups, horseshoe groups and syndicates; (Chapters 21 and 22).

C. Teacher-centred, and subject-centred, groups such as group tutorials, seminars and plenary classes which are led by a teacher and where the tasks are cognitive (see the first part of Chapter 23).

D. Student-centred groups in which the tutor is non-directive and where the learning is affective and interpersonal, such as free group discussions, counselling sessions and T-groups (see the last part of Chapter 23).

Now what you may notice about this sequence is that (A) it assumes limited skills and then moves from (B) small tightly structured cognitive tasks in tutorless groups, through (C) tutored groups with larger less structured cognitive tasks, to (D) unstructured affective tasks in groups where the tutor does not lead in a directive way. In short, there is a move from cognitive to affective tasks, from structured to unstructured procedures, from a directive to a non-directive style of teaching, and from dependency to mature independence demanded of the students. Yet, as we move from (A) to (D), there is an overlap on all these criteria. The skills demanded from the teachers and the students at each stage can be built upon those at the previous stage. They are progressive and developmental. That's part of the rationale for the maxim.

A. What norms do students assume?

We can't know the answer to this question before we meet them. They come from many backgrounds. But we can make some reasonable assumptions. If they have plenty of experience of learning through discussion, little adjustment will be needed anyway. From the teachers' point of view there's no great problem. So let's assume the opposite.

Even if students come from the most formal backgrounds where discussion methods are never used, they can hardly have avoided working on their own, either in class or at home. They will have some experience of 'independent study'. (They will also have experienced teaching in which the teacher controls a whole class and teaches from the front. This may be called 'class teaching' of a 'plenary group'. If a 'plenary discussion' is used the method is sometimes called 'class discussion'.)

Because they will have experienced independent study, teachers will not break convention or have to establish a new norm if they set a task to be done independently. Independent study can then provide information to share in dyads or a small group. In this way the beginnings of discussion techniques can be built upon students' previous practice combined with their natural desire to talk, which we considered in Chapter 12. I therefore contend that the background of independent work plus motivation, makes my maxim *'Start with simple tasks in small groups for short periods of time, and then gradually increase their respective complexity, size and duration'* feasible even for students with no previous experience of group work.

B. Patterns of development in tutorless groups

The classic work on the development of tutorless groups was by Bales and his colleagues in the early 1950s. They gave decision-making problems to 22 groups of Harvard students and classified the contributions according to the categories shown in Table 18.1. Bales confirmed that during the discussion there was a steady move from categories (a) through to categories (f). That is to say that at the beginning of the discussion, the groups spend a lot of time seeking and giving information because the amount of relevant knowledge possessed by the groups is limited. This orientation phase (a) gives way to expressions of feeling, opinion and judgement (b). These evaluations naturally lead to suggestions (c). Group members will either agree or disagree with the suggestions (d). Understandably, disagreement will result in some tension, while agreement allows tension to be released in socially acceptable ways such as humour (e). Constant disagreement can result in antagonism, while frequent agreement produces friendship (f).

Considered in this way, the sequential pattern observed by Bales and his colleagues seems very natural. It also explains a number of findings which might otherwise seem paradoxical. For example, it has often been observed that the most successful decision-making groups spend more of their time in the socio-emotional areas than focusing on the task itself. While one explanation is that socio-emotional discussion removes the blocks to agreement, Bales has shown that agreement also produces socio-emotional discussion. So categories 2 and 3 each tend to be followed by the other.

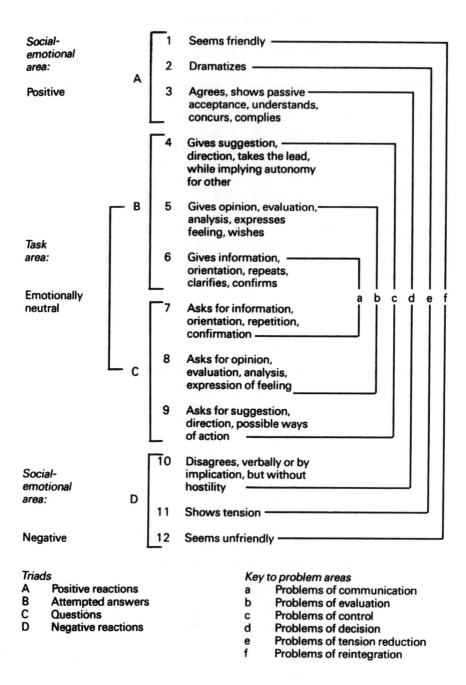

Social-
emotional
area:

Positive

A

1 Seems friendly
2 Dramatizes
3 Agrees, shows passive
acceptance, understands,
concurs, complies

B

4 Gives suggestion,
direction, takes the lead,
while implying autonomy
for other

5 Gives opinion, evaluation,
analysis, expresses
feeling, wishes

6 Gives information,
orientation, repeats,
clarifies, confirms

Task
area:

Emotionally
neutral

C

7 Asks for information,
orientation, repetition,
confirmation

8 Asks for opinion,
evaluation, analysis,
expression of feeling

9 Asks for suggestion,
direction, possible ways
of action

Social-
emotional
area:

D

10 Disagrees, verbally or by
implication, but without
hostility

11 Shows tension

Negative

12 Seems unfriendly

a b c d e f

Triads
A **Positive reactions**
B **Attempted answers**
C **Questions**
D **Negative reactions**

Key to problem areas
a **Problems of communication**
b **Problems of evaluation**
c **Problems of control**
d **Problems of decision**
e **Problems of tension reduction**
f **Problems of reintegration**

Table 18.1. Bales's analysis of verbal behaviour in tutorless groups (1970)

Bales (1965) also observed that as discussion continued, more time was spent on the lower numbers. For example, more time was spent on giving information, opinions and suggestions than on asking for them. In particular, the socio-emotional environment of groups tended to become more 'positive' and mutually supportive the longer the groups continued.

The work reported here describes the pattern of interaction amongst leaderless groups that met only once. Most buzz groups, brainstorming and horseshoe groups are this kind; but syndicates and some case study groups are not. They may meet over several sessions.

Bales has also studied the development of leaderless groups of different sizes over 4 meetings. Apart from increases in tension release and expressions of agreement, he found almost no significant trends. What he did find was increasing variability amongst the contributions of individuals in larger groups. It seems as if the larger the group, the more likely it was that individuals would take on different roles at successive meetings. This is contrary to what one might expect in tutorless groups. (Tutored groups are different.) It might be expected that the same individuals, placed in the same company with similar problems to solve, would behave in a consistent way. An important factor here may be the time interval between successive sessions. It seems possible that, after a week, a group virtually has to start again with its orientation phase. If so, the assumptions of timetablers about what may be expected from weekly seminars and group tutorials may be quite erroneous.

C. Patterns of development in subject-centred groups

There have been very few studies of the sequence of development in subject-centred groups led by a tutor. Table 18.2 summarises the sequence of four studies where the objectives were academic learning rather than interpersonal awareness and sensitivity. Here the discussions were more firmly led and (except for Zurcher, 1969) the objectives were more cognitive than affective. Nevertheless, there are some similarities with the sequence of sensitivity groups (especially LaCoursiere, 1974).

Johnson et al (1987) have claimed that 'learning groups typically move through seven stages'. They based their sequence upon that of Tuckman (1965), but because the initial leadership of the tutor is more directive, the period of frustration and rebellion is delayed until after some norms have been established.

1. Structure
In the first stage 'defining and structuring procedures and becoming oriented', students expect the tutor to explain what is expected of them. The tutor defines procedures, allocates the students to groups, assigns their tasks, attempts to establish co-operative interdependence and takes responsibility for the organisation of the groups' work. It's what you might expect in group tutorials and student seminars at the beginning of the academic year.

2. Conformity
In the second stage, 'conforming to procedures and getting acquainted', the group is task-centred and dependent upon the tutor for the clarification of goals and procedures.

The tutor obliges by setting group norms and values such as taking responsibility for one's own learning, assisting each other, developing trust and consensus and being open without any problems in the way the group functions. As in the Bennis and Shepard study, students may interact with each other at this stage, but their reasons for doing so (their goals) are personal to them. They are not oriented to each others' goals, nor to maintaining the group, because the tutor has taken that responsibility.

3. Mutuality
In the third stage, 'recognising mutuality and building trust', students increasingly recognise their interdependence and as they increasingly disclose their thoughts, ideas, opinions and feelings, disclosure is reciprocated. Consequently, acceptance, support and trust are increased.

Many group tutorials never get beyond this stage because the tutors squash signs of rebellion and challenges to their authority, rather than negotiating and adjusting to it. Consequently the tutor remains responsible for the students' learning.

4. Rebellion
It is only natural as the students get greater trust in each other, that the fourth stage (rebelling and differentiating) is characterised by challenging the authority of the tutor. This is a necessary step towards students taking responsibility for their own learning. That independence also involves independence from the other students. Student–student relationships may show some contradictions. They will be sorting out in what ways they are independent and interdependent. Johnson et al (1987) say 'relationships among group members are often built through a cycle of becoming friendly, establishing independence through disagreement and conflict, and then committing oneself to a relationship' again.

In effect, students are going through a phase of having to adjust the boundaries between their independence and autonomy on the one hand, and their commitment to fellow students on the other. Different students will draw different boundaries at different times. If their boundaries don't coincide there will be conflicts until adjustment is made. Johnson et al give the following advice to tutors.
i) Do not tighten control and try to force conformity to prescribed procedures. Reason and negotiate.
ii) Confront and problem-solve when students become counter-dependent and rebellious.
iii) Mediate conflicts among members, helping the group establish members' autonomy and individuality.
iv) Work toward students taking ownership of the procedures and committing themselves to each other's success.

5. Commitment
We shall see in a moment that the remaining stages are the same as those following 'rebellion' in sensitivity groups. Dependence upon the teacher and conformity to procedures he prescribes are replaced by dependence on other students. The group begins to establish its own norms and because students now feel the aims of the group

are their aims, there is a greater personal commitment to group co-operation. Participants are now self-motivated rather than motivated by the teacher. Johnson et al call this stage 'committing to, and taking ownership for, goals, procedures and other members'.

6. Productivity

As group members become personally committed and supportive of each other, a sense of group identity develops. Most important, the group alternates between socio-emotional contributions that help to maintain the group as a group, and contributions to the task. Thus the group 'functions maturely and productively'. This helps to explain the seeming paradox that the most effective and most productive groups are those that spend least time on the task and most time on the group maintenance. Students freely ask for, and give, help to each other. Consequently they are more influenced by each other than by the teacher. The teacher recedes to become a consultant.

Most group tutorials never reach this stage because most tutors do not have the skills to let go of their responsibility. Building trust is difficult. Accepting, listening to, and tolerating the criticism and hostility in the fourth stage conflicts with their

RESEARCHERS				
Johnson &Johnson 1987	Dunphy 1974	LaCoursiere 1974	Spitz & Sadock 1974	Zurcher 1969
PHASES REPORTED				
1. Structure 2. Conformity 3. Mutuality 4. Rebellion	1. External norms maintained 2. Individual rivalry 3. Conflict Frequent aggression 4. Negative moods	1. Orientation anxieties Expectations 2. Dissatisfaction Anger Frustration	1. Guardedness Anxiety Dependency Confusion	1. Orientation 2. Catharsis
5. Commitment 6. Productivity	5. Increasing concerns with feelings	3. Production More realism about learning	2. Group interaction. Trust. Cohesion. Inter-dependence	3. Focus 4. Action 5. Unproductive limbo 6. Testing 7. Purposive
7. Termination	6. High affection Reflection Sadness	4. Termination	3. Disengagement Separation anxiety Good feelings for teacher	
SOURCES OF INFORMATION				
Tuckman's data applied to learning groups	Content analysis of 2 sections of a relations course	Student psychiatric nurses meeting 90 mins for 10 weeks	Trainee nurses and 3rd year medical students	174 meetings of neighbourhood action committees

Table 18.2. Phases in group development – groups with leaders

conception of a teacher who should structure and control. This highlights the difficulty of moving from teacher-centred to student-centred teaching. All group development involves changing group norms. In this case the norms to be changed are those established by the teacher, and teachers find that difficult.

7. Termination

Every class must come to an end. As Johnson et al point out, the 'more mature and cohesive the learning group, and the stronger the emotional bonds that have been formed among group members, the more potentially upsetting the termination period is'.

The sequence put forward by Johnson et al is rather like growing up. At first children need to be told what is expected of them, what they should do and how they should behave. Not only is trust built up, but so is a mutual recognition that children and parents should help each other. In adolescence there is a rebellion against the rules and the norms that have been established while the children are struggling for independence. If these adjustments can be made, a family with young adults can be very productive. Finally there is a further period of emotional adjustment when the children leave the home.

D. Patterns of development in student-centred groups

The vast majority of these studies deal with sensitivity groups, often called T-groups or encounter groups. The earliest of these was by Bennis and Shepard (1956). They observed sensitivity groups developing in two phases, each of which was sub-divided in three. A major characteristic of sensitivity groups is that the trainer does not take an authority role. Consequently, initially the group is concerned with authority, power relations and the establishment of group norms and structure. Since the Bennis and Shepard study, a great many others have looked at the sequence of behaviour in sensitivity groups. There is a common pattern.

1. Dependency

At first, the group seeks dependence upon the trainer. The group is submissive and expects him to establish the rules and group goals. There is an expectation that the leader will lead, and there is a lack of structure because he does not.

2. Rebellion

When he doesn't do this, the group becomes disenchanted with him and then rebellious. The group is said to be counter-dependent. This is a phase of conflict, rebellion, hostility, resistance or frustration and anxiety. Very commonly the group splits into two factions about the problems of leadership and structure. A state of indecision may remain for some time. Indeed some groups might never progress beyond this stage.

3. Resolution

However, most groups learn to be independent and take more responsibility for their own learning by coming to terms with their own rebellion. But how? Rebellion usually occurs following some emotional event in which individuals express their repressed feelings. When those feelings are expressed, crucially they become part of the business of the group. The showdown in which personal hostilities are expressed demands resolutions for the future working of the group. It is the group that makes and eventually accepts proposals for how they should work together. In this way they jointly take responsibility for their own conduct.

4. Harmony

So in the fourth sub-phase there is concern with personal relations. Relationships improve, there is increased communication and expression of feelings, interaction is on a more personal level, and there is greater harmony in the group. This is a period of interdependency with closer trust, warm feelings and cohesiveness with mature and productive work. It is a happy, relaxed and productive phase. It is a period of greater openness.

RESEARCHERS				
Bennis & Shepard, 1956	Tuckman & Jensen, 1977	Braaten, 1974	Mann, 1975	Yalom, 1975
PHASES REPORTED				
1. Submission	1. Forming	1. Lack of structure	1. Dependency upon leader 2. Initial anxiety or resistance	1. Orientation Hesitant participation
2. Counter dependence Factions	2. Storming	2. Sub-groups with conflict Hostility	3. Frustration Hostility	2. Conflict Dominance Rebellion
3. Resolution 4. Personal interaction Expression of feelings Harmony 5. Harmony illusory Open and Closed factions 6. Irrational defences against sad parting	3. Norming 4. Performing 5. Adjourning	3. Mature work Interdependence Trust develops 4. Regrets at disengagement	4. Intimacy Integration Mutual synthesis 5. Separation phase	3. Closeness Warmth Cohesion 4. Termination concerns
SOURCES OF INFORMATION				
Laboratory studies	Reviewed 50 studies mostly sensitivity groups	Survey of 14 studies	Factor analysis of observations	Psychotherapy groups

Table 18.3. Phases in group development – T-groups

5. Divisions and anxieties

Openness during the period of harmony results in expressions of feeling about each other. Things may be said about oneself that one didn't know. Consequently, in the fifth sub-phase there is more concern with studying oneself. Self-confrontation can be threatening and members differ in their tolerance of openness. The feelings of harmony dissipate. Very often two groups are formed: those who wish to be open and those who either do not want to explore themselves anymore, or who wish to do so privately. The latter tend to become anxious. The anxiety is only resolved by each person describing their perceptions, possibly including their limits to openness and privacy, and these perceptions being accepted by the group. It is a phase that requires courage by these speakers; and maturity, understanding, empathy and warmth from their listeners.

6. Departure and separation

Finally, because the group is now a place of warmth and trust, when the course comes to an end, there is a sense of loss that the relationships will not be maintained.

These stages can be discerned in Table 18.3. The table summarises two review articles and two more recent studies. As a result of Tuckman's, 1965 article, the stages of forming, storming, norming and performing became particularly well known. 'Adjourning' was added to the 1977 reprint of the same paper.

E. Conclusion

I said in the introduction that these three types of discussion show a progression with regard to the skills they demand. What can now be seen is that that progression occurs within each type as well. For example, Bales pointed out that in tutorless groups, the prevalent contributions to discussion progressively shift from task to group maintenance and from cognitive to affective. The progression is also from simple to complex tasks. Broadly speaking, the same progression distinguishes the chapters in Part II. It is consistent with the principles that underlie my maxim: *Start with simple tasks in small groups for short periods of time, and then gradually increase their respective complexity, size and duration.*

Chapter 19
The influence of the environment

A. Seating position

B. The room

C. College environments

D. Conclusion

A. Seating position

It is of the essence of a group and of discussion that members interact with each other. That is to say, group members respond to stimuli from others. It is obvious that in discussion some of those stimuli are auditory. Others are visual, for example most non-verbal behaviour. Consequently, being able to see other group members as well as hearing them is pretty important.

1. The arrangement of chairs

For this reason, how the teacher arranges the chairs will affect interaction. It is clear that chairs in a circle allow each group member to interact with every other person, provided the circle is not too big. So now focus on your discussion groups. How do you arrange the chairs? What are the distances between them? Do they differ in comfort or height? Which are high status chairs? How is interaction influenced?

Sommer (1969) conducted an extensive experiment on the connection between classroom layout and student participation. Six rooms were chosen: two seminar rooms which offered horseshoe or open square arrangements of chairs, two laboratories which offered extreme examples of straight row arrangements, one windowless room with starkly modern decor, and one room with a long wall composed entirely of windows. Two teaching assistants were responsible for three groups, each of 25 students. In order to control for student differences, groups were asked to change rooms half-way through the course. Sommer was surprised and saddened by how passively the students accepted the room changes. Escape behaviours were immediately evident in the laboratories and the windowless room. On the first day of the classes, one teaching assistant asked to change rooms, and when no action was taken, took the matter into his own hands. Another showed her distaste for the laboratory by comments to her students, and eventually moved outside on to the lawn, where Sommer was fascinated to see that the students lined themselves up in three straight rows in front of the tutor! There were more contributions in the seminar arrangements than in the laboratories, but they came from fewer people.

What affects where group participants choose to sit? There are two background psychological factors: territoriality and personal space. 'Territoriality' refers to a sense of ownership of an area by an individual or a group. Having a sense of ownership is quite different from having a legal right to it. 'Personal space' refers to having an area round a person's body. Hence it moves with the person.

2. Territoriality

Many of the most striking examples of territoriality are not in educational contexts. For example, Lipman (1968) noticed in old folk's homes that people made claims to own a particular chair, and to have it in a particular place. These claims were respected and reinforced by other members, and newcomers would be told very firmly, if not with anger, if they in any way challenged the claim. Whyte (1949) noticed that individuals had a lower status when they entered another person's territory. For example, if one person visits another person's office, he will feel he is there by permission of the 'owner'.

Taylor and Lanni (1981) experimented with triads, each composed of a low-, medium-, and high-dominance man meeting in one of their rooms to reach consensus on a budget problem. They found that the solution eventually adopted most commonly reflected a proposal originally presented by the regular occupant of the office, regardless of whether he was high, medium or low in dominance. In other words, the territorial effect overpowered the effect of personality.

Altman and Haythorn (1967) noticed that pairs of students in discussion gradually increased the physical distance between each other, and established preferences for a particular chair, table or bed. As in the old folk's home, these preferences were then strongly respected by the other person.

Sommer (1969) found that students said they would take different seating positions according to the context. For example, when shown a diagram of a rectangular table with 3, 4 or 5 chairs per side, the vast majority chose end positions when they wanted to be as far away as possible from any distraction, but they chose middle positions if they wished to discourage other people from sitting at the same table. Sommer also noticed that students could defend their ownership of a table, even when they were not sitting at it, provided they informed invaders soon after they arrived. If, however, there was a delay when someone sat at a vacant table, the intruder would not move when a claim was made. Sommer also noticed that non-verbal signals can communicate to others where they should not sit. For example, a young lady apparently studying at a table in a cafe will be more likely to be left alone than if she sits without any apparent preoccupation.

It is a fairly common observation that in learning groups the teacher, or others with high status, will be accorded a larger territory than others. For example, the seats either side of the teacher are frequently the last to be occupied, and latecomers will go to considerable lengths to avoid sitting in them. In an experiment by Sommer, students avoided chairs alongside the teacher, even when there weren't any others – they sat on the floor or went out to get more chairs. The interpretation of this behaviour is, of course, a matter of inference. It could be that teachers are seen as having a larger personal space, or that there is uncertainty about the extent of the territory they might claim. Alternatively, individuals may fear that other class members would perceive them as teacher's pet, or as trying to acquire some of the teacher's status if they were to sit at the same end of the table.

3. Personal space

An individual's personal space is invaded if another person gets uncomfortably close to him. The distance at which an approach becomes uncomfortable varies. For intimate people it will be quite close; for those who are hostile, more distant. There are also cultural differences. It is said that at cocktail parties in the Egyptian Embassy, Englishmen move slowly backwards round the room pursued by Egyptians, who can tolerate a closer personal distance in conversation than Englishmen, who constantly back away. In crowded conditions, closer distances are tolerated for a while, but ultimately they lead to aggression. This can occur in crowded tutorial rooms, particularly if the territorial space occupied by the tutor leaves even less space for the students.

Willis (1966) has looked at the distance between individuals when they interact. In general, the closer the relationship, the closer the distance. Mean distances varied from 21" to 27" for the different groups. Compared with men, women stood nearer to close friends when speaking, but further away from 'just good friends'. People of the same age stood closer than people of contrasting ages. Curiously, however, parents stood at a distance comparable to perfect strangers.

Baxter (1970) noticed that the interaction distance increases with chronological age, and the contrast between the different cultures also increases with the age of the participants.

Sommer has engaged in a number of experiments in which he has invaded an individual's personal space. For example, if he went and sat close to someone on a park bench or sat at a library table in a way contrary to conventional norms, the individual would show signs of stress and would fairly soon leave the scene. However, in teaching situations it is not so easy to take flight from the classroom. Students can either retreat or, as it were, stand and defend themselves. According to Sommer, three-quarters of those who retreat choose a chair with its back to the wall, whereas only half as many do so if they take a defensive attitude.

4. How seating position affects participation

Sommer has observed that participation from students directly opposite the teacher is greater than from those at the side tables. Those sitting away from tables participated even less.

In the experiment by Sommer where discussions were held in laboratories, the benches posed a problem to the teaching assistants. One sat in front of her own desk and encouraged students to bring their stools up to the front bench in an unsuccessful attempt to approximate a semi-circular arrangement. Participation corresponded to the ease of eye contact with the teacher. Both in this and another experiment, students in the front row participated more than others, and those at the sides who had a clear view, participated more than students in any other row but the first. Interestingly, the front row is considered to be too close to the teacher, and was avoided by students who came on time. Of 51 latecomers, 41 ended up in the front row. Lest it should be thought that latecomers are more likely to be talkative, participation was greater from people in the front row when latecomers were removed from consideration. Sommer's interpretation is that seating in the front row gives students greater 'stimulus value', but it is not clear what this means, and an explanation coherent with general psychological theories is still awaited. Nonetheless, the relevance of Sommer's observation is unaffected. Later, Sommer talks about these students being 'psychologically closer' to the teacher than students at the sides. He concludes that what we need are 'conference rooms rather than lecture halls'.

Social and personality factors affect seating position. Strodtbeck and Hook (1961) observed that jurors from managerial and professional classes were more inclined to take head of the table positions than were people from other classes.

Observations of triads in natural settings show that the person seated most centrally speaks most often (Silverstein and Stang, 1976). Similarly, Hare and Bales (1963) noticed that people who score high on tests of dominance are more likely to take central seating positions in group discussions. Compare the seating arrangements in Figures 21.4, 21.5 and 21.6 for their effects upon participation.

However, Michelini et al (1976) have concluded that assertive people will not dominate a group unless they are also highly visible. They found that seating position facilitated initiating communications but did not affect the number received.

Sommer asked students where they would prefer to sit relative to another person at a rectangular table if they were conversing, co-operating, coacting or in competition. In conversation they preferred a corner-to-corner or face-to-face arrangement; for co-operation they preferred to be side by side; in coaction they preferred to be as far apart as possible; while those in competitive discussion wanted to be face-to-face across the table. These findings were confirmed by Myers (1969) who also reported that people preferred to be knee-to-knee when being counselled, not in a formal face-to-face confrontation. This is interesting because Egan (1982) recommends that counsellors sit face-to-face with their clients in order to be challenging and confronting when appropriate. Myers also produced evidence that formal seating arrangements caused much greater anxiety, and we have seen that this can strongly inhibit learning. When Sommer asked students why they chose to sit where they did, their answers tended to be in terms of eye contact, proximity and the position most suitable for the task.

It is clear that eye contact is important for communication in groups, and that any teacher who wishes to encourage group discussion should ensure that everyone in the group can see everyone else. What is less obvious is the consequence that ease of eye contact influences who talks to whom in a group. As long ago as 1950, Steinzor observed that people sitting opposite were more likely to respond to each other than people sitting side-by-side. The same thing has been observed in 12-person juries sitting at rectangular tables (Strodtbeck and Hook, 1961). People at the end of rectangular tables talked more and were seen as being more influential. Steinzor suggests that over-talkative individuals should be sat opposite a quiet one, and that two people who monopolise discussion should be placed next to each other.

Hearn (1957) confirmed the 'Steinzor effect' but found that if there was a strong leader, many more comments were directed to neighbours rather than those sitting opposite. When students are feeling sensitive to being rejected, they are more likely to talk to others sitting close to them and those sitting opposite if they are not too far away. Ask yourself, does this happen in your tutorials? Russo (1967) reported that the greater the distance between two people at a rectangular table, the less friendly, acquainted and talkative they were perceived as being.

B. The room

Most teachers believe that the classroom environment has an important influence on teaching and learning; but few take many steps to create the environment they want. Of course, that is partly because there are many aspects of the classroom they cannot change. So stop a moment and think about the rooms you use. What's good about them? What's bad? What can you change?

1. Windowless rooms

It is increasingly fashionable to build classrooms in large buildings without windows. Teachers are rarely involved in the discussions at which such decisions are taken. They are taken by an architect in local government, by the college buildings officer, or by a committee at a planning stage before the teachers were appointed. Those who take these decisions frequently know little about teaching and learning. Windowless rooms are easier to design, are cheaper to build, are more efficient to heat, can be lit to reduce eye strain and are less susceptible to outside noise.

There is little evidence that students learn either better or worse in windowless rooms. The simple fact is that people don't like being in them. As Sommer has shown (1969), both teachers and students try to escape from them, either to other rooms or to the open air. This is critical in continuing education or in any aspect of education that is voluntary.

Similarly, there is little evidence either way that students in windowless rooms participate more or less than those in rooms with windows. On the face of it one might think that rooms with windows would be more stimulating, with more fresh air and natural light, while windowless rooms would be more claustrophobic and likely to induce sleep. Using classrooms with seating in straight rows, Sommer (1969) found no significant difference in the amount of participation between windowed and windowless rooms. Seating position in both types of room was important. In particular, students spoke more if they sat at the front, sat in the middle of the row or were free to choose where they sat. They also spoke more as the course progressed.

2. Aesthetic appeal

One of the first investigators to look at the effects of rooms upon dyadic discussion was Mintz (1956). He had two examiners, one in a beautiful room and one in an ugly room. Examiners' ratings of photographs on 'well-being' and 'energy' were consistently more favourable in the beautiful room than in the ugly room. Moreover, when they were in the ugly room, examinees complained of fatigue, monotony, headaches, discontent, irritation and hostility. Furthermore, they usually got out of the room by finishing the examination quicker.

3. Distractions

Mehrabian and Diamond (1971) showed that the presence of objects in a room can either act as a distraction leading to reduced interaction between group members, or it can act as a focus for discussion if members have a common interest in the objects.

Guyot et al (1980) have made the interesting observation that students often sit in the same seat and are surprised, offended and even angry when this consistent behaviour is pointed out to them. In asking why students choose a particular seat, Guyot et al distinguish between a person's biological sex and their degree of masculinity or femininity on psychological tests. Psychological gender correlated with reasons given for choosing a particular seat. Biological gender seemed to correlate with motives of territoriality.

4. Memory by association

In the 1980s there was a flurry of studies suggesting that students memorise in association with their physical environment. Smith (1985) reported that if students are told to memorise word lists in three different rooms, they do better than those memorising in only one room, because they associate the words with the rooms. If they are not told to memorise, there is no advantage in using the three different rooms. Fernandez and Glenberg (1985), however, failed to obtain an advantage for students who memorised and were then tested in the same environment. But Canas and Nelson (1986) found that when students were given a surprise test by telephone at home, they performed less well than controls who were tested in the laboratory setting. Clearly, a great deal more research will be needed to sort out all the environmental influences in this kind of experiment.

C. College environments

The last section has emphasised the physical environment of discussion groups. It said nothing about their academic and social context. Studies of college environments, as distinct from small group discussion environments, emphasise quite different factors. For example, Pace (1962) described four groups of college environmental factors which he called College Characteristics Index. The first of these was the intellectual, humanistic and aesthetic climate of the college; the second coupled personal status and vocational orientation; the third was the extent of group, community and social responsibility; and the fourth factor was the college's independence, rate of change and scientific emphasis. Subsequently Pace (1969) developed seven scales with which to characterise colleges: practicality, community, awareness, propriety, scholarship, campus morale, and teacher-student relationships.

Stern (1963) formed six scales:
i)   intellectual orientation,
ii) social effectiveness,
iii) the amount of play,
iv) friendliness,
v) the degree of constraints, and
vi) dominance-submission.
Using questionnaire and interview techniques, Ramsden (1979) identified and isolated eight dimensions which students thought characterised their learning environment, in order of their perceived importance:
i)   student-centred relationships,
ii) tutor commitment,
iii) student workload,
iv) formality of teaching methods,
v) vocational relevance,
vi) social climate,
vii)goals and standards, and
viii)freedom in learning.

There's a lot to think about here. Take one of these scales and mark your institution out of ten on each item. Then ask, 'How do these features influence student discussions?'

The important contrast with the work on physical environments of classrooms is that research into college environments emphasises psychological and social factors, not physical ones. Yet one might have expected that psychological factors would be more important in learning groups, while physical factors would be most prominent in a student's image of his college.

This may yet be true because there is very little work on teaching environments as such. (There is, of course, a great deal of research into teaching, teachers, teaching methods and student characteristics.) One exception is a review by Fraser (1986) where he classifies the variables of the classroom environment:
i)   the evaluation of educational innovations, programmes and curricula,
ii) differences between students' and teachers' perceptions of actual and preferred environments, and
iii) determinants of classroom environment including class size, teacher personality, grade level, subject, sex of the teacher, and type of institution.

D. Conclusion

Overall, the study of physical and psychological learning environments in public education is still very limited. It is probable that the costs of creating attractive spaces is one limiting factor – the learning environments in industry are very different. Another reason may be the failure of authorities to rethink the austere assumptions of school education handed down from the 19th century. Much remains to be done.

Chapter 20
Patterns of interaction in small group discussion

A. Interpersonal perception

B. Verbal communication

C. Non-verbal communication

D. Patterns of communication

E. Group cohesion

F. Conclusion

In a sense the eight factors so far considered in Part III are all artificial. The essence of small-group teaching is that students interact. The essence of discussion is that students communicate one with another. Obviously, this is also an interaction process. The way the eight factors combine gives the enormous complexity and subtlety of small-group teaching. This section cannot possibly deal with that complexity in the detail in which it has been researched by people in many different fields. All I can do is to signal five areas to which the teacher should pay attention: interpersonal perception, verbal communication, non-verbal communication, communication networks and group cohesion. The first four are major areas of study in their own right.

A. Interpersonal perception

Interaction in groups depends upon how group members see each other and how they see themselves. Such perception and self-images are, for many reasons, subject to error. We form impressions of other people upon very limited data. Our observations are often casual and strongly influenced by our own experiences, personality, the norms we are used to, the roles we are taking and the contexts in which the observations were made. We also tend to ignore information that does not confirm our prejudices.

Let us imagine two people A and B, and consider their perception of B. Perhaps you are A counselling a student, giving an individual tutorial, or offering some feedback. Alternatively, you are B and A is a student whose motivation is strongly influenced by what he thinks of you. Figure 20.1 shows three circles: A's image of B, B's image of himself and B in reality.

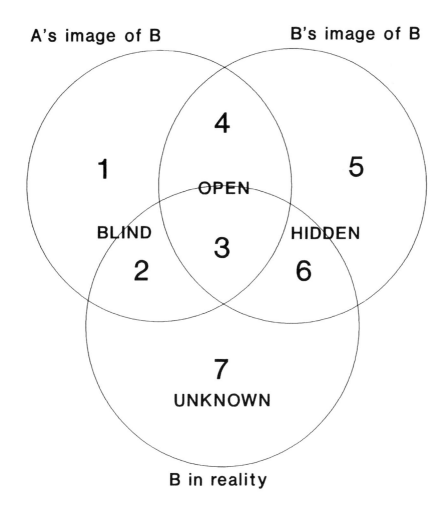

Figure 20.1.Perceptions and misperceptions of group members

1. A has some misperceptions of B that B does not have.
2. He also has some realistic perceptions of B which B does not have.
3. Shows correct perceptions by both A and B.
4. Represents misperceptions by A which are shared by B.
5. B has misperceptions about himself which are not shared by A.
6. He also knows some things about himself which A does not know.
7. There are some things about B that neither A nor B knows.

This elaborates Johari's window which we saw in Chapter 4, by adding a representation of objective reality. To make the connection I have inserted the Johari labels.

A similar diagram could be produced regarding perceptions of A. When A and B interact, they do so with reference to their perceptions of themselves and each other. The interaction may modify each others' perceptions. Accordingly, there are 14 different truth conditions with reference to changing mutual perceptions, and only two of them (the area represented by 3 in each case) where their perceptions are both in agreement and true. All the others represent either misperceptions or disagreements. Of course, in any given case we don't know how many perceptions or items are represented in any one area, but misperceptions and disagreements may not seem like a very firm foundation for a productive interaction. Yet discussion methods are better than any other for dealing with such misperceptions because interaction creates an opportunity for disagreements to become evident, so that misperceptions can be corrected by a constant process of adjustment, provided there is an accepting attitude in searching for the truth.

It can readily be appreciated that with groups larger than 2, the pattern of realistic perceptions and misconceptions is even more complex. Zajonc (1960) showed that it is communication between individuals that reduces conflicts between their perceptions, particularly when they expect there to be differences from the start. So let's briefly consider elements of communication in tutorials and other discussion groups.

B. Verbal communication

This subject alone has been studied by philosophers, anthropologists, sociologists and linguists, as well as psychologists. As if those were not enough, it has also spawned its own new disciplines, such as semiotics, semantics, cybernetics and linguistics.

1. The functions of language in discussion
It is fundamental for teachers to appreciate that with any utterance or message in small group discussion, there is a sender, a medium such as sound, vision or touch through which the message is sent, and several different receivers. As we saw in Chapter 6, the sender may intend one meaning, but the receivers may each interpret what they perceive to have several different meanings. For example, the meanings of words are primarily determined by individuals' experiences, and since they have all had different experiences, there is no guarantee that all individuals will mean the same thing by the same words. Indeed, there is a high likelihood that they will mean something different. There is evidence that when people speak they activate cognitive relationships that are more differentiated, complex and organised than those activated by the receivers (Zajonc, 1960).

The importance of discussion methods for the development of thinking is that by a process of successive interchanges, incompatible interpretations become evident and are increasingly difficult to maintain. Thus discussion facilitates a consensus of understanding which is not achieved by one-way communication as in a lecture. Argyle (1969) says that the main purposes of speech are to influence the behaviour of others, to convey information, to establish and sustain social relationships, to ask questions and to benefit oneself.

Allen and Brown (1976) have said that language has five different functions:

i) *Informing.* Textbooks, lectures and video recordings are amongst the teaching methods that assume the teacher has something to tell the student that the student does not know already. Hollander (1967) and Bales (1952 and 1970) have shown that information-giving is also the most common contribution to decision-making discussions.

ii) *Controlling.* Controlling behaviour includes arguing, questioning, nagging, correcting, criticising and giving reasons. Controlling is not only a function of teachers and discussion leaders. Everyone attempts to control others to some extent whenever they speak, because they seek the attention of others and want to influence what they know.

iii) *Expressing feelings.* As any actress will know, we express feelings whenever we speak, not only when the content of what we say is about our feelings. This aspect of discussion sets its tone.

iv) *Ritualising.* A great deal of everyday language is a ritual. Rituals are particularly evident in stereotyped greetings. Characteristically, the sequence of interactions is highly predictable, yet they are part of a process of mutual acceptance. They are part of the process of interaction. Curiously, they are often omitted from discussion groups in the classroom, and that may be one reason why interpersonal barriers sometimes take a long time to come down.

v) *Imagining.* Although imaginative communications may sound like the opposite, they contain an element of unreality. They require some confidence in the speaker and some mental flexibility in the listeners. They are essential for creativity and criticism.

There is a sense in which all communications in discussion involve these five elements. Students are receptive to these elements insofar as they know the rules and codes of language.

2. The need to learn both rules and strategies when using language

There are a great many other rules of language, such as knowing when to speak and when not to, how to speak to strangers, which words to use in what company, and so on. Learning groups include these rules but they also have their own and they are different in different teaching methods and in different cultures (cf difficulties of foreign students). They are part of the norms of the groups. For example, in leaderless groups they are quite different from group tutorials. Skilled interaction in the classroom involves learning the acceptable social pattern of language and interaction.

Communication in discussion is more than a repertoire of rules. It includes strategies for selecting which rules apply at any given time and context. As in chess, where the rules of strategy are quite different from the rules of the game, so in discussion the strategies and tactics for interaction are quite different from the rules of grammar. The strategies and tactics have to be learned. When children first go to school, they learn tactics quite different from those relating to their parents. They learn by experience. In the same way, as I have repeatedly argued, a developmental sequence of experience is required to learn how to learn from a discussion.

How are the rules of language learned? Gilmore (1977) has shown that questioning skills can be learned by positive modelling. That is to say, copying someone who has performed the skill well, rather than avoiding a model they see as ineffective (negative modelling).

C. Non-verbal communication

As Argyle (1969) points out, when two people talk to each other, there must be continuous evidence that each is attending and reacting to the other. These indications are given by eye movements, gestures, nods of the head, facial expressions, changes in position, and so on. In order to transmit these signals they take up positions so that they can be sent and received. (Conversely, the student who doesn't want to take part in a discussion, or who resents being there, takes up a position where they can't.) The end of a conversation is signalled by withdrawal from these positions and cessation of the non-verbal signals. These signals are different in different social classes and cultures, so presumably they are learned. Yet most of them are below the level of consciousness, both for the senders and the receivers. We have impressions of people which contribute to our judgements of them, but we can't always say why we make the judgements we do.

Apart from indicating attention and responsiveness, non-verbal signals have other functions. They signal when one person will stop talking and another will start. (See Figure 20.2.) These are mostly eye movements, including the use of eye contact and its withdrawal, head nods, hand movements and turning the body to face the next sender. Eye contact in dyads is different from larger groups. In groups, eye contact with the speaker is used as a signal that one wants to respond. In dyads that's unnecessary.

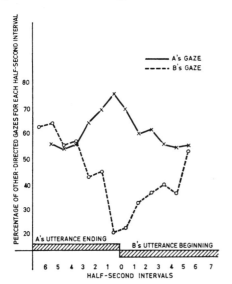

Figure 20.2. Direction of gaze at the beginning and end of contributions (Kendon, 1967)

These skills are important in discussion, particularly for the teacher, because they are mechanisms of control. You don't have to control by talking. It's usually better not to. Use gestures instead.

Non-verbal signals indicate attitudes which are crucial to discussion. Verbal language is quite ineffective for this purpose. The signals include tone of voice, dominance and submission postures, changes in interpersonal distance, and movements of the hands, legs and head. Again, these skills are crucial to any discussant, but particularly to a leader or teacher. The non-verbal language communicating emotions and language is partly innate, but is modified by a superstructure of cultural norms.

Non-verbal signals in discussion also give feedback to contributors on how people react to what they have said. Disbelief, agreement, annoyance, and surprise are all conveyed quite differently and they set a constant stream of mini problems on how contributors should express their next point.

Particularly in learning groups, where explanation forms an important part of discussion, non-verbal signals may contribute to the content of discussion. For example, gestures can illustrate the shape of a graph or the magnificence of a work of art.

In addition to these functions of non-verbal behaviour, there are many other types of non-verbal signal. These include paralinguistic factors which are part of speech itself, such as its variations in pitch, speed, rhythm and volume, in addition to sounds that are not words, such as laughing, 'uh-huh', accent and pauses.

When combined with language, non-verbal communications can have four functions:

i) they can *reinforce* what is being said, for example, by pointing to a blackboard,

ii) they can *substitute* for language. For example, shrugging the shoulders can mean 'I don't know',

iii) they can add to, or *complement*, what is being said, or

iv) they can *contradict* the words that are being spoken by apparently giving a different message.

Love and Roderick (1971) have identified ten 'teacher behaviours' which they regard as non-verbal. In fact, with minor adaptations, they could equally well apply to students and verbal communication as well:

i) Accepting another person's behaviour, for example, smiling or raising the eyebrows as if to say 'yes'.

ii) Praising, eg. nodding approval.

iii) Displaying another person's ideas, either visually or by repeating and elaborating them.

iv) Showing interest in another person, eg. by establishing and maintaining eye contact.

v) Facilitating students' interacting, eg. by a gesture inviting John to reply to Mary.

vi) Giving directions, for example by pointing or raising a hand to stop someone.

vii) Showing authority, eg. by staring, shaking the head or even snapping the fingers.

viii) Focusing attention, perhaps by giving emphasis with downward beats of the forearm.

ix) Demonstrating or illustrating, as in performing a physical skill.

x) Ignoring another person by lack of non-verbal or verbal response when one would be expected.

There have been several research studies showing that teachers who give more non-verbal cues, and who are more physically active are judged to be more effective, but gestures and facial expressions are not effective on their own. They must be used in combination with other behaviour. There is also evidence that, although many aspects of non-verbal behaviour are innate, teachers can be trained to enhance their non-verbal skills, particularly by micro-teaching. (The repeated practice of specific skills in miniature following feedback on previous performance.)

D. Patterns of communication

The efficiency of groups is reduced if their sources of information are reduced. So if there is an interaction pattern such that group members can only get their information from one or two other members, their discussion will be ineffective. Indeed, it will cease to be a group at all if individuals cannot interact.

This is what happens when most students come to a seminar without proper preparation. There comes a point where the tutor must abandon the seminar, or remove students who have not prepared, pointing out that members cannot benefit if students don't prepare. In the long run this may be more beneficial than frequent periods in which the teacher struggles to keep a conversation going by providing information rather than promoting thought. A considerable volume of research has also been carried out in industry and other occupational situations showing that small groups of workers who can all interact with each other will be more efficient and productive than groups of workers amongst whom interaction is less possible (Argyle, 1969; and Handy, 1987).

Leavitt (1951) attempted to study interaction patterns in a laboratory. Leavitt's purpose was to explore experimentally the relationship between the behaviour of small groups and the patterns of communication which groups operate. He wanted to consider the psychological conditions that are imposed on groups by various communication patterns and the effects of these conditions on the organisation and behaviour of its members.

Leavitt asked five people seated at a table and separated by partitions that prevented face-to-face contact, to communicate only by written messages. The partitions were connected to a centre post in which there were slots like letter boxes, through which the messages were passed. Leavitt could control who could communicate with whom, and he confined his investigation to four structures: a circle, a chain, a wheel in which four members could only communicate through one central member, and the Y, in which three people could only communicate through a central person, and the fifth member only through one of these. Subjects were given a problem to solve and Leavitt took a number of measurements, including the time taken, the number of errors, and the number of messages needed to achieve a solution.

While there were inconsistencies on any one measure, the general order of efficiency was wheel, Y, chain, and circle. Members of the circle were judged to be leaderless, very active, unorganised and erratic, but nonetheless enjoyed the task, while members of the wheel had a distinct leader, were less active, and had a good, stable organisation but found the task unsatisfying. Members of the wheel, Y and chain channelled the information into the centremost person, who tended to evolve as the decision-maker almost regardless of his or her personality. People in the central positions tended to send more messages, to make fewer errors, to solve the problem more quickly, and to be better satisfied than those situated more peripherally.

Personally I find the Leavitt experiment very artificial. Its significance is to show the importance of the central person, and to show how lines of communication can affect both the group performance and the group process in a fairly systematic way. Consequently, one of the things for teachers to observe in horseshoe groups, syndicates and case discussion, as well as in their own group tutorials, is who is central and which students are peripheral. People in highly central positions have considerable freedom in choosing with whom they will communicate (consider the chairman of a committee), while those on the periphery have much more limited channels of communication. This factor becomes more crucial the larger the group.

Shaw (1981) has also pointed out that people in central positions can suffer from overload, or what he calls 'saturation'. This is a particular problem for teachers who place themselves at the centre of a wheel in group tutorials. If they insist on responding to every student's contribution and then controlling who shall be next to speak, they will easily become overloaded by having to monitor both the content and the process of the discussion simultaneously. Stasser and Taylor (1991) have shown that in 6-person mock juries, just half the contributions were responded to by the person to whom they were a response. Over-dominant tutors perpetuate this pattern.

E. Group cohesion

Group cohesion is usually defined in terms of the desire of group members to remain members of a group. Another criterion is the extent to which group members work together – that is, the degree of co-ordination. The attractiveness and co-ordination of the group will be greater when there are fewer conflicts within it. So a negative criterion of group cohesion is the presence of group conflict. If conflicts are very great, cohesion will be so low that members may split up with the result that the group ceases to exist.

In cohesive groups in continuing education, members maintain their attendance, they arrive on time, they display mutual trust and support, they accept each other's individuality, and they enjoy coming to class and having fun.

Shaw (1981) gave a learning task to triads varying in cohesion. A teacher who did not know the basis of the groupings observed that members of cohesive groups praised each other more, initially spent more time planning their method of study, were more democratic, and were generally more co-operative and friendly. Groups low in cohesion were more hostile, aggressive, pleased when others made mistakes, did not plan their method of study and contained more autocratic leaders. Although both types of group were task-oriented to begin with, by the third task the cohesive groups spent more time saying things that were supportive and maintained the group, rather than directly on the task.

Because of the importance of establishing group cohesion, Zander (1982) devotes his first chapter of *Making Groups Effective* to this subject. He says that responsible members make their groups stronger, that they help participants recognise that they constitute a whole and want to do what the group needs. He recommends a number of techniques to give this sense of unity:

- Ensure that members of a group are within easy reach of each other.
- Group people who are already alike, or help them to become alike.
- Physically separate groups from other groups in the class so that each is perceived as a distinct entity.
- Give each group unique characteristics, such as a name, a logo, a song, a flower, a flag, or a uniform.
- Demonstrate to members that their group has an interdependent relationship with other groups and that each group depends upon the other.

He argues that a group is attractive if it satisfies the needs of its members (see needs of personalities on page 141*ff*). Therefore:

❍ Help members to identify individual needs that they may satisfy in the group. Start with a questionnaire.

❍ Increase the group's ability to meet these needs.

❍ Determine how well the group meets these needs.

❍ Help members understand how well their needs are being met in the group, and

❍ Give members a chance to make sacrifices for the group.

Then, recognising the importance of task accomplishment, Zander recommends task-based strategies to develop cohesion founded upon achievement.

● Develop standards for the group's purposes, activities, goals, procedures and beliefs.

● Encourage each member to abide by these standards.

● Stimulate a disposition amongst members to experience pride and satisfaction with the group if it successfully accomplishes a group task.

Blakeman and Helmreich (1975) think this is because researchers have assumed that cohesiveness causes good performance, rather than the other way round; while Magin (1982) thought that it was group pressure in collaborative learning that enhanced the performance of decision-making groups.

An experiment by Schachter et al (1951) suggests that group cohesiveness is more easily destroyed than established. If this is generally true, it should influence teachers not to take risks that might make groups less attractive because they may have long-term effects upon the attractiveness of group methods. It seems as if group cohesion is a delicate flower which needs constant nurture. Tziner (1982) emphasises the distinction made throughout this book between group processes concerned with the task and those concerned with the socio-emotional characteristics of a group that maintain its existence. He says these two factors make different kinds of group cohesion.

Back (1973) has noticed that the characteristics of cohesive groups vary with the basis of their mutual attraction. When it was based upon an achievement motive, they wanted to complete the task quickly and efficiently. When the basis was interpersonal attraction, they wanted to continue the discussion after the task was completed. And where the cohesion was based upon the group's high prestige, the group performed cautiously for fear of errors that might lower it.

F. Conclusion

Although the influences upon any of the nine factors considered in Part III can be described in terms of the other eight, there is a sense in which the interaction of group members is the major synthesis. By definition, learning groups have members who interact.

What I have tried to do in Part III is to separate the nine factors and to consider the influences upon them as revealed by psychological research. That is not an end in itself, and we must now turn to consider skills and teaching methods that apply these factors.

Part IV

A Developmental Sequence Of

Discussion Methods

A. Learning to think requires a developmental sequence of discussion methods

B. A developmental sequence is needed to learn and teach discussion skills

C. What that developmental sequence is

In Part I, I reviewed a number of experimental studies comparing small group discussion methods with presentations and other methods of teaching. It emerged that the major function of small group discussions is to teach students to think. They are also effective for teaching perceptual, attitudinal and inter-personal skills, particularly when there can be discussion of a common experience. This common experience can be provided by using other, preferably active, methods such as role plays, simulations and demonstrations. We shall see that the value of discussion for perceptual, attitudinal and inter-personal skills depends upon the fact that some thought is necessary when taking part in discussion. So it is the thinking component where discussion is important.

The review treated small group discussion methods as if they were mostly of one type. That was a crude generalisation. We all know that there are many different kinds of small group discussion method. Indeed, Huczynski (1983) has described over a hundred.

One purpose of this chapter is to review a number of these methods so that the tasks and factors influencing group process described in Parts II and III can be placed in a practical context.

There is also a second important purpose. It is to convince you that the variety of small group discussion methods should be introduced in a developmental sequence, both because students can only develop their thinking skills gradually and because they need to develop the skills of how to interact in groups. These are skills to do with the tasks and the processes of group work respectively.

Because these two sets of skills need to be learned in a developmental sequence, small group discussion methods need to be introduced in a carefully planned developmental sequence. The arguments are as follows.

A. Learning to think requires a developmental sequence of discussion methods

1. Students need to learn to think
They are not born with, and do not arrive with, all their thinking skills.

2. Complex thoughts develop upon simple ones
This is not a logically necessary truth for every conceivable thought, but reflection will show that most complex thoughts consist of relating, or distinguishing between, ideas previously developed by more simple thoughts.

3. Students learn to think when trying to answer questions in discussion
Evidence for this has been produced in Chapter 2. If it seems obvious, you should remember that many teachers behave as if students will only learn to think by listening to them. I'm using the word 'question' with a very wide definition here. Most statements can be formulated as answers to a question. It includes most of the skills I considered in Part II, particularly chapters 7 to 10. Judgements, conclusions, interpretations, inferences, decisions and solutions to problems are all answers to questions.

4. Discussion methods should vary with the question(s) to be answered
In all tasks from carpentry to man management it is fairly evident they require different methods to achieve different objectives. A carpenter's tools to cut wood are different from tools to make it smooth. Teaching methods are tools to achieve learning. In the same way learning of different kinds and in various contexts requires different methods. I may seem to labour the point, but it is remarkably common in higher education for teachers to try to use the same method, seminars for example, regardless of what they want to achieve. If a carpenter did that, you'd think him crazy. Yet university teachers are supposed to be intelligent!

How come university teachers get away with this stupidity? One reason is that their failures are not obvious. It's immediately obvious if a carpenter fails to cut a plank of wood in two with sandpaper. It's not so obvious when half a class continues to reason illogically, cannot apply principles in practice, remains uncreative and can't take decisions.

A second reason is that university teachers don't think psychologically. They think in terms of their own subject. But they need to do both. That's why I wrote Part II. It gives examples of tasks that answer various kinds of question. No doubt there are other examples that might have been given.

5. Students should learn to think in a developmental sequence of discussion methods
I believe this is a reasonable conclusion from propositions 1–4.

However I do admit that the sequence required by the content of a subject may conflict with the sequence of thought processes I have described in Part II. If that is the case, I would ask you to look again at the curricula you have designed. There are cases where there can be no reconciliation. It may be, for example, that the most difficult leap of the imagination comes at the beginning when learning calculus or quantum mechanics for the first time. In these cases premise 2 is false. Even in these cases I think teachers should look for analogies, metaphors and similar devices that provide stepping stones for the imaginative leap.

I accept that that the conflict can exist. Teaching is not an exact science. This is simply one of those cases where teachers have to work out the best compromise between conflicting generalisations and then monitor their success.

B. A developmental sequence is needed to learn and teach discussion skills

So far as the use of group processes and the development of skills in group work are concerned, there are two arguments each with three propositions. The first concerns students' discussion skills; the second is about the teacher's teaching methods. But in essence they are the same argument.

1. Students need to learn how to learn discussion skills

These are also not inborn. They include the ability to express or articulate thoughts, to do so in a way that others can understand, to try to understand others, to listen, to have confidence, to admit one was wrong, to respect others, to accept others as they are, and so on. There are very many of them. These skills are qualities of maturity. They are not learned quickly or easily, and it is part of the teacher's job to foster them.

2. Students learn new skills by practice based upon old ones

In other words, learning to learn in groups is a process of progressive adaptation of existing skills and techniques. We learned many of the basic skills of discussion when we were toddlers. We learned to talk, to observe reactions to what we said and to respond accordingly. These skills have been greatly developed since then by everyday practice. Whenever we enter a new environment, in this case the learning group, we have to adapt to it. We need to adapt the skills we already have. In other words, a further developmental process is needed.

3. Discussion skills are best learned in developmental sequences, each building upon others

This is a reasonable conclusion from propositions 1 and 2.

4. Different discussion methods require different learning and teaching techniques

This is almost a truism. Methods consist of combinations of skills and techniques. So different methods must require a different combination of skills and techniques even when some of their skills and techniques are the same.

5. New discussion skills and teaching techniques can gradually be developed upon old ones

Group techniques need to be developed one out of another. More subtle techniques are learned by the refinement of cruder ones. Learning to learn in groups is a process of progressive adaptation of existing skills and techniques. Consequently, though in Part IV I talk about discussion methods and techniques as if they were separate and distinct procedures, they are not. The art of developing students' abilities to learn in discussion groups involves blending one method into the next so that the transition is gradual and almost imperceptible. For convenience, different discussion methods and techniques are given names. But in the last analysis they are artificial labels for points on a variety of continua.

6. Teachers need to learn small group skills and teaching techniques in a developmental sequence

This follows from 3, 4 and 5. In theory there could be conflict between the three sequences: the sequence required for students to learn how to think, the sequence for students to learn how to participate in discussion, and the one for teachers to develop their teaching skills. In practice, I don't think there is much conflict. The sequences required are much the same and in any case they are not absolutely rigid. There is not a single sequence in each case. There are alternative sequences for development.

C. What that developmental sequence is

1. The sequence in outline

Figure 21.1 shows the complex of sequences that could be used. It follows the maxim, *'Start with simple tasks in small groups for short periods of time, and then gradually increase their respective complexity, size and duration'*. There is a general drift starting in Chapter 21 with individual work and the nominal group technique, followed by short discussions in pairs (dyads). Buzz groups ideally have only three or four members also meeting for only a short period of time. Horseshoe and cross over groups are larger and are also tutorless.

In Chapter 22, brainstorms, case discussion and syndicates meet for longer, require more structure amongst group members, will be visited by the teacher and each have their characteristic objectives.

They are transitional toward tutorial groups (Chapter 23) where the teacher is present all the time. Perhaps controversially, I shall regard seminars, free group discussions, counselling and T-groups as particular kinds of group tutorial each with their own types of objectives. Finally there are several varieties of plenary class with large numbers and where, realistically, little more than the acquisition of information is achieved.

Fortunately the broad sequence is the same whether it is students learning to think and feel, or a teacher learning to use discussion methods.

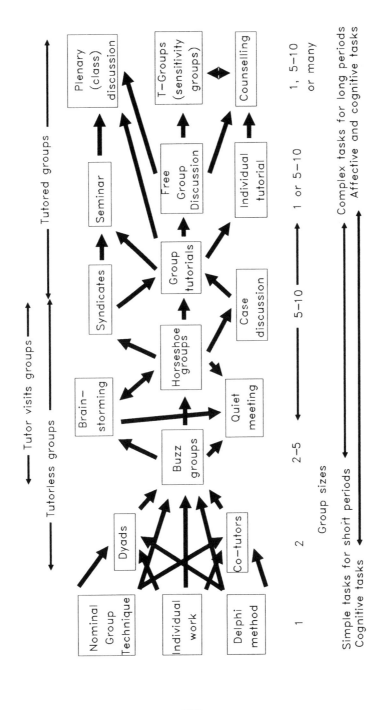

Figure 21.1. Sequences to follow the maxim

2. Progressively increase your available repertoire of methods

I do not mean to say that once one has progressed some way along a sequence that one may abandon earlier methods, never to return. Quite the contrary. The sequences should be seen as a process of widening one's repertoire so that, for example, teachers will continue to use pyramid and buzz groups even when they have matured sufficiently to use free group discussions. Why? Once again because different methods achieve different objectives. In any case, if you don't want your teaching to fall into a dull routine, there is great merit in constantly varying your methods and techniques. Variety also sends a message to students that you care and think about what you are doing.

Nor do I mean to say that teachers and students must be well practised in *each* method of the sequence before proceeding to the next. The skills of successive methods overlap, so it is possible to skip one, or even two, and perhaps go back and use them later when more appropriate. There are several paths of development.

Nor am I claiming that *every* skill used in earlier methods is a prerequisite of later ones. Not all the special procedures in brainstorming, for example, are necessarily required for later methods; but they help. They give a freedom to be ridiculous and not be chastised for it.

Nonetheless, I maintain my broad maxim: '*Start with simple tasks in small groups for short periods of time, and then gradually increase their respective complexity, size and duration*'. To put that negatively, there are far too many university and college teachers who plunge their students into seminars, or who try to develop attitudes and social skills long before their students have basic discussion skills. This is particularly true when the student groups come from family backgrounds where discussion of everyday issues does not occur (let alone everyday discussion of serious issues).

Chapter 21
Tutorless groups

A. Individual work plus small tutorless discussion

The first basic skill is not a group skill at all, but the ability to work individually. The product of that work then needs to be shared and discussed in a small group so that it can be developed, criticised, applied, related to other knowledge and ideas, or thought about in some other way. The small group may be a dyad, a buzz group or possibly a slightly larger group. I will describe these in a moment.

As I suggested in Chapter 18, most students learn to work on their own in class at school or at other times. Thus it is a skill they have when they arrive in higher education. Being asked to work individually for a short time in class is therefore a normal practice in their experience and should be acceptable to them. So it is a basic skill that can be built upon.

1. Establish the norms and expectations you want early
In fact if you don't use it in class when students first arrive, from its neglect, they

195

might get the idea that individual work in class is never required at university. They will mistakenly adduce a false norm and resent being made to work later.

I don't mean that I make them work individually for a long time – 3 minutes at the very most – but I don't apologise for making my students work. If my students get the idea that they don't have to work when they come to my classes, I've failed badly.

2. The advantages of using individual preparation before group work

Ask students to work individually on a problem before suggesting that they share their thoughts in groups.

Apart from what they learn doing the task, this has another purpose. It ensures that each group member brings something to the group and has something to contribute. It makes passive non-participation less likely. It does not prevent it, but at least there is a moral sanction when students cannot tell their group what they prepared individually. This sanction is greater if individuals prepare in the presence of others. That's the coaction effect I discussed in Chapter 12 (page 112 *ff*). Conversely, every teacher knows that if you say, 'Prepare this at home and come next time prepared to talk about it', there are always some students who don't do so.

The trick is to set a task sufficiently small that it can be accomplished in a couple of minutes in class, but which opens up the topic they need to think about. A smaller task prepared in class, before forming dyads or buzz groups of 3 or 4 members, gives a higher preparation rate.

Consequently, the use of individual work is a technique leading to more even participation in groups and enabling each participant to 'break the ice'. The preparation reduces fear (see page 107 *ff*). This is crucial. It's a confidence builder. The longer students remain silent whilst others talk, the more difficult they find it to contribute later, and the less notice is taken of what they say when they do.

Contributing early in a discussion has another advantage for hesitant students. It makes their thoughts part of the agenda. If they delay, it is more difficult to contribute relevantly later. Can every student contribute early in the subsequent discussion? Yes, if the group is small enough. That's one reason why I recommend 2 to 4 members.

Individual preparation is important in another way. It forces the students to begin to use the language of their subject. As we saw in Chapter 6, this is an important basis for later thought.

More than that, I think it is important to get the message across to students at an early stage that any discussion is going to be more productive if members are well briefed and well prepared. It is worth explaining for later group tutorials that lectures, reading and personal planning may set out the facts. The purpose of discussion is to use the facts and reason with them. To have to spend long in discussion setting out the facts, when that should have been done in preparation, is to waste the scarce time when the group can be together.

You may think it is a waste of valuable class time, even at this early stage, to give students work that they could do at home; but if it establishes students' confidence to take part in discussions early in a course, it is time well spent. In any case, remember, I am proposing tasks that only take two or three minutes. There is a coaction effect, and it is quite a good idea to set an expectation of intensive work by saying, 'You will only have 3 minutes for this task' and then, half way through say, 'You have 90 seconds more'. Far from wasting time, the use of time pressure raises students' arousal levels and creates a greater sense of urgency with spin-off benefits later. Again, I make no apology for creating an atmosphere in which students come expecting to be put under pressure to work intensively.

As I shall mention later when describing buzz groups, tasks drawing on students' personal experience are good for starters. They are non-threatening because each student is the authority about their experience. No one can say 'You're wrong; you never experienced that'. I shall also recommend the use of listing tasks, for example, 'List as many reasons as you can for ...' That may seem simple, but listing tasks can be creative and intellectually demanding. Instead of 'reasons', students could be required to list examples, applications of a principle, or criticisms of an experiment, a theory, a piece of legislation or a proposal.

B. The nominal group technique (NGT)

NGT is one way of pooling all the products of individual work without discussion until they have all been collected and summarised. Hence the 'group' is only nominal. It's not a group. Its work and products are individual. The NGT is commonly used with classes between 6 and 20 members, but could be used with more or less. The procedure is as follows:

1. Steps in procedure
i)   Participants work individually and silently on a problem or some other task. For some tasks this period could be 3 minutes; for others, virtually no time at all.
ii) Going round the class, each member presents one solution or idea.
iii) Typically these are summarised on a flipchart or blackboard.
iv) When everyone has contributed, go round again until all ideas are summarised. Individuals pass if they have nothing new.
v)   Participants can then act as a group, discussing the ideas mostly to clarify and evaluate them. Some new ideas may be added; others discarded. Very often at this stage or when the method is completed, sheets from the flipchart are torn off and displayed round the walls of the teaching room for later reference as matters arise.
vi) In the commercial world where the task is a decision, members may rank order the suggestions. The company's decision is the one ranked highest on average. In university teaching, the teacher needs to take the ideas submitted, bind them into a lecture or in some other way relate them to underlying theory or principles.

2. The merits of NGT
● NGT is an easy method for beginning teachers to use, provided they can summarise contributions succinctly and accurately to the contributor's satisfaction.
● It can elicit ideas forming the material for later work (depending on the task individuals are set). For example, a range of attitudes, values or perceptions can then be the source for developing mutual understanding and tolerance using free

group discussion (see Chapter 23). Alternatively, competing decisions could form the material for a case study.

● NGT obliges participants to contribute early ('break the ice') and this helps to facilitate later contributions from naturally silent members.

● By requiring everyone to contribute before there is a general discussion, it prevents early over dominance by some members.

● NGT is useful for 'getting to know each other'. Depending on the task set, used early in a short course, NGT can reveal participants' background experience, interests, prejudices and other characteristics that the teacher could use, or may need to be aware of (cf. Chapter 15). Consider, for example, the task, 'What made you enrol on this course?'

3. Warnings about NGT – consider the follow up

○ *Use as a starter.* As you see, the merits of NGT are that it is a good starter. The danger with its overuse is that it is not used to start anything. If possible, plan the follow up. I've seen too many teachers who use one NGT after another.

○ *Know when to let go.* Steps (ii), (iii) and (iv) on page 197 require some control by the teacher. I notice that, in practice, many teachers cannot let go of control when it is time for step (v). Alternate contributions continue to be by the teacher. Communication is in a radial pattern in and out from the teacher at the centre. True discussion involves group members talking to each other and this is not achieved

○ *Place ideas in their theoretical context.* It is important that step (vi) is carried out, otherwise NGT becomes nothing more than collecting ideas from those who came to learn and no intellectual advancement or rigor is achieved. You've collected ideas from the class: use them; show their significance. Otherwise you beg the question, 'So what?' Particularly in continuing education, using the expertise amongst class members is important but don't forget that you, the teacher, are one of the group's main experts. And as a teacher, your expertise is to relate a collection of separate ideas to a context, a set of principles, or generalisations. It's a process of synthesis.

○ *Use the initiative you've created.* If you use it to break the ice, make sure you use discussion methods before the pool freezes over again. If you use it to get to know your students, then make sure you use that knowledge and show a personal interest in them, use their background experience, or whatever advantage that knowledge gives. If you stick the summary sheets around the wall, make sure you integrate the students' learning later in the course, by referring to the ideas and building upon them.

All these errors in the use of NGT arise from not planning the follow-up properly.

C. The Delphi method

So far as I know, the Delphi method doesn't have much to do with the Oracle, except that it is a consultation procedure for taking a decision. It has been described as 'a systematic way of encouraging individuals to arrive at a consensus, and of identifying those views which differ from the majority' (David Jaques, private communication).

1. Steps in procedure

i) A problem is identified. Sometimes the first problem is identifying what the real problem is. Participants anonymously submit their solutions or relevant ideas. These could be obtained formally by using a questionnaire.

ii) The solutions and ideas are analysed and collated by the teacher or leader.

iii) A summary of the results is fed back to participants who are again asked for their solutions. The results usually evoke new solutions and ideas which are again submitted to the teacher or leader.

iv) Steps (ii) and (iii) are repeated until responses are stable. That is to say, either consensus is reached or minority opinions are not changing.

2. Features of the Delphi method

i) Like individual work and the nominal group technique, the Delphi method is not a discussion method in the normal sense. Nonetheless, participants make contributions and others respond to them, or at least to analysed and collated summaries of them.

ii) Participants do not meet each other face to face. The consensus-taking is traditionally done on paper. However (although without the anonymity), the method could now be used for distance teaching using e-mails and the Internet or for consultation with the capitals of the world by the head of a multinational company.

iii) Contributions are anonymous. This is useful for a king organising his own palace revolution! But there are other embarrassing situations when consensus is required without personal opinions being public. Collecting students' opinions about their teacher could be a similar example. This contention assumes there are opinions that can be expressed anonymously that would not be expressed openly in a group. However, the opposite has also been argued, namely, ideas will be expressed in the heat of discussion that would not emerge from a formal procedure.

iv) Although the Delphi method could save time and travel costs, in itself, it is very time consuming.

v) It depends upon the competence (not to say, integrity) of the leader.

vi) The method tries to achieve convergence of opinions. So you won't get the diversity of opinions that you might get from NGT or brainstorming. Consequently there is a tendency to eliminate creative solutions proposed by a single individual.

D. The use of dyads

Dyads are very special groups. Some people would not call them groups at all. Obviously they are the smallest size of group you can get. That fact influences the skills they practise and the skills they don't practise effectively. It influences the objectives dyads can achieve. They practise the lower level cognitive skills I discussed in Chapters 5 and 6 and the formal reasoning in Chapter 7.

1. The merits of dyads

i) *Dyads are natural ice breakers.* They quickly provide everyone with someone to whom they can report the fruits of their individual work. After a class has done some work individually, it's very easy to say 'Compare what you have done with your neighbour'. Indeed that may well happen spontaneously. If so, encourage it. Say something like, 'Yes, discuss it with your neighbour while the others are finishing'. Fear in pairs is at a minimum (see Chapter 12) because dyads provide everyone with a minimal audience. But dyads are more than that.

ii) *Dyads are good for teaching the language of a subject.* When a speaker in a dyad finishes speaking, assuming there is to be a response, it can only come from one person. That means there is no competition about who will respond or who can choose not to respond. The listeners know they will have to practise the language of the subject being discussed.

iii) *They practise listening.* Consequently the listener will listen with an expectation to reply and the speaker also speaks with that expectation. So the listener will be thinking about his response as well as listening.

iv) *They work with parallel processing.* This means that listeners have to listen and think at the same time. Knowing they have to reply, social loafing (see page 125) is not possible. Consequently dyads demand some concentration and teach it in preparation for other discussion methods.

Students have to operate the attention switching mechanism I described in Chapter 5 on page 33 to manage the information load. White et al (1994) found MBA students' thinking surprisingly restricted by the load in dyads. In a simulation, students had to negotiate a price for some goods. Three items of information were supplied, but they tended to negotiate focussing only on one. Using a similar task, Mannix and Innami (1993) found that student negotiators who only prepared their own arguments and did not anticipate counter arguments from their adversary were less flexible in their thinking. Preparation eased the thinking load.

v) *They have formal reasoning.* For this reason dyads are all right for getting students to work on a prescribed reasoning task such as working through some calculations. They are not so good for reasoning of a less formal kind where much more information has to be managed.

vi) *They develop interpersonal trust.* If in larger groups some members are not going to reply, those people are observers of the interaction between those who do, at least temporarily while the interaction takes place. To put that another way, there is a privacy in dyads that does not apply to other groups. This is of great importance in counselling and personal tutoring. It also favours a kind of paired bonding early in the life of a class when all members are strangers. Trust can develop in pairs.

It's interesting that when that trust is threatened, dyads tend to explore the problem, whilst larger groups are more likely to repress it (Ruscher and Hammer, 1994). The more concrete the exploration, the more specific are the plans to deal with it (Waldron et al, 1995).

2. Difficulties with dyads

i) *Not so good for higher cognitive skills?* In dyads there is only one other person to whom one's ideas can relate. There is a single relationship of ideas. It is a relationship, AB, between A and B. But if there are three members, ideas can be related between AB, AC, BC and ABC. One more person results in four times as many idea relationships. With larger groups the number rises exponentially. This means that, compared with larger groups, dyads are not much good for relating ideas. They won't be much good for creativity or receiving (either constructive or negative) criticism. Similarly, two people will not see all the pros and cons of a decision so easily as a larger group.

However, there are doubts about this criticism. Instead of a single dyadic discussion, Kuhn, Shaw and Felton (1997) set up a whole series of dyadic discussions on capital punishment with the same students. They found the range of arguments used increased, the quality of reasoning improved, arguments were based within a framework of alternatives including both sides of an argument and they showed awareness of how different views could coexist at a metacognitive level. We cannot know how much thought took place outside the classroom between one discussion and the next, but what does it matter anyway? It's the cognitive development that matters. To explain these effects of a series of dyads will require a new line of research and could lead to quite new ideas about cognitive development.

ii) *The random composition of dyads.* For the teacher to choose who pairs with whom is likely to cause an adverse reaction amongst students. But that raises the question of how their composition affects performance. In some subjects the ethnic and cultural mix can produce discussions that are difficult for teachers to build upon (cp Williams and Halgin, 1995).

iii) *Is there over-dominance by one partner?* One might think that dominant personalities could be over-powerful when there is only one other person in the group (see Chapter 15). It's true that people with strong attitudes are more effective persuaders, produce more arguments and more valid arguments than their partners (Shestowsky et al, 1998). It is also true that aggressive boys in dyads at secondary level have been found to be unaware of their aggression (Lochman and Dodge, 1998). But on the whole this is not a big problem.

iv) *Do men over-dominate?* In mixed-sex dyads, men tend to speak first, louder and more of the time than women. Whilst women look at their partner more when speaking, there's no significant connection between their visual dominance and assertiveness (Kimble and Musgrove, 1988). Men are more likely to change the topic of discussion unilaterally, but in general men and women agree to do so (West and Garcia, 1988).

E. The pyramid technique

In this technique, individuals' thoughts on a topic are first shared with one other person. Depending on the topic, the sharing may or may not be preceded by individual work. Pairs are then merged to form groups of 4, and in theory, quartets may be used to form groups of 8, then 16 and so on, until the whole class is involved. This procedure is sometimes called 'snowballing'.

In practice I find it accelerates the group size too rapidly, and early in the life of a class I don't wish to form groups larger than 4. Repeated doubling up also results in the same people saying the same thing in each new group and that does not progress matters very much. So in the early stages of group development I usually stick at size 4, though I might sometimes merge three pairs to form groups of six instead of four. I'm more likely to do this if I want to bond the groups for joint project work (syndicate method) later. As we shall see, I may double up as far as groups of 8 when I want to form brainstorming or horseshoe groups. There are lots of pyramid variations. Be flexible according to what you want to achieve. You can use your knowledge of factors influencing participation in groups (see Part III) to try variations on this theme.

The pyramid technique can be used on the first meeting of a class or conference delegates, as shown in Figure 21.2. It can be used in large classes. Participants are instructed to introduce themselves to one other person, not only giving factual information about themselves, but expressing some of their thoughts, hopes and expectations about the course or conference, and in particular their feelings now that they have arrived.

An essential feature of this task is that participants speak on a subject on which they alone are an authority. Furthermore, in the case of students, the teacher (who is all too often perceived as a powerful and threatening) is not a member of the group. The students learn to conquer any fears they may have on speaking to a stranger. Partners are usually supportive. They can empathise because they are in the same situation.

The listeners begin to learn the skills of listening and attending that we considered in Chapter 5. They know that in three minutes' time they will be asked to summarise what they have heard, and the accuracy of their summary will be checked by their partner. They are told not to interrupt during those three minutes. This helps to establish the independence of the speaker.

The enforcement of a time control sets a businesslike tone to the course. Notice the whole exercise only takes just over 12 minutes, yet its effect upon the friendliness of the class, compared with giving an introductory talk, which is so often the custom, is difficult to overestimate.

When each individual introduces their partner to another pair, they repeat the summary that has already been checked. By the end of this exercise each person should know three other people, and that is as many friends as most people can acquire at one time. It is sufficient upon which to build buzz groups.

You don't have to confine the use of pyramid groups to the 'getting-to-know-you' at the first meeting. On the contrary, they have value throughout a course. In particular, after merging into groups of 4, they are very good at making students present a partner's point of view accurately, in their presence, to a couple who have not heard it before. Students have to present it fairly and rationally. That is a powerful academic discipline in any subject, particularly for budding barristers, managers or anyone who wants the skills of leadership. Furthermore, they will then hear how someone else perceives their point of view. This can be sobering too. Imagine having to present the

– *Tutorless groups* –

	A	B	C	D
3 Minutes	Talks to B	Listens to A	Talks to D	Listens to C
1 Minute	Checks	Summarises A	Checks	Summarises C
3 Minutes	Listens to B	Talks to A	Listens to D	Talks to C
1 Minute	Summarises B	Checks	Summarises D	Checks
	Merge pairs to form groups of four			
1 Minute	Introduces B	Listens to A		
1 Minute	Listens to C		Introduces D	Listens to C
1 Minute	Listens to B	Introduces A	Listens to B	
1 Minute	Listens to D			Introduces C

Figure 21.2. A pyramid technique

perceptions of a partner from another racial group. It forces the beginning of understanding all sides of an issue. It is laying the basis of maturity – of tolerance and considered judgement.

So far as the timing is concerned, be strict and flexible. That sounds like a contradiction. The technique is this: listen and observe students so that you learn by experience how long they need for the task(s) you have given. Give them that amount and no more. As soon as you give students too long, you ease the pressure to work hard. As I said before, I don't apologise for working students intensively. With a bit of praise, they get a sense of achievement as well as enjoyment, and that's the potent combination.

F. Co-tutoring

Co-tutoring is a variant of peer tutoring, but I would not recommend other methods of peer tutoring this early in the sequence.

1. The procedure
It builds upon individual work. Set a short piece of writing to be done individually in class (not more than half a page maximum). Then put students together in pairs with a minute for each to look at their partner's written work. You might say, 'Comment on what your partner has written as if you were a tutor. Praise its merits first. Then ask questions about it.' Each student then tutors the other on what the other has written. *Keep the task small and the periods of time short.* Teachers tend to give tasks that are far too big. Then they get into time trouble. You must give yourself time to follow up on this

task – that is (i) say what you observed while they were doing the task, (ii) receive feedback and (iii) respond to it.

2. Advantages

Co-tutoring has advantages. It can be used in large classes. Tutoring someone else is an effective way of learning. So students learn from each other and with each other. The praise reinforces their merits. Yet they learn to accept criticism with minimum exposure and, where partners are good friends, they learn to separate criticism of their work from criticism of themselves as persons. This is a lesson that needs to be learned before placing students in larger groups. (We shall return to it again in the next chapter.) They learn to see their written work as their teachers see it. They learn to express themselves more accurately and to appreciate how their written work is perceived. So far as their written style in concerned, the feedback raises standards quickly at first where there are shortcomings, but after that the benefits are slight.

	A	B
3 Minutes	Writes short answer	Writes short answer
1 Minute	Checks B's answer	Checks A's answer
2 Minutes	A tutors B	
2 Minutes	B tutors A	
However long it takes	Feedback and correction of errors by teacher	

Figure 21.3. Co-tutoring on short written task

3. Plan your follow up

Particularly in the physical sciences, teachers will worry that co-tutors will teach errors or omit vital points, but, of course, the teacher should follow up with what is expected and will probably have got some feedback by eavesdropping on some conversations from a distance. Have your own 'perfect' answer prepared on an overhead transparency and don't be too modest in pointing out the features in your answer that you were looking for in the students'.

G. Buzz groups

Of all methods of teaching in higher and continuing education, buzz groups are the most important. If you don't use buzz groups you are not developing your students to their full potential and you are not doing your job. That's because they are

Figure 21.4. Arrangement for buzz groups in a typical classroom

fundamental to the development of small group teaching and hence to the most effective development of thought and attitudes. Lectures, reading, films, TV, the Internet and all other presentation methods are mere servants providing the information to inform attitudes and values, and to be applied in thought. It is upon such thought and values that our humanity and civilisation depend. The whole idea of a 'college' is that people seek knowledge and understandings together as a community. Buzz groups are the way to maintain that ideal in large classes.

In my book, *What's the Use of Lectures?*, I have argued in some detail that limitations in what lectures can achieve, factors influencing memory, attention spans and students' motivation and difficulties in lecturing all make the combination of buzz groups with lectures imperative. Important as those arguments are, I shall not repeat them here.

1. The techniques are relatively easy to learn

i) *Forming the groups.* Buzz groups are groups of 2 to 6 participants meeting for half a minute to 15 minutes to discuss an issue or problem. It has been used in lecture classes of up to 400 students. Ideally, as we saw in Chapter 16, each group should have 3 or 4 members. In a formally arranged, horizontally floored room, the technique is to ask alternate rows to turn round and face the row behind. In this way groups of 3 or 4 will naturally form. If there is an odd number of rows, some people may have to move. (See Figure 21.4.)

Where the class is in a terraced lecture theatre, turning round may be difficult and groups of 2 or 3, but not 4, may be formed on a single row. (See Figure 21.5.) Four in the same row encourages shouting between the two at either end and noise then escalates. To limit noise, it's a useful tip to check that the distance between members in every group is less than the distance between any two individuals in different groups. If that is not true, speech from outside a group may be more easily heard than what is said in it. (For ways to use buzz groups in lectures, see my book *What's the Use of Lectures?*)

More commonly, buzz groups are used in more informal seating arrangements. In group tutorials, buzz groups of 3 can be quickly formed by every third person pulling out their chair to face the two people on their left. (See Figure 21.6.) Once a teacher has used this technique a few times, students move readily into groups and it is organisationally very easy. Indeed, the buzz group method is probably the easiest of all teaching methods and that is why it is fundamental to the development of others.

One technique is to give a task that everyone can do individually in a short period of time, and give slightly too much time for it. When students have finished they will naturally begin to talk to their neighbour. As with dyads, this can be encouraged by saying, 'Yes, compare notes with your neighbour while others are finishing'. In this way pairs or triads develop naturally. They do not have to be formally introduced as a duty. Having established the pattern of behaviour, the groups can then be used rather more formally as buzz groups.

ii) *Giving the task.* The teacher should present the task so that it is visually present throughout the period of discussion. For this reason it should be on an overhead projector, a blackboard, or a sheet of paper in front of every student. The use of a sheet

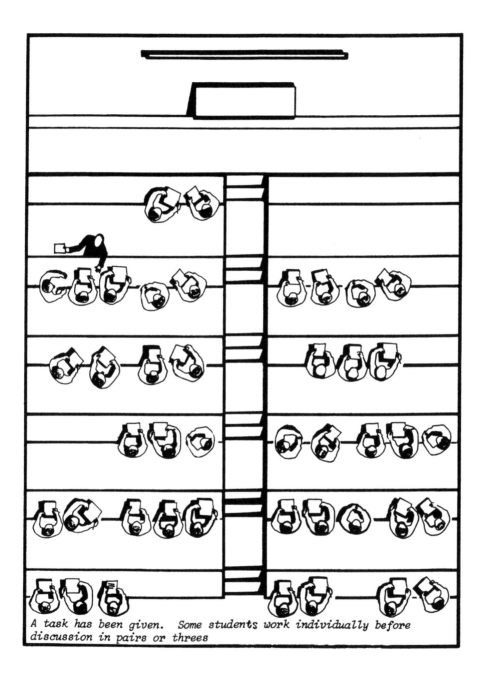

Figure 21.5. Arrangement for buzz groups in a terraced lecture theatre

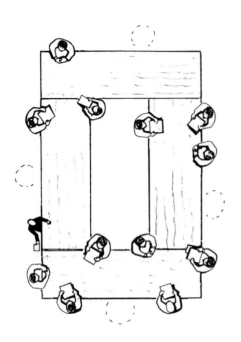

Figure 21.6. Format for buzz groups in group tutorials. Students sit round the tables, but then move chairs to the centre, particularly the corners, to get best eye contact in discussion. The tutor visits groups to give support and to build relationships

of paper is a good idea if students are asked to write their conclusions upon it. This provides a focus to the discussion. It makes sure the students know how productive their discussion is being, and it enables the teacher to observe the students' work rate at a distance without entering and interrupting the group.

Tasks that everyone can do are typically ones based upon their own experience. They are very suitable early in a course. Tasks drawing on individuals' experiences are also less threatening than tasks that test their knowledge, so they are very useful to start getting students used to discussion methods. Later on the tasks can be more demanding.

Listing tasks are particularly effective because they require the students to crystallise their thoughts. You might think that all listing tasks would be at the same cognitive level. That's not true at all. To list examples teaches powers of application. To list the components or elements of something practises powers of analysis. To list positive and negative criticisms teaches judgement and discernment. And so on. Nearly all the tasks given in Part II can be used in buzz groups.

iii) *Monitor the discussions from a distance.* Having set the task, the teacher's first job is to make sure that it has been clearly understood and that students are getting on with it, not something different. Accordingly, cast your eye around the class to ensure that all groups have been formed and there is no-one who cannot proceed. If there are several groups with difficulties, you may need to clarify the task and the procedures from the front. If there are one or two groups with difficulties move to them quickly to get their discussion under way.

Otherwise, keeping your distance is crucial. There is no-one who can kill a discussion like the teacher! Too often teachers are a threat and a source of criticism. If you wish to enter a group, try to do so, not by standing, looking down upon the students, but with your head height at the same level or lower than theirs. This may require you to crouch down. That may seem unconventional, but it reduces the perception of threat.

If you set listing tasks, feedback from groups can be obtained in a very succinct form. Lists also make it very easy for the teacher to see the extent of progress from a distance, without entering the groups. Buzz groups provide a golden opportunity for the teacher to observe the students when one is not obliged to concentrate on the subject matter being taught all the time. The buzz group technique is one that takes some of the pressure off the teacher and for that reason it is particularly appropriate for new teachers. Hence, again, its fundamental place in the staff development of teachers.

It is customary to tell the students a little in advance when you expect to close the groups. This may spur the slower groups to crystallise their thoughts and focus on the central issues. Particularly when first introducing buzz groups to a class, I put the students under time pressure by telling them, at intervals, how much time they have left. It teaches them that discussions mean business.

iv) *Feedback and pooling.* There is nothing more tedious than listening to one group after another report on their discussion. Particularly when there are a lot of groups, don't let it happen. Students pay little attention except to the report of their own group. Students' disenchantment with the process tends to be transferred to the buzz group technique itself, even though one advantage of the technique is that students normally enjoy it.

There are a number of ways of getting feedback. One is for teachers to observe discussions and to collect the main points being raised so that they can give the summary themselves, followed by a request for other points that the students might raise. Another technique is to ask for one quick point from each group in the class. This minimises the feeling of groups that report later, that everything worthwhile has already been said. If later groups have nothing new to add, they should say so.

2. A very wide range of objectives can be achieved

Buzz groups may be used for virtually all the objectives and tasks considered in Parts I and II of this book.

The golden rule when designing tasks is to require the students to practise the pattern of skill to be developed. When designing tasks for buzz groups or any other small group discussion, teachers need to be able to recognise the component skills they expect from their students. For example, it is no good giving tasks that apply principles if your aim is to promote powers of analysis. Part of their skill in observing small group discussions is to recognise with which component skills the students have most difficulty. In my opinion the capacity to identify the psychological component skills required by students should become one of the hallmarks of the professional teacher of the future. It requires the teacher to operate at a meta-level relative to his students.

I have no need to describe all the objectives and tasks that buzz groups can be used for. Part II does that. But there are two exceptions concerned with the acquisition of information.

i) Clarification. Almost any buzz group following a presentation such as the first part of a lecture, or reading a text, will include students asking others about things they did not understand. It is not unusual for students to be able to explain things to each other more clearly than the teacher can do, especially when the students come from a common background of professional experience. Clarification also comes from appreciating different perspectives upon the same subject matter expressed by various group members.

ii) *Consolidation of learning.* The very act of going over information that has previously been presented requires retrieval of that information from students' memories, and we have already seen in Chapter 1 that this enhances the retention of information. Thus although the information has already been acquired, the ability to retrieve it is practised.

3. Buzz groups develop the group dynamics for learning

In addition to practising the cognitive and affective skills described in Part II, buzz groups also use factors considered in Part III to foster a community of scholars. It is worth mentioning six of them:

i) *They encourage reticent students.* We have already seen on pages 108–109 that small groups without the presence of a teacher are less threatening than large tutored groups. Buzz groups create a context in which students can develop their confidence and their powers of expression without feeling they are being judged. These two things support each other.

ii) *They foster a cohesive class spirit.* Buzz groups establish working relationships. They also meet for short periods of time so that new groups can be constituted, building more working relationships. To do this in horizontally floored lecture rooms, ask a different row to turn round the second time (see Figure 21.4). The cross-over technique enhances this process systematically. (See page 214 *ff.*) Consequently, buzz groups are particularly quick at developing working relationships throughout a whole class. This is a most satisfying aspect of teaching and learning, particularly for adults.

iii) *Feedback to both teacher and students.* If buzz groups are used in combination with other teaching methods (and this is how they should normally be used), students will obtain feedback on their learning during the other methods. Feedback motivates students. For example, if a buzz group task requires students to use information acquired from reading or a lecture, they will obtain feedback on how far they acquired that information. If they haven't, you can see from observation where students are having difficulty and can offer assistance. This can give you feedback upon the effectiveness of your teaching and students in need appreciate the personal contact.

iv) *Buzz groups can release students' tensions.* Because buzz groups place students in an expressive situation, they provide opportunities for frustrations and opinions to be expressed. They are particularly useful in lectures for this purpose.

v) *Revive and maintain students' attention.* It is notorious that students' attention wanders during lectures and group tutorials. The use of buzz groups provides an intensive activity and a break in the monotony.

vi) *Gives the teacher a breathing space.* Lectures are a long performance, particularly for new lecturers. Group tutorials can also be intensive hard work. The buzz group technique can provide a break for lecturers and tutors to collect their thoughts and recover their composure, if necessary. If in doubt, there is one task that can always be set at a moment's notice: 'In your groups, decide on a question to ask me!'

4. Combining buzz groups with other methods

Buzz groups are essentially a method to combine with others, particularly presentation methods. Presentation methods present information. Buzz groups get students to think about it. There are various ways of doing this.

i) *Lecture, class discussion, individual work, buzz groups, plenary.* This seems a natural sequence. The lecturer lectures for 25 minutes by which time attention is beginning to wander. For 5 minutes there is a period for questions, clarification and feedback to the teacher. A few minutes is then allocated for each student to apply the lecture information to a problem or another related task. Next, individuals join to discuss their answers more critically in a buzz group. Feedback to a plenary session follows, concluding with a summary by the teacher, who may then continue the lecture if there is time.

ii) *Buzz group, feedback to teacher, followed by lecture.* This combination collects students' opinions on a topic and then the lecturer lectures on the topic considering the various opinions as the topic is developed. It makes students search their existing knowledge (something discouraged by passivity in lectures) and relates new knowledge to it. That is equivalent to saying, 'understanding is promoted'. It also makes the lecture more personal to the individual student – potentially a powerful motivation.

iii) *Introduce task, buzz group, practical, buzz group, feedback/plenary.* This combination is useful in laboratory teaching. After practical work has been introduced, it is sensible for students to talk over and plan what they are going to do. This reduces errors and has the logistic advantage that not every student starts the practical element at the same time. (I always feel it's a bit chaotic when they do.) The buzz group after an experiment is completed makes the students' write-ups more thoughtful. It has the logistical advantage that students don't drift away at various times as social loafers are tempted to do. The teacher can pull strands together (observations, thoughts and advice) and finish the laboratory class in a businesslike working atmosphere.

iv) *The step-by-step lecture.* This method was developed by McCarthy (1970) when teaching medicine which was examined by multiple choice questions (MCQs). But it can be used in any subject, provided the teacher keeps the buzz group tasks small and short. In effect, it is a rolling sequence of buzz group, lecture, buzz group, lecture. McCarthy set an MCQ for individuals or a group and then lectured on why the right answer is correct and, importantly in medicine, why the distractors are wrong. By this combination, anything up to 10 buzz groups can be held in a one hour lecture period. Five is more normal – but the tasks must be kept short. This combination has the same advantages as (ii) and maintains attention very well.

Teaching methods in general can be combined in a vast variety of ways. Contemporary practice is stultifying. Much more flexibility is needed. With the exception of (iii), each of these combinations can also be used with horseshoe groups. Many conferences, which delegates attend not knowing each other, would be far more successful if combinations (i) and (ii) were used almost as standard.

H. Horseshoe groups

As you know, my maxim for the progressive development of group skills is '*Start with small groups with simple tasks for short periods of time and gradually increase their size, complexity and duration*'. Horseshoe groups are a natural development from buzz groups. They are twice the size (4 to 12, but preferably 6 to 8) and could be formed from the merger of two buzz groups. They may be used for the same types of objectives, but, working on bigger or more difficult tasks, they will take longer. Like buzz groups, they may be used within a lecture or between other presentations.

1. Furniture arrangement and the teacher's intervention techniques
Their distinguishing feature, the arrangement of furniture, requires preparation, so they cannot be used in quite the same impromptu fashion as buzz groups. The chairs are arranged in a series of horseshoe shapes with the open end toward the blackboard or screen. There are normally tables within the horseshoe, on which a problem sheet, specimens or apparatus may serve as the focus of discussion. (See Figure 21.7.)

The tables have another function – they encourage participants to lean forwards. This position maintains attention and promotes involvement much better than leaning

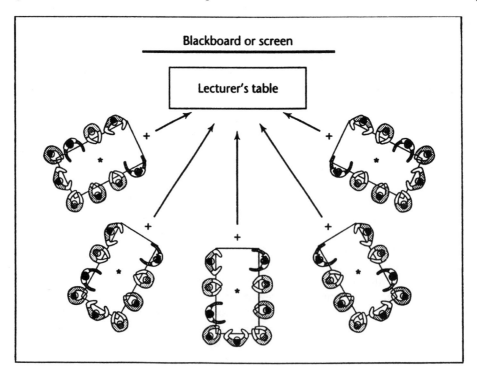

Figure 21.7. Furniture for horseshoe groups

back. Leaning back encourages detachment. Leaning forward shortens the distance between participants, allowing voices to be softer and relationships to be more intimate.

The teacher may move from group to group, closing the circle by sitting at the open end of the horseshoe. In this way, groups are gradually introduced to the presence of the teacher for short periods of time. The teacher should enter a group as unobtrusively as possible, averting eye gaze until one or two interactions have taken place between the students. If you don't do this, your arrival will interrupt the flow of conversation and all students will turn to you to hear what you have to say. Years of schooling have made students dependent. The teacher must foster their independence.

The flexibility of this arrangement is that, if several groups have the same misconception or difficulty, the teacher can interrupt from the front, correct the point, and then let the groups resume their task.

If you don't intend to lecture or address the class from the front, the horseshoes can be arranged radiating from a central point. With both arrangements there is a focal point from which the teacher can selectively listen in to the groups' conversations without obviously doing so and without entering a group, closing the circle and being a group member. The advantage of the focal point being central is that the distance from a central point to the closing position is usually shorter. You can sit on a chair in that position and move very unobtrusively in and out of groups as help is required.

I have used horseshoe groups with classes of 90 students, making 9 groups of 10 students, but for me, that is near the limit. If I wanted to know what is going on in all those groups I would need to structure the task(s) quite tightly so that I could see what they have done and not done when I visit. Usually I don't want to know that amount of detail. I don't need to. By the time I have developed the students' discussion skills sufficiently to use groups of 6 or larger, I expect to have developed a working atmosphere.

Nonetheless, particularly when first using the method with a group, it is a good idea to be quite precise about what you want them to do. It is often better to have prepared a list of questions requiring short answers that lead students through the minefield of your subject, rather than give a broader question that allows them to wander more freely and get lost. (The latter is more appropriate to group tutorials, free group discussion and seminars when a tutor is present to help them. See Chapter 23.) Put the questions spaced on a sheet of paper (either one each, or one in the centre of the table) on which you expect the answers to be written. As I've already said (see page 197), listing tasks can also be quite stretching and they allow you to see how much work has been done when you visit.

How can the fruits of discussion be shared amongst the whole class? It's not always necessary. You have to judge what will be learned by doing so. Of all teaching methods, stand-up reports by a nominated group member 'of what we discussed', are rated most unfavourably. They are liable to be repetitious. There are alternatives that keep them brief and confined to what is important.

i) One is for you, the teacher, to extract from group visits and report what you think is useful. Then ask generally for additional points.

ii) Where the task was to write a list on torn out flip chart paper, the list can be displayed on the wall with brief additional comments.

iii) A method I favour is to ask each group to write their answers on an overhead transparency. Then I display them and can draw attention to what is important. Furthermore, if I have structured the discussions with a series of short questions, I can photocopy them on to the transparency in advance. This keeps discussions tightly relevant.

iv) The cross-over technique. See the next section.

2. Some practical uses for horseshoe groups

Horseshoe groups have an advantage over buzz groups when students need the wider resources that a larger group offers. They are therefore suitable for informal reasoning (latter parts of Chapter 7), problem-solving, creative tasks, decision-making and sharing diverse attitudes and opinions (Chapters 8 to 11).

As indicated, horseshoe groups can be used for students to observe specimens, apparatus or maps. Since colleges cannot afford or store separate specimens for every student, this is a cost-effective method. More important, it teaches perceptual skills more thoroughly than independent work.

I also use horseshoe groups at the end of the year for students to discuss examination questions or other topics that review the whole course. Students are often surprised to find how others would answer questions. They discover that others perceive the course quite differently. Hence the method has an important role in broadening perspectives. It helps students see other people's points of view. This is an important step to open-mindedness, which I see as a major function of higher, adult and continuing education.

I have used this arrangement of furniture at the beginning of the year to introduce students to the literature available in the college library. I bring in a large collection of books relevant to the course and give tasks practising library reference skills, in which the students have to find their way around these references to find specific information and answer particular questions. Strictly, this is not a horseshoe *group* because new students do that task either individually or in twos and threes. But it does familiarise them with the furniture arrangement so that it is not such a surprise when I introduce horseshoes later.

3. Some limitations on their use

There is clearly a limitation in that the method requires a horizontally floored room with suitable furniture. The teacher must prepare the furniture in advance, and some timetables make this difficult. What is required in further, higher and adult education is a new attitude towards the use of furniture. Staff development is required with teachers, caretakers and cleaners! There is so little understanding of the need for flexible teaching methods, that furniture is sometimes screwed to the floor. However, given the facility, students themselves will move furniture to the right place, if a diagram as in Figure 21.7 is presented on an overhead projector. Students will do this quickly and easily after the method has been used once or twice.

I. The cross-over technique

This is a technique for sharing knowledge or opinions between groups.

1. Its procedure

Ideally, take the square root of the number of people in the class. Suppose it's 25. Then form 5 groups with 5 members. I do this by giving everyone a small card on which is written one of A1, A2 to A5 through to E5. (See Figure 21.8.) If I am using buzz groups or horseshoe groups I will say, 'If you have an 'A' on your card come to this table; a 'B' to this table …' and so on. When they have settled at their table and after I have set the task, I will warn them, 'After a while I shall recompose the groups so that those of you with a '1' on your card will come to this table; those with a '2' to this table…' and so on. The cards are labelled according to latin square designs (see Figure 21.9). 'I shall then ask each of you to report briefly on what you have decided (or said, or concluded, etc.) to your new group. So you will each need to make a note of it in your first group.'

With this procedure I sometimes call them 'square root groups'. Admittedly, if there are 26 or 27 in the class, one or two people won't have to report. If there are 24 in the class you may decide to form 6 groups of 4 members to start, and then 4 groups each with one person from the previous six groups.

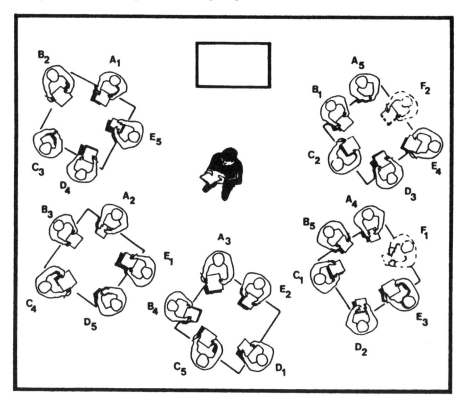

Figure 21.8. Arrangement for cross-over groups

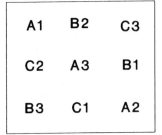

A1	B2	C3
C2	A3	B1
B3	C1	A2

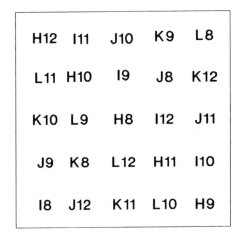

M	S	R	P	O	N
N	M	S	R	P	O
O	N	M	S	R	P
P	O	N	M	S	R
R	P	O	N	M	S
S	R	P	O	N	M

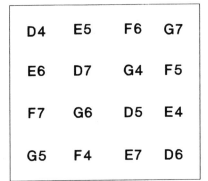

D4	E5	F6	G7
E6	D7	G4	F5
F7	G6	D5	E4
G5	F4	E7	D6

H12	I11	J10	K9	L8
L11	H10	I9	J8	K12
K10	L9	H8	I12	J11
J9	K8	L12	H11	I10
I8	J12	K11	L10	H9

Figure 21.9. Latin squares designs for cross-over group cards. Notice that each column and row could be given a number or letter. This allows two more cross overs without a student meeting the same person twice – a useful way to mix groups.

Should you use smaller or larger groups first? If you want to trawl all the expertise in the class, it pays to have the smaller sized groups first, because smaller groups give a better chance for everyone to contribute. In addition, members more nervous of contributing can gain some confidence after testing their ideas in a smaller group before having to speak in a larger one. The disadvantage this way round is that the second groups start with a lot of reports.

The timing of the cross over depends on your purpose in using the technique. If it is a way of groups reporting their discussion, then obviously you must wait until they have finished their task. But if you want to develop individuals' powers of thought, cross over after knowledge has been trawled, but before any group comes to a conclusion. Theoretically at least, after knowledge has been shared in the second group, every person has the necessary knowledge to do the thinking. Furthermore, by this timing the second groups all finish more or less at the same time, and that makes the class easier to manage.

2. What's the use of cross-over groups?
i) It might be a method of group reporting.
ii) It can be a way, in mixed ability classes, of enabling everyone to do some thinking.
iii) Knowing that they have to report on their first discussion forces every student to concentrate. It's a technique that forces 'social loafers' to pay attention.
iv) Each (silent) student is obliged to 'break the ice' and say something.
v) It can build up relationships in the class. After crossing over once, every student has met two less than two times the square root of the number of students in the class.

But there is no reason why they should only cross over once. If you have a series of tasks, they can cross over any number of times. I use cards of various colours with several styles of numbers and letters so that I can repeatedly mix the groups. When the number of cross over equals the square root of the number of participants, everyone in the class will have met everyone else. (eg. In the class of 25, each participant meets four others in every group. After one cross over they will have met 8. After five cross overs they will have been in 6 groups of 4. Those 24 plus themselves = 25.) This process of building contacts and relationships is particularly important for part-time, evening and short course students, who have little opportunity for extra-curricula contact. It has also been used to advantage with foreign students and other language classes where conversation is to be encouraged.

J. Conclusion – applying the maxim

Dear reader, if you have ploughed through 20 chapters before seeing how the maxim is applied, you have been very patient. Teaching by discussion is like most disciplines. You have to learn quite a bit of theory before you can see how it is applied and why.

Perhaps you can see that the progression I've described starts by using the *norms* of individual work that students acquired at school. It then uses their natural *motives* of *affiliation* – the desire to talk and socialise with each other – to break that norm by encouraging conversation with their neighbour. Conversation is then progressively formalised, establishing new *norms* by modifying one procedure into another. Casual conversation is formalised into dyads; dyads enlarged into buzz groups; buzz groups into horseshoe groups.

You may also have noticed that I have been concerned with establishing a *norm* of another kind – students' expectation that if they come to lectures, they must expect to work. Lectures are not events where they can sit back passively and watch the teacher work. They may be entertained and discussions should be fun; but students must work as well.

By demanding specific work, the teacher's *role* and style at this stage is quite controlling. That implies a very definite social *structure* with the teacher as leader. Yet within it there is a freedom too. The teacher does not control every move within the discussions. Students are free to do the *task* in their own way. Many tasks in employment are managed that way. Teaching is a management profession. Teachers manage learning opportunities. As the complexity and duration of the tasks gradually increases from individual tasks to horseshoe groups, the teacher's control is being slowly and subtly released. We will see in the next two chapters that, even with the teacher's presence, control is slackened until it is minimal in free group discussions and T-groups.

If one person in a horseshoe group is deputed to report on their discussion, there is just the beginning of a *social structure* within the groups we have considered. But with that exception, so far there have been no special *roles and structure* within the groups. Everyone has had the same responsibilities and the use of very small groups has been a means to ensure that they take them. Equality has been assumed.

Of course, the *characteristics of group members* make a difference. Even in dyads (which are intended to minimise these effects), we have had to recognise the effects of *gender* and *dominant personalities*. In the next chapter personalities may express themselves more freely as we develop groups in which members have particular *roles* and responsibilities. Their responsibilities for their own learning also gradually increase as the maxim is progressively implemented.

This progression of *group sizes* uses what we know about motivation. Dyads and buzz groups are quite cosy. The *fear* of talking in a group is reduced to the minimum. Then as friendships, confidence and *language* skills develop, the groups are gradually enlarged.

Notice, too, how *fear* of teachers is gently reduced by gradual acclimatisation to their presence. They are not present in dyads. They may occasionally help a buzz group. And visits to horseshoe groups are slightly more sustained. This trend is continued in Chapter 22; and in Chapter 23 the teacher is present all the time.

In this chapter you will have seen how successive discussion methods roughly correspond to the sequence of *tasks* outlined in Part II. Whilst elements of *creativity*, *decision-making* and *affect* development are applied in buzz groups and horseshoe groups, this chapter has primarily been concerned with the application of Chapters 5 to 8. It is concerned with developing all the skills for solving fairly standard *problems*. Complex decisions and creative tasks are considered further in the next chapter and personal development in Chapter 23.

The classroom *environment*, too, has been gradually evolving. At first individual students are lost in a conventional classroom or auditorium. They are one in a crowd. Gradually the conventional classroom is being changed from rows facing the front. In dyads the students look sideways. In buzz groups some will turn round; they might even move a chair! When we reach horseshoe and cross over groups, the teacher and the teaching methods are beginning to control the learning environment, not the other way round.

The factors at work in discussions are intricate. I hope this summary shows how they all come together in the application of the maxim. It's a moot point how quickly you can move students along this progression. It could take the 'freshers' fortnight or a whole year. That depends on your students, their background and you.

Chapter 22
Tutorless groups with procedures for particular tasks

A. Brainstorming for creative solutions

B. Pyramid decision groups for facing criticism

C. Case discussion for complex decisions

D. Group projects or 'syndicate method'

E. Role plays in rotating triads for observing interpersonal skills

F. Quiet meeting for reflective thought

G. Conclusion

The skills required for the methods in this chapter build upon those learned in the last. It should not be thought that when teachers and students can use these methods, that dyads, buzz groups and so on should no longer be used. Quite the contrary. The intention should be to progressively increase the repertoire of both the teachers and the students and to use and combine the techniques in new and original ways – always providing they serve the students' learning needs. Don't see the progression too rigidly.

A. Brainstorming for creative solutions

Brainstorming is a word that has entered the language since Osborn introduced it in 1953. As so often happens, popular usage has changed its meaning. What is described here is the correct technique, not its popular misrepresentation.

The objectives of brainstorming are to produce creative solutions to problems and/or to produce creative people. There is no doubt that it produces creative solutions to problems, but there is some doubt as to how far it changes people. (Parnes and Meadow, 1959.) Obviously the latter is more difficult to assess. Levels of personal creativity are not something that can change quickly, but brainstorming probably does produce more flexible minds if frequently used.

A brainstorming group usually has 6 to 12 members. So it is a natural development from a horseshoe group. As I said in Chapter 16, a larger group has more resources and potential originality and association of ideas, but in my experience it becomes too large for everyone to be heard before ideas go out of their mind.

The procedure is as follows:

1. Describe the problem that needs a creative solution

Keep the description of the problem as simple as possible. This is not as easy as you might suppose. At least, there is a trap to avoid. The task might be 'Think of all the facilities that should be provided when building a centre for a children's play group'.

Resist giving further details. The students may ask questions that they think are clarifying the task. 'What age groups will attend?' 'How many children is it for?' 'What's the size of the site where it is to be built?' 'Is it in a rural or an urban area?' As soon as you start to answer questions of this kind, you narrow the scope of students' thinking. The aim is the opposite – to make students think as widely as possible and to consider all manner of possibilities.

2. Explain the rules and that brainstorming is fun

There are two important rules, both based upon psychological assumptions.

The first is that participants should be non-judgmental at the first stage of the discussion. This rule is based upon the assumption that many creative ideas will never be voiced in discussion for fear that they may seem ridiculous. It aims to unblock repressed thoughts. In this respect, education has been too successful in developing powers of criticism. If participants suspend their judgement, others will be more likely to express half-formed ideas and to utter thoughts without having to put them in a sentence.

The second rule is that participants should be encouraged to associate ideas freely, so that each idea sparks off another. This is based on the belief that the mind works by association and that new and original thoughts are produced by new and original associations of ideas. That is why stupid suggestions can be very helpful.

Both these rules are concerned with establishing a free and permissive atmosphere. It is advisable to explain their psychological purpose. Brainstorming is great fun when groups enter into the spirit of free association of ideas. The fun can be encouraged by choosing a task, relevant to your subject, but also slightly ridiculous. Perhaps it should have been 'Think of all the facilities that should be provided when building a centre for an Alzheimers' play group'. The slightly odd concept of 'an Alzheimers' play group' would probably produce more creativity than 'an Alzheimers' day centre', yet many of the ideas could well be pertinent.

3. Appoint a scribe

When the creative problem-solving task has been set, the group should appoint a secretary to jot down as fast as he or she can, all the ideas that should come tumbling out into the discussion.

4. Brainstorm discussion
Next there is the brainstorming discussion itself. Typically, the secretary may note down 200 ideas, but the number may vary greatly.

5. Review and highlight potentially useful ideas
When the group can no longer think of any more relevant ideas, the secretary should read out the list of ideas and highlight items that the group thinks are potentially useful. This second stage in the discussion is quite different from the brainstorming session itself. Participants are being more critical and selective. The psychological assumption is that by this time the ideas have become disassociated from the person who mentioned them. Thus there should be no stigma attached to ideas that are rejected. It is the fear of criticism that the brainstorming method aims to eliminate.

6 Work towards solution
Once a selective list of potentially useful ideas has been formed, the group should use them to work towards a solution to the problem. This third phase of discussion is focussed on the practicalities of the problem.

7. Implementation
Once a solution has been agreed, the group will need to work out how it can be implemented.

B. Pyramid decision groups for facing criticism

I am now going to suggest combining the pyramid technique with buzz groups.

1. Invent transition methods as you need them
You may ask, 'Why are you putting it this late in the sequence? Surely you could have introduced it immediately after buzz groups? Both students and teachers would have learned the necessary discussion skills by then'. Yes possibly, but remember the sequence must cater for cognitive development as well as the development of discussion skills. The students may not have had sufficient cognitive development at that stage. It depends what cognitive skills they came with and what you developed with the tasks you gave to buzz groups.

This is an example where we need to invent a transition method. The cognitive skills I am beginning to approach are decision-making tasks of rather more complexity than students have hitherto faced, but they are not as complex as those considered in case discussion.

I don't know the curriculum you teach. Maybe you teach in a medical school. The students have had their heads stuffed with anatomy, biochemistry and the rest. Soon you want to get them one step closer to diagnosis – a decision-making task – or even more complex, to decide what treatment to offer a patient with complications. Perhaps you're a lawyer. You've given plenty of exercises which required simple application of the law, but you want your students to be able to decide the probable outcome of much more subtle and complex cases if they are to be able to advise their clients. Or maybe you teach architecture and in the same way you want your students to be able to synthesise information varying from engineering to aesthetics. If you are a historian, you may want your students to come to a decision after consulting a wide variety of sources. Almost no matter what your discipline, there is a big jump from the tasks given to buzz groups where I emphasised 'give them simple tasks in small groups for short periods of time', to these decision-making tasks requiring considerable synthesis.

Invent transition methods for tasks at an intermediate level of complexity. It's true that horseshoe groups have increased the group size and the size of the tasks and there could have been decision-making tasks amongst them. A particular example is the critical incident task in which members are asked either to identify the cause of an incident (an analytical task) or to decide what ought to be done in the circumstances. But it's still quite a step from there to the decisions taken in case conferences and in joint research projects (syndicate method).

2. A procedure
In this method, first set a decision-making task at a level of difficulty that your students should now be able to achieve. They should write their decision at the top of a sheet of

	A	B	C	D
3 Minutes	Writes short answer	Writes short answer	Writes short answer	Writes short answer
1 Minute	Checks B's answer	Checks A's answer	Checks D's answer	Checks C's answer
4 Minutes	A & B agree and write a common answer		C & D agree and write a common answer	
Merge pairs to form groups of four				
1 Minute	Reads C & D's answer		Reads A & B's answer	
2 Minutes or longer	C and D ask questions about A and B's answer			
2 Minutes or longer	A and B ask questions about A and B's answer			
As long as the teacher thinks necessary	Teacher gets feedback and shows preferred answer, pros and cons			

Figure 22.1. Pyramid decision groups

paper and then list below it first their reasons for it, and second their reservations or reasons against it. After (say) 3 minutes they should meet with a partner and have a minute to read their partner's decision and reasons for it. Then they should write down a joint decision with reasons and reservations. This produces a different kind of discussion from what we saw in pyramid groups or dyads because it requires constructive criticism of their own and their partner's work in some detail. (See Figure 22.1.)

As with pyramid groups, they will join another pair. There are two possibilities: you may have set the same decision task to the second pair or a different one. Either way, each pair criticises the other's decision – constructively, of course. The purpose of the merger is to get a wider perspective. If all four students agree about everything, this aim is not achieved, so the students may need some encouragement to consider the decision from various points of view. There are, of course, many variations on these procedures.

However, I have another important reason for suggesting this method.

3. An important objective – learning to take criticism

Students need to learn to accept criticism of what they say without taking umbrage that it is personal criticism of them. This is a hard lesson to learn. It is to do with emotions. I should like to think that seasoned academics will have learned it long ago, but I don't think that is always true. If the reviews to this book are harshly critical and show me how wrong I am, I must confess I shall feel a little hurt. But I should not. I should be grateful that someone wiser than I has shown a better way. I should be grateful that the students of tomorrow will be better cared for than I have been able to suggest. The students are more important than my ego.

In the same way we should try to help students to value the truth, to value their work as the pursuit of it, and not to feel that they and their contributions are not valued by others. This emotional stability is important if students are to get the best out of discussion methods where their opinions are criticised. That includes nearly all the methods remaining in this chapter and the next.

4. The rationale

The rationale behind this method is similar to what we have already seen. Let students first make up their minds without the instantaneous pressure of having to speak in a group. Let the ideas be tested by only one other person in a reciprocal relationship. Have an opportunity to defend one's opinion, accept the other's, or negotiate a compromise (see section B in Chapter 11, 'Seven responses in discussion', pages 99–101), then let opinions be tested by two more of their peers in a reciprocal relationship.

It is the same kind of strategy for students gradually building confidence in their own opinions and the ability to express them.

C. Case discussion for complex decisions

Case discussion is particularly popular in medicine, management and, increasingly, in economics and education. Groups are given the details of a case, usually requiring a decision. Hence case discussion is usually a decision-making task. The information upon which the decision is to be based may be presented in the form of professional documents, such as case records, or in a descriptive account. In economics there may be tables of figures that need interpretation. The group may need to find out more information by calculation or further enquiry.

1. The objectives of case discussion
Case discussion can be used for one or more of eight objectives.

i) *The analysis of a complex case.* Cases usually require an inter-disciplinary approach. Each individual is implicitly asked to use inter-disciplinary skills. They have to break down all the pigeonholes in their mind. Two kinds of analysis are required. One is to sort out which facts are important and get the issues in proportion. The other is recognising the order in which sub-decisions have to be taken, or the order in which the implementation of a decision must be carried out. This requires the reasoning skills discussed in Chapter 7 – 'If X is the case, then we can do Y; and when Y is finished we can do Z, etc.'

ii) *The use of group members' experience.* If the case is carefully designed, the case discussion method requires individuals to dig into the depth of their knowledge and personal professional experience.

iii) *Selection of evidence.* It is not unusual for groups to be given irrelevant information, from which they must sift what is important. In professional practice, that is the situation.

iv) *Recognition that evidence is missing or required.* Similarly, an important professional skill is to know what you don't know. There is the ability to ask pertinent questions.

v) *Handling information.* A great deal of case discussion is concerned with interpreting and applying available information. This may include the use of statistics on the one hand and empathy on the other.

vi) *Evaluation and judgement.* To interpret and apply information to take decisions requires evaluation and judgement.

vii).*To defend one's judgement against criticism.* It is the defence of one's judgement that makes discussion go deeper.

viii)*To listen open-mindedly.* When group members make different judgements or recommend different decisions, the need to gain consensus will force at least some members to entertain the merits of other people's opinions.

2. Stages in case preparation
The stages in preparation of case discussion and the stages of the discussion itself are similar. Nonetheless, I shall deal with them separately.

i) *Identify the key issue.* It is important that the decision alternatives are evenly balanced, otherwise the group may come to a decision quickly and not consider the issue in depth. For this reason it is quite a good idea for the case writer not to have any preconceived idea of the best decision. That doesn't mean that writers should not decide what the key issue is. Of course they should. I find it is best to have a central issue and then, according to the students' level and the skills I want to teach, I embellish the case with as many or as few complications as required.

ii) *Decide what issue will be presented.* There is a separate question of what problem should be presented to the students. If they are beginners, it will probably be the real problem. Students with better analytical skills should be expected to recognise that in real life the problem presented is often not the real problem. There are underlying issues that need to be sorted out first. Also in real life, one is presented with a situation (as in Figure 11.1) and you have to decide what the key issues are. Case writers must decide which of these three they will present.

iii) *Identify relevant facts.* Case writers need to prepare documents or some other presentation that gives the facts of the case. They will include some facts that are relevant and, particularly with more advanced students, some that are irrelevant to the eventual decision. Inevitably, the presentation will be selective but writers should ask themselves 'Are there facts that a person taking this decision should reasonably be expected to know?' In most cases those facts should be included, where relevant.

Prepare the facts in as realistic a way as possible. For example, if it's a medical decision, submit genuine looking reports and patient's case notes. Encourage participants to play various roles (doctor, nurse, consultant, health visitor, etc.). It's much more fun that way.

iv) *Identify facts and data not known.* From the teacher or case writer's point of view, these facts are of two kinds: those that cannot be known and those that could be given if the students bothered to ask or find out. Both kinds of facts are typical of everyday life. It is our ignorance that gives us uncertainty. It is uncertainty that makes decisions difficult.

v) *List key assumptions about the situation.* These assumptions may well include values. The difficulty with assumptions is that we don't know we are making them. So this task requires some self-awareness by the writer.

vi) *Identify the causes of problems.* This has the effect of bringing out the important factors in a case.

vii) *List possible decisions.*

viii) *Calculate the consequences of alternative decisions.* This process requires using the interpretations and calculations from the information given.

ix) *Modify the case.* If case writers discover that the data is very one-sided and leads to one obvious decision, they may wish to change or omit certain facts or, more commonly, introduce more facts which complicate the decision. Of course, it is not necessary to do this if the educational objectives will have been achieved without it. It is only necessary if quick decisions mean superficial decisions.

Case discussions can take a long time to prepare. There is a danger that learning from the discussion itself will not justify that effort. It is therefore advisable to keep cases short, and have many of them, rather than rely upon the momentum of a single case to teach a large number of different skills. Using many short cases also has the advantages of building from the simple to the complex and of giving repeated practice at basic skills in many and varied situations.

3. Stages in case discussion

To ensure an efficient use of time, it is best to teach students these nine stages in holding a case discussion. Note that the teacher may or may not be present during case discussion. Very likely, teachers will visit their groups for longer periods than with horseshoe groups, but not intervene very much and not be present all the time. It is therefore possible to run three, perhaps four, case discussion groups at the same time; but five does not leave sufficient visiting time.

i) *Teacher presents the information according to (ii) above.* I find it best to run case studies as if they were simulations. That is to say, I suggest they should regard themselves as a committee, a research team, a multi-disciplinary case conference, or whatever is appropriate. State the time available.

ii) *Group identifies the key issue(s).*

iii) *Identify relevant facts.* Students should ask themselves 'Which facts are most relevant?' They may also need to ask themselves about their values. What would be their own priorities in this case? What should be their goals in that case? The case writer may have presented the objectives of a company, but in many cases, the values may not be explicit. In a medical case, the health of the patient will be assumed. In other cases, the values may be ambiguous. So, indeed, may the facts, and there is no reason why the case writer should not present the facts in an ambiguous way. Cases in real life are like that. Uncertainty is an important element in the psychology of decision-making (see Chapter 10).

iv) *Identify facts and data not known.* The teacher can play the role of a further source of information, or even simulate a visiting professional consultant available to be called upon by the groups. As indicated in (iv) above, there will be some information consultants can provide and some they cannot.

v) *List key assumptions about the situation.* These assumptions may well include the values mentioned in (iii) above. Periods of reflection in the middle of case discussion may be valuable to uncover assumptions and to foster self-awareness of them.

vi) *Identify the causes of problems.* This is a useful step. As when writing the case, it has the effect of revealing the important factors in a case.

vii) *List possible decisions.* Again, both the case writer and the students may undertake this stage. The decisions will probably depend upon different interpretations of the facts, or different predictions based upon them. These predictions will be based upon analyses and predictions based upon the given data. Many cases will require knowledge and imagination to decide what calculations and interpretations are appropriate. Consequently, case discussion requires mastery of one's subject.

viii) *Calculate the consequences of alternative decisions.* Depending on the subject, this may involve statistics, the use of computers or other equipment and data.

ix) *Weigh and decide.* The students will need to weigh the evidence and agree upon their decision. They should agree by consensus, not by a vote. It is the discussion for consensus that teaches criticism, depth of enquiry and appreciation of other students' views. The teacher should be careful not to come to a decision too soon. Indeed, it is usually better not to commit oneself to one point of view at all, lest a bias is injected in the presentation of the case.

x) *Plan implementation.* For the case writer, preparation often stops at stage (viii). For the student, case discussion often stops at stage (ix). However, the discussion can be taken a stage further, to plan how the decision would be implemented. This stage may be particularly important in medicine and management. The product at this stage is therefore a series of steps.

4. Conclusion

Notice that to use case discussion, students will need to have matured considerably since their first buzz group, but that is not to say that students experienced in group work will not continue to use buzz groups. They should. Development in group work involves continually adding to one's repertoire of skills, not discarding easier and earlier ones.

Case discussions can take a long time to prepare. There is a danger that learning from the discussion itself will not justify that effort. It is therefore advisable to keep cases short, and have many of them, rather than rely upon the momentum of a single case to teach a large number of different skills. The discussions could take anything from 5 minutes to half a year, but for most cases it is best to allow 20 to 40 minutes with 10 to 20 minutes follow-up plenary discussions with the teacher.

D. Group projects or 'syndicate method'

Syndicate groups typically consist of 5 or 6 students engaged upon a joint project to *agree* a report with specific conclusions or recommendations. Agreement is imperative. If the some members cannot agree, they should write a minority report. It is possible for a teacher to manage five such groups, but no more. Give each group a different project.

1. Choosing a topic

The sizes of tasks given to syndicates and case discussions are similar and equally wide ranging. They are bigger than those given to horseshoe groups. I sometimes compare a syndicate group to a miniature 'commission of enquiry' because the project requires specific conclusions or recommendations based upon a variety of specialist knowledge. Accordingly it is an inter-disciplinary task.

'Make recommendations as to whether there should be a Bloggsbridge bypass, and if so what route it should take.' This kind of task requires students to turn their minds to several specialist fields of knowledge – calculating present and future traffic flows, surveying geological conditions, estimating costs of land purchase and road construction, considering commercial and social consequences for local citizens, and so on.

Provided the obligation to make recommendations or specific conclusions is clear, you can set up syndicate groups with general titles like 'The treatment of Crohn's disease' or 'The qualities of Jane Austen as a novelist'. Alternatively you can narrow the group's options a bit by posing the topic as a problem such as 'What were the consequences of the Cold War?' I recommend the latter at first, so that the students learn to focus on a problem. Some teachers leave the topic wide open for the students' choice, but in my experience students tend to choose topics that are unmanageably wide or inadequately resourced. Then at the start, the teacher has to visit every group at once to persuade them to be more realistic.

2. The objectives of syndicate method

The objectives achieved by these groups are very relevant to employment:

i) *To foster an inter-disciplinary approach to decisions and problem-solving.*

ii) *To harness the potential of each individual student.* The best groups are those where students have varied experience and expertise so that each has something unique to contribute.

iii) *To be able to work as a team.* Because the students have to work together, the vocational relevance of this objective hardly needs elaboration. With a large and wide-ranging subject, the groups usually subdivide the tasks and each student will go away and find out what they can that is relevant. This achieves three inter-related objectives:

iv) *The ability to find information* by the use of study and library skills.

v) *To develop powers of relevance.*

vi) *To introduce students to research techniques.* This objective is important. Too often, the first time students face the need for research techniques is when they have to do a large-scale dissertation. Research skills too need to be learned gradually, starting with small tasks and gradually increasing their size.

vii) *To generate motivation.* The syndicate method can be very motivating, particularly with mature students. It uses their experience and their independence. Because younger students have less of both, they require more careful handling by the teacher.

3. Typical procedure

Typically syndicate method has several stages.

i) *Planning the procedure.* First there is usually a brief stage in which group members discuss the topic with reference to the tasks necessary to carry out the project.

ii) *Allocating sub-tasks.* The first stage usually passes quite quickly to allocation or choice of tasks. In other words, each student takes on a specific role. Some will go to the library, others will conduct an experiment, a couple may do some fieldwork, one will search the Internet, and so on. They need to agree when they will come together again. I usually put a lot of relevant resources on my table at the front, including a selection of library books.

iii) *Discuss, form and integrate recommendations.* If the method is not carefully handled, it has a serious weakness at this stage. When students have gathered their information, there is a temptation for them to write the final drafts of their report too soon, rather than to report back to the group for intense critical discussion. The report of a commission should be agreed by every one of its members. So should the report of a syndicate group. It is better to have a short report intensively discussed with agreed conclusions and recommendations than a lengthy document presenting a great deal of collected information about which there has been little thought or criticism.

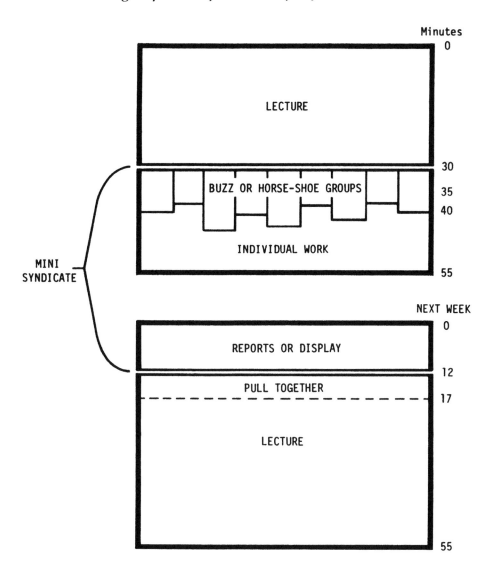

Figure 22.2. Technique to introduce syndicate work to students gradually

Thus the teacher should make it crystal clear that any student in the group should be able to justify *any single sentence* in the report. Passive acceptance should be discouraged. When teachers circulate amongst the groups, (now for rather longer periods of time than with the horseshoe groups), they should challenge group members to make these justifications. If the teacher does not achieve this, the method can waste a lot of time on relatively low level objectives.

For this reason, the method is often best introduced on a very small scale at first.

Give a mini-project at one meeting to be displayed or reported the following week (see Figure 22.2). This requires students to work together outside the classroom. It therefore encourages the teamwork that is so crucial. It is wise for the teacher to check the feasibility of outside meetings when the groups are first established.

4. Write preliminary drafts
The next stage is to write drafts to be subjected to intense discussion by the rest of the group. Notice, as I discussed earlier, this requires group members to have sufficient maturity not to think that criticism of what they have written is criticism of them personally. The value of a student and the ideas he has expressed should be sharply distinguished.

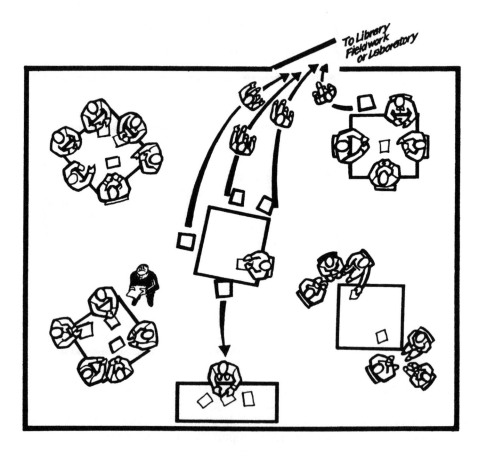

Figure 22.3. Representation of the syndicate method. Note that the students plan how they will work. One group is out gathering data. (The tutor has put some on his desk.) Another group has split into two teams. Another has sent one member on an errand. The tutor is quizzing a group to justify what they have written.

5. Final editing

Finally, the report is edited jointly by the whole group. Sometimes it is a good idea for the 'report' to be a visual display. In this case we have what I call a 'museum session' during which the class goes round looking at what other groups have produced. Alternatively there can be a period in which each group presents its report orally. If this course is adopted, keep the oral reports brief. This can be done if the presentations are confined to the recommendations or specific conclusions followed by questions eliciting justification for them.

6. Conclusion

When the syndicate method is successful, it is very rewarding for everyone including the teacher. When it fails, it is a disaster. So it is not a method for taking big risks. It works best with mature and professional students including part-time ones. To begin, run it on a small scale and abide by the maxim, *Start with simple tasks in small groups for short periods of time, and then gradually increase their respective complexity, size and duration.* With joint projects, there can be injustice in awarding the same grade to all group members when there are 'social loafers'. One way over this is to let each student be assessed by his peers (perhaps with the teacher giving a tentative average). If so, students would need to be told so at the beginning.

E. Role plays in rotating triads for observing interpersonal skills

The emphasis in this book is upon the development of students' thinking. I have not said a lot about the development of affect, perceptual skills or behavioural skills. They make up interpersonal skills. James Kilty's excellent book on this topic deals with these more thoroughly. His approach is more experiential and covers methods such as role-plays, simulations, games and socio-dramas. He also accepts the need for a developmental sequence of teaching methods.

1. Why this method fits here or earlier

So how does his sequence fit into mine, or doesn't it? I claim that it fits in, and branches off, here, and that the same maxim applies: *Start with simple tasks in small groups for short periods of time, and then gradually increase their respective complexity, size and duration.*

The reasons for the maxim are the same but even more powerful. Many people are intensely afraid of role playing at first. Interpersonal skills, of their nature, are more personal than cognitive ones.

So why begin with triads? A triad is the smallest and most intimate group for developing self-awareness for skills that are so personal.

There is another reason for introducing this method no later than at this point. (It might be introduced earlier.) In this method students are beginning to be faced with their own feelings more directly than hitherto. They need to deal with their fears of 'going public' before they enter larger groups with the continuous presence of the teacher.

2. A common procedure

i) *Forming the triads.* The class divides into triads and moves to positions where their conversation will not disturb others, and arranges furniture. In a typical role play in a rotating triad, two members interact and the third person is an observer who will sit a little apart from the others.

ii) *Setting the task.* The task for two members might be to role play an interview, a negotiation, a conflict, making a request, consoling the bereaved, or any of a thousand other possibilities depending on the attitude, perception or behaviour being developed and all the standard tasks anyone in their profession should be expected to perform. Leave the task open to some interpretation so that role players display themselves.The observers may be tasked to look for particular interpersonal attitudes, perceptions and behaviours or more generally. By observing, they are themselves developing their powers of perception.

iii) *Evaluation and feedback.* Afterwards, the role players (out of role) are first asked to reflect upon their experience. The observers will then report on their observations, all such evaluations being discussed by the triad.

iv) *Rotate and repeat.* After that members of the triads take a different role, normally within a repeat of the same exercise. Then roles rotate again so that everyone has played each role, has observed, and has been observed with feedback.

v) *Class debriefing.* Thereafter, the teacher will debrief the whole exercise, not in triads, but in a plenary session. It is important to give time for everyone to reflect upon their experiences in order to be fully aware of them and to learn from them.

F. Quiet meetings for reflective thought

1. Procedure

A quiet meeting can last from 3 to 60 minutes, but in education it is usually nearer 3. Ideally, ask participants to sit in a circle so that all members can see everyone else. In practice I usually use the method at the end of a lesson and students don't move the chairs very much from where they happen to be. Typically, I use it at the end of a workshop or some other activity, but it is also very useful at the end of a formal lecture.

My instructions may be something like this: 'I should like us to finish by sitting quietly for a bit. Think over what you have learned this morning. Think what was good about it; then what was not so good. Consider your feelings about this morning's work. Plan how you might follow it up. I call this method 'a quiet meeting' and I finish it by shaking hands. Very often the most beneficial meetings are those when no one speaks and our thoughts are uninterrupted. But if you want to share any thought or concern, please do so. Otherwise let us reflect in silence upon what we have learned, relate it to other parts of the course, and perhaps take our thoughts a little further. Please don't speak immediately after someone else has spoken. Leave ample time for others to appreciate and reflect upon it first.'

When you finish and shake hands with your neighbour, don't speak straight away.

Let others reach a convenient point in their reflections. The quiet rustle of clothing when changing posture will also communicate that the meeting has closed. Very often the shaking hands becomes general and that is heart warming.

If students say anything, they should not expect a reply. The temptation to argue or justify oneself should be resisted (particularly by the teacher). With some students this will need to be explained too. The quiet meeting is not a conversation or a discussion in the usual sense. It is a period of constructive critical reflection. The ethos should be constructive and empathic, a search for truths and reconciliations. It is an opportunity for one's thought to take a journey, to try roads that get nowhere, as well as a journey of maturation.

Very often students look over their notes and add personal comments. They focus on issues that are personal to them. This may result in them forming new goals and in seeing the subject matter or the course in a new light. Students who use a quiet meeting to review the whole course are more likely to get an overall view of the subject.

I also use this method at the beginning of a day during intensive courses and workshops. It not only gives an opportunity for the students to think over yesterday's activity, but it prepares their minds for the activity to come. It has a reorienting role.

2. The purpose of quiet meetings
The psychological objectives of a quiet meeting are:

i) *To promote cool reflection and profound thought*. A quiet meeting is an opportunity to clarify one's thoughts, to recognise inconsistencies, to relate one person's comment to another's, or one part of the course with another, to take decisions, and to originate new thoughts or courses of action. Insofar as the quiet meeting offers a period without interruption, it provides an opportunity to follow one's thought through to a natural conclusion, with only a little extra stimulation. It also provides an opportunity for constructive comment on issues under discussion, rather than initial superficial reactions.

ii) *To express concerns.* There are many things that can undermine the success of a workshop or course, particularly when they are intense. One person may have a personal anxiety that interferes with his learning and his relationships with other group members. A course without a quiet meeting provides no opportunity to express these concerns, to obtain the understanding and support of the group. Another student might choose to express his inability to understand something, another might express an appreciation or a criticism of some part of the course. Sometimes a student uses the quiet meeting to make a public apology. To express these things takes courage, but they also earn the warmth of the group, and build its harmony.

When working intensively with police officers, they sometimes used the morning meeting to make 'public' apologies, confessions or expressions of feeling that they had been mulling over since the day before. These were accepted with empathy and set a constructive tone to the day's group work.

iii) *Fellowship.* It can be seen from the last point that the regular use of a quiet meeting can gradually develop harmony and fellowship amongst a group. This is very important when the learning objectives are to do with inter-personal and perceptual skills.

iv) *'To cool it'*. A quiet meeting can also be used to promote calm reflection when a group is highly emotional. For example, if some group members are extremely angry or even hostile to each other, after these feelings have been expressed in the ordinary course of discussion, the teacher may move that the group has a quiet meeting for reflection. If sufficient time has been allowed for the feelings to emerge, the quiet meeting will give an opportunity for members to look at themselves as well as others.

These objectives suggest that the purposes of a quiet meeting are mostly to do with emotions. They can be, but in my experience that is not usually the case. The most important objective is (i), which is primarily to do with the promotion of thought.

It will be evident that the quiet meeting makes unusual demands upon group members. They normally need to be previously acquainted. To get the best out of it, the method requires considerable maturity, but children can learn to use it. Lives in Western societies are full of noise and bustle. Some people cannot tolerate silence and that adjustment may have to be learned. The method requires considerable self-discipline and a suitable physical setting.

G. Conclusion

This chapter has seen a progression towards the skills needed for group tutorials including the free group discussions and seminars that we will meet in the next chapter.

At the end of Chapter 21 we had developed students to be well practised with problems such as I considered in Chapter 8. In this chapter students' cognitive skills have been developed further to include creativity (brainstorming), decision-making (case discussion) and the beginning of some research skills (syndicate method). These skills are necessary for writing a good introduction for a seminar. The tasks produce contrasting styles of discussion each with different norms.

The length of time that the teachers have spent in student discussion groups has gradually increased. The intention has been to gradually decrease the fear of speaking in the teacher's presence that is experienced by some silent students.

In the final chapter, I consider methods in which the teacher is present all the time. So far, teachers' interventions have been minimal, but in the syndicate method the teacher has to be quite insistent that the final reports are jointly agreed. At this stage of the syndicate method the teacher is quite controlling about the content of discussion. Hitherto tutorless discussions have been quite free in this respect. The teacher has controlled procedure and the goal, but not how the content was managed to achieve the goal.

This chapter describes methods that gradually increase the demand for students to defend their point of view. Discussions considered in Chapter 21 were generally co-operative, but we must anticipate that strong differences of opinion will arise in group tutorials considered in Chapter 23. These could undo the growing confidence of the initially silent student. The methods in this chapter ease the transition from co-operation to defence against academic criticism. Brainstorming invites original opinions without the obligation to defend them. In case discussion and pyramid decision groups, students need to say why they agree or disagree with a decision. In syndicates, they must defend every word they have written and argue about what others have written. In the rotating role plays they will receive, and have little option but to accept, judgements and observations about their personal behaviour.

Unlike Chapter 21, the groups in this chapter involve students taking specific roles. Personal characteristics have freer rein. Leadership and other group structures emerge more strongly.

Apart from the quiet meeting and brainstorming, the size of the groups has not increased over horseshoe groups. The overall class size has decreased. I should regard 30 as the maximum class size to be sub-divided using the methods described in this chapter if they are to be managed by only one teacher. There still tends to be a world-wide norm that only one teacher manages a class at once. The convention is wholly unnecessary, restrictive and unimaginative. If you have never done so, try teaching with a colleague. It is far more stimulating, rewarding and less pressured. In the next chapter, the class size will be smaller still.

Chapter 23
Tutor participation in discussion

A. What to do before a group tutorial

B. Techniques and skills during a group tutorial

C. Subject-centred group tutorials

D. Seminars

E. Free group discussion (FGD)

F. Individual and personal tutorials

G. T-groups, sensitivity groups, and encounter groups

H. Conclusion to the book as a whole

Any teaching method involves learning a large number of techniques and skills. A technique is a smaller unit of activity than a method. The methods considered in this chapter differ in that they combine techniques and skills in different ways, nonetheless, many of the techniques are the same. Similarly, a skill is a smaller unit of performance than a technique. Several skills may be necessary for any particular technique.

Perhaps controversially, I regard subject-centred tutorials, the seminar method, free group discussion and T-Groups all as different kinds of group tutorial. Although their objectives are different, they have a family resemblance in that the teacher uses many of the same techniques and skills in each, but in different proportions. Therefore the first question I must answer is 'What are these techniques and skills that are used in differing amounts in these various methods?' Sections A and B in this chapter describe a selection of these. I don't pretend it could be a complete list. The remaining sections give the common objectives of each method and some of their specific procedures and techniques.

One reason why I hold this controversial view is itself a matter of techniques and skills. Professional and perceptive teachers vary techniques according to the needs of the class. When there is an emotional need they will use more of the skills associated with FGD. When patterns of thought need to be developed, the skills of the subject-centred tutorial will be more in evidence. Hence in practice, whatever the definitions, there is no sharp division between the methods. The skilful teacher subtly blends into one from another as the needs arise.

A. What to do before a group tutorial

1. Say what you want your students to be able to do

The first question for teachers to consider is 'What are my objectives?' These are broadly classified in Part I. The decision must take account of enquiries into what the students want and need. In the light of that decision, teachers can decide whether a presentation method, discussion, a more active method or some combination of these is the most appropriate. So teachers' second decision is about the broad class of teaching method, not necessarily a specific one. (See Part I.) They then need to identify the precise task that will practise skills they want their students to learn. (See Part II.) In the context of this book I am assuming that the task will involve some thought, or thought combined with self-awareness, attitude change or the development of interpersonal skills.

2. Consider feasibility in terms of the likely group dynamics

In choosing the precise teaching method to facilitate students in developing the chosen abilities, the teacher will need to do a feasibility check. This requires criticism and imagination – two activities that sometimes don't go together. Part III and Part IV this far provide the feasibility check. It consists of asking oneself questions such as:

- 'Will the students be motivated to accomplish the task?' (Chapter 12)
- 'How many students are there?' (Chapter 16)
- 'What are the characteristics of group members that will affect task performance?', 'Are there "silent students", over-talkative ones, or others who need particular help?' (Chapter 15)
- 'Are there leaders in the group and if so are they task or socio-emotional leaders?', 'Are there other roles and relationships of which I should be aware?' (Chapter 17)
- 'What is the past experience of the group? How will it influence what they do?' (Chapter 18)
- 'What norms and expectations do they have resulting from that experience?' (Chapter 14)
- 'How can the physical arrangements of the room be arranged to best advantage?' (Chapter 19) and so on.

When considering the past experiences of group members, it is worth looking up their personal file and keeping a record of things that interest you for yourself. You may have to write a reference for them later, so it's not time wasted. What is their previous academic performance? What school did they go to? What jobs did they have before going to college? What are their interests and can they be related to what you teach?

Learn their names and how to spell them. Then you don't have to learn them when they come. You only have to learn to associate the face with the name.

3. Check the feasibility of the task(s)

In particular the teacher needs to analyse the task from the students' point of view.
- ○ 'What sub-tasks does it contain?' (Part II and Chapter 13)
- ○ 'What prerequisite knowledge and intellectual skills do they assume?'
- ○ 'Can the students be expected to have that knowledge and those skills?'
- ○ 'How might the task affect the group dynamics?' (Chapter 13)

Although it is now fashionable to be dismissive of Bloom's Taxonomy of Educational Objectives (1956), I still find it a useful checklist.
- ● 'Does the task require simple understanding – the ability to relate two ideas together and draw a conclusion?' (Chapter 7)
- ● 'Does it involve knowledge of a generalisation, or principle, and its application to a particular instance?' (Chapter 8)
- ● 'Does it require analysis of a proposition, situation or set of circumstances?' (Chapter 8)
- ● 'Is it necessary to relate a large number of facts (synthesis)?' (Chapters 9 and 10)
- ● 'Is evaluation or judgement required, and if so, what values and principles have to be applied?' (Chapters 10 and 11)

Having chosen the precise task and the method by which students will accomplish it, the teacher will need to visit the room in order to conceive how to arrange the physical environment. The physical arrangement of furniture is a major decision on which the teacher should spend some time during preparation. (I sometimes spend up to half my preparation time planning the sequence of movements of furniture for a class.) Yet it is not uncommon for visiting teachers to be given a room they have never seen before, and for full-time teachers to be allocated rooms where the furniture cannot be moved, or where the janitors control its arrangement. It is small wonder teachers resort to didactic methods. Notice that while most teachers assume that furniture is never moved during a period of teaching, I make the opposite assumption. Furniture can and ought to be moved to create new learning environments as required. Students soon learn to assist when they know the teaching methods and appreciate the reasons for them. I prepare overhead transparencies to show them what is needed and this reduces moving time (normally less than one minute).

Some of the points to be checked when inspecting a room may seem very obvious, even banal, but they are often overlooked so that teaching does not proceed as smoothly as it might. They include seeing what blackboard, screen and other facilities are available; setting up, operating and focusing projection facilities; and knowing where light switches and electric power points are, and how to operate room blackout if it will be required. When checking the furniture, make sure the room arrangement can hold the number of students expected when using the various discussion methods planned.

4. *The informal welcome*

Particularly at the first meeting, teachers should be there to welcome participants. More than any other time, it is the time when the norms of the group are set. It is an opportunity for teachers to show personal respect for students and to create an atmosphere of mutual support and co-operation.

Not everyone will arrive at the same time. Therefore teachers need to decide what they want early arrivals to experience before they begin more formally. Adjustment to a group is easier if members have something to do such as drinking coffee, completing a form, or engaging in small talk. Much will depend on the circumstances. It may be an opportunity to get to know participants at a more individual level than is possible when the whole group has arrived. In other circumstances participants may want to review in silence the work they have prepared. It may be a time when participants can raise matters with the teacher semi-privately. There could be many uses for this short period of time.

In addition to the physical environment, other factors influencing the group's behaviour will have been determined before members arrive, in particular the group size, members' personalities and backgrounds, and their past experiences of this group or others. It might be helpful to acknowledge these experiences so that the group is more open. When group members already know each other, some aspects of group structure will also be established. These few minutes may be an opportunity to relate to, support, and privately raise the self-esteem of less dominant members.

Regarding their motivation, one participant may arrive with some anxieties, another with ambitions. The first may seek friendship, the other achievement. How openly does the teacher want these expressed and how should they be handled? When we consider that responses to issues such as these may require split second decisions, the extreme subtlety of small group teaching becomes evident. Yet it is often given to beginners as if group teaching is an easy option!

Many norms are set at this time. For example, with what style will participants' names be introduced? Names can influence the group's social climate. Conformity is usually quite strong at the beginning, but to what does the teacher want them to conform?

People who are new to a group normally look for clues as to how they are to behave. These are the norms. The physical set-up, the teacher's behaviour and other participants' behaviour will all be influential. Are other participants seated or standing? Isolated or in groups? Smoking or refraining? Reading preliminary material or with nothing to do? Do they speak with hushed tones or riotous laughter? All these things, and more, give signals to new arrivals about the norms and social climate of the group. They are influenced by the teacher's behaviour and strongly influence what can be achieved later.

5. *The opening*

Compare an introduction in which the teacher defines the group's goal, key concepts in the task, the criteria for exam success and so on, with one who seeks consensus on how the group should proceed. One sees himself as a task leader; the other as a socio-emotional leader. Which will contribute most to achieving the goal efficiently and which to maintaining group processes? (That's a trick question. In the long-run, the socio-emotional leader is better at both. Did you fall into the trap?)

The formal leader may begin with a statement of the purposes of the meeting, his own name and official position, the objectives of this particular meeting and how it fits into a wider context of objectives. He may then outline what is going to happen at this meeting, or indeed later. A formal introduction of this kind outlines tasks, sets norms, limits the range of motives that are evoked and sets up a group structure and a controlling leadership style. If the style is brisk, it may have the effect of setting a businesslike tone.

For my taste, it is far too formal. It could destroy trust, create tension and could silence the 'silent student' for ever. It would make FGD, T-Groups and personal tutorials ineffective, if not impossible. It is almost a message saying, 'I don't want to know you personally'.

Alternative introductions will also affect these things, but, of course, differently. Compare a formal introduction with a practical activity, such as jotting down answers to a question, or even completing a very short questionnaire on one side of a sheet of paper, to form the basis of a discussion.

Another possibility is to start with a discussion, either in pyramid groups, buzz groups, or, if the group is small enough, in a plenary session. Some leaders ask members to introduce themselves going round the circle in turn. There is psychological evidence that once the group is larger than 6 to 10 members (that is 7 ± 2 plus yourself), names presented by this method will forgotten. Members will feel embarrassed that they should have remembered. Embarrassment is just the opposite of what the leaders intend. So either don't use this methods with larger groups, or point out the difficulty and encourage members to jot down the names in roughly a circle like a clockface (or whatever the shape of the group is) with themselves at 6 o'clock. In this way those to the right or left of them in the group are to the right or left on the clockface.

When new participants introduce and describe themselves, they tend to give only factual information about their past, their job, their status and so on. But getting to know someone involves knowing their anxieties, enthusiasms, attitudes and dislikes. These things they tend not to mention. They are about their values, motives and feelings – 'affect'. It is therefore necessary to guide their self-report with tasks such as saying why they came on the course, what they want to get from the discussions, or other contributions indicating their affective qualities.

B. Techniques and skills during a group tutorial

1. Listening skills
This section overlaps with what I said in Chapter 5 except that here I am concerned with listening by the tutor rather than the students.

i) Elements of listening.
Barker et al (1971) says listening has four elements: hearing, attending, understanding and remembering.

Hearing is here regarded as a non-selective physiological process. I considered it very briefly at the beginning of Chapter 5. It is influenced by physical factors such as background noise and fatigue.

Attention is necessarily selective. It is active and psychological. This activity is demonstrated by non-verbal behaviour such as eye contact and a forward posture. But it is more than that. It includes an effort to understand. That is, to obtain meanings from the sounds that are heard. In small group discussion there is social pressure upon students to pay attention, because they know they are more likely than in some other situations to have to respond. The smaller the group, the higher the probability. As we saw in Chapter 21, in dyads it is certain that they must respond and no one else. For that reason, when fatigue begins it is a good idea for the tutor to break up the group and give a task to dyads. (Resist the expected norm that tutorial groups can never be split into sub-groups.)

Understanding involves interpretation of what is heard. It requires several skills that have to be learned: recognition of the logical and grammatical rules being used by the sender, some knowledge of the sender and the social context of the message, and an ability to relate the information so obtained to ideas the receiver already possesses. An important selective listening skill is to identify the sender's key points and then look for supporting evidence – both that which speakers give and that which they do not. To present the omitted supporting evidence early in one's response assists empathy.

Short-term remembering. A response is not part of listening (as Barker et al, 1987, claim), but it is evidence of having listened and remembered. An appropriate response usually shows that the receiver has heard, paid attention, understood and remembered what was said. So to know that someone has listened, he must have remembered what he understood at least long enough to respond. For example, counsellors are sometimes taught to *paraphrase* what their clients say, partly to maintain attention and to demonstrate that they are attending, and partly so that the client can correct them if their interpretations are inaccurate. The latter is known as *'reflecting back'* (see later). The latter is also achieved by *'perceptual checking'*, a skill in which the tutors check their understanding by responses like, 'What I understand you to be saying is ...' Another skill that has the same effect is to *relate* two or more things that the students have said. I shall return to these three response skills – paraphrasing, perceptual checking and relating – later.

ii) Reasons why some tutors listen badly.

'Message underload' because tutors are so familiar with their subject, their brains have spare capacity. The topic at the students' level has no novelty and appears boring.

Mind wandering onto the tutor's personal concerns rather than the students'.

Over-familiarity with a topic can result in believing that the sender makes the same assumptions.

A common problem is that tutors *do not respect their students* sufficiently to pay close attention to what they say.

iii) Consequent bad listening habits.

'Pseudolistening'. Tutors nod but don't give students their full attention.

Insensitive listening. Tutors fail to interpret feelings and non-verbal communications because they are not vigilant. Sensitive listening is an art. It needs constant practice and no one ever reaches perfection.

Interrupting. Some tutors talk, but don't listen because they are too busy thinking of what they are going to say next. This is a particular fault in a group tutorial when tutors chip in before students have finished speaking. This happens when tutors think they know what the student is going to say, when the tutor's mind works quicker than the student's speech, when teachers unconsciously feel they have less control as students are speaking, and when tutors think that what they have to say is more valuable than their students' contributions. It shows disrespect for the students.

Selective listening is misapplied when tutors only listen to bright students, to what they want to hear, or to what interests them at the time.

'Ambushing' in order to attack what is said is common in the cut and thrust of academic debate. It is unconstructive and inconsiderate at any level. We have seen that co-operation is better than competition to foster learning. And tutors ambushing students is unfair competition.

Mistaken self-concept. Unfortunately, teachers are often worse listeners than their students when they see their job as giving, not receiving. Unlike tutors, students have more to lose if they don't listen. Teachers should try to learn from their students.

2. Orienting skills

Orienting skills try to make the group pay attention to a particular issue or topic. There are four of them, but they differ in degree rather than being sharply distinct. They can be placed on a continuum from being directive to non-directive.

When considering these four techniques, the teacher needs to bear two questions in mind:

- How can I build the students' learning upon concepts, knowledge and skills they already have? and
- How can I develop the students' self-esteem?

i) *Redirecting.* At the most directive end of the continuum, the teacher or leader might say, 'I want us now to leave that topic and consider the question of … ' Such a statement exhibits a very controlling style, expressed in terms of what the teacher wants, not in terms of what the students need. While some groups may welcome and expect a directive style, others would require this statement to be softened by an explanation of why one topic is now being rejected and why it is desirable to consider another. It is always important to give reasons when being directive with adult groups. The explanation would be more persuasive if the reasons are expressed in terms of the students' needs.

ii) *Invitation to consider.* A softer approach is to ask the group whether they would like to consider a second topic. The fundamental difference from redirecting is that the wishes of the group are being consulted and acted upon, rather than the wishes of the leader. Notice that this approach involves a shift from attending to a task, or a topic, to discussion of the group's own processes. The shift may be transitory and brief, but it is nonetheless a significant feature of teaching technique. McKeachie (1978) drew attention to research showing that groups that spend longer considering their own processes learn and achieve more than groups that never do anything but attend to their task. This only seems paradoxical if learning is conceived as something purely cognitive, rather than something that is also emotional. Groups work better if they are motivated and co-operative than if they are treated as cognitive machines. Groups achieve by working together. They develop this cohesiveness by openly discussing and working at the process of how to work together. This includes making the process visible. T-Groups in particular are designed for this purpose.

iii) *Focusing.* The technique of focusing is to take a point that a participant has raised and draw the group's attention to it. This technique has a number of advantages and it is crucial to making a discussion run smoothly.

Firstly, by focusing on something a participant has said, the discussion flows smoothly without a sharp break. It is not a sharp shift from one topic to another.

Secondly, the discussion uses a conception held by one of the participants, rather than imposing a perspective held by the teacher. This ensures that the continuing discussion is in terms understood by at least one participant, and presumably more if his point was understood when he made it. So it is a technique that builds new learning upon concepts participants already have. It makes learning a process of development, not injection.

It is also a technique that leaves the previous contributor explaining or defending what he said. In this way the teacher is able to move the discussion on without dominating it. The contributor takes ownership of his contribution and has to be involved with what follows.

Finally, by accepting a point raised by a participant, the teacher is valuing what the participant has said. This tends to be associated with valuing the participant as well. Even if the teacher has focused on the point in order to correct it, it is done in such a way as to be respectful to the individual.

iv) *Open questions.* An open question is one that has many possible answers. Those who respond select from many possibilities. If the discussion then focuses on the answer participants have selected, the reorientation of the discussion has, within the bounds of the question, been chosen by the participants. The more closed the question, the more restrictive its bounds, but even the most open question is restrictive to some extent. Open questions have some of the same advantages as focusing in that they produce discussions developing a framework of understanding possessed by participants. Rather than ideas neatly pigeon-holed and sparsely related, it thereby integrates new ideas with their previous knowledge.

Some teachers use open questions in a closed way. They don't accept the answers that come until they get the one they want, and then they focus upon it. This 'guess what I'm thinking' approach may encourage students to undertake a mental search, but otherwise it is convergent. I don't recommend it. If early respondents feel rejected, there will be a motivational turn-off. Consequently acceptance of the merits of responses is crucial. When the answers are plain wrong that may seem difficult. That necessitates focusing on them at least briefly, before, in effect, re-posing the question again. The brief focusing has two aspects. The first is to empathise with the way the participant was thinking, and then to select what was good about it.

In describing these techniques I have assumed that the reorientation is by the teacher or discussion leader if there is one. This is an over-simplification. Not only may any participant use any of these four techniques, but insofar as discussion consists of responding to the previous contributor, it consists of focusing on a point made by that contributor. Discussion is a process of focusing and constantly re-focusing. It is by re-focusing that participants learn new perspectives.

3. *Reflecting back*

i) *Reflecting feelings and experiences.* Where the leader's purpose is to encourage participants to express their perceptions, thoughts and feelings there is a problem. We have seen that any listener needs to show that they are hearing, attending, understanding and remembering. This is communicated by making a response. Yet we have now seen that any response will have an element of reorientation. In that case there is a danger that the agenda will shift to the leader's concerns, not those of other participants. If, on the other hand, the leader makes no response at all, he will be perceived as uninterested.

This problem arises in any non-directive teaching method such as free group discussion, counselling, mediation and T-Groups, but the technique to deal with it may be used in any discussion.

Carl Rogers' (1951) solution in counselling was to say back to his client what he or she had said to him. He called this 'reflecting' and I shall use that term as distinct from 'reflection', a process of inner thought.

Reflecting has many of the same features as focusing. It is selective (and admittedly in this respect it is consciously agenda setting). But it stays within the other person's framework of thought and does not break its flow. It encourages them to go deeper.

It is important to recognise that teachers may reflect back feelings as well as thoughts. This is well understood as a Rogerian counselling technique, but it is not well recognised as a teaching technique. Yet many of the most important aspects of education are about feelings.

What Rogers has done is to show that the techniques of counselling are applicable to teaching. Indeed, counselling is a method of teaching. More precisely, it is a method of learning about oneself. As in all teaching, the teacher merely strives to make the learning possible. For too long, counsellors, teachers and doctors have been seen as distinct professions requiring different knowledge and a different training. That is because their training has concentrated upon the content of their professional discussions, not their processes.

Reflecting is related to two techniques that I mentioned as part of listening behaviour: perception checking and paraphrasing.

ii) *Perception checking.* In perception checking in effect the teacher says, 'What I hear you saying is ...' or 'If I understand you correctly you are saying ...' or in some other way checking his understanding of what the student meant.

Perceptual checks can also help the students to refine their thoughts more accurately – and a lot of education consists of that. When students correct their tutor's perception by saying 'No, I didn't mean that, I meant …' they must analyse and distinguish their thoughts from their tutor's representation of them.

The verification of meanings is a fundamental part of discussion. Perception checking is an under-used technique. It may seem to hold up the flow, but it has the great advantage that the discussion proceeds with a fuller and more thorough understanding by participants. It creates a firmer base for understanding. The confidence that results from a firmer understanding encourages more members to take an active part.

iii) *Paraphrasing.* In paraphrasing, a contribution is re-expressed in the speaker's own words. This has several functions. It creates the base of understanding I have just described. It may enable the subject to be discussed more accurately. And re-expression in different words sometimes allows wider relationships in the subject matter to be made more easily.

One danger with reflecting, perceptual checking and paraphrasing is that they become too mechanical. If this happens they no longer show the warmth and attention that group members have a right to receive. In all three, what is reflected, perceived and paraphrased may be feelings, experiences or understandings of the subject matter.

Again, although I have described these as contributions by the teacher, any participant could make them. Indeed the more responsibility learners take for their own learning, the more likely it is that leadership will be distributed.

4. Summarising

As with reflecting, paraphrasing and perception checking, summaries may include the content of discussion, the feelings expressed or both. Sometimes teachers think that summaries should only come at the end of a discussion. That is far from the case. Summaries have many different functions:

i) *To warm up.* A summary is very appropriate at the beginning of a discussion. In a seminar it is useful to summarise the argument of the initial presentation. In a syndicate it may be important to review the tasks that have been carried out. In a lecture-initiated buzz group the content of the lecture may be usefully summarised. In a group tutorial or a committee, a reminder of where the group got to last time will set the discussion in context.

ii) *Structuring by taking stock.* Taking stock in the middle of a discussion is a useful way of showing how the discussion has developed so far. It is not unusual for participants to think that a discussion has got nowhere and, so painless is their learning, they are surprised when taking stock reveals their progress.

Taking stock permits a bird's eye view of the discussion, which many students find difficult to see whilst in the thrust and parry of the discussion itself. The review structures the discussion by placing ideas in context and often makes it easier to relate the topic to others in the course.

iii) *Focusing.* Summaries are necessarily selective. They focus on some issues and not others. They are particularly useful in focusing upon the general feelings of a group without any one person taking full responsibility for them. In this way they can help self-awareness without group pressure being applied.

iv) *A springboard.* Summaries that take stock of where a discussion has got to so far, may help to show the group that certain issues are outstanding and thereby get consensus to tackle them. This can be particularly useful if the group, at some level of consciousness, has been deliberately avoiding crucial questions.

v) *To check understanding.* A summary can be used as a perception check to verify consensus and understanding up to that point. This may be very necessary when used as a springboard. In other words, a summary can establish the foundations upon which to use a springboard before plunging into deeper issues.

vi) *To give assurance.* Summaries can be useful in unstructured discussions, not only to give a structure, but to give assurance to group members that they are covering the major issues and that they have not been wandering aimlessly or going round in circles. Thus summaries have a motivational function.

vii) *To close discussion.* The summary at the close of a discussion may have many of the functions already described – showing its structure, providing a springboard for future work, checking understanding, and so on. Summaries at this stage also give what Gestalt psychologists call 'closure' – they can tie up all the loose ends so that the issues discussed are seen as a unity and are understood as a whole.

5. Information relating

Researchers and systems that have analysed group discussions usually have information-giving as a major category (eg. Bales, 1970; and Flanders, 1970). Indeed, no matter what the category system, most discussions seem to have more information giving than any other single kind of contribution.

However, small group discussion methods are procedures for interaction, and this means it is the way the information is related that is important, not its delivery, receipt and storage. In short, it is thinking that matters, not memory. Consequently, the crucial skill with information lies less in the techniques of presentation, and more in the techniques of relating one idea with another.

The information given commonly consists of facts, suggestions or advice. To be understood, they must be related to ideas a person already has using a pattern of reasoning (Chapter 7). These ideas are usually one or more of several kinds:
i)   *Purposes or intentions.*
ii) *Moral principles and values.*
iii) *Experiences and mental activity.*
iv) *Causes or consequences.*
v)   *A set of rules as in mathematics, logic, law or scientific principles.*
vi) *Functional relationships including scientific generalisations.*
vii) *Distributions in space.*
viii)*Differences in time.*

So when someone has difficulty in understanding a point in discussion, it is worth asking oneself, 'In which of these categories is my understanding? Now, can I explain the point by a simple analogy in that category?'

6. Interpretation

Obviously an important skill in discussion is to interpret what is being said. The skill here is to match the speaker's framework of ideas to one's own. One's own framework may be a hypothesis, a theory or one's pet explanation. If the match could be exact there would be complete mutual understanding. In practice no two people will ever have exactly the same framework of ideas – their lifetime of experiences are different. So complete understanding never occurs. In practice, we have mutual understanding up to some level determined by a criterion. The function of discussion is to make that criterion more rigorous.

The problems start when the mismatch is so great that we don't understand what the speaker is saying. Either the speaker's or one's own ideas are mistaken, or both, or possibly neither, when it is one of those topics where more than one point of view is viable. The usual difficulty is that neither framework is totally explicit. There are unexpressed assumptions on both sides.

Consequently, discussions to remove failures of understanding often consist of trying to analyse other members' frameworks of understanding. That is why representation is so important in problem-solving. (See Chapter 8.) Representation of a problem permits its relationships to be displayed and understood more easily.

Notice it is not necessarily the concepts that are different; it may be the way different members relate them. For example, at a social work case conference, a mother and a social worker might have all the same facts and concepts, but have quite different interpretations of why the daughter behaves that way. They relate cause and effect differently.

That problem of interpretation is quite different from when the social worker interprets the daughter's behaviour using a framework of theory not possessed by the mother. This is the situation in a discussion when some members can relate what is said to a framework of understanding, whilst others have no such framework to do so. This commonly occurs in tutorials and seminars where the tutor or presenter has specialist knowledge not possessed by others. In seminars the initial presentation is supposed to give that framework; in practice it often doesn't or its implications are too complex to take in straight away.

In this situation there are two possibilities. In one, those who have a framework may make relatively long reasoned contributions to explain it. This can result in teachers giving mini lectures in tutorials. Alternatively, a tutor or group members may try to help others develop the framework for themselves. For example, the social worker is not going to give a mini lecture on psychoanalysis; she will try to help the mother realise for herself why her daughter behaves as she does. A similar approach would be used in free group discussion, counselling and T-Groups (cp the area that is 'Blind' in Figure 4.1).

7. Note-taking to unscramble a discussion

As a result of discussions being spontaneous, their subject matter is not organised. Sometimes discussions go round in circles, or several issues are discussed, if not confused, at the same time. Consequently, an important skill is to unscramble the mixture of issues being discussed and sort them out into some kind of order or structure.

The technique to do this is first to ask oneself 'What are the issues, questions or problems being discussed?' This requires the participant, particularly the leader, to analyse and classify the points being made, and to place them in a wider context. The classification is a conception of the central issues.

A note of these issues may then be written as headings on different parts of a sheet of paper. As points are made that are worth noting, they are placed under the appropriate heading. This is the process of unscrambling. If they might go under more than one heading, draw a line linking points under the headings. (See Figure 23.1.) These lines can be used for a refocusing technique I'll mention in a moment.

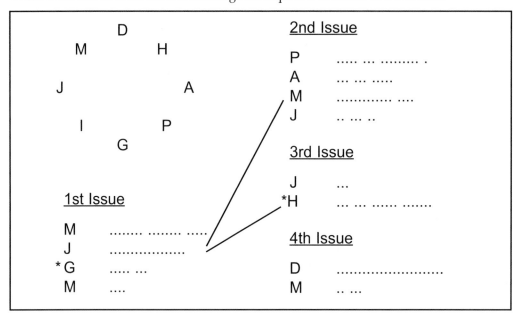

Figure 23.1. Note-taking technique to unscramble a discussion

Notes of this kind are not for the purpose of a permanent record of the meeting, but for monitoring and managing the discussion at the time. Note points in your personal shorthand, as a reminder of what has been said, only for the duration of the discussion. Being very brief notes or jottings, the process of noting should not be very time-consuming or very obtrusive. If a permanent record is required, the notes should be written up in more detail as soon as possible afterwards, filling in the gaps that could not be noted at the time before memory of a fuller account fades. The kind of notes I am describing here are rough notes used only to monitor the discussion and to permit a very orderly summary when appropriate. Normally they are thrown away at the end of the discussion.

There are two subsidiary techniques with this procedure. One I alluded to earlier is to draw a small seating plan of the group, with individual's names or initials in the appropriate place. I use initials so as to note quickly who made each of the points I might want to refer to later (see Figure 23.1).

The second technique is to draw light lines across the page linking points that could be connected. These two techniques enable the teacher to say, 'That point, John, about …, can you see how it might be related to what Mary said about …?' In other words, it enables the teacher to get students to make links for themselves and not do all the thinking himself. It also enables the teacher to refocus the discussion onto another issue, whilst leaving the discussion in John's hands.

8. Questioning

Of all the skills considered in this brief review, questioning is the most heavily researched. Yet, for our purposes the research has two major limitations. With the exception of the work by Brown and Atkins (1988), it is almost entirely at school level.

Secondly, the research focuses on how teachers use questions in practice, rather than how they ought to use them. Even the helpful suggestions of Brown and Atkins rely somewhat upon Brown's work in schools with Edmondson (Brown and Edmondson, 1984). In some areas of educational research, findings can be transferred with some assurance from school to adult level. But research on questioning at school level assumes that the teacher is controlling the class in a way that would be quite patronising with adults. Doneau (1986) views research showing that the vast majority of questions at school test students' memory and low-level understanding. Such questions result in the next response being confirmation or rejection by the teacher. The repeated use of such questions produces a quizzing, testing style which adults will quickly reject as humiliating and failing to use their breadth of experience.

With adults, questions can be used to draw upon the experience of group members for orienting, to stimulate wonderment and motivation, to draw out and encourage deep thought, to cross-relate subject matter, and to elicit values for general discussion. Questions for diagnosing weaknesses or to structure the discussion are less appropriate, though they may be used in science, engineering and other subjects with a relatively fixed structure.

Questions are a particular kind of task. I describe tasks to develop cognitive processes in Part II and nearly all of them could be expressed as questions; for example, to ask students to represent a problem as they see it, to ask them to relate the problem to something familiar, and questions to lead students towards successful heuristics. We also saw that questions which encourage students to challenge habitual patterns of thought are more likely to lead to creativity.

Questions that go deeper into a subject following previous contributions are known as '*probes*'. Brown and Atkins list examples such as, 'How is that relevant?', 'Can you give me an example?', 'What is the underlying principle, then?' and 'What distinguishes the two cases?'

'*Prompting*' is the technique of giving supplementary information, or in some other way leading the students to give answers that are acceptable when an initial response has been unsatisfactory.

At school level teachers sometimes ask the same question of many different pupils in order to widen the number of pupils involved. This is known as 'distributing' the question. It is inappropriate at adult level and other techniques, such as buzz groups, must be used to widen involvement.

The most important feature of questions at post school level is that most of them should be asked by the students, not the teacher. Skills to encourage questions are not easy, and they mostly lie in the art of task design rather than during the discussion itself. Alison King (1991) developed a set of question stems of the kind shown in the Table below. Students were required to fill in gaps to produce three questions on a given topic. She found that students who generated and answered their own questions in buzz groups of three members, performed better than those who answered the same questions generated by someone else. Both these groups obtained higher scores than those who reviewed the topic without questions either in buzz groups or individually.

- What values are assumed by ...?
- What's the connection between ... and ...?
- What is the function of ...?
- Which is the best ... and Why?
- Do you agree or disagree with the statement ... and Why?
- Compare ...and ... with regard to ... .
- What is the main purpose of ...?

Table 23.2. Typical stems used to generate questions Adapted from King (1991)

High level tasks such as those requiring evaluation, criticism, decision-making and creativity are more likely to evoke questions from students. In the discussion itself open probes such as 'What questions do we need to consider in order to answer that?', 'What are the main issues here?', and 'What problems are most likely to arise?' can lead to further questioning by students though they are not always openly expressed.

9. Gatekeeping

The art of widening participation in a discussion is known as 'gatekeeping'. It has many subsidiary skills.

The most direct approach is to stipulate a norm at the first meeting that all members should participate; but on its own, this will not produce an even distribution of contributions.

A more common approach is to look for incipient contributions indicated by non-verbal behaviour such as a change in posture, leaning forward, signs of slight agitation or attempts to catch the leader's eye. This is known as 'scanning' the group. Then the leader, or indeed any group member, may use eye contact, a motion of the hand, or even a spoken invitation to contribute just as the previous speaker is drawing to a close. The accuracy of the timing of these invitations to speak is quite subtle.

How do you know that the previous speaker is drawing to a close? Most people have a characteristic variation in pitch. For most, but not all, dialects it is a drop in pitch. It's a bit like the final note of a piece of music returning to doh, the keynote of the scale.

As Argyle has shown, it is also possible to get an indication that a speaker is coming to the end of his contribution because, statistically, most speakers make greater eye contact at the beginning and end of their contribution. They are more inclined to avert their gaze in the middle whilst thinking of what they are saying and how to say it. See Figure 20.2 on page 184. If you wish to control who speaks next, when you see that a contribution is coming to an end, invite the person non-verbally. This can be done by shifting eye contact to them, physically turning to them, or by an open-handed gesture in their direction.

Since people tend to speak across a group seated in a circle, quiet members can be induced to speak a little more if they are seated opposite talkative ones. Conversely talkative members can be discouraged from dominating if they sit next to each other. Because teachers are usually the most talkative group members, over talkative students can be discouraged from speaking if the teacher sits next to them. (See the Steinzor effect in Chapter 19 page 176–177.)

Gate-keeping can also be achieved by the techniques with which I began in Chapter 21, namely, giving individual work followed by very small groups for preliminary discussion so that each group member brings something to contribute to a wider group.

The essence of gatekeeping is to recognise that human beings naturally communicate with one another. If they don't, something is preventing them. So what is probably required is the removal of an inhibition, not a stimulus to respond. As we saw in Chapter 12, the most common inhibitions are fear and anxiety. Consequently, praise, acceptance and support are essential skills for small group leadership.

10. Responding to feelings
There are three ways of responding to feelings:
i) Make a mental note of the feeling, but decide to make no response to it at the time.
ii) Briefly acknowledge, verbally or non-verbally, that you recognise and understand the feeling.
iii) Reorient the discussion and focus on the feeling or the issue which has caused it.

i) *No overt response at the time.* The leader only makes a mental note of the feeling
- when to do so would embarrass the individual,
- when the group has a full agenda,
- when a more active response would be too risky emotionally, or
- when no useful purpose would be served by doing so. Since every contribution to a discussion has some emotional content, a perceptive leader will be adept at sensing these feelings.

ii) *Acknowledging the feelings.* Acknowledging the feelings would be more appropriate
- when they are impossible to ignore, but cannot appropriately be considered at the time,
- when the feelings are well known to the group and have been considered on another occasion, and
- when the teacher feels uncertain that he can handle the feelings at the time.

iii) *Discussing the feelings.* A criterion for whether a feeling should be discussed by the group, is whether it would help the progress of the group, either because the group would learn from it, or because learning would be blocked if it was not.

A great deal has been written in the counselling literature on techniques of responding to feelings, but it is doubtful whether those techniques can be transferred into the educational context because the relationship between teacher and student has elements of authority and power which should be absent in a counselling situation. Virtually all the discussion methods described in Part IV, with the exception of T-Groups, have a programme with some cognitive content, in addition to discussing the feelings of group members.

I believe it is important that teachers develop the skill to fade from one teaching method to another, such as from a teaching role to a counselling one and back again. However, I accept that there are basic conflicts between those roles that make this ideal hard to accomplish. Like much in teaching, blending one set of techniques into another is a skill that has to be worked at.

11. Feedback

Feedback in this context consists of obtaining information about oneself. It may be about one's feelings, thoughts or opinions. Feedback is constantly available to all participants, particularly the leader, during the interaction process. Usually there is no shortage of feedback to participants if they are able to observe it. The skill to be learned by students and teachers alike is to see and hear what is there to be seen and heard. It is a matter of having the necessary concepts to perceive and interpret what is there to be perceived. Parts II and III provide such concepts. The skills of observing and using non-verbal behaviour are typical of those requiring the developmental practice for which I argued at the beginning of Part IV.

It is, of course, possible to obtain feedback formally outside the discussion process by means of grades, evaluation questionnaires and interviews. These methods are beyond the scope of this book

C. Subject-centred group tutorials

A group tutorial is a discussion group led by a tutor. Its objective is learning. It is a general name for many such meetings, including free group discussions, some seminars and T-Groups. When the learning focuses on an academic subject, it is a subject-centred group tutorial. Some tutors may conduct their subject-centred group tutorials in the form of a seminar; that is, a discussion initiated by a presentation. The two methods overlap but they are not identical. Some seminars are group tutorials. Those held by learned societies at conferences typically are not.

1. The general purposes of subject-centred group tutorials
The general objectives of subject-centred group tutorials are:
i) *To promote thought.* The tutor may wish to take a subject deeper than is possible by presentation methods. He may do this by questioning, or by introducing new ideas

to be cross-related to others already expressed. In higher education, one group of thinking skills is particularly important in subject-centred tutorials. That's criticism. So I'll try to be a bit more specific and return to that in a moment.

ii) *To clarify.* They provide an opportunity for tutors to detect misconceptions, and for students to seek clarification.

iii) *To provide feedback on learning for both the tutor and the students.*

iv) *To assist private study.* An under-used purpose of group tutorials is to give students guidance on how to read a book, in what order to read the literature, and on other ways to make learning easier.

v) *To provide teacher-student contact.* In some institutions, the group tutorial is almost the only regular contact between a student and his tutor. In this case the tutor may need to devote some time to the social and emotional conditions of learning. Because 'group tutorial' is a general name, there is no one technique that can be described.

2. Tell students the elements of criticism you want them to learn

I said a general aim of a tutorial is to study a specific subject in depth. And this involves using all the relevant canons of criticism. What are the canons of criticism? According to Ennis (1962), critical thinking includes discerning whether:

- there is ambiguity in a statement or a line of reasoning,
- certain statements contradict each other,
- a conclusion necessarily follows,
- a statement is precise and specific enough,
- a statement is an application of a certain principle,
- an observation is reliable,
- an inference is warranted,
- the real problem has been identified,
- something is an assumption,
- a definition is adequate, and
- an authoritative statement is acceptable.

These eleven aspects of critical thinking assume a twelfth: the ability to grasp the meaning of a statement.

Ennis says there are three 'dimensions' to these judgements. A logical dimension is one where students relate terms or statements. A criterial dimension is exercised when students apply standards, for example, when interpreting statistical significance in social and medical sciences. And a pragmatic dimension is employed when students judge that they have enough evidence for a particular purpose (cp. a jury's decision).

Each of these twelve 'aspects' could be re-expressed as a question. Those are the kind of questions students should constantly be asking themselves. The problem for tutors is how to get them to do so. By constantly asking these kinds of questions in group tutorials, tutors expect students to anticipate them and then to ask the questions of themselves. As we saw in Figure 23.2, King achieves this more effectively by directly requiring students to ask questions using question stems. Alternatively, when criticism is not forthcoming in a group tutorial, a task to check one of these aspects of a theory or argument could be given to dyads or buzz groups.

A critical mind is always testing and judging the truth of what is said or written. It is a mark of an educated mind. A great deal of higher education strives to develop this quality. The aim of criticism is not to be negative; but to establish the truth. It's an attitude of mind.

D'Angelo has elaborated Ennis's list of 12 aspects to 50 skills and 10 attitudes. The attitudes are as follows:

○ intellectual curiosity,
○ objectivity,
○ open-mindedness,
○ flexibility,
○ intellectual scepticism,
○ intellectual honesty,
○ being systematic,
○ persistence,
○ decisiveness, and
○ respect for other viewpoints.

Tutors often try to develop these attitudes and 'aspects' of criticism as if by a process of osmosis. They seem to expect students to absorb them from the climate of discussion. But learning to think is not an absorption process. The attitudes and aspects are learned by practice. The practice will be most effective if they know what they are practising. So it is a good idea for tutors to tell students about Ennis's aspects and D'Angelo's attitudes.

3. Group tutorial skills

Group tutoring is a method that demands all the skills covered in sections A and B of this chapter. There's no need to repeat them here. Tutors must be able to handle the subject matter from any point of view, at a moment's notice, and at the same time be unerringly perceptive of the group dynamics, including an accurate awareness of themselves. Yet in spite of the difficulties, it is not unusual for new teachers to be given group tutorials, while lectures are given by more experienced staff. To give a good lecture is easier than to lead a good tutorial.

The skill of group tutors lies in their style of leadership. A common error amongst teachers is to over-dominate the group by establishing a centralised power structure with themselves at the centre. This is exemplified by a tutorial style in which alternate contributions are by the teacher, the teacher's contributions are longer, students answer questions but do not ask them, and contributions are controlled by the teacher. When tutors find themselves doing this, it is time to form dyads or small buzz groups and get out of the limelight. Better still, get out of the room, become a servant, and bring the students some tea.

D. Seminars

A seminar is a discussion initiated by a presentation. The presentation may use a lecture, one or more articles, other reading material, a video, an audio recording, or some other means. A 'seminar' is sometimes confused with a 'group tutorial'. A tutor may use the seminar method, in which case his method in a group tutorial happens to be the seminar method. Not all group tutorial begin with a presentation. And not all seminars, such as those held by learned societies, are group tutorials. But in this book, I am confining myself to seminars that are group tutorials.

I have argued that criticism is a fundamental objective of post-school education. For this reason it is pertinent to all discussion methods. It is particularly relevant to the seminar because, as I have just described, critical thinking is the process of evaluating statements, arguments and experiences. The seminar method is designed to provide an opportunity to evaluate statements and arguments made in the presentation.

1. Use seminars only with experienced discussants

Don't use the seminar method with inexperienced undergraduates. It's a postgraduate method. It assumes participants have all the skills I have described in Parts II, III and IV. It assumes the language of the subject. More than the ability to solve standard problems, it assumes the capacity to pursue a line of reasoning. It demands a balanced knowledge of the subject and its associated values. The fears of participation must have been overcome.

Furthermore, the undergraduate seminar in which students take it in turns to make the initial presentation destroys the natural development and dynamics of the group. It is artificial. Everyone, when giving the presentation, must suddenly acquire powers of a task leader they did not have the previous week. They must lead in the presence of the student who had to do so then, and of the teacher who everyone knows is the real task leader with real power. The motives, norms, structure, group development and patterns of interaction are wholly artificial until such a time that students have learned confidence to be themselves in discussion. That takes time and maturity.

2. Don't use the adversarial system

When the seminar method is used before students are ready for it, tutors struggle with silent students – and little wonder! In a misguided attempt to overcome this, some tutors contrive to set up a debate between students representing different points of view. This only compounds the artificiality.

We have already seen (in Chapter 12 and Figure 12.2) growing evidence that co-operative groups are more effective, for a whole variety of purposes, than competitive ones. Competition inevitably produces defensive behaviour. Competition increases fear; it does not reduce it. There's no genuine search for the truth; only a desire to win. When the people aim to win an argument, rather than pursue the truth together, it is the truth that suffers. Ideas and information are hidden. (Too often, hiding the truth has serious consequences for justice in the law courts and decisions in politics.) In other words, the first casualty of debate is open communication (cf Gibb, 1961). But that is precisely what discussion methods should aim to provide!

3. Bear Hill's 'Cognitive Map' in mind

How can the difficulties in using a seminar method with undergraduates be overcome? Hill (1977) has argued that discussion following a presentation should proceed through nine steps, which he calls his 'Group Cognitive Map'.

i) Define the term and concepts used in the presentation.

ii) Make a general statement of the presenter's message.

iii) Identify the major themes of sub-topics.

iv) Allocate the available time between the themes and sub-topics.

v) Discuss the themes and sub-topics.

vi) Integrate the discussion with other topics in the curriculum.

vii) Consciously apply the information and other material.

viii) Evaluate the presentation

ix) Evaluate the performance of group members and the group as a whole.

Hill has a point. The Group Cognitive Map may be a useful 'map' of procedure for the beginning tutor. But it risks being a formula that is too prescriptive and mechanical. If so, seminars may become boring and unimaginative. It could be far too restrictive. Seminar discussions should be free to wander to enthusiasms in the light of what has been said, not inflexibly pre-planned. Furthermore, it underplays the role of criticism. There is an undertone that the presentation is authoritative, to be understood and memorised, rather than understood and criticised. Stage (viii) looks like an evaluation of style, not content.

On the other hand, it does provide a guide for students on what to consider before criticism. It provides a focus. It is an agenda and it might be argued that there is an opportunity within that agenda for students to say anything relevant.

4. Scriven's seven steps for analysing arguments

If beginning tutors need some guidance, they need something more concerned with thought and criticism. Essentially, a seminar should analyse the argument in a presentation. Scriven says there are 7 steps in argument analysis:

i) Clarify the argument so that the meaning of each of its component steps is understood.

ii) Identify the stated and unstated conclusions of the argument.

iii) Represent the structure of the argument. (We saw in Chapter 8 that representation is an essential aspect of problem-solving).

iv) Make explicit the unstated premises and assumptions of the argument.

v) Criticise the premises and the inferences of the argument.

vi) Consider other relevant arguments both for and against the presenter's conclusions.

vii) Make an overall evaluation of the presenter's argument in the light of (i) – (vi).

Steps (i) to (iv) bear some resemblance to Hill's Cognitive Map, but they are explicitly preparing the ground for balanced criticism in steps (v) to (vii). Once again, if you are not careful, a formula of this kind restricts what can be discussed and lacks spontaneity. Nevertheless, a beginning teacher may find it a useful guide. Furthermore, students themselves might take more responsibility for their own development if they knew about this sequence of steps. Therefore it might be worth tutors acquainting their students with it.

E. Free group discussion (FGD)

In her pioneering work on free group discussion, 'The anatomy of judgement', Abercrombie hypothesises that we may make better judgements if we know the factors that influence their formation. In FGD more attention is paid to the *processes* of observing and thinking than to their results. Her ideas, which had origins in psychoanalysis, have in turn influenced ideas on facilitation techniques and self-directed learning. Weaker forms have long been called 'student-centred learning'.

1. The purpose of free group discussion (FGD)
The purposes of a free group discussion are:
i)   *to become aware of preconceptions,*
ii) *to discover other people's patterns of thinking and perception, and*
iii) *to provide opportunities for attitude change and development.*
In essence, the method is simple; in practice it is extremely subtle and delicate.

2. Processes in FGD
There are three steps in the psychological process. They have their analogies in Rogerian counselling and psychoanalysis. Look also at the four steps in Section A of Chapter 11.

i) *Expression.* A climate is created in which students feel free to express their *own* ideas, feelings, perceptions and attitudes. The students themselves, not the teacher, are the authorities, each in their own case, of what these are. This climate is created by a tutor who is tolerant, open-minded, with a humble, enquiring mind. Listening is crucial. Domination is fatal. The teacher's chief activity is to listen, to speak only when necessary, and then to appreciate and relate what he or she hears. Thus the first thing for the teacher is to encourage spontaneity. That means avoiding, so far as possible, the behaviour, symbols and associations of authority. It means avoiding the correction of mistakes unless they are dangerous. It means refraining from expressing one's own opinion.

The refusal to be an authority can result in a period of rebellion, and indeed the other stages, described in Table 18.2. Accepting rebellion, rather than resisting it, is something many teachers find very hard. The tutor must be careful not to summarise the discussion in too final a way, because the journeys of self-exploration must be allowed to continue long after the group has ceased meeting.

Figure 23.3. The subjectivity of perception

ii) *To consider what has been expressed.* The essential climate for considering perceptions and attitudes is one of rationality and reasonableness. Discussion provides an opportunity for perceptions by group members to be compared and distinguished, for their implications to be followed through, and for their personal nature to be recognised and valued by each individual.

The teacher mostly listens. Interventions at this stage will be relating others' contributions, an occasional steer (orienting), some reluctant gate-keeping if necessary, reflecting back and so taking stock at the end. (See pages 242–245 and 250–251.)

It is the personal nature of perceptions that is a revelation to most students. They have been taught that science is objective – that everyone observing an experiment sees the same thing. (See Figure 23.3.) They slowly discover that all perceptions are interpretations in the light of previous experience, that everyone's history of experiences is different, and that consequently their interpretations are different, but each in their way may have some validity. This leads to a recognition that there are many valid perspectives on facts they previously saw as incontrovertible. It leads to open-mindedness. Students start like six blind men and the elephant. (See Figure 23.4.)

Understanding information consists of relating it to frameworks of ideas (sometimes called 'schemata') that the individual already possesses. Education partly consists of building such associations of ideas. The oldest frameworks were formed and reinforced before the individual acquired language. Indeed they were necessary to do so. Because students are unaware of them, they don't question their validity when used inappropriately. Recently received information is more easily verbalised. Free group discussion uses language and the contrasting perceptions of group members, to

> It was six men of Indostan
> To learning much inclined,
> Who went to see an elephant
> (though all of them were blind)
> That each by observation
> Might satisfy his mind
>
> [The first felt its side, the second its tusk, the third its trunk, the fourth a leg, the fifth its ear and the last its tail. They each had a different experience. Consequently they had different perceptions and different conceptions of what an elephant is.]
>
> And so these men of Indostan
> Disputed loud and long,
> Each in his opinion
> Exceeding stiff and strong,
> Though each was partly in the right
> And all were in the wrong
>
> So oft in theologic wars,
> Disputants, there I ween
> Rail on in utter ignorance
> Of what each other mean,
> And prate about an elephant
> Not one of them has seen!
>
> After J. G. Saxe, The Blind Men and the Elephant

Figure 23.4. Extracts from 'The Blind Men and the Elephant'

reveal to individuals their previously unidentified frameworks and their assumptions. This conscious recognition allows ideas to be separated from previous frameworks and assumptions, and associated with others more appropriately. It is a process of dissociation and re-association elsewhere.

A similar process applies to the individual's attitudes. Indeed, an attitude usually entails the disposition to use certain assumptions and frameworks of ideas in preference to others. By creating a secure climate, students feel able to express their attitudes, values and feelings. Once expressed they can be compared with others' and open to rational consideration.

iii) *To change*. Only when perceptions, attitudes and feelings have been expressed, recognised and considered, can individuals, of their own free will, change their attitudes or chose to see things differently. Personal change is on the basis of freedom. The process of change is the dissociation and re-association I have just described.

3. The tutor's techniques
The sequence of expression, self-recognition, consideration and self-directed change is a fundamental, yet insufficiently appreciated, educational procedure. As described in Chapter 3, Paulo Freire and Abercrombie have each, in very different contexts, used this technique first by discussing issues or objects that are visually familiar. The teacher's techniques include listening, orienting students' attention, summarising, seeking interpretations of what has been said, occasionally questioning, and giving feedback to help students' self-awareness. The timing of the teacher's contributions is crucial. The same utterance at different points in a discussion can have quite different effects.

An important skill when leading a free group discussion is not to control it, but to let it run. British television has long had a programme discussing moral problems, called 'The Heart of the Matter'. On any question that is raised it always fails to get to the heart of the matter because the leader keeps posing new questions rather than letting one be tackled in depth. Constant intervention by a leader prevents interaction between participants. For example, in a discussion where participants disagreed whether pets have moral rights, she kept seeking their opinions on different, though related questions such as 'Do pets have moral duties?', 'Does it make a difference whether the pets are intelligent?', 'What do eastern religions think?' and so on. Consequently the premises of any viewpoint, and their successive premises, were never considered. If the leader had kept quiet and let those who disagree examine the premises that underlie each others' beliefs, deeper principles would become explicit. These would then be available to answer the other questions that the leader asks. Without the deeper principles first becoming explicit, discussion consists of expressions of opinion one after the other without any serious explanations or justifications. The discussion remains superficial.

4. Can you fade from one method to another?
Controversially, I believe it is possible to fade in from a subject-centred tutorial to FGD and back again as the need arises. In other words, when I see a need for feelings or perceptions to be expressed, I find I can listen using FGD techniques while the group

works at them. I think a tutor has to work in this flexible way. Whilst I can set tasks that will beg questions of attitudes, values, feelings and perceptions, many of the most pregnant ones from the students' points of view, will not be artificially induced. They need to be worked upon when they emerge and that time cannot be planned in advance.

The argument against this, which I fully acknowledge, is that tutors using their authority in a subject-centred tutorial cannot suddenly remove that aura. Certainly there are situations in counselling when one judgmental remark can undo hours of patient building of trust. But counsellees are uncommonly vulnerable. I can't deny that some students may be too. I think it depends how authoritarian and judgmental tutors choose to be in subject-centred phases and with what norms students expect tutors to act. As we saw in Table 12.1, a highly supportive tutor conveying a sense of achievement can remove many anxieties.

F. Individual and personal tutorials

1. Types, terms and structures

Like 'group tutorial', I shall use 'individual tutorial' as a general name, in this case a name for discussions between a tutor and one student. I see an individual tutorial as having a beginning and an end, and in between there is discussion towards solving one or more (usually more) problems. The problems may be academic or personal. That is not the same as saying they are cognitive or affective, but these contrasts have some overlap.

If the discussions are about academic matters, their content may not be very different from group tutorials, but their structure will be. Group tutorials are more likely to be thematically prepared by the teacher. The topics discussed in individual academic tutorials are more likely to be a series of problems initiated by the students to improve their understanding. In an academic tutorial initiated by the student presenting a piece of work, the discussion may be structured like a seminar.

When the problems discussed in individual tutorials are personal, the tutorial has a counselling element. Most tutors are not trained counsellors and when the problems are big, they should not attempt to do what only a trained counsellor can do. Nonetheless, every tutor knows that students have personal problems that require their help. I shall call this element 'personal tutoring' or 'a personal tutorial'.

In practice, individual tutorials are a mixture. Academic tutorials, personal tutorials and individual counselling are methods that blend into each other in the way described at the beginning of this chapter and in the last section. This concept is important because the competent tutor glides imperceptibly from the skills used in academic work to skills a counsellor might use, and back again as different problems arise. (Again, I recognise that the controversy raised in section E4 above has its counterpart here. But in practice, I don't think a tutor has any alternative. Some personal problems have to be dealt with as they arise.)

2. Procedures for an individual academic tutorial

Tutorial teaching is more exhausting than you might expect. A tutor's approach is very much a personal matter. What follows are matters for consideration, not a blueprint.

i) *Preparation before the tutorial.* Before the first tutorial, find out as much as you can about the tutee, yet keep an open mind. Check out the student's application, history, references and academic performance at college so far. What evidence do you have about the student's motivation? How far do you want to set norms and what are they?

Regarding later tutorials, are there academic objectives regarding specific subject matter that you want the student to achieve, or is the student to set the agenda? Set the physical environment. In particular, make sure your chair and theirs are the same. If equality is not possible, let the tutor's be the more humble. How controlling do you think you should be, and how far should the student take control?

ii) *The welcome.* First impressions can be influential. You will probably want your welcome to be warm and informal. If so, how will you move to business – abruptly or gradually? How will that warmth be conveyed? (See also sections A4 and A5 of this chapter.)

iii) *The beginning.* The beginning might include a review of 'where we got to last time'. More challenging for *students* is to review what they have learned since last time. The latter soon reveals academic problem areas requiring help. Perhaps more important, it reveals aspects of the students' study methods where advice could be helpful, provided the tutor has some knowledge of research in that field (which most tutors do not).

iv) *Tackling the academic problems.* Clearly, it is difficult to say much when the way to tackle academic problems will depend upon the discipline. But for many disciplines, particularly in science and engineering, I recommend you look again at Polya's 'How to solve it' in Table 8.1, page 58. Encourage the students to go through the four stages by themselves, even though they will need help at first, on which question to ask themselves.

When criticising patterns of reasoning in the humanities, Scriven's sequence for analysing arguments (see page 256) might be more appropriate.

It goes without saying that virtually all the skills described in sections A and B of this chapter are applied at this stage of a tutorial. These include listening, orienting, reflecting back, summarising in its various forms, relating information, understanding the student's frame of mind, questioning, responding to feelings and so on.

What style do you expect to adopt?
- Will it be *authoritarian* in which you tell the student what they ought to know?
- Will it be the *Socratic* style in which answers to your questions trigger another question so that the students explore their own knowledge deeper? If so, beware of the danger that your style becomes an authoritarian interrogation with the teacher supplying information when ignorance is found.
- Will it be the 'Let's explore this together' *heuristic* approach? This pays more attention to thinking and other skills, including research and manual skills in some cases.

● Or will it be a *counselling* style which may also be heuristic, but in which there is much greater attention to interpersonal skills and self-exploration? If so, will a shortage of time leave important parts of the curriculum unexplored?

Each style has its merits and disadvantages.

v) *Drawing to a close.* The tutor has several small duties as the end of the tutorial draws near. First, it is useful to summarise the issues that have been raised. Second, couple the summary with advice upon where and how to follow up. Third, agree a contract with the student on what each will do for next time. Persuasion to agree the contract will include an explanation of why it is beneficial

vi) *Evaluation after the tutorial.* Write a note of the issues covered, any student difficulties that might indicate how certain areas of knowledge could be better taught in future. Include an impressionistic evaluation of your tutorial teaching.

3. Counselling skills within personal tutorials

When students present problems that are personal, rather than academic, tutors need an approach that employs many of the same skills that professional counsellors are trained to use. The problem presented and the tutor's skills will probably be more concerned with feelings, motivation, emotions and personal relations than knowledge. With that adjustment, I shall assume that the preparation, welcome, beginning, closure and evaluation will not be so very different from those we have just considered.

The procedure in that phase of an individual tutorial concerned with personal problems is analogous to the three phases of free group discussion: expression, rational consideration, and action for change. Egan (1982) calls them (i) Problem exploration and clarification, (ii) Developing new perspectives and setting goals, and (iii) Action.

i) *Problem exploration and clarification.* In this phase the tutor uses all the listening skills described in B1 above. Particular emphasis is placed upon eye contact and forward posture. Assurance of confidentiality is offered.

The tutor reflects back what the student says in a non-judgmental way, and responds and empathises with the feelings observed in order to elicit further elaboration of the problem. The student is to be valued as a person and their self-esteem cherished. Rogers (1951) would say that the tutor should offer 'unconditional positive regard'. Most counsellors use prompts, such as uh-uh. The reflecting should be frequent, but always brief and tentative so that the student can freely confirm, deny, explain or change the emphasis.

Although there is some taking stock and reflecting back results in some focusing, the tutor does not use orientation skills that might divert the student to the tutor's agenda and away from their own. Nonetheless, there is a gradual shift from the facts of the problem to feelings about it, or that are part of it.

Inevitably the tutor must interpret what the student says, but it is important to avoid imposing one's own personal frameworks of ideas (schemata). The aim is to empathise as accurately as possible with the student's. Resist giving advice; it is the student who must take the decisions.

It is sometimes necessary to ask questions, particularly open questions, but if you ask too many, the student feels interrogated and empathy suffers. Later when trust is well developed it is possible to use a probe (see pages 249–250) so long as it is followed by empathy or greater control of the conversation by the student.

ii) *Developing new perspectives and setting goals.* A lot of students' personal problems result from not knowing how some aspect of the educational system works. It may be something about student loans or university regulations. Students can decide what to do when given the appropriate information. They don't need counselling.

There are other problems, for example, to do with study skills and the use of computer facilities, where the tutor can give helpful information and then needs to give students help in acquiring the skill that uses the information. Regrettably, failure to follow up in this way is so common as to be normal!

The tutor's note in Figure 23.5 summarises a problem exploration and clarification. The individual tutorial started as an academic tutorial, but it soon developed into a personal one. Indeed the note may well summarise more than one personal tutorial, because exploration and clarification is often a slow process.

> *Jackie is a second year student of French Literature. The quality of Jackie's work has deterio-rated recently. She's been quiet and inattentive in group work. I have tried to find out why. It emerges that she is the first member of her wider family to go to university and since she came, her parents' marriage has been under strain. Jackie feels guilty that she has not been with her parents when it mattered and has been going home late on Fridays, returning tired early on Monday mornings. She is in financial difficulties because she cannot afford the rail fares. Lacking university weekend social life, she feels she has no friend close enough to confide in. She says she feels ashamed because 'Everyone else comes from secure families'.*

Figure 23.5. Tutor's note

'Would Jackie might prefer to consult the university counsellor?' the tutor might tentatively ask. Ultimately Jackie has to take some decisions and act upon them. That has to be her goal, but at the moment she is confused by too many questions and cannot sort out her priorities. 'Can I stop them separating? Should I leave university? Could I come back if I did? Would the same thing happen if I did? How can I pay back my student loan? What job would I do if I went home?'

Before she can do that, it might be helpful if she could see herself and the situation in new ways. For example, her perception of her 'guilt' and 'shame' need to be challenged, preferably by herself, otherwise by her tutor or counsellor. There is quite a lot of work for her to consider what her responsibilities are, and what they are not.

Challenging is a difficult skill. Challenges need to be tentative and not made too early. They consist of helping the student to consider facts and feelings she has, at some level of consciousness, ignored so that she will see matters from a different perspective. (See the Johari window in Chapter 4 and Figure 20.1.) Accurate information about the situation at home, the student loans scheme and university regulations might help. Sometimes a new perspective can be prompted by a summary that puts things in proportion. New perspectives can be encouraged by helping the student to reach conclusions by relating information, saying explicitly what she implies, or recognising recurring themes in what she says. At this stage it is acceptable for tutors to share their feelings and experiences if they help to show other perspectives.

When new perspectives enable Jackie to decide her priorities, she can clarify her goals. They need to be realistically achievable within a reasonable time and compatible with her values. It is important that she, and no one else, decides her goals.

iii) *Action.* Having decided what she wants to achieve, Jackie will need to plan her course of action. Talking this through with her tutor is helpful. What sequence and timing of activities is planned? What resources are needed?

G. T-groups, sensitivity groups and encounter groups

As in Chapter 4, where I discussed the empirical evidence that these groups can teach inter-personal skills, I regard them as different names for the same thing. I do not recommend that teachers use them until they have experienced them as participants on several occasions.

1. Their purpose
The central task of these groups is to become a group, to observe the processes involved, and to learn about their own inter-personal behaviour, the feelings and perceptions of others, and how groups and group members interact. These groups enhance self-awareness by adding the perspective of others. That is the process I described in Chapter 4. There is evidence that to explore the interaction of a small group as a group member can be personally rewarding and lead to permanent changes in behaviour. (Dies, 1979; Lakin, 1979; Lieberman, 1976; and Smith, 1975.)

Participants are usually managers, social workers, clerics and others who want to understand how people interact, improve their social skills and facilitate their skills of interpersonal perception. They usually meet several times for around two hours in groups of about a dozen members.

2. The procedure
There is no procedure laid down. Trainers usually introduce themselves, state the purpose of the group much as in my first sentence in section 1 above, and then sit down.

The fact that no specific instructions are given about how to achieve these tasks, itself poses a problem about how to proceed. Consequently, the group is immediately plunged into a discussion about how to proceed. This means that they start discussing how groups behave, and how they intend to behave, or would like to behave, in the group. The data for discussion is their experience at the time. So comments are personal about each other.

By putting forward suggestions or guidelines about how the group should conduct its affairs, individuals are, in effect, imposing rules. Inevitably, they make assumptions. The proposals they make are commonly based upon experience they have brought from other groups. How each member thinks and feels will affect the way the group develops. So a major task for the group is to allow individuals and sub-groups to express differences. Then the differences must he resolved or integrated.

The trainer participates as a full group member, but has some special responsibilities. The trainer needs to encourage members to contribute freely. Free expression of thoughts and feelings requires a permissive atmosphere. The trainers' role ultimately is more passive than in most educational groups, yet they must observe and monitor the group process very actively. They should avoid imposing their own preferences because that will prevent other group members from learning about theirs.

From time to time the trainer may intervene to:

- interpret or explain his perceptions of what is happening (the group dynamics),
- show how to make non-judgmental contributions about the behaviour of other members,
- show how to learn from such contributions and not receive them defensively,
- apply the group's experiences to real life situations, or to
- teach members to have less authoritarian attitudes towards both their superiors and inferiors in the workplace.

As we saw in Chapter 18, T-Groups go through stormy periods and the trainers must have the self-assurance and maturity to weather these storms. In particular, they should resist the insistence of a group to take control and rescue them from the discord and other problems of their own making.

3. How do T-groups work?

T-groups are unlike other groups. Their norms and procedures are unexpected. The leader seems to shirk a leader's responsibilities. The task – to study the group itself – seems odd. To talk at all creates the subject matter you are talking about. Insofar as members are learning about themselves, they are all learning about something different from the others. There is no criterion of when the task is accomplished. The discussions feel awkward and all kinds of escape mechanisms are employed. They fail at once because they become the immediate topic of discussion.

Yet it is precisely because the usual conventions and inhibitions of discussion are removed that T-groups provoke intense self-examination. It is a process of expanding the open area shown in Johari's window (Figure 4.1). The procedure is like the sequence 'expression', 'consideration' and 'change' employed in free group discussion (pages 257–259) except that it is other group members who may express their perceptions of an individual, not the individuals themselves. It is the 'blind' area in Johari's window, that becomes more 'open'. The perceptions are of others 'here and now'. So, although subjective at one level, they are objective insofar as they can be confirmed or denied by other members of the group. That can apply group pressure for individuals to accept what others perceive about them.

Accepting that you are the sort of person others say you are is a learning process that can be emotionally painful. Consequently, follow up support is essential if the group does not reach the supportive stages shown in Table 18.3. Time must be available. In my experience the mutually supportive stages are often reached quite suddenly, perhaps as a result of a particularly tense incident. Individuals then adjust their self image and, knowing it is relatively congruent with how others see them, they are able to face the world with greater confidence and understanding. That is why it is a method particularly used in management training.

H. Conclusion to the book as a whole

There are other books on teaching students in groups; in fact, I've written a couple myself. So how is this one different?

It is not a collection of tit bits. It has a logical structure that forms an argument. It asks what can discussion achieve, then what factors influence that achievement, and finally, how can those factors best be used to achieve it? The diagram in the Preface illustrates that structure.

It does not rely on subjective opinions. The answers are grounded in empirical research where available. The first question is answered by finding that educational and psychological research reach the same conclusions, namely, discussion methods are best for teaching students to think and, particularly when preceded by role plays or some other relevant common experience, are good at helping students to develop their attitudes and values.

The factors referred to in the second question are divided in two: the content of a discussion (its task) and its processes (its group dynamics). The answers are mostly based upon experimental psychology or logic.

The logic and psychology have repeatedly led me to the conclusion set out formally in the introduction to Part IV, namely, that both students and their teachers will best acquire their respective discussion skills by using a developmental sequence of discussion methods. This sequence is summarised by my maxim, *Start with simple tasks in small groups for short periods of time, and then gradually increase their respective complexity, size and duration.* The sequence moves from groups without tutors, through groups intermittently visited by tutors, to group tutorials and groups with tutors taking a non-dominant role. It also moves from simple cognitive tasks to complex ones and then to tasks that are concerned with feelings, attitudes and values. However, the sequence I have suggested stops short of methods to teach interpersonal skills. That is is taken up by James Kilty's book.

I shall consider this book a success if teachers apply the maxim by increasing and diversifying their repertoire of discussion methods. That way, teaching will turn from a drudge to a joy.

Appendices

Key to abbreviations

C	Centred	Pr-tut	Peer tutoring
D	Discussion	Q	Questionnaire
FGD	Free Group Discussion	Q&A	Question and answer
Gp	Group	R	Reading and private study
L	Lecture	Sem	Seminar
MMPI	Minnesota Multiphasic Personality	St	Student
	Inventory	StCD	Student Centred Discussion
P	Problem	T	Teacher
PBL	Problem Based Learning	TCD	Teacher Centred Discussion
PCD	Problem Centred Discussion	Tut	Tutorial
PL	Programmed Learning		

The following tables list published comparisons of discussions with other teaching methods. Each comparison gives the author(s), the methods compared and the criteria used. Where the method described is identifiable as one dealt with in this book, I have used the same name. If not, I have given the name used by the researcher.

Appendix 1.1
Discussion is at least as effective as other methods for teaching information

Studies finding discussion is more effective than other methods for teaching information

Tutored Groups

1	Bane (1925 & 1931)	D v. L	Delayed recall
2	Bond (1956)	D v. L	Delayed test
3	Gerberich & Warner(1936)	D v. L	Less able students on MCQ tests, matching true/false questions and examinations
4	Huffaker (1931)	D v. L	Immediate & delayed tests of recall
5	Kirby (1931)	D v. L	Immediate & delayed tests of recall examinations
6	Rickard (1946)	D v. L	Delayed recall test
7	Walker (1986)	D v. L	Vocabulary & written material

8	Ward (1956)	D v. L	Understanding of information by more able students
9	Beach (1960)	Class D v. L	Less sociable students MCQ
10	Erskine & Tomkin (1963)	Two Ds v. nine Ls	Objective tests, total time
11	Boeding & Vattano (1976)	Seminar v. L-D	Facts learned
12	Fontenot (1996)	L v. L+Coop learning v. L	Science achievement test
13	Carter (1995)	L + D v. L	4 week delayed 20 item MCQ
14	Beilin & Rabow (1979)	L+D v. L	Scores on final exams by whites
15	Dawson (1956)	Problem-solving gps v. L+Demo	Test of recall of information
16	Abdul-Munim (1988)	Video panel/D L v. Video L	7 mostly memory tests
17	Whitehurst (1972)	Individual tutorials v. Written assignments	Weekly tests
18	Knowles (1975)	Tut v. Trad teaching	Quality of assignments
19	Keilman (1971)	Tut v. PL	Speed, amount & delayed retention
20	Edmondson & White (1998)	Tut v. Controls Tut+Counselling v.Tut	Knowledge gains Knowledge gains
21	Webb (1968)	Gp & indiv tut mix v. Trad	75-item pre & post objective test

Tutorless Groups

1	Roach et al (1983)	Dyads v. Trad teaching	Gains on standardised maths tests
2	Schermerhorn et al (1975)	Dyads	Gains on probability theory
3	Malone & McLaughlin (1997)	Reciprocal peer-tut v.controls	Weekly vocabulary quizzes
4	Gibb (1993)	Teach to learn v. L	Knowledge retention
5	Dineen (1977)	Giving &receiving peer-tut Peer-tut v. Trad teaching	Spelling tests
6	Coyne (1978)	Peer-tut v. R	Performance on intro course
7	Levine (1990)	Peer-tut v. controls	Writing & mastery of psychology
8	Riggio et al	Reciprocal peer-tut v. controls	Cognitive gains
9	Gaynor & Wolking	PSI proctors v controls	Course assessment
10	Zimmer et al (1974)	Proctor led D v. Quiz	Concepts & principles
11	Romaneeva et al (1980)	Mixed ability triads v. L-D	Comprehension & grammar problems
12	Stone (1997)	Inquiry+D v. L-tour	Long-term retention
13	Beach (1960)	Tutorless small-gp D v. L	More sociable students on MCQ
14	Gore (1962)	Problem-centered gps v. L	Final examinations, retention, tests, job sheets
15	H.C.Smith (1955)	Syndicates v. L	Achievement test, not clearly specified

Studies finding discussion is equally effective as other methods for teaching information

Tutored Groups

1	Bane (1925 & 1931)	D v. L	Immediate recall
2	Becker & Dallinger (1960)	D v. L	Factual knowledge
3	Carlson (1953)	D v. L and L v. L-D	Gains on test of knowledge
4	Dubes (1987)	D v. L	3 week delayed test
5	Fitzgerald (1960)	D v. L	Objective tests
6	Gadzella (1977)	D v. L	Essay exams
7	Gerberich & Warner (1936)	D v. L	Heterogeneous gps on exams, MCQ tests, matching true/false Q
8	Gotke (1931)	D v. L	Immediate & delayed tests
9	Guetzkow et al (1954)	D v. L	Misconception tests and USAF standard exam
10	Hill (1960)	D v. L	Concepts & principles
11	Hudelson (1928)	D v. L v.	Type of test not specified Q&A sessions
12	Rickard (1946)	D v. L	Recognition of facts
13	Robbins (1931)	D v. L	Immediate & delayed recall
14	Rohrer (1957)	D v. L	Terminology, facts & principles
15	Ruja (1954)	D v. L	Tests of knowledge on two out of three courses
16	Smith J.P. (1954)	D v. L	Recognition of facts
17	Spence (1928)	D v. L	Tests of facts
18	Ward (1956)	D v. L	Retention of information by able students
19	Palmer & Verner (1959)	D v. L v. L+D	MCQ
20	Connolly (1992)	D v. L+D	1/3 gps post test
21	Joyce & Weatherall (1957)	D v. L v. L+	Short answer tests & MCQ Practicals v. L+R
22	Lifson et al (1956)	L+D v. L	MCQ on facts
23	Beilin & Rabow (1979)	L+D v. L	Scores on facts & final exams for ethnic minorities
24	Deignan (1956)	L+D v. L+StCD	MCQ & sentence completion
25	Benson (1996)	L+D in small gps v. L	Claydon course exam: knowledge
26	Heller & Dale (1976)	L-D v. Competency based	Achievement gains
27	Beach (1960)	Class D v. L	MCQ
28	Erskine & Tomkin (1963)	Two Ds v. nine Ls	Essays
29	Barnard (1936)	1L & 2Ds per week v. 3Ls	MCQ
30	Gauvain (1968)	Seminar v. L	MCQ & essay exams
31	Bills (1952)	L v. StC D v. L	Objective tests
32	Di Vesta (1954)	L v. StC D v. L	Knowledge of principles
33	Haigh & Schmidt (1956)	StC v. TC	Horrocks-Troyer test

34	Patton (1955)	StC v. trad. TC	Measures not clearly described
35	Eglash (1954)	FGD v. L	Examinations
36	Jenkins (1952)	FGD v. L	Standard examination
37	Johnson & Smith (1953)	FGD v. L	Test on terminology & facts
38	Garcia-Werebe & Reinert (1976)	Free D v L	Sex education
39	Martenson et al (1992)	PBL v.L	Knowledge
40	Poole & Wade (1985)	TV+D v. TV	Number & quality of ideas
41	Watts (1977)	R+D v. L	Sex Knowledge & Attitude Q
42	Wieder (1954)	L-Demo v. FGD	Objective tests
43	Ott (1996)	Expert-led reflective D v. L	Physiologic concepts
44	Husband (1951)	Large L [Av 200] v. small L [av 55] + questions + D	Hourly quizzes & final examinations
45	Whitehurst (1972)	D v. Written assignment	Weekly tests
46	Watts (1977)	R+D v. L	Sex knowledge
47	Knowles (1974)	Weekend tut v.Trad.	9 performance variables

Tutorless Groups

1	Casey and Weaver (1956)	Small-gp Ds v. L	Objective tests
2	Churchill (1960)	Small gps v. L-D and Private study	MCQ
3	Churchill and John (1958)	Small L-D gp v. large L class	Objective test
4	Leton (1961)	Case Discussion v. L	Tests of knowledge, not clear
5	Tillman (1993)	Case Discussion v. L-D	Course content
6	Carter (1995)	Case study method v. L	Immediate 20 item MCQ
7	Watson (1975)	L v. Case study method	Knowledge of principles
8	Carsrud (1979)	Tut v. Peer-tut v. L	Final examination
9	Diflorio (1996)	Coop learning v. L-D	MCQ
10	Randolph (1993)	Coop learning v. L-D	Introductory biology
11	Robinson (1995)	Coop learning v. L	Home assignments, class tests
12	Smith D.L. (1995)	Coop learning v. L-D	Knowledge test
13	Andrews (1996)	Coop learning + CAL v. L	Mechanics Baseline test + exam
14	Dutt (1994)	2 wks' Coop learning v. L	Quizzes
15	Courtney et al (1994)	D (Coop learning) v. L	MCQ
16	Stone (1997)	Inquiry+D v. L-tour	Short-term retention

Studies finding discussion is less effective than other methods for teaching information

Tutored Groups

1	Bloom (1953)	D v. L	Stimulated recall of attention to simple comprehension
2	Gadzella (1977)	D v. L	MCQ
3	Gerberich & Warner (1936)	D v. L	More able students on MCQ tests, matching true/false questions & examinations
4	Guetzkow et al (1954)	D v. L	University exams
5	Ruja (1954)	D v. L	Tests of knowledge on one of three courses
6	Ward (1956)	D v. L	Retention & understanding by less able students
97	Walker (1986)	D v. L	Recall & comprehension
8	Spence & Watson (1928)	Class D v. L	Objective tests
9	Jha & Baral (1973)	L+D v. D	Retention
10	Beilin & Rabow (1979)	L+D v. L	Scores on facts by whites
11	Connolly (1992)	L+D v. D	2/3 gps posttest
12	Burke (1955)	FGD v. L-D	Exams & Course work
13	Asch M.J. (1951)	'Non-directive' FGD v. L-D	MCQ, Essay examinations
14	Dawson (1956)	L-Demo v. problem-solving gps	Test of recall of information
15	Barnard (1942)	L-Demo v. problem C D	Tests on specific information
16	Marr et al (1960)	L v. Quizzing of teacher v. L by students	Course tests, final examinations
17	Peterson (1980)	L+Q&A v. Class D	Experimenter designed test
18	Metz (1987)	'Interactive instruction' v. L	2 of 19 measures

Tutorless Groups

1	Tans et al (1986)	PBL v Direct instruction	MCQ
2	Beach (1960)	Tutorless D v. L	Less sociable students on MCQ
3	Beach (1960)	Tutorless small gp D v. L	Less sociable students on MCQ
4	Brooks (1993)	Coop learning v. L	Knowledge gain scores
5	Smith D.L. (1995)	Coop learning v. L-D	Time spent in private study
6	Byers and Hedrick (1976)	D (small gp) v. L	Test scores/exams

Appendix 2.1
Discussion is more effective than presentation methods to promote thought

Comparisons showing discussion more effective

1	Asch M.J. (1951)	L v.`Non-directive' FGD	Breadth of thinking, consider more than one authority
2	Bloom (1953)	D v. L	Stimulated recall of thinking
3	Bond (1956)	D v. L	Decision-making
4	Brinkley (1952)	Gp D v. L	Stimulated recall of thought
5	Guetzkow et al (1954)	D v. L	McCandless Test of Scientific Attitudes, analytical thinking
6	Katz (1990)	D v. L	Problem-solving with active learning style, time taken
7	Lam (1984-5)	D v. L	Depth of question
8	McKeachie & Hiler (1954)	D v. L	Application of knowledge
9	Perkins (1950)	D v. L	Application of knowledge
10	Rickard (1946)	D v. L	Giving examples of generalisations
11	Ward (1956)	D v. L	Understanding by more able students
12	Erskine & Tomkin (1963)	Two Ds v. Nine Lectures	Oral examinations
13	Cabral-Pini (1995)	Coop learning v. L	Understanding a case study Flexible, creative (2-yr case study)
14	Mohr (1996)	Coop learning v. L	Cognitive Complexity Index
15	Smith D.L. (1995)	Coop learning v. L-D	Application questions
16	Hingorani (1996)	Case study + CAL v. L	reasoning, criticism, problem identification/solving, decisions
17	Tillman (1993)	Case Study v. L-D	Problem-solving, reserved judgement, multiple perspectives
18	Watson (1975)	Case study v. L	Application of principle
19	Self et al (1989)	L+Case D v. L	Moral reasoning
20	Khoiny (1995)	PBLearning v. L	Critical thinking
21	Eisenstaedt (1990)	PBL v. Trad instruction	2 year delayed test
22	Thompson (1987)	PBL v. Computer presentations	Diagnosis speed, responsiveness
23	Dawson (1956)	PB gps v. L-Demo	Problem-solving
24	Barnard (1942)	Problem D v. L-Demo	Problem-solving & scientific attitudes
25	Burns & Jones (1967)	Lecture-tutorial v. L	Sharper focus in written work more intense communication
26	Johnson & Smith (1953)	StCD v. TCD	Reasoning & creativity tests, case analysis
27	Greeson (1988)	StCD v.TCD	Questions asked; ideas.

28	Gibb & Gibb (1952)	'Participative action gps' v. L-Demo	Role flexibility in thinking
29	Sawyer & Sawyer (1981)	Microcounselling v. L	Decision-making
30	Carpenter (1956)	Small-gp D v.Ls, films and Demos	Problem-solving, scientific thinking
31	Zimmer et al (1974)	Proctor led D v. Quiz	Ability to generalise
32	Knowles (1975)	Tutorials v. Trad instruction	Verbal thinking
33	Hooper (1992)	Dyads v. Individual study	Computer based maths
34	Mill et al (1994)	Traditional+Tut v. Traditional Statistics & research methods	Reasoning & criticism in
35	Levin (1995)	D v. Reading & writing	Metacognitive & clear thought
36	Gibb (1993)	Teach to learn v. L	Application of knowledge
37	Jensen (1996)	Experiential learning v. L	Skills of Kolb's learning cycle

Comparisons showing no significant difference

1	Bloom (1953)	D v. L	Stimulated recall of application of knowledge
2	Davis & Horne (1986)	Gp Counselling v. L+D+tests	Career decision-making

Comparisons showing discussion less effective

1	Katz (1990)	D v. L	Problem-solving with reflective learning style, time taken
2	Millett (1969)	Unstructured D v. L	Student-teacher translation tactics
3	Eisenstaedt (1990)	PB Tutorial v. Traditonal instruction	Immediate test

Appendix 3.1
Discussion is more effective than presentation methods to promote attitude change

Studies showing discussion more effective

1	Barnard (1942)	ProblemC D v. L+Demo	Scientific attitude
2	Bennett (1955)	Consensus +individual decisions in D v. L	Expressed willingness to volunteer
3	Bovard (1951)	StCD v. TCD	Application of principles
4	Casey & Weaver (1956)	D v. L	Minnesota Teacher Attitude Inventory
5	Courtney et al (1994)	D v. L (Coop learning)	Self efficacy.

273

6	Gibb & Gibb (1952)	'Participative action gps' v.L	Role flexibility & self insight
7	Johnson & Smith (1953)	FGD v. L	Democratic attitude scale
8	Kelley & Pepitone (1952)	StCD v. TCD.	Ratings of empathy by peers.
9	Levine & Butler (1952)	Gp decision v. L	Objectivity in supervision of employees
10	Lewin (1943)	D v. L	Behaviour in response to persuasion
11	Metz (1987)	'Interactive instruction' v. L	Felt challenged
12	Mitnick & McGinnies(1958)	D v. L	Delayed attitude test
13	Pederson (1993)	D v. L (Debate)	Understanding suicidal factor
14	Pelz (1958)	D v. L v. control	Implementation of decision
15	Pennington et al (1958)	Gp decision by D v. L	Opinionnaire
16	Walton (1968)	Seminar v. L	Willingness to see patients, understand their emotional attachments
17	Wanlass et al (1983)	D v. L	Greater tolerance
18	Connolly (1992)	D v. D+L	1/3 gps' questionnaire on retirement
19	Diflorio (1996)	Coop learning v. L-D	sense of responsibility to others
20	Galbraith & Jones (1977)	D v. Reading	Moral development

NSD

1	Becker & Dallinger (1960)	D v. L	'Liberal democratic' attitudes
2	Bennett (1955)	D v. L	Willingness to volunteer
3	Corey (1967)	D v. L	Authoritarianism, perception of self & others
4	Di Vesta (1954)	D v. L	Leadership skills
5	Eglash (1954)	D v. L v. FGD	Rokeach Dogmatism Scale
6	Hill (1960)	D v. L	Liberal attitudes & tolerance of ambiguities, insight
7	Johnson & Smith (1953)	FGD v. L	Social sensitivity
8	Kriner & Vaughan (1975)	Structured D v. L Unstructured D v. L	Attitude to drugs
9	Leton (1961)	Case D v. L	Minnesota Teacher Attitude Inventory, Shoben's Parent Attitude Survey
10	Boroffice (1992)	L+D v. L	Attitude to patients
11	Connolly (1992)	D v. D+L	2/3 gps' questionnaire on retirement

Discussion less effective

1	Gerberich & Warner (1936)	D v. L	Tests of liberal attitudes
2	Pederson (1993)	D(Debate) v. L	Care for others
3	Wanlass et al (1983)	D v. L	Reduced anxiety
4	Benson (1996)	L+D in small gps v. L+L	Claydon responsibility scores

Appendix 3.2
Discussion is more effective than presentation methods to stimulate interest in a subject

Discussion more effective

1	Asch M.J. (1951)	Non-directive D v. L	Amount read
2	Byers & Hedrick (1976)	D (small gp) v. L	Greater interest, better attendance for D
3	Courtney et al (1994)	D (Coop learning) v. L	Motivation
4	Geiger (1996)	Coop learning gps v. L	Engagement with set task
5	Winteler (1974)	Seminar v. L	Motivation
6	Martenson et al	PBL v. Traditional methods	Attitude toward medicine
7	Levine J.R. (1990)	Tut for writing v. None	On time performance; work hard

NSD

1	Smith D.L. (1995)	Coop learning v. L-D	Gable-Roberts subject interest Q. Motivated Learning Strategies Q.
2	Austin (1996)	Coop learning v. L	Attitude to mathematics
3	Geiger (1996)	Classroom discourse v. L	Engagement with set task
4	Firstman (1983)	TV + D v. L	Expressed interest dropout rates

Discussion less effective

1	Firstman (1983)	TV + D v. L	Attendance rates

Appendix 3.3
Discussion is more popular than other methods

Studies showing discussion more popular

1	Walton (1968)	Sem v. L	Ratings of teaching & knowledge acquired
2	Winteler (1974)	Sem v. L	Questionnaire
3	Hale Report (1964)	Sems v. Tuts v. L	Questionnaire survey
4	McLeish (1968 & 1970)	Sem v. Tut v. L	Agree/disagree questionnaire
5	Stones (1970)	Sem v. Tut v. L	Questionnaire on preferred method
6	Saunders et al (1969)	Sem v. Tut v. L	Ratings as 'very effective', Preferred amount time spent on D, Criticisms of teachers
7	Burns & Jones (1967)	L-Tut v. L	Anonymous questionnaire
8	Metz (1987)	Interactive instruction v. L	Preferred method
9	Lam (1984-5)	D v. L	Interaction, teacher & St sociability, sharing experience
10	Mackie (1973)	StCD v. L	Attitude to content instruction achievement
11	Flood Page (1970)	Small Gps v. D v. L	Mean rank order for 'efficiency' and 'enjoyment'
12	Reid-Smith (1969)	Syndicate Gps v. L	5-point rating scale

NSD

1	Reid Smith (1969)	Seminar v. L	5-point rating scale

Discussion less popular

1	Gauvain (1968)	Seminars v. L	Questionnaires to postgraduates

References

Numbers printed after @ refer to the citation pages in this book

ABDUL-MUNIM, A.M. (1988) Dissertation Abstracts International, vol.50/03A p.607. **@ 268**

ABERCROMBIE, M.L.J. (1969) The Anatomy of Judgement. Penguin, Harmondsworth, Middlesex. **@ 21, 24, 256, 259**

ABRAHAM, A. and SCHUTZENBERGER, A.A. (1982) The problem of change according to the mode of teaching. Psychologie Francaise, vol.27 (1), pp.21–36. **@ 25**

ADAMS, G.L., TALLON, R. J. AND RIMELL, P. (1980) A comparison of lecture versus role-playing in the training of the use of positive reinforcement. Journal of Organizational Behavior Management, Summer vol.2, no.3, pp.205–212. **@ 26**

ADAMS, L.T. (1985) Improving memory: can retrieval strategies help? Human Learning: Journal of Practical Research and Applications, vol.4 (4), pp.281–297. **@ 7**

ALLEN, V.L. and WILDER, D.A. (1979) Group categorization and attribution of belief similarity. Small Group Behaviour, vol.10 (1), pp.73–80. **@ 150**

ALLPORT, F.H. (1920) The influence of the group upon association and thought. Journal of Experimental Psychology, vol.3, pp.159–182. **@ 113**

ALTMAN, I. and HAYTHORN, W.W. (1967) The ecology of isolated groups. Behavioral Science, vol.12, pp.169–182. **@ 174**

AMABILE, T.M. (1983) Social Psychology of creativity. New York Springer, Verlag. **@ 77**

ANDERSON, J.R. (1995) Cognitive psychology and its implications (4th edn). Freeman and Co., New York. **@ 70**

ANDREWS, S. (1996) The effects of a constructivist learning environment on student cognition of mechanics and attitude toward science: a case study (attitudes toward science). Dissertation Abstracts International-A, vol.56, no.08, February, p.2981. **@ 270**

ARGYLE, M. (1969) Social Interaction. Tavistock Publications. **@ 184, 186**

ASCH, M.J. (1951) Nondirective teaching in psychology: an experimental study. Psychological Monographs, vol.45, pp.1–24 (whole no. 321). **@ 25, 271, 272, 275**

ASCH, S.E. (1951) Effects of group pressure upon the modification and distortion of judgments, in Guetzkow, H., ed. Groups, Leadership and Men, Carnegie Press. pp.177–90. **@ 136–138, 155**

ASCH, S.E. (1956) Studies of independence and conformity: a minority of one against a unanimous majority. Psychological Monographs, vol.70 (whole no.416). **@ 134, 137**

AUSTIN, D.A. (1996) Effect of cooperative learning in finite mathematics on student achievement and attitude. Dissertation Abstracts International-A, vol.56, no.10, April, p.3868. **@ 275**

AUSTIN, M.F. and GRANT, T.N. (1981) Interview training for college students disadvantaged in the labor market: Comparison of five instructional techniques. Journal of Counseling Psychology, January, vol.28, no.1, pp.72–75. **@ 26**

BABAD, E.Y. and KURILOFF, P.J. (1986) Learning from trainer interventions in small groups. A function of participant and observer roles. Small Group Behaviour, vol.14 (4), pp. 427–443. @ **108**

BACK, K.W. (1973) Beyond Words: The story of sensitivity training and the Encounter movement. Penguin Books, Harmondsworth, Middlesex. @ **188**

BALES, R.F. (1952) Some uniformities of behaviour in small social systems. In G.E. Swanson, T.M. Newcomb, and E.L. Hartley, eds. Readings in Social Psychology (2nd edn). Holt. @ **121, 165, 167, 183**

BALES, R.F. (1965). The equilibrium problem in small groups. A.P. Hare, E.F. Borgatta and R.F. Bales, eds. Small Groups: Studies in Social Interaction (New edn). Knopf, New York. @ **167**

BALES, R.F. (1970) Personality and Interpersonal Behaviour. Holt, Rhinehart and Winston, New York. @ **141–144, 158, 166, 183, 246**

BALES, R.F., STRODTBECK, F.L., MILLS, T.M. and ROSEBOROUGH, M. (1951) Channels of communication in small groups. American Journal of Sociological Review, vol.16, pp.461–468. @ **152, 153, 156, 172**

BANE, C.L. (1925) The lecture vs. the class-discussion method of college teaching. School and Society, vol.21, pp.300–302. @ **267, 269**

BANE, C.L. (1931) The Lecture in College Teaching. Badger. @ **267, 269**

BARKER, L.L. (1971) Listening Behaviour. Prentice-Hall, New Jersey. @ **240**

BARKER, L.L., WAHLERS, K.J., WATSON, K.W. and KIBLER, R.J. (1987) Groups in Process: An introduction to group communication. Prentice Hall, New Jersey. @ **241**

BARNARD, H.S. (1982) A small group programme to facilitate identity information. Small Group Behavior, vol.13, no.1, pp.387–393. @ **17**

BARNARD, J.D. (1942) The lecture-demonstration vs. the problem- solving method of teaching a college science course. Science Education, vol.26, pp.121–132. @ **271, 272, 273**

BARNARD, W.A., MASON,W.A., and CEYNAR, M.L. (1993) Level of interaction and reciprocal influence in supportive and critical male discussion groups. Journal of Social Psychology, vol.133 (6), pp.833–838.

BARNARD, W.H. (1936) Note on the comparative efficacy of lecture and socialised recitation versus group study method. Journal of Educational Psychology, vol.27, pp. 276–284. @ **269**

BARNLUND, D.C. (1959) A comparative study of individual, majority, and group judgment. Journal of Abnormal and Social Psychology, vol.58, pp.55–60. @ **11**

BARON, R.M. (1963) A cognitive model of attitude change. Unpublished Doctoral Dissertation, New York University (see Cohen A.R. 1964). @ **104**

BARTON, W.A. (1926) The effect of group activity and individual effort in developing ability to solve problems in First Year Algebra. Journal of Educational Administration and Supervision, vol. 12, pp. 512–518. Cited in Shaw, M.E. (1981) Group Dynamics: Psychology of Small Group Behaviour. McGraw-Hill Press. @ **10**

BASS, B.M., PRYER, M.W., GAIER, E.L. and FLINT, A.W. (1958) Interacting effects of control, motivation, group practice and problem difficulty on attempted leadership. Journal of Abnormal and Social Psychology, vol.56, pp.352–358. @ **123**

BAXTER, J.C. (1970) Interpersonal spacing in natural settings. Sociometry, vol.33, pp.444–456. **@ 175**

BEACH, L.R. (1960) Sociability and academic achievement in various types of learning situations. Journal of Educational Psychology, vol.51, pp.208–212. **@ 268, 269, 271**

BECHTEL, L. P. (1963) Comparative Effects of Differentiated Teaching Methods on Certain Personality Characteristics of College Students. Doctoral Dissertation, New York University. **@ 25**

BECKER, S.L. and DALLINGER, C.A. (1960) The effects of instructional methods upon achievement and attitudes in communication skills. Speech Monographs, vol.27, pp.70– 76. **@ 269, 274**

BEEM, A.I. and BRUGMAN, D. (1986) The effects of value development lessons on pupils' wellbeing, pleasure in school, mutual relationships, and on pupils' valuational behaviour during classroom dialogues. Theory and Research in Social Education, vol.14 (2), pp.97–112. **@ 19**

BEILIN, R. and RABOW J. (1979) Effects of ethnicity and course structure on factual learning and critical ability. Annual Meeting of the American Sociological Association, Boston. August. ERIC ED180902. **@ 268, 269, 271**

BEM, D.J. (1967) Self-perception: An alternative interpretation of cognitive dissonance phenomena. Psychological Review, vol.74, pp.183–200. **@ 97**

BENNETT, E.B. (1955) Discussion, decision, commitment and consensus in 'group decision'. Human Relations, vol.8, pp.251–273. **@ 18, 19, 26, 273, 274**

BENNE, K.D. and SHEATS, P. (1948) Functional roles of group members. Journal of Social Issues, vol.4, pp.41–49. **@ 121**

BENNIS, W.G. and SHEPARD, H.A. (1956) A theory of group development. Human Relations. Reprinted in G.S. Gibbard, J.J.Hartman and R.D.Man, vol.9, pp.415–437. **@ 160, 170, 171**

BENSON, S. B. (1996) A comparison of the effects of short-term small groups and lectures on the knowledge, attitudes and behavior of pharmacy students concerning alcohol/alcoholism. Dissertation Abstracts International, vol.57-A, no.06, December, p.2353. **@ 269, 275**

BERNE, E. (1964) Games People Play. Penguin Books. **@ 100**

BILLS, R.E. (1952) Investigation of student centred teaching. Journal of Educational Research, vol.46, pp.313–319. **@ 269**

BLAKE, R. and MOUTON, J. (1964) The Management Grid. Gulf. **@ 163**

BLAKEMAN, R., and HELMREICH, R. (1975) Cohesiveness and performance: covariation and causality in an undersea environment. Journal of Experimental Social Psychology, vol.11, pp.478–489. **@ 188**

BLIGH, D.A. (1998) What's the Use of Lectures? (5th edn). Intellect Books, Bristol. **@ vii, 206**

BLIGH, D.A. (1974) Are varied teaching methods more effective? PhD Thesis of the University of London. **@ 7, 51**

BLOOM, B. S., ed. (1956) Taxonomy of Educational Objectives: I. Cognitive Domain, Longman. **@ 238**

BLOOM, B.S., ed. (1953) Thought-processes in lectures and discussions. Journal of General Education, vol.7, pp.160–169. @ **10, 271, 272, 273**
BOEDING, C.H. and VATTANO, F.J. (1976) Undergraduates as teaching assistants: A comparison of two discussion methods. Teaching of Psychology, vol.3 (2), pp.55–59. @ **268**
BOND, B.W. (1956) Group discussion-decision: an appraisal of its use in health education. Minnesota Department of Health. Reported in Ruth Eckert (ed.) Encyclopaedia of Educational Research (3rd edn). 1960, College and University Programs. @ **267, 272**
BOOKMAN, A.B. and IWANICKI, E.F. (1983) The effects of method of test preparation on standardized mathematics achievement test performance. Journal of Research and Development in Education, Summer, vol.16, no.4, pp.46–51. @ **26**
BORG, W.R. (1960) Prediction of small group role behaviour from personality variables. Journal of Abnormal and Social Psychology, vol.60, pp.112–116. @ **142**
BOROFFICE, O.B. (1992) Fostering medical compliance in some Nigerian sickle cell disease patients. Journal of Applied Rehabilitation Counseling, Spring, vol.23, no.1, pp.33–37. @ **274**
BOVARD, E.W. (1951) The psychology of classroom interaction. Journal of Educational Research, vol.45, pp.215–224. @ **273**
BRAATEN, L.J. (1974) Developmental phases of encounter groups: a critical review of models and a new proposal. Inter Personal Development, vol.75, pp.112–129. @ **171**
BRAZA, J., KREUTER, M.W. (1975) Journal of School Health, vol.45 (6): 353–355. @ **17**
BRECKHEIMER, S.E. and NELSON, R.O. (1976) Group Methods for reducing racial prejudice and discrimination. Psychological Reports, vol.39 (3, Part 2), pp.1259–1268. @ **15**
BRINKLEY, S.G. (1952) Mental activity in college classes: student estimates of relative value of ten learning situations. Journal of Experimental Education, vol.20, pp.373–378. @ **272**
BROOKS, V.S. (1993) Alcohol education pedagogy: effects on knowledge and locus-of-control (health knowledge). Dissertation Abstracts International, January, vol.53-A, no.07, p.2256. @ **25, 271**
BROWN, G.A. and ATKINS, M. (1988) Effective Teaching in Higher Education. Methuen. @ **249**
BROWN, G.A. and EDMONDSON, R. (1984) Asking Questions. In Wragg, ed. Classroom Teaching Skills. London. Croom Helm. pp.97–120. @ **249**
BRYANT, N. (1975) Petitioning: dress congruence versus belief congruence. Journal of Applied Social Psychology, vol.5, pp.144–149. @ **150**
BURKE, D.M., McKAY, D.G., WORTHLEY, J.S. and WADE, E. (1991) On the tip of the tongue: What causes word finding failures in young and older adults? Journal of Memory and Language, vol.30, pp.542–579. @ **39**
BURKE, H.R. (1955) An experimental Study of Teaching Methods in a College Freshman Orientation Course, doctoral dissertation, Boston University. Dissertation Abstracts, vol.16, pp.77–78. @ **271**

BURKE, V.M. (1977) The veil and the vision. Black American Literature Forum, vol.11, no.3, pp.91–94. ERIC EJ 171476. **@ 22**

BURNS, R.S. AND JONES, R.C. (1967) Two experimental approaches to freshman composition–lecture-tutorial and team teaching. Central Missouri State College, Warrensburg. ERIC ED510214. **@ 272, 276**

BUTLER, R. and NISAN, M. (1986) Effects of no feedback, task- related comments, and grades on intrinsic motivation and performance. Journal of Educational Psychology, vol.78 (3), pp.210–216. **@ 110**

BYERS W. S. and HEDRICK R.E. (1976) A comparison of two teaching strategies: lecture vs. discussion in a small class environment at Florida Southern College, Report. ERIC ED136741. **@ 271, 275**

CABRAL-PINI, A.M. (1995) Cooperative learning: its effect on math education. Dissertation Abstracts International-A, June, vol.55, no.12, p.3772. **@ 25, 272**

CAMP, D.L., HOLLINGSWORTH, M.A., ZACCARO, D.J., CARIAGA L.L.D. et al (1994) Does a problem based learning curriculum affect depression in medical students? Academic Medicine, October, vol.69, no.10, Suppl. pp.S25–S27. **@ 25**

CANAS, J.J. and NELSON, D.L. Recognition and environmental context: the effect of testing by 'phone. Bulletin of the Psychonomic Society, vol.24 (6), pp.407–409. **@ 178**

CARLSON, C.R. (1953) A study of the relative effectiveness of lecture and directed discussion methods of teaching tests and measurements to prospective Air Force Instructors. Dissertation Abstracts, vol.13, pp.112–113. **@ 269**

CARPENTER, F. (1956) Educational significance of studies on the relation between rigidity and problem solving. Science Education, vol.40, pp.296–311. **@ 273**

CARSRUD, A.L. (1979) Undergraduate tutors: Are they useful? Teaching of Psychology, vol.6 (1) pp.46–49. **@ 270**

CARTER, L.D. (1995) Effectiveness of case-based method versus traditional lecture in the retention of athletic training knowledge. Dissertation Abstracts International-A, vol.56, no.06, December, p.2164. **@ 268, 270**

CARTER, L.F. (1953) On defining leadership. In M. Sherif and M.O. Wilson, eds. Group relations at the crossroads. Harper and Row, New York, pp.262–265. **@ 159**

CARTWRIGHT, D., and ZANDER, A. (1968) Leadership and performance of group functions: introduction. In Cartwright, D. and Zander, A., eds. Group Dynamics: Research and Theory (3rd edn). pp.301–317. **@ 125**

CASEY, J.E. and WEAVER, B.E. (1956) An evaluation of lecture method and small group method of teaching in terms of knowledge of content, teacher attitude, and social status. Journal of Colorado-Wyoming Academy of Science, vol.4, p.54. **@ 270, 273**

CHAPMAN, L.J. and CHAPMAN, J. (1971) Test results are what you think they are. Psychology Today, Nov., pp.106–110. **@ 88**

CHAPPEL, J.N. and VEACH,T.L. (1987) Effect of a course on students' attitudes toward substance abuse and its treatment. Journal of Medical Education, vol.62 (5), pp.394–400. **@ 17**

CHASE, W.G. and SIMON, H.A. (1973) Perception in Chess. Cognitive Psychology, vol.4, pp. 55–81. **@ 64**

CHI, M.T.H., FELTOVICH, P. and GLASER, R. (1981) Categorization and representation of physics problems by experts and novices. Cognitive Science, vol.5, pp.121–152. **@ 61**

CHU, G.H. and SCHRAMM, W. (1967) Learning from television: what the research says. Stanford Institute for Communication Research. **@ 3**

CHURCHILL, R. and JOHN, P. (1958) Conservation of teaching time through the use of lecture classes and student assistants. Journal of Educational Psychology, vol.49, pp.324–327. **@ 270**

CHURCHILL, R.D. (1960) Evaluation of independent study in college courses. Doctoral dissertation, University of Minnesota. **@ 270**

CLABBY, J.F. and BELZ, E.J. (1985) Psychological barriers to learning. An approach using group treatment. Small Group Behaviour, vol.16 (4), pp.525–533. **@ 108**

CLAXTON, C.S. and RALSTON, Y. (1978) Learning styles: their impact on teaching and administration. American Association for Higher Education and ERIC Clearinghouse on Higher Education. **@ 147**

COHEN, A.R. (1959) Situational structure, self-esteem, and threat-oriented reactions to power. Cartwright, D., ed. Studies in social power. Ann Arbor, Michigan Institute for Social Research. **@ 123**

CONNOLLY, J. (1992) Participatory versus lecture/discussion preretirement education: a comparison. Educational Gerontology, vol.18, no.4, pp.365–379. **@ 26, 269, 271, 274**

COOK, D.W., KUNCE, J.T. and SLEATER, S.M. (1974) Vicarious behaviour induction and training psychiatric aides. Journal of Community Psychology, vol.2 (3), pp.293–297. **@ 26**

COOPER, C.L. and MANGHAM, I.L. (1971) T-Groups: A survey of research. Wiley, New York. **@ 23**

COREY, G.F. (1967) An investigation of the outcomes of an introductory psychology course in a junior college. Doctoral dissertation, University of Southern California, School of Education. **@ 274**

COSTANZO, M. (1992) Training students to decode verbal and nonverbal cues: Effects on confidence and performance. Journal of Educational Psychology, September, vol.84, no.3, pp.308–313. **@ 26**

COTA, A.A. and DION, K.L. (1986) Salience of gender and sex composition of ad hoc groups: an experimental test of distinctiveness theory. Journal of Personality and Social Psychology, vol.50 (4), pp.770–776. **@ 146**

COTTRELL, N.B. (1972) Social facilitation. In McClintock, C.G., ed. Experimental social Psychology, pp.185–236. **@ 111**

COURTNEY, D. P., COURTNEY, M. AND NICHOLSON, C. (1994) The effect of cooperative learning as an instructional practice at the college level. College Student Journal, December, vol.28, no.4, pp.471–477. **@ 25, 270, 273, 275**

COYNE, P.D. (1978) The effects of peer tutoring with group contingencies on the academic performance of college students. Journal of Applied Behavior Analysis, vol.11 (2), pp.305–307. **@ 268**

CRAIK, F.I. and McDOWD, J.M. (1987) Age differences in recall and recognition.

Journal of Experimental Psychology: Learning, Memory and Cognition, vol.13 (3), pp.474–479. **@ 8**

CROCKENBERG, S.G. (1972) Creativity tests: a boon or boondoggle for education? Review of Educational Research, vol.42, no.1, pp.27–45. **@ 71**

CROSS, K.P. (1981) Adults as Learners: Increasing participation and facilitating learning. Jossey-Bass. **@ 147**

DALY, J.A., BELL, R.A. and KORINEK, J. (1987) Interrelationships among attitudes toward academic subjects. Journal of Contemporary Educational Psychology, vol.12 (2), pp147–155. **@ 146**

D'ANGELO, E. (1971) The Teaching of Critical Thinking. B.R. Gruner, Amsterdam. **@ 254**

DAVIS, J.H. and RESTLE, F. (1963) The analysis of problems and production of group problem solving. Journal of Abnormal and Social Psychology, vol.66, pp.103–116. **@ 12**

DAVIS, R.C. and HORNE, A.M. (1986) The effect of small-group counseling and a career course on career decidedness and maturity. Vocational Guidance Quarterly, vol.34 (4), pp.255–262. **@ 273**

DAWES, R.M. (1971) A case study of graduate admissions: applications of three principles of human decision making. American Psychologist, vol.26, pp.180–188. **@ 87**

DAWSON, M.D. (1956) Lecture vs. problem-solving in teaching elementary social sciences. Science Education, vol.40, pp.395–404. **@ 268, 271, 272**

de GROOT, A.D. (1966) Perception and memory versus thought: some old ideas and recent findings. In Kleinmuntz, B., ed. Problem Solving: Research, method, and theory. pp.19–49. Wiley, New York. **@ 64**

DEIGNAN, F.J. (1956) A comparison of the effectiveness of two group discussion methods. Dissertation Abstracts, vol.16, pp.1110–1111. **@ 269**

DEUTSCH, M. and GERARD, H.B. (1955) A study of normative and informational social influence upon individual judgement. Journal of Abnormal and Social Psychology, vol.51, pp.629–636. **@ 135**

DEUTSCH, M., CANAVAN, D. and RUBIN, J. (1971) The effects of size of conflict and sex of experimenter upon interpersonal bargaining. Journal of Experimental Social Psychology, vol.7, pp.258–267. **@ 171, 146**

Di VESTA, F.J. (1954) Instructor-centred and student-centred approaches in teaching human relations course. Journal of Applied Psychology, vol.38, pp.329–335. **@ 269, 274**

DIES, R.R. (1979) Group psychotherapy: refections on three decades of research. Journal of Applied Behavioural Science, vol.15, pp.361–373. **@ 264**

DIFLORIO, I.A.S. (1996) Cooperative learning: a study of nursing students' achievement and perceptions. Dissertation Abstracts International-A, vol.56, no.09, March, p.3431. **@ 25, 26, 270, 274**

DOENAU, S.J. (1984) Soliciting. In M.J. Dunkin, ed. International Encyclopedia of Teaching and Teacher Education, pp.407–413. **@ 249**

DUBES, M.J. (1987) Comparison of lecture, discussion and poster modes of instruction of adults ages 59 to 90 attending nutrition sites. Dissertation Abstracts International, vol.49-A, no.06, p. 1344. **@ 269**

DUBIN, R. and TAVEGGIA, T.C. (1968) The teaching-learning paradox. Centre for the Advanced Study of Educational Administration. Monograph No. 18. University of Oregon. **@ 3**

DUBIN, R. and HEDLEY, R. A. (1969) The medium may be related to the message: college instruction by TV. Eugene Oregon. Center for the study of Advanced Study of Educational Administration. **@ 3**

DUNPHY, D.C. (1974) The Function of Fantasy in Groups. In G.S. Gibbard, J.J. Hartman and R.D. Mann, eds. Analysis of Groups. Jossey Bass, San Francisco. **@ 169**

DUTT, K. M. (1994) The cognitive and affective outcomes of cooperative learning in four college education courses (cognitive outcomes). Dissertation Abstracts International-A, vol.54, no.08, February, p.2986. **@ 270**

EDMONDSON, J.H. and WHITE, J. (1998) A tutorial and counselling program: Helping students at risk of dropping out of school. Professional School Counseling, vol.1 (4), pp.43–47. **@ 268**

EGAN, G. (1982) The Skilled Helper. Brooks/Cole. **@ 176, 262**

EGLASH, A. (1954) A group discussion method of teaching psychology. Journal of Educational Psychology, vol.45, pp.257–267. **@ 270, 274**

EHRLICH, H.J. and LEE, D. (1969) Dogmatism, learning and resistance to change: a review and a new paradigm. Psychological Bulletin, vol.71 (4), pp.249–260. **@ 142**

EISENSTAEDT, R.S., BARRY, W.E and GLANZ, K. (1990) Academic Medicine, vol.65 (9, Suppl), S11–S12 **@ 272, 273**

EKEHAMMAR, B.O. (1985) Women and men and research: perceptions, attitudes, values, and choice. Reports from the Department of Psychology, University of Stockholm. Suppl. 64., p.34. **@ 146**

EMERY, M. (1986) Toward an heuristic theory of diffusion. Human Relations, vol.39 (5), pp.411–432. **@ 16**

ENNIS, H.R. (1962) A concept of critical thinking. Harvard Educational Review, Winter, vol.32, no.1, pp.83–111. **@ 253**

ERICSSON, A. and SIMON, H.A. (1980) Verbal reports as data. Psychological Review. vol.87, pp.215–225. **@ 87**

ERLICH, R. (1979) Anxiety reduction in small groups learning and in frontal instruction classroom. Israeli Journal of Psychology and Counseling in Education, February, pp.1038–44. **@ 25**

ERSKINE, C.A. and TOMKIN, A. (1963) Evaluation of the effect of the group-discussion method in a complex teaching programme. Journal of Medical Education, December, vol.38, pp.1036–1043. **@ 268, 269, 272**

EVANS, R.D. and EVANS, G.E. (1989) Cognitive mechanisms in learning from metaphors. Journal of Experimental Education, Fall, vol.58, no.1, pp.5–19. **@ 26**

EYSENCK, M.W. and KEANE, M.T. (1990) Cognitive Psychology: A student's handbook. Laurence Erlbaum Associates. **@ 70**

FALVO, D.R., SMAGA, S., BRENNER, J.S. AND TIPPY, P.K. (1991) Lecture versus role modeling: A comparison of educational programs to enhance residents' ability to communicate with patients about HIV. Teaching and Learning in Medicine, vol.3, no.4 , pp.227–231. **@ 26**

– References –

FELSON, R.B. and REED, M.D. (1986) Reference groups and self- appraisals of academic ability and performance. Social Psychology Quarterly, vol.49 (2), pp.103–109. @ **148**

FERNANDEZ, A. and GLENBERG, A.M. (1985) Changing environmental context does not reliably affect memory. Memory and Cognition, vol.13 (4), pp.333–345. @ **178**

FESTINGER, L. (1957) A Theory of Cognitive Dissonance. Row Peterson, Evanston. @ **96, 135, 138**

FEU (1987) See Further Education Unit. @ **126**

FIEDLER, F. (1967) A Theory of Leadership Effectiveness. McGraw-Hill, New York. @ **162–163**

FIRSTMAN, A. (1983) A comparison of traditional and television lectures as a means of instruction in biology at a community college. Unpublished. ERIC ED230264. @ **275**

FISS, H. (1978) A dynamic conceptual approach to the teaching of psychotherapy in the classroom. Professional Psychology, Nov., vol.9 (4), pp.646–649. @ **17**

FITZGERALD, A.I. (1960) A study of the relative effectiveness of selected instructional procedures in a college course in children's literature. Doctoral Dissertation, University of Missouri. @ **269**

FLANAGAN, S., ADAMS, H.E. AND FOREHAND, R. (1979) A comparison of four instructional techniques for teaching parents to use time out. Behavior Therapy, January, vol.10, no.1, pp.94–102. @ **26**

FLANDERS, N.L. (1970) Interaction Analysis. Addison Wesley. @ **246**

FLEETWOOD, R.S. and PARISH, T.S. (1976) Relationship between moral development test scores of juvenile delinquents and their inclusion in a moral dilemma discussion group. Psychological Reports, vol.39 (3, Part 2), pp.1075–1080. @ **17**

FLOOD PAGE, C. (1970) Students' reactions to teaching methods'. Universities Quarterly, July, pp.266–72. @ **276**

FODOR, E.M. and SMITH, T. (1982) The power motive as an influence on group decision making. Journal of Personality and Social Psychology Bulletin, vol.9, p.587–9.

FONTENOT, D.W. (1996) The effects of cooperative learning methods in conjunction with traditional lectures in seventh-grade earth science classes. Dissertation Abstracts International-A, July, vol.57, no.01, p.86. @ **268**

FORTNER, V.L. (1986) Generalization of creative productive thinking training to LD students' written expression. Learning Disability Quarterly, Fall, vol.9 (4), pp.274–284. @ **71**

FRASER, B.J. (1986) Determinants of classroom psychosocial environments: a review. Journal of Research in Childhood Education, vol.1 (1), pp.5–19. @ **179**

FREIRE, P. (1970) Pedagogy of the Oppressed. Herder and Herder. New York. @ **16, 259**

FURST, E.J. and STEELE, B.L. (1986) Motivational orientations of older adults in university courses as described by factor and cluster analyses. Journal of Experimental Education, vol.54 (4), pp.193–201. @ **146**

FURTHER EDUCATION UNIT (1987) Stretching the mind: increasing support for intellectual development. A discussion document. Department of Education and Science.

FYFE, B. (1979) Effects of a sexual enhancement workshop on young adults. Journal of Clinical Psychology, vol.35 (4), pp.873–875. **@ 17**

GADZELLA, B. M. (1977) Performance on objective and essay tests by individualized study, lecture, and group discussions in educational psychology. Perceptual and Motor Skills, vol.44, no.3, pt 1, June, pp.753–754. **@ 269, 271**

GALBRAITH, R.E. and JONES, T.A. (1977) Teaching for moral reasoning in the social studies: a research report. Counseling Psychologist, vol.6 (4), pp.60–63. **@ 274**

GALL, M.D. and GALL, J.P. (1976) The discussion method in: Gage N.L., ed. The Psychology of Teaching Methods. 75th Year Book of the National Association for the Study of Education, Part I. University of Chicago Press. **@ 14**

GALOTTI, K.M. (1995) Reasoning about reasoning: a course project. Teaching of Psychology, vol.22, pp.66–68. **@ 10**

GARCIA-WEREBE, M.J. and REINERT, M. (1976) Sex education: Results of an experimental study with adolescent sample. Bulletin de Psychologie, vol.30 (1 Supplement 2), pp.46–58. **@ 270**

GARDNER, H. (1985) Frames of Mind. Palladin Books. **@ 71**

GAUVAIN, S. (1968) The use of student opinion in the quality control of teaching. British Journal of Medical Education, vol.2, no.1, pp.55–62. **@ 16, 269, 276**

GAYNOR, J.F. and WOLKING, W.D. (1974) The effectiveness of currently enrolled proctors in an undergraduate special education course. Journal of Applied Behavior Analysis, vol.7 (2), pp.263–269. **@ 268**

GEERLIGS, T. (1994) Students' thoughts during problem-based small-group discussions. Instructional Science, vol.22 (4), pp.267–278. **@ 10**

GEIGER, W. M. (1996) The comparison of student engagement rates during classroom discourse, cooperative learning, and lecture methods of instruction in secondary schools. Dissertation Abstracts International, vol.57-A, no.03, September, p.1086. **@ 275**

GERARD, H.B., WILHELMY, R.A. and CONOLLEY, E.S. (1968) Conformity and group size. Journal of Personality and Social Psychology, vol.8, pp.79–82. **@ 155**

GERBERICH, J.R. and WARNER, K.O. (1936) Relative instructional efficiencies of the lecture and discussion methods in a university course in American National Government. Journal of Education Research, vol.29, pp.574–579. **@ 267, 269, 271, 275**

GERGEN, K.J. and BAUER, R.A. (1967) Interactive effects on self-esteem and task difficulty on social conformity., Journal of Personality and Social Psychology, vol.6, pp.16–22. **@ 124**

GERSON, J.M. (1985) Women returning to school: the consequences of multiple roles. Sex Roles, vol.13 (1–2), pp.77–92. **@ 147**

GETZELS, J. and CSIKSZENTMIHALYI, M. (1976) The Creative Vision: A longitudinal study of problem finding in art. Wiley, New York. **@ 77, 79**

GIBB, J.R. (1961) Defensive communicaton. Journal of Communication, vol.11, pp.141–148. **@ 255**

GIBB, L.M. and GIBB, J.R. (1952) The effects of the use of 'particpative action' groups in a course in general psychology. American Psychologist, vol.7, p.247 (abstract). @ **273, 274**

GIBB, S.A. (1993) Evaluating first-year education students for retention and application of knowledge through a comparison of two teaching strategies: the lecture method and teaching-for-learning (knowledge retention). Dissertation Abstracts International-A, vol.53, no.10, April, p.3500. @ **268, 273**

GICK, M.L. and MCGARRY, S.J. (1992) Learning from mistakes: inducing analogous solution failures to a source problem produces later success in analogical transfer. Journal of Experimental Psychology: Human Learning and Memory, vol.18, pp.623–639. @ **65**

GILES-GEE, H.F. (1989) Increasing the retention of black students: a multimethod approach. Journal of College Student Development, vol.30 (3), pp.196–200. @ **16**

GILMORE, S. (1977) The effects of positive and negative models on student-teachers' questioning behaviours. In McIntyre et al. @ **183**

GOLDMAN, M. (1965) A comparison of individual and group performance for varying combinations of initial ability. Journal of Personality and Social Psychology, vol.1, pp.210–216. @ **10, 149**

GOOD, K.J. (1973) Social facilitation: effects of performance anticipation, evaluation and response competition on free associations. Journal of Personality and Social Psychology, vol.28, pp.270–275. @ **111**

GORDON, W.J. (1961) Synectics: The development of creative capacity. Harper and Row, New York. @ **78**

GORE, A.E. (1962) Individualised instruction through team learning in a college course in general psychology. Doctoral dissertation, Boston University. Reprinted in Dissertation Abstracts, no. 23/04/1273. @ **268**

GOTKE, E. (1931) cited in C.L. Bane, The Lecture in College Teaching, Badger. @ **269**

GRABOWSKY, S.M. (1970) Teaching catechetics with role playing. Catholic Educator, vol.40(8), pp.30–32. @ **17**

GREENWOOD, C.R. (1984) Teacher versus peer mediated instruction: An ecobehavioral analysis of achievement outcomes. Journal of Applied Behaviour Analysis, vol.17, no.4, pp.521–538. @ **3**

GREESON, L.E. (1988) College classroom interaction as a function of teacher- and student-centered instruction. Teaching and Teacher Education, vol.4 (4), pp.305–315. @ **10, 272**

GUERIN, B. (1986) Mere presence effects in humans: a review. Journal of Experimental Social Psychology, vol.22 (1), pp.38–77. @ **135**

GUETZKOW, H., KELLY, L.E. and McKEACHIE, W.J. (1954) An experimental comparison of recitation, discussion and tutorial methods in college teaching. Journal of Educational Psychology, vol.45, pp.193–207. @ **269, 271, 272**

GUILFORD, J.P. and HOEPFNER, R. (1971) The Analysis of Intelligence. McGraw-Hill, New York. @ **74**

GURNEE, H. (1937) Maze learning in the collective situation. Journal of Psychology, vol.3, pp. 437–443. @ **5**

GURNEE, H. (1939) The effect of collective learning upon the individual participants. Journal of Abnormal and Social Psychology, vol.44, pp.491–504. **@ 5**

GUYOT, G.W., BYRD, G.R. and CAUDLE, R. (1980) Classroom seating: an expression of situational territoriality in humans. Small Group Behaviour, vol.11 (1), pp.120–128. **@ 178**

HACKMAN, J.R., and VIDMAR, N. (1970) Effects of size and task type on group performance and member reactions. Sociometry, vol.33, pp.37–54. **@ 154**

HAIGH, B.V. and SCHMIDT, W.H. (1956) Learning of subject matter in teacher-centred and group-centred classes. Journal of Educational Psychology, vol.47, pp.295–301. **@ 269**

HALE, R.E. and CAMPLESE, D.A. (1974) Assessing the effectiveness of a mastery teacher education program. Western Carolina University Journal of Education, Winter, vol.5, no.3, pp.26–32. **@ 26**

HALE, Sir E. (University Grants Committee) (1964) Report of the Committee on Teaching Methods. HMSO. **@ 16, 276**

HANDY, C.B. (1987) Understanding Organisations. Penguin Books, Harmondsworth, Middx. **@ 186**

HARACKIEWICZ, J.M. and LARSON, R. (1986) Managing motivation: the impact of supervisor feedback on subordinate task interest. Journal of Personality and Social Psychology, vol.51 (3), pp.547–556. **@ 110**

HARE, A.P. (1952) Interaction and consensus in different sized groups. American Sociological Review, vol.17, pp.261–267. **@ 155**

HARE, A.P., and BALES, R.F. (1963) Seating position and small group interaction. Sociometry, vol.26, pp.480–486. **@ 176**

HARVEY, O.J., HUNT, D.E., and SCHRODER, H.M. (1961) Conceptual Systems and Personality Organisation. Wiley, New York. **@ 149**

HASKELL, R.E. (1991) An analogical methodology for analysis and validation of anomalous cognitive and linguistic operations in small group (fantasy theme) reports. Small Group Research, vol.22 (4), pp.443–474. **@ 30**

HEARN, G. (1957) Leadership and the spatial factor in small groups. Journal of Abnormal and Social Psychology, vol.54, pp.269–272. **@ 177**

HELLER, B. and DALE, M. (1976) Traditional teaching and learning modules. Exceptional Children, vol.42 (4), pp.231–232. **@ 269**

HERRMANN, D.J. (1982) Know thy memory: the use of questionnaires to assess and study memory. Psychological Bulletin, vol.92, pp.434–452. **@ 87**

HERSEY, P. and BLANCHARD, K. (1977) Management of Organisational Behaviour: Utilising human resources (3rd edn). Prentice Hall, New Jersey. **@ 169**

HEVERIN, J. P. (1993) Marital preparation: a comparison of skill training and lecture on factors related to marital success (communication skills training, premarital intervention). Dissertation Abstracts International, vol.53-A, no.12, June, p.4254. **@ 25, 26**

HILL, R.J. (1960) A comparative study of lecture and discussion. New York Fund for Adult Education **@ 269, 274**

HILL, W. (1977) Learning thru discussion. Sage Publications, Beverley, California. **@ 255**

HINGORANI, K.K. (1996) Information technology supported case studies for teaching higher level cognitive skills: a comparative evaluation of methodologies (professional development). Dissertation Abstracts International, vol.56-A, no.12, June, p.4852. @ **272**

HOFFMAN, L.R. and MAIER, N.R.F. (1961) Quality and acceptance of problem solutions by members of homogeneous and heterogeneous groups. Journal of Abnormal and Social Psychology, vol.62, pp.401–407. @ **145**

HOGG, M.A. (1985) Masculine and feminine speech in dyads and groups: a study of speech style and gender salience. Journal of Language and Social Psychology, vol.4 (2), pp.99–112. @ **137**

HOLLAND, J.G. and SKINNER, B.F. (1961) Analysis of Behavior. McGraw-Hill, New York. @ **39**

HOLLANDER, E.P. and WILLIS, R.H. (1967) Some current issues in the psychology of conformity and nonconformity. Psychological Bulletin, vol.68, pp.62–76. @ **135**

HOLLANDER, E.P. (1967) Principles and Methods of Social Psychology. Oxford University Press, New York. @ **183**

HOLLIDAY, G. (1985) Addressing the concerns of returning women students. New Directions for Student Services, vol.29, pp.61–73. @ **147**

HOLTZCLAW, L.R. (1985) Adult learners' preferred learning styles, choice of courses and subject areas for prior experimental learning credit. Lifelong Learning, April, pp. 23–27. @ **147**

HOLYOAK, K.J. and SPELLMAN, B.A. (1993) Thinking. Annual Review of Psychology, vol.44, pp.265–315. @ **65**

HOOPER,S. (1992) Effects of peer interaction during computer-based mathematics instruction. Journal of Educational Research, vol.85 (3), pp.180–189. @ **273**

HOUSE, J.D. and WOHLT, V. (1991) Effect of tutoring on voluntary school withdrawal of academically underprepared minority students. Journal of School Psychology, vol.29 (2), pp.135–142. @ **16**

HUCZYNSKI, A. (1983) Encyclopaedia of Management Development Methods. Gower Press. @ **189**

HUDELSON, E. (1928) Class Size at the College Level. University of Minnesota Press. @ **269**

HUDSON, L. (1966) Contrary Imaginations: A psychological study of the English schoolboy. Methuen. @ **74**

HUFFAKER. (1931) Cited in C.L. Bane, The Lecture in College Teaching. Badger. @ **276**

HUSBAND, R.W. (1940) Cooperative versus solitary problem solution. Journal of Social Psychology, vol.11, pp.405– 409 @ **12**

HUSBAND, R.W. (1951) A statistical comparison of the efficiency of large lecture versus smaller recitation sections upon achievement in general psychology. Journal of Psychology, vol.31, pp.297–300. @ **270**

ITSKOWITZ, R., ALON,M. and STRAUSS, H. (1989) Increasing sensitivity in teachers toward pupils' behavior by means of structured sensitivity training. Small Group Behavior, vol.20, pp.302–319. @ **26**

JANIS, I.L. and MANN, L. (1977) Decision Making. Free Press, New York. @ **118**

JANIS, I.L. (1972) Victims of Groupthink. Houghton Mifflin, Boston. **@ 118**

JANIS, I.L. (1982) Groupthink. Houghton Mifflin, Boston. **@ 118**

JENKINS, R.L. (1952) The relative effectiveness of two methods of teaching written and spoken English. Unpublished Doctoral Dissertation, Michigan State University. Reprinted in Dissertation Abstracts, 1952, vol. 12, p.268. **@ 270**

JENSEN, A.R. (1984) Test validity: versus the specificity doctrine. Journal of Social and Biological Structures, vol.7, pp.93–118. **@ 71**

JENSEN, P.H. (1996) The application of Kolb's experiential learning theory in a first semester college accounting course. Dissertation Abstracts International, vol.56-A, no.08, February, p.3201. **@ 273**

JHA, P. N. AND BARAL, J. R. (1973) Relative effectiveness of some group methods in agricultural information communication in Nepal. Indian Journal of Psychology, September, vol.48, no.3, pp.65–74. **@ 271**

JOHNSON, D.M. and SMITH, H.C. (1953) Democratic leadership in the college classroom. Psychological Monographs, vol.67, pp.1–20. (Whole no. 361). **@ 270, 272, 274**

JOHNSON, D.W. and JOHNSON, F.P. (1987) Joining Together: Group theory and group skills (3rd edn). Prentice Hall International Editions. **@ 114, 137, 167–169**

JOHNSON, D.W. (1980) Group processes: influences on student-centred interaction on school outcomes. In J. McMillan, ed. Social Psychology of School Learning. Academic Press, New York. **@ 10**

JOHNSON, D.W. and PANCRAZIO, S.B. (1971) The effectiveness of 3 microteaching environments in preparing undergraduates for student teaching. Paper presented at Annual Meeting of AERA, February, New York. **@ 10**

JOHNSON, S.D. and BECHLER, C. (1998) Examining the relationship between listening effectiveness and leadership emergence: Perceptions, behaviors and recall. Small Group Research, vol.29 (4), pp.452–471. **@ 161**

JOHNSON-LAIRD P.N. and BYRNE, R.M.J. (1991) Deduction. Lawrence Erlbaum Associates. **@ 42**

JOYCE, C.R.B. and WEATHERALL, M. (1957) Controlled experiments in teaching. Lancet, vol.2, pp.402–407. **@ 269**

KAHNEMAN, D. and TVERSKY, A. (1973) The psychology of prediction. Psychological Review. vol.80, pp.237–251. **@ 89**

KAHNEY, H. (1993) Problem Solving: Current issues. Open University Press. **@ 67**

KANEKAR, S. and ROSENBAUM, M.E. (1972) Group performance on multiple-solution task as a function of available time. Psychonomic Science, vol.27, pp.331–332. **@ 11**

KAPLAN, T. (1988) Group field instruction: rationale and practical application. Social Work with Groups, vol.11 (1–2), pp.125–143. **@ 26**

KATZ, N. (1990) Problem solving and time: Functions of learning style and teaching methods, Occupational Therapy Journal of Research, Jul–Aug, vol.10, no.4, pp.221–236. **@ 272, 273**

KEILMAN, P.A. (1971) Effects of presentation modes on paired associate learning of retardates. Psychonomic Science, vol. 24 (2), pp.57–58. **@ 268**

– References –

KELLEY, H.H. and PEPITONE (1952) An evaluation of a college course in Human Relations. Journal of Educational Psychology, vol. 43, pp.193–209. @ **274**

KELLEY, H.H. and THIBAUT, J.W. (1969) Group Problem Solving. In G. Lindzey and E. Aronson, eds. The Handbook of Social Psychology (2nd edn). vol.4, pp.1–101. Addison-Wesley, Reading, Mass. @ **113**

KENDON, A. (1967) Some functions of gaze direction in social interaction. Acta Psychologica, vol.26, pp.22–63. @ **184**

KENT, R.N. and McGRATH, J.E. (1969) Task and group characteristics as factors influencing group performance. Journal of Experimental Social Psychology, vol.5, pp.429–440. @ **146**

KHOINY, F.E. (1996) The effectiveness of problem-based learning in nurse practitioner education. Dissertation Abstracts International, vol.57-A, no.01, July, p.88. @ **272**

KHOURY, R.M. (1985) Norm formation, social conformity, and the confederating function of humour. Social Behaviour and Personality, vol.13 (2), pp.159–165. @ **138**

KIMBLE, C.E. and MUSGROVE, J.I. (1988) Dominance in arguing mixed-sexed dyads. Visual dominance patterns, talking time and speech loudness. Journal of Research in Personality, vol.22, March (1), pp.1–16. @ **201**

KING, A. (1991) Improving lecture comprehension: Effects of a metacognitive strategy. Applied Cognitive Psychology, July–August, vol.5, no.4, pp.331–346. @ **250**

KING, K. (1980) Modeling vs lecture/discussion in training undergraduates as teachers. Perceptual and Motor Skills, vol.51, no.2, October, pp.527–531. @ **26**

KIRBY (1931) Cited in C.L. Bane. The Lecture in College Teaching. Badger. @ **267**

KLEIN, M. A. (1983) An experiential versus a didactic approach to training counselors in interpersonal conflict management: a comparative study. Dissertation Abstracts International, vol.43-A, no.10, April, p.3218. @ **25**

KNIGHT, H.C. (1921) A comparison of the reliability of group and individual judgments. Unpublished Master's thesis, Columbia University. Cited in Shaw (1981). @ **12**

KNOWLES, L. (1974) The traditional and tutorial classrooms compared: Academic performance amongst undergraduate students in basic statistics courses. Journal of Instructional Psychology, vol.1 (4), pp.18–25. @ **270**

KNOWLES, L. (1975) The relationship between academic performance and the tutorial versus traditional teaching modes in evening classes. Journal of Instructional Psychology, vol.3 (1), pp.23–25. @ **268**

KNOWLES, L. (1975) The tutorial and traditional classroom formats: A comparison of background and academic performance variables. Journal of Instructional Psychology, vol.2 (3), pp.37–40. @ **273**

KNOX, A. B. (1986) Helping Adults Learn. Jossey Bass @ **147**

KOHLER, W. (1957) The Mentality of Apes. Penguin. Harmondsworth, Middx. @ **57**

KOTOVSKY, K., HAYES, J.R. and SIMON, H.A. (1985) Why are some problems hard? Evidence from the tower of Hanoi. Cognitive Psychology, vol.l7, pp.248–294. @ **65**

KRINER, R. E. AND VAUGHAN, M. R. (1975) The effects of group size and presentation method on the impact of a drug presentation. HumRRO Technical Report, June, no.75, p.11. @ **274**

KUHN, D., SHAW, V. and FELTON, M. (1997) Effects of dyadic interaction on argumentative reasoning. Cognition and Instruction, vol.15 (3) pp.287–315. @ **201**

KUNKLE-MILLER, C. and BLANE, H.T. (1977–8) A small group approach to youth education about alcohol. Journal of Drug Education, vol.7 (4), pp.381–386. @ **17**

KUSHELL, E. and NEWTON, R. (1986) Gender, leadership style, and subordinate satisfaction: an experiment. Sex Roles, vol.14 (3–4), pp.203–209. @ **146**

LaCOURSIERE, R. (1974) A group method to facilitate learning during the stages of a psychiatric affiliation. International Journal of Group Psychotherapy, vol.24, pp.342–351. @ **167, 169**

LAKIN, M. (1979) Epilogue. Journal of Applied Behavioural Science, vol.15, pp.265–270, 424–427. @ **264**

LAM, Y.J. (1984) Logitudinal relationships of selected course structure, cognitive and affective factors, and classroom behaviours of adult learners. Educational Abstracts Search, vol.9 (3), pp.28–36. @ **272, 276**

LANEY, J.D. (1984) Creative thinking techniques and the writing process. Creative Child and Adult Quarterly, Winter, vol.9 (4), pp.259–264. @ **76**

LANZETTA, J.T. and ROBY, T.B. (1956) Effects of work-group structure and certain task variables on group performance. Journal of Abnormal and Social Psychology, vol.53, pp.307–314. @ **123**

LANZETTA, J.T. and ROBY, T.B. (1957) Group learning and communication as a function of task and structure 'demands'. Journal of Abnormal and Social Psychology, vol.55, pp.121–131. @ **123**

LARKIN, J.H., McDERMOTT, J., SIMON, D.P. and SIMON, H.A. (1980) Expert and novice performance in solving physics problems. Science, vol.208, pp.1335–1342. @ **63**

LATANE, B. and WOLF, S. (1981) The social impact of majorities and minorities. Psychological Review, vol.88, pp.438–453. @ **139**

LAUGHLIN, P.R. and DOHERTY, M.A. (1967) Discussion versus memory in cooperative group concept attainment. Journal of Educational Psychology, vol.58, pp.123–128. @ **11**

LAUGHLIN, P.R., BRANCH, L.G. and JOHNSON, H.H. (1969) Individual versus triadic performance on an undimensional complementary task as a function of initial ability level. Journal of Personality and Social Psychology, vol.12, pp.144–150. @ **149**

LEARY, M.R. and ATHERTON, S.C. (1986) Self-efficacy, social anxiety, and inhibition in interpersonal encounters. Special Issues: Self-efficiency theory in contemporary psychology. Journal of Social and Clinical Psychology, vol.4 (3), pp.256–267. @ **102**

LEAVITT, H. (1951) Some effects of certain communication patterns on group performance. Journal of Abnormal and Social Psychology, vol.46, pp.38–50. @ **186**

LETON, D.A. (1961) An evaluation of course methods in teaching child development. Journal of Educational Research, vol.55, pp.118–122. @ **270, 274**

LEVIN, B.B. (1995) Using the case method in teacher education: The role of discussion and experience in teachers' thinking about cases. Teaching and Teacher Education, vol.11 (1), pp.63–79. @ **273**

LEVINE, J. and BUTLER, J. (1952) Lecture vs. group decision in changing behaviour. Journal of Applied Psychology, vol.36, pp.29–33. @ **19, 274**

LEVINE, J.R. (1990) Using a peer tutor to improve writing in a psychology class: One instructor's experience. Teaching of Psychology, vol.17 (1), pp.57–58. @ **268, 275**

LEWIN, K. (1943) Forces behind food habits and methods of change. Bulletin of the National Research Council, no.108, pp.35–65. Cited in Cohen, A.R. (1964) Attitude Change and Social Influence. Basic Books. @ **18, 274**

LEWIN, K., LIPPITT, R. and WHITE, R.K. (1939) Patterns of aggressive behaviour in experimentally created 'social climates'. Journal of Social Psychology, vol.10, pp.271– 299. @ **161**

LIEBERMAN, M.A. (1986) Change induction in small groups. Annual Review of Psychology, vol.27, pp.217–250. @ **264**

LIFSON, N., REMPLE, P. and JOHNSON, J.A. (1956) A comparison between lecture and conference methods of teaching physiology. Journal of Medical Education, vol.31, pp.376– 382. @ **269**

LIGHT, L.L. and SINGH, A. (1987) Implicit and explicit memory in young and older adults. Journal of Experimental Psychology: Learning, Memory and Cognition, vol.13 (4), pp.531–541. @ **8**

LIPMAN, A. (1968) Building design and social interaction. The Architects Journal, vol.147, pp.23–30. @ **174**

LOCHMAN, J.E. and DODGE, K.A. (1998) Distorted perceptions in dyadic interactions of aggressive and non-aggressive boys: effects of prior expectations, context and boys' age. Development and Psychopathology, vol.10, Summer (3), pp.495, 512. @ **201**

LORGE, I., AIKMAN, L., MOSS, G., SPIEGEL, J. and TUCKMAN, J. (1955) Solutions by teams and by individuals to a field problem at different levels of reality. Journal of Educational Psychology, vol.46, pp.17–24. @ **11**

LOVE, A. and RODERICK, J. (1971) Teacher non-verbal communication: the development and field testing of an awareness unit. Theory into Practice, vol.10, pp.295–299. @ **185**

LUBIN, B. and LUBIN, A.W. (1971) Laboratory training stress compared with college examination stress. Journal of Applied Behavioural Science, vol.7, pp.502–507. @ **24**

LUFT, J. (1984) Group Processes: An introduction to group dynamics (3rd edn). Mayfield Publishing Company. @ **22**

MABRY, E.A. (1985) The effects of gender composition and task structure on small group interaction. Small Group Behaviour, vol.16 (1), pp.75–96. @ **146**

MACKIE, J. B. (1973) Comparison of student satisfaction with educational experiences in two teaching process models. Nursing Research, vol.22, no.3, pp.262–266. @ **276**

MAGIN, D.J. (1982) Collaborative peer learning in the laboratory. Studies in Higher Education, vol.7 (2), pp.105–117. @ **188**

MALONE, R.A. and McLAUGHLIN (1997) The effects of reciprocal peer tutoring with a group contingency on quiz performance in vocabulary with seventh and eighth grade students. Behavioral Interventions, vol.12 (1), pp.27–40. @ **268**

MANN, R. (1959) A review of the relationship between personality and performance in small groups. Psychological Bulletin, vol.56, pp.241–270. @ **148**

MANN, R.D. (1975) Winners, losers and the search for equality in groups. In C.L. Cooper, ed. (1975) Theories of group processes. @ **171**

MANN,L. and JANIS, I.L. (1983) Decisional conflict in organisations. In Tzosvold, D. and Johnson, D., eds. Productive conflict management. Irvington, New York. @ **119**

MANNIX, E.A. and ANNAMI, I. (1993) Group Decision and Negotiation, vol.2 (4), pp.347–362. @ **200**

MANSFIELD, R.S. and BUSSE, T.V. (1981) The Psychology of Creativity and Discovery. @ **74, 77**

MARGULIS, Y.D. (1984) Psychological characteristics of the teaching of group activity: 1. Experimental teaching of group problem solving. Novye Issledovaniya v Psikhologii, vol.30 (1), pp.65–69. @ **10**

MARR, J. N., PLATH, D. W., WAKELEY, J. H., and WILKINS, M. (1960) The contribution of the lecture to college teaching. Journal of Educational Psychology, vol.51, pp.277–284. @ **271**

MARTENS, R. and LANDERS, D.M. (1972) Evaluation potential as a determinant of coaction effects. Journal of Experimental Social Psychology, vol.8, pp.247–259. @ **111**

MARTENSON, D., MYKLEBUST, R. and STALSBERG, H. (1992) Implementing problem based learning within a lecture-dominated curriculum: Results and process. Teaching and Learning in Medicine, vol.4 (4), pp.233–237. @ **270, 275**

MATSUI, T., KAKUYAMA, T. and ONGLATCO, M.U. (1987) Effects of goals and feedback on performance in groups. Journal of Applied Psychology, vol.72 (3), pp.407–415. @ **125**

McCARTHY, W. H. (1970) Improving large audience teaching: the 'programmed' lecture, British Journal of Medical Education, vol.4, no.1, pp.29–31. @ **211**

McDANIEL, M.A. (1986) Encoding difficulty and memory: toward a unifying theory. Journal of Memory and Language, vol.25 (6), pp.645–656. @ **7**

McGUIRE, M. S. (1984) A comparison of three methods to teach medical students sex history taking. Dissertation Abstracts International, vol.44-A, no.09, March, p.2623. @ **26**

McGUIRE, S.Y. (1985) Authoritarian holistic education: Efficient and effective. In SONNIER, I. L. et al, eds (1985) Methods and techniques of holistic education. pp. 133–137. Charles C. Thomas, Publisher. Springfield, IL, USA. @ **72**

McKEACHIE, W.J. (1978) Teaching Tips: a guide book for the beginning college teacher (7th edn). Heath Lexington, Massachusetts. @ **14, 243**

McKEACHIE, W.J. and HILER, W. (1954) The problem oriented approach to teaching psychology. Journal of Educational Psychology, vol.45, pp.224–232. @ **272**

McKEACHIE, W.J. and KULIK, J.A. (1975) Effective college teaching. In Kerlinger, F.N., ed. A Review of Research in Education, vol.3, Peacock, Itasca, Illinois. @ **14**

McLEISH, J. (1968) The Lecture Method, Cambridge Monographs on Teaching Methods, no.1. Cambridge Institute of Education. @ **276**

McLEISH, J. (1970) Students' Attitudes and College Environments. Cambridge Monographs on Teaching Methods, no.3. Cambridge Institute of Education. @ **16, 276**

McPECK, J.E. (1981) Critical Thinking and Education. Martin Robertson, Oxford.

MEDNICK, S.A. (1962). The associative bases of the creative process. Psychological Review, vol.69, pp.220–232. **@ 74**

MEHRABIAN, A. and DIAMOND, S. G. (1971) Effects of furniture arrangement, props and personality on social interaction. Journal of Personality and Social Psychology, vol.20, pp.18–30. **@ 178**

MENDELSOHN, G.A. (1976) Associative and attentional processes in creative performance. Journal of Personality, vol.44, pp.341–369. **@ 74**

METZ, P.A. (1987) The effect of interactive instruction and lectures on the achievements and attitudes of chemistry students. Dissertation Abstracts International, vol.49–A, no.03, p.474. **@ 271, 274, 276**

MICHELINI, R., PASSALACQUA, R. and CUISMANO, J. (1976) Effects of seating arrangement on group participation. Journal of Social Psychology, vol.99, pp.179–186. **@ 176**

MILL, D, GRAY, T. and MANDEL, D.R. (1994) Influence of research methods and statistics on everyday reasoning, critical abilities, and belief in unsubstantiated phenomena. Canadian Journal of Behavioural Science, vol.26 (2), pp.246–258. **@ 273**

MILLETT, G.B. (1969) Comparison of four teacher training procedures in achieving teacher and pupil 'translation' behaviours in secondary school social studies. American Educational Research Association, ERIC ED027256. **@ 273**

MINTZ, N.L. (1956) Effects of aesthetic surrounding: II, Prolonged and repeated experience in a 'beautiful' and 'ugly' room. Journal of Psychology, vol.41, pp.459–466. **@ 177**

MITNICK, L.L. and McGINNIES, E. (1958) Influencing ethnocentism in small discussion groups through a film communication. Journal of Abnormal and Social Psychology, vol.56, pp.82–90. **@ 14–15, 274**

MOHR, P. H. (1996) Cognitive development in college men and women as measured on the Perry scheme when learning and teaching styles are addressed in a chemical engineering curriculum. Dissertation Abstracts International, vol.56-A, no.08, February, p.3020. **@ 272**

MOORE, O.K. and ANDERSON, S.B. (1954) Search behaviour in individual and group problem solving. American Sociological Review, vol.19, pp.702–714. **@ 11**

MOSCOVICI, S. and PERSONNAZ, B. (1986) Studies on latent influence by the spectrometer method: I The impact of psychologization in the case of conversions by a minority or a majority. European Journal of Social Psychology, vol.16 pp.345–360. **@ 139**

MULLEN, B. (1983) Operationalising the effect of the group on the individual: a self-attention perspective. Experimental and Social Psychology. vol.19, pp.295–322. **@ 155**

MYERS, R.K. (1969) Some effects of seating arrangements in counseling. Dissertation Abstracts, University of Florida, Gainesville. **@ 176**

NAOR, M. and MILGRAM, R.M. (1980) Two preservice strategies for preparing regular class teachers for mainstreaming. Exceptional Children, vol.47 (2), pp.126–129. **@ 17**

NELSON-LE GALL, S. and DECOOKE, P.A. (1987) Same-sex and cross-sex help exchanges in the classroom. Journal of Educational Psychology, vol.79 (1), pp.69–71. @ **145**

NEWELL, A. and SIMON, H.A. (1972) Human problem solving. Prentice-Hall, Engelwood Cliffs, New Jersey. @ **68**

NISBETT, R.E. and WILSON, T.D. (1977) Telling more than we know: verbal reports on mental processes. Psychological Review, vol.84, pp.231–259. @ **87**

NUTHALL, G.A. (1968) An experimental comparison of alternative strategies for teaching concepts. American Educational Research Journal, vol.5 (4), pp.561–584.

OAKSFORD, M. and CHATER, N. (1994) A rational analysis of the selection task as optimal data selection. Psychological Review, vol.101, pp.608–631. @ **50**

OSBORN, A.F. (1953) Applied Imagination. Scrivener, New York. @ **78, 219**

OTT, B. A. (1996) The effect of expert-led, reflective discussion on academic achievement among health science students. Dissertation Abstracts International, vol.56-A, no.08, February p.2971. @ **270**

PACE, C.R. (1962) Methods of describing college cultures. Teachers' College Record, vol.63, pp.267–277. @ **178**

PACE, C.R. (1969) CUES Technical Manual (2nd edn). Educational Testing Service, Princeton, New Jersey. @ **178**

PALMER, R.C. and VERNER,C. (1959) A comparison of three instructional techniques. Adult Education, vol.19, pp.232–238. @ **269**

PANCRAZIO, J.J. and CODY, J.J. (1967) A comparison of role-playing and lecture-discussion instructional methods in a beginning course in counseling theory. Counselor Education and Supervision, vol.7 (1), pp.60–65. @ **17**

PARNES, S.J. and MEADOW, A. (1959) Effects of 'brainstorming' instructions on creative problem solving by trained and untrained subjects. Journal of Educational Psychology, vol.50, pp.171–176. @ **219**

PATTERSON, M.L. AND SCHAEFFER, R.E. (1977) Effects of size and sex composition on interaction distance, participation, and satisfaction in small groups. Small Group Behavior., vol 8 (4), Nov., pp.433–442 @ **154**

PATTON, J.A. (1955) A study of the effects of student acceptance of responsibility and motivation on course behaviour. Dissertation Abstracts, vol.15, pp.637–638. @ **270**

PAVITT, C. (1993) What (little) we know about formal group discussion procedures: a review of relevant research. Small Group Research, vol.24 (2), pp.217–235. @ **90**

PEDERSON, C. (1993) Promoting nursing students' positive attitudes toward providing care for suicidal patients. Issues in Mental Health Nursing; Jan–March vol.14, pp.67–84. @ **274, 275**

PELZ, E.B. (1958) Some factors in 'group decision'. In E. Maccoby, T. Newcomb and E. Hartley, eds. Readings in Social Psychology, New York. @ **18, 274**

PENNINGTON, D. HARAVEY, F. and BASS, B. (1958) Some effects of decision and discussion on coalescence, change and effectiveness. Journal of Applied Psychology, vol.42, pp.404–408. @ **19, 274**

PERKINS, H.V. (1950) The effects of climate and curriculum on group learning. Journal of Educational Research, vol.41, pp.269–286. @ **272**

– *References* –

PERLMUTTER, H.V. (1953) Group memory of meaningful material. Journal of Psychology, vol.35, pp.361–370. @ **6**

PERLMUTTER, H.V., and De MONTMOLLIN, G. (1952). Group learning of nonsense syllables. Journal of Abnormal and Social Psychology, vol.47, pp.762–769. @ **5**

PETERSON, A.J. and CLARK, A.W. (1986). Using group decision to reduce adolescent girls' smoking. Psychological Reports. La Trobe University, Melbourne, Australia. vol.58 (1). @ **17**

PETERSON, P.L., JANICKI, T.C. and SWING, S.R. (1980) Aptitude treatment interaction effects of three social studies teaching approaches. American Educational Research Journal, vol.17 (3) pp.339–360. @ **271**

PETTY, R.E. and CACIOPPO, J.T. (1986) The elaboration, likelihood model of persuasion. In Berkowitz, L., ed. Advances in Experimental Social Psychology, pp 123–205. New York Academic Press. @ **97**

PITTS, J.H. (1975) SATChL: An approach to self-awareness. Personnel and Guidance Journal, vol.54, no.3, pp.167– 169. @ **22**

PLASS, H., MICHAEL, J.J. and MICHAEL, W.B. (1974) The factorial validity of the Torrance Tests of Creative Thinking for a sample of 111 sixth-grade children. Educational and Psychological Measurement, vol.34, pp.413–414. @ **74**

POOLE, R. and WADE, B. (1985) Pupils' perceptions of topics in educational broadcasts: A case study. vol.11 (2), pp.119–125. @ **270**

POPPER, K.R. (1968) The Logic of Scientific Discovery. Harper and Row, New York. @ **49**

POULTON, E.C. (1982) Biases in quantitative judgements. Applied Ergonomics, vol.13, pp.31–42. @ **89**

POWELL, C. L. (1987) A comparison of lecture versus discussion method in teaching assertiveness. Dissertation Abstracts International. @ **26**

POWELL, C. L. (1988) A comparison of the lecture versus group discussion method in teaching assertiveness. Dissertation Abstracts International. @ **26**

POWELL, J.P. (1974) Small Group Teaching Methods in Higher Education. vol. 16 (3), pp. 163–171. @ **156**

RAMSDEN, P. (1979). Student learning and perceptions of the academic environment. Higher Education, vol.(8), pp.411– 427. @ **179**

RANDOLPH, W. M. (1993) The effect of cooperative learning on academic achievement in introductory college biology. Dissertation Abstracts International, vol.53-A, no.08, February, p.2756. @ **270**

RAVEN, B.H. and RIETSEMA, J. (1957) The effects of varied clarity of group goal and group path upon the individual and his relation to the group. Human Relations, vol.10, pp.29–44. @ **123**

REEVE, J., COLE, S.G. and OLSON, B. (1986) The zeigarnik effect and intrinsic motivation: are they the same? Motivation and Emotion, vol.10 (3), pp.233–245. @ **110**

REID-SMITH, E.R. (1969) The measurement of level of student satisfaction by means of a course assessment questionnaire. Research in Librarianship, vol.10, no.2, pp. 100–107. @ **16, 276**

REYNOLDS, S.B. and HART, J. (1990) Cognitive mapping and word processing: Aids to story revision. Journal of Experimental Education, vol.58 (4), Summer, pp.273–279 **@ 76**

RICKARD, P.B. (1946) An experimental study of the effectiveness of group discussion in the teaching of factual content. Summaries of Doctoral Dissertations, Northwest Universities, no.14, pp.72–77. **@ 267, 269, 272**

RIGGIO, R.E., WHATLEY, M.A. and NEALE, P. (1994) Effects of student academic ability on cognitive gains using reciprocal peer tutoring. Journal of Social Behavior and Personality, vol.9 (3), pp.529–543. **@ 268**

ROACH, J.C., PAOLUCCI, W.P., MEYERS, H.W. and DUNCAN, D.A. (1983) The comparative effect of peer tutoring in math by and for secondary special needs students. Pointer, vol.27 (4), pp.20–24. **@ 268**

ROBBINS (1931) in C.L. Bane, The Lecture in College Teaching, Badger. **@ 269**

ROBINSON, P. (1995) A comparison of the effect on college students' academic achievement and course satisfaction by three teaching methods: cooperative learning, reciprocal peer tutoring and lecture only, Masters' Abstracts International, vol.33, no.02, April, p.677. **@ 270**

ROE, A. (1963) Psychological approaches in science. In Coler, M.A. and Hughes, H.K., eds. Essays on Creativity in the Sciences. University Press, New York. **@ 77**

ROE, A. (1952) The Making of a Scientist. Dodd Mead, New York. **@ 77**

ROGERS, C.R, (1951) Student-centred Teaching in Client-centred Therapy. Houghton Mifflin, Boston, Constable, London. **@ 69, 244, 257, 262**

ROHRER, J.H. (1957) Large and small sections in college classes. Journal of Higher Education, vol.28, pp.275–279. **@ 269**

ROMANEEVA, M.P., TSKERMAN, G.A. and FOKINA, N.E. (1980) The role of peer cooperation in mental development of elementary school children. Voprosy Psikhologii, Nov–Dec. no.6, pp.109–114. **@ 268**

ROMER, L.T., BUSSE, D.G., FEWELL, R.R. and VADASY, P.F. (1985) The relative effectiveness of special education teachers and peer tutors. Education of the Visually Handicapped, vol.17, no.3, pp.99–115.

RONCELLI, J.M. (1980) An imagery exercise in self-awareness and literary sensitivity. Paper presented at the Annual Meeting of the Central States Speech Association. Chicago, USA. ERIC ED 185623. **@ 22**

ROSENBAUM, M.E. (1986) The repulsion hypothesis: on the development of relationships. Journal of Personality and Social Psychology, vol.51, pp.626–642. **@ 135**

ROSENBERG, L.A. (1961) Group size, prior experience, and conformity. Abnormal and Social Psychology, vol.64, pp.436–437. **@ 155**

ROTHENBERG, A. (1979) The Emerging Goddess: The creative process in art, science and other fields. University of Chicago Press. **@ 79**

RUJA, H, (1954) Outcomes of lecture and discussion procedures in three college courses. Journal of Experimental Education, vol.22, pp.385–394. **@ 25, 269, 271**

RUMAIN, B., CONNELL, J. and BRAINE M.D.S. (1984) Conversational comprehension processes are responsible for reasoning fallacies in children as well as adults: IF is not biconditional. Developmental Psychology, vol.19, pp.471–481. **@ 47**

RUMSEY, M.G. and RUMSEY, J.M. (1977) A case of rape: sentencing judgments of males and females. Psychological Reports, vol.41 (2), pp.459–465. @ 19

RUSCHER, J.B. and HAMMER, E.D. (1994) Revising disrupted impressions through conversation. Journal of Personality and Social Psychology, vol.66 (3), pp.530–541. @ 200

RUSS, R., and GOLD, A. (1975) Task expertise and group communication. Journal of Psychology, vol.91, pp.187–196. @ 148

RUSSO, N.F. (1967) Connotations of seating arrangements. Cornell Journal of Social Relations, vol.2, pp.34–37. Cited by Shaw, M.E. (1981). @ 177

SANSONE, C. (1986) The effects of competence and task on intrinsic interest. Journal of Personality and Social Psychology, vol.51 (5), pp.918–931. @ 110

SAUNDERS, M. et al (1969) Report of the Commission on Teaching in Higher Education. National Union of Students. @ 16, 276

SAUNDERS, W., NIELSON, E., GALL, M. AND SMITH, G. (1975) The effects of variations in microteaching on prospective teachers' acquisition of questioning skills. Journal of Educational Research, vol.69, no.1, September, pp.3–8 @ 26

SAWYER, H. W. AND SAWYER, S. H. (1981) A teacher-parent communication training approach. Exceptional Children, vol.47, no.4, January, pp.305–306   @ 273

SCHACHTER, S. (1951) Deviation rejection and communication. Journal of Abnormal and Social Psychology, vol.46, pp.190–207 @ 136

SCHACHTER, S. ELLLERTSON, N. MCBRIDE, D. and GREGORY, D. (1951) An experimental study of cohesiveness and productivity. Human Relations, vol.4, pp. 229–238. @ 188

SCHACHTER, S., NUTTIN, J., de MONCHAUX, C., MAUCORPS, D.H., OSMER, D., DUIJKER, J., ROMMETVEIT, R. and ISRAEL, J. (1954) Cross-cultural experiments on threat and rejection. Human Relations, vol.7, pp.403–439. @ 138

SCHERMERHORN, S.M., GOLDSCHMID, M.L. and SHORE, B.M (1975) Learning basic principles of probability in student dyads: A cross age comparison. Journal of Educational Psychology, vol.67 (4), pp.551–557. @ 268

SCHLENKER, B.R. and LEARY, M.R. (1985) Social anxiety and communication about the self. Jornal of Language and Social Psychology. Special Issue: Cognition in social interaction: Production principles, vol.4 (3–4), pp.171– 192. @ 110

SCHUTZ, W.C. (1958) FIRO: A three-dimensional theory of interpersonal behaviour. Rinehart, New York. @ 141

SCRIVEN, M. (1976) Reasoning. McGraw-Hill. New York. @ 256, 261

SELF, D. J., WOLINSKY, F. D. AND BALDWIN, DE W. C. (1989) The effect of teaching medical ethics on medical students' moral reasoning. Special Issue: Teaching medical ethics. Academic Medicine, December, vol.64, no.12, pp.755–759. @ 272

SHAW, M.E. (1954) Group structure and the behaviour of individuals in small groups. Journal of Psychology, vol.38, pp.139–149. @ 124

SHAW, M.E. (1954) Some effects of problem complexity upon problem solution efficiency in different communication nets. Journal of Experimental Psychology, vol.48, pp.211–217. @ 124

SHAW, M.E. (1954) Some effects of unequal distribution of information upon group performance and various communication nets. Journal of Abnormal and Social Psychology, vol.49, pp.547–553.

SHAW, M.E. (1981) Group dynamics: the psychology of small group behaviour. McGraw-Hill, New York. @ **13, 143, 144, 187**

SHAW, M.E. and BRISCOE, M.E. (1966) Group size and effectiveness in solving tasks varying in degree of cooperation requirements. @ **124**

SHAW, M.E., ROTHSCHILD, G.H., and STRICKLAND, J.F. (1957) Decision processes in communication nets. Journal of Abnormal and Social Psychology, vol.54, pp.323–330. @ **137**

SHAW, Marjorie E. (1932). A comparison of individuals and small groups in the rational solution of complex problems. American Journal of Psychology, vol.44, pp.491–504. @ **10**

SHERIF, M. and SHERIF, C.W. (1956) An outline of social psychology (Revised edn). Harper and Row, New York. @ **137**

SHERIF, M. and SHERIF, C.W. (1967) Attitude as the individual's own categories: the social judgement-involvement approach to attitude and attitude change, in Sherif C.W. and Sherif M. Attitude, ego-involvement and change. Reprinted in Warren N. and Jahoda M., eds. (1973) Attitudes. Penguin Modern Psychology Readings. @ **97**

SHESTOWSKY, D., WEGENER, D.T. and FABRIGAR, L.R. (1998) Need for cognition and interpersonal influence: Individual differences in impact on dyadic decisions. Journal of Personality and Social Psychology, vol.74 (5), pp.1317–1328. @ **201**

SIAU, K.L. (1995) Group creativity and technology. Journal of Creative Behavior, vol.29 (3), pp.201–216 @ **77**

SILVERSTEIN, C.H. and STANG, D.J. (1976) Seating position and interaction in triads: a field study. Sociometry, vol.39, pp.166–170. @ **176**

SIMON, D.P. and SIMON, H.A. (1978) Individual differences in solving physics problems. In Siegler, R.S., ed. Childrens' Thinking: What Develops? Erlbaum, Hillsdale, New Jersey, pp.325–348.

SKON, L., JOHNSON, D.W. and JOHNSON, R.T. (1981) Co-operative peer interaction versus individual competition and individualistic efforts: Effects on the acquisition of cognitive reasoning strategies. Journal of Educational Psychology, vol.73, pp.83–92. @ **11**

SMITH, D. L. (1995) The effects of cooperative learning in a short-term, intensive, adult, religious education seminar. Dissertation Abstracts International, vol.56-A, no.07, January, p.2549. @ **270, 271, 272, 275**

SMITH, E.R. and MILLER, R.S. (1978) Limits on perception or cognitive processes: a reply to Nisbett and Wilson. Psychological Review, vol.85, pp.355–362. @ **87**

SMITH, H.C. (1955) Team work in the college class. Journal of Educational Psychology, vol.46, pp.274–286. @ **268**

SMITH, J.P. (1954) A study of outcomes of instruction in a psychology class with specific reference to two teaching methods. Doctoral Dissertation, Ohio State University. @ **269**

SMITH, K., JOHNSON., D.W. and JOHNSON, R.T. (1982) Effects of co-operative and individualistic instruction on the achievement of handicapped, regular, and gifted students. Journal of Social Psychology, vol.116, pp.277–283. **@ 4**

SMITH, P.B. (1975) Controlled studies of the outcome of sensitivity training. Psychological Bulletin, vol.82, pp.597–622. **@ 23, 264**

SMITH, S.M. (1985) Effects of number of study environments and learning instructions on free-recall clustering and accuracy. Bulletin of the Psychonomic Society, vol.23 (6), pp.440–442. **@ 178**

SMITHERS, A. and GRIFFIN, A. (1986) Mature students at university: entry, experience and outcomes. Studies in Higher Education, vol.11 (3), pp.258–268. **@ 146**

SMYTH, M.M., COLLINS, A.F., MORRIS, P.E. and LEVY, P. (1994) Cognition in Action (2nd edn). Lawrence Erlbaum Associates. **@ 70**

SOMMER, R. (1969) Personal Space: The behavioural basis of design. Prentice-Hall, Englewood Cliffs, New Jersey. **@ 173–177**

SPENCE, R. B., and WATSON, G. B. (1928) Lecture and class discussion in teaching educational psychology, Journal of Educational Psychology, vol.19, pp.454–462. **@ 271**

SPENCE, R.B. (1928) Lecture and class discussion in teaching educational psychology. Journal of Educational Psychology, vol.19, pp.454–462. **@ 269**

SPITZ, H. and SADOCK, B.J. (1973) Small interactional groups in the psychiatric training of graduate nursing students. Journal of Nursing Education, vol.12, pp.6–13. **@ 169**

STAGER, P. (1967) Conceptual level as a composition variable in small-group decision making. Journal of Personality and Social Psychology, vol.5, pp.152–161. **@ 150**

STASSER, G. and TAYLOR, L.A. (1991) Speaking turns in face to face discussion. Journal of Personality and Social Psychology, vol.60 (5), pp.675–684. **@ 187**

STEINER, I.D. (1972) Group Process and Productivity. Academic Press, New York. **@ 120, 127–131**

STEINZOR, B. (1950) The spatial factor in face-to-face discussion groups. Journal of Abnormal and Social Psychology, vol.45, pp.552–555. **@ 176, 177, 251**

STEITZ, J.A. (1985) Issues of adult development within the academic environment. Lifelong Learning, April, pp.15–18, 27–28. **@ 147**

STENHOUSE, L. (1979) Curriculum Research and Development in Action. Heinemann Educational, London. **@ 120**

STERN, G.G. (1963) Characteristics of the intellectual climate in the college environment. Harvard Educational Review, vol.33, pp.5–41. **@ 179**

STERNBERG, R.J. (1985) Beyond I.Q.: A triarchic theory of human intelligence. Cambridge University Press. **@ 79**

STIFF, J.B. (1986) Cognitive processing of persuasive message cues: A meta-analytic review of the effects of supporting information on attitudes. Communication Monographs, vol.53 (1), pp.75–89. **@ 19**

STOGDILL, R. (1974) Handbook of Leadership. Free Press, New York. **@ 160, 161**

STONE, D.L. (1997) A comparative study of two art museum tours and their impact on adult learning. Visual Arts Research, vol.23 (1), pp.142–150. **@ 268, 270**

STONES, E. (1970) Students' attitudes to the size of teaching groups. Educational Review, vol. 21, no.2, pp.98–108. **@ 16, 276**

STRODTBECK, F.L. and HOOK. L.H. (1961). The social dimensions of a twelve-man jury table. Sociometry, vol.24, pp.397–415. @ **176, 177**

SUBOTNIK, R.F. (1984) Emphasis on the creative dimension: Social Studies curriculum modifications for gifted intermediate and secondary students. Roeper Review, Sep., vol.7 (1), pp.7–10 @ **76**

TAIT, A. N. (1993) A comparison of didactic and modeling instruction in grief intervention skills training (didactic instruction, death education). Dissertation Abstracts International, vol.53-B, no.11, May, p.6000. @ **26**

TALBERT, E. E., WILDEMANN, D. G., ERICKSON, M. T. (1975) Teaching nonprofessionals three techniques to modify children's behavior. Psychological Reports, vol.37, no.3, pt.2, December, pp.1243–1252. @ **26**

TANS, R.W., SCHMIDT, H.G., SCHADE-HOOGEVEEN, B.E. and GIJSELAERS, W.H. (1986) Problem based learning: A field experiment. Tijdschrift voor Onderwijsresearch, vol.11 (1), pp.35–46. @ **271**

TAYLOR, D.W. and FAUST, W.L. (1952) Twenty questions: Efficiency in problem solving as a function of size of group. Journal of Extenal Psychology, vol.44, pp. 360–368. @ **12**

TAYLOR, R.B. and LANNI, J.C. (1981) Territorial dominance: The influence of the resident advantage in triadic decision making. Journal of Personality and Social Psychology, vol.41, pp.909–915. @ **174**

TEEVAN, K. G. AND GABEL, H. (1978) Evaluation of modeling role playing and lecture-discussion training techniques for college student mental health professionals. Journal of Counseling Psychology, vol.25, no.2, March, pp.169–171. @ **26**

THOMPSON, D.G., JOLLY, B., MACDONALD, M.M., COOKSON, J. et al (1987) Students' approaches and attitudes to solving computer presented problems. Journal of Computer Assisted Learning, vol.3 (4), pp. 240–249. @ **272**

THORNDIKE, R.L (1938) On what type of task will a group do well? Journal of Abnormal and Social Psychology, vol. 33, pp.408–412. @ **12**

TILLMAN, B. A. (1993) A study of the use of case methods in preservice teacher education. Dissertation Abstracts International, vol.53-A, no.11, May, p.3877. @ **270, 272**

TIMMEL, G. B. (1954) A study of the relationship between methods of teaching a college course in mental hygiene and changes in student adjustment status, Doctoral Dissertation, Cornell University. Reprinted in Dissertation Abstracts, vol.15, no.90. @ **25**

TOBIAS, S. (1985) Test anxiety: interference, defective skills, and cognitive capacity. Educational Psychologist, vol.20 (3), pp.135–142. @ **111**

TOMM, K. AND LEAHEY, M. (1980) Training in family assessment: a comparison of three teaching methods. Journal of Marital and Family Therapy, vol.6, no.4, pp.453–458. @ **26**

TORRANCE E.P. (1966). The Torrance tests on creativity: norms (technical manual). @ **71**

TORRANCE, E.P. (1972a) Career plans and peek creative achievements of creative high school students 12 years later. Gifted Child Quarterly, vol.16, pp.75–88. @ **71, 74**

TORRANCE, E.P. (1972b) Predictive validity of the Torrance Tests of Creative Thinking.

Journal of Creative Behavior, vol.6, pp.236–252. Cited in R.J. Sternberg and E.E. Smith. (1988). The Psychology of Human Thought. **@ 71**

TORRANCE, E.P. (1981) Predicting the creativity of elementary school children (1958–80). The teacher who 'made a difference'. Gifted Child Quarterly, Cited in Sternberg, R.J. and Smith, E.E., eds (1988). The Psychology of Human Thought, vol. 25, pp. 55–62. **@ 71, 74**

TOULMIN, S., RIEKE, R. and JANIK, A. (1979) An Introduction to Reasoning. MacMillan, New York. **@ 42–46**

TRIANDIS, H., BASS, A., EWEN, R. and NIEKSELE, E. (1963) Teaching creativity as a function of the creativity of the members. Journal of Applied Psychology, vol.47, pp. 104–110. **@ 150**

TRIANDIS, H.E., HALL, E.R. and EWEN, R.B. (1965) Member heterogeneity and dyadic creativity. Human Relations, vol.18, pp.33–55. **@ 148**

TRIPATHI, K.N. and AGARWAL, A. (1985) Effects of verbal and tangible rewards on intrinsic motivation in males and females. Psychological Studies, vol.30 (2), pp.77–84. **@ 111**

TUCKMAN, B.W. (1965) Developmental sequence in small groups. Psychological Bulletin, vol.63, pp.384–399. **@ 167, 172**

TUCKMAN, B.W. and JENSEN, N.A.C. (1977) Stages in small group development revisited. Group and Organisational Studies, vol2, pp.419–427. **@ 171**

TUCKMAN, J. and LORGE, I. (1962) Individual ability as a determinant of group superiority. Human Relations, vol.15, pp.45–51. **@ 11**

TVERSKY, A. and KAHNEMAN, D. (1973) Availability: A heuristic for judging frequency and probability. Cognitive Psychology, vol.5, pp.207–23. **@ 88**

TVERSKY, A. and KAHNEMAN, D. (1974) Judgement under uncertainty: heuristics and biases. Science, vol.185, pp.1124–1131. **@ 52**

TVERSKY, A. and KAHNEMAN, D. (1980) Causal schemas in judgements under uncertainty. In Fishbein, M., ed. Progress in Social Psychology. Lawrence Erlbaum Associates. @ 51

TZINER, A. (1982) Differential effects of group cohesiveness types: a clarifying overview. Social Behaviour and Personality, vol.10, pp. 227–239. **@ 188**

VAN DAM, G., BRINKERINK-CARLIER, M. and KOK, I. (1985) The influence of embellishment and prequestions on free recall of a text. Journal of General Psychology, vol.112 (2), pp.211–219. **@ 7**

VAN REETH, P.CH and SOURIS, M. (1972–3) Sensitization of medical students to medical psychology. Psychotherapy and Psychosomatics, vol.21, nos.1–6, pp.222–226. **@ 17**

WALKER, C. A. (1986) Effects of the lecture teaching method and discussion teaching method on the reading success and attitudes of bright learning disabled adolescents (secondary). Dissertation Abstracts International, vol.47-A, no.04, p.1286. **@ 267, 271**

WALKER, K. B. (1985) The comparison of three instructional techniques for teaching interaction management skills and rhetorical sensitivity (modeling, T-groups, lecture-discussion). Dissertation Abstracts International, vol.45-A, no.08, February, p.2304. **@ 26**

WALLACH, M.A. (1976) Tests tell us little about talent. American Scientist, vol.64, pp.57–63. **@ 74**

WALLACH, M.A. and KOGAN, N. (1965a) The roles of information, discussion and consensus in group risk taking. Journal of Experimental Social Psychology, vol.1, pp.1–19 **@ 88**

WALLACH, M.A. and KOGAN, N. (1965b) Modes of Thinking in Young Children. Holt, Rinehart and Winston, New York. **@ 74**

WALLACH, M.A. (1970) Creativity. In Mussen, P.H., ed. Carmichael's Manual of Child Psychology. Wiley, New York, vol.1, pp.1211–1266. **@ 74**

WALLACH, M.A., KOGAN, N. and BEM, D.J. (1962) Group influence on individual risk taking. Journal of Abnormal and Social Psychology, vol.65, pp.75–86. **@ 87**

WALTON, H.J. (1968) An experimental study of different methods for teaching medical students. Proceedings of the Royal Society of Medicine, Feb., vol.61, no.2, pp.109–112. **@ 274, 276**

WANG, Z. (1985) Memory and Stress. Information on Psychological Sciences, no.2 pp.38–33. **@ 110, 111**

WANLASS, R. L. (1983) Sex education: A comparison of instruction formats. Dissertation Abstracts International, vol.43–B, no.07, January, p.2363. **@ 25**

WANLASS, R. L., KILMANN, P. R., BELLA, B. S. AND TARNOWSKI, K. J. (1983) Effects of sex education on sexual guilt, anxiety, and attitudes: A comparison of instruction formats. Archives of Sexual Behavior, December, vol.12, no.6, pp.487–502. **@ 274, 275**

WARD, J.M. (1956) Group-study versus lecture-demonstration method in physical science instruction for general education students. Journal of Experimental Education, vol.24, pp.199–210. **@ 268, 269, 271, 272**

WARREN, T.F. and DAVIS, G.A. (1969) Techniques for creative thinking: an empirical comparison of three methods. Psychological Reports, vol25, pp.207–214. **@ 76, 78**

WASON, P.E (1966) Reasoning. In Foss, B.M. ed. New Horizons in Psychology. Penguin. Harmondsworth. **@ 49, 50**

WATSON, C. E. (1975) The case study method and learning effectiveness. College Student Journal, April–May, vol.9, no.2, pp.109–116. **@ 270, 272**

WATSON, G. and JOHNSON, D.W. (1972) Social Psychology: Issues and Insights (2nd edn). Lippincott, Philadelphia. **@ 10**

WATTS, P.R. (1977) Comparison of three human sexuality teaching methods used in university health classes. Research Quarterly, vol.48 (1), pp.187–190. **@ 270**

WEBB, C. and BAIRD, J.B. (1968) Learning differences resulting from teacher- and student-centred teaching methods. Journal of Higher Education, vol.39 (8), pp.456–460. **@ 268**

WEBB, N.M. (1980a) Group process: The key to learning in groups. New Directions for Methodology of Social and Behavioural Science, vol.6, pp.77–87. **@ 126**

WEBB, N.M. (1980b) A process-outcome analysis of learning in group and individual settings. Educational Psychologist, vol.15, pp.69–83. **@ 126**

WEST, C. and GARCIA, A. (1988) Conversational shift work: A study of topical transitions between men and women, vol.35 (5), pp.551–575. **@ 201**

– References –

WHITE, S.B., VALLEY, K.L., BAZERMAN,M.H., NEALE, M.A., et al (1994) Alternative models of price behavior in dyadic negotiations: Market prices, reservation prices, and negotiator aspirations. Organizational Behavior and Human Decision Processes, vol.57 (3), March, pp.430–447. @ 200

WHITEHURST, G.J. (1972) Academic responses and attitudes engendered by a programmed course in child development. Journal of Applied Behavior Analysis, vol.5 (3), pp.283–291. @ 268, 270

WHYTE, W.F. (1949) The social structure of the restaurant. American Journal of Sociology, vol.54, pp.302–308. @ 174

WICKER, A.W. (1969) Attitudes v. actions: The relationship between verbal and overt responses to attitude objects. Journal of Social Issues, vol.25, pp.41–78. Reprinted in Warren N. and Jahoda M., eds. (1973) Attitudes. Penguin Modern Psychology Readings. @ 97

WIEDER, G.S. (1954) Group procedures modifying attitudes of prejudice in the college classroom. Journal of Educational Psychology, vol.45, pp.332–344. @ 25, 270

WILLIAMS, J.M., HADDEN, K. and MARCAVAGE, E. (1983) Experimental study of assertion training as a drug prevention strategy for use with college students. Journal of College Student Personnel, vol. 24 (3), pp. 201–206. @ 26

WILLIAMS, R.H., STOCKMYER, J., WILLIAMS, S.A. (1984) The left and right of creativity: A cognitive (hemispheric co-operation) based program for teaching creative thinking. Creative Child and Adult Quarterly, 1984, Sum., vol.9 (2), pp.69–81   @ 72

WILLIAMS, S. and HALGIN, R.P. (1995) Issues in psychotherapy supervision between a white supervisor and black supervisee. Clinical Supervisor, vol.13 (1), pp.39–61. @ 201

WILLIS, J. and GUELDENPFENNING, J. (1981) The relative effectiveness of lecturing, modeling, and role playing in training paraprofessional reading tutors. Psychology in the Schools, vol.18, no.3, July, pp.323–329. @ 26

WINTELER, A. (1974) Factors in the effectiveness of the organization of academic learning. Psychologia Universalis, vol.30, pp.1–180. @ 275, 276

WOLFE, D.E. (1970) A study to determine the feasibility of including the direct experiences of microteaching and team teaching and interaction analysis training in the pre-service training of foreign language teachers. PhD thesis, Ohio State University. @ 138

WOOD, W. (1987) Meta-analytic review of sex differences in group performance. Psychology Bulletin, vol.102 (1), pp.53–71. @ 145

WRIGHT, R.A. (1986) Attitude change as a function of threat to attitudinal freedom and extent of agreement with a communicator. European Journal of Social Psychology, vol.16 (1), pp.43–50. @ 19

WYER, R.S. and MALINOWSKI, C. (1972) Effects of sex and achievement level upon individualism and competitiveness in social interaction. Journal of Experimental Social Psychology, vol.8, pp.303–314. @ 146

YAGER, S., JOHNSON, D. W., JOHNSON, R. T. (1985) Journal of Educational Psychology, Feb., vol.77(1), pp.60–66 @ 4

YALOM. I D, (1975) The Theory and Practice of Group Psychotherapy (2nd edn). Basic Books, New York. **@ 171**

YAMAMOTO, K. (1965) Effects of restriction of range and test unreliability on correlation between measures of intelligence and creative thinking. British Journal of Educational Psychology, vol.35, pp.300–305. **@ 71**

YORDE, B. S. AND WITMER, J. M. (1988) An educational format for teaching stress management to groups with a wide range of stress symptoms. Biofeedback and Self Regulation, vol.5, no.1, March, pp.75–90 **@ 25**

YUKER, H.E. (1955) Group atmosphere and memory. Journal of Abnormal and Social Psychology, vol.51, pp.17–23. **@ 6**

ZAJONC, R.B. (1960) The process of cognitive tuning in communication. Journal of Abnormal and Social Psychology, vol.61, pp.159–167. **@ 182**

ZAJONC, R.B. (1965) The requirements and design of a standard group task. Journal of Experimental and Social Psychology, vol.1, pp.71–88. **@ 113**

ZANDER, A. (1982) Making Groups Effective. Jossey-Bass. **@ 126, 187**

ZANDER, A. (1980) The origins and consequences of group goals. In L. Festinger, ed., Retrospections on Social Psychology. Oxford University Press, New York. **@ 125**

ZIMET, C.N. and SCHNEIDER, C. (1969) The effects of group size on interaction in small groups. Journal of Social Psychology, vol.77, no.2, pp.77–187 **@ 154**

ZIMMER, J.W. (1985) Text structure and retention of prose. Journal of Experimental Education, vol.53 (4), pp.230–233. **@ 7**

ZIMMER, J.W., WILSON, E.D. and BRUNING, R.H. (1974) Proctor-led discussion groups: A further look. Journal of Educational Research, vol.67 (8), pp.378–381. **@ 268, 273**

ZIOLKOWSKA, R E. (1977) Development of active thinking in children aged 10 to 12. Psychologia-Wychowawcza, vol.20 (1), Jan–Feb, pp.1–15. **@ 72**

ZURCHER, L.A. Jr. (1969) Stages of development in poverty programme neighbourhood committees. Journal of Applied Behavioural Science, vol.5, pp.223–251. **@ 167, 169**

Subject Index

Authors are indexed within the References.
Bold numbers below indicate key pages.

intellect BOOKS

EDUCATION SERIES

Seven Decisions when Teaching Students	Donald Bligh, David Jaques and David Warren Piper
What's the Use of Lectures?	Donald Bligh
Understanding Higher Education	Donald Bligh, Harold Thomas and Ian McNay
What's the Point in Discussion?	Donald Bligh
Personal Transferable Skills	Ray McAleese
Communication Skills	Richard Ellis

Selected Titles on Education Technology

Evaluation of CALL Programs	Keith Cameron (ed.)
Computers and English Language Learning	John Higgins
Learning With Computers	Robert Lawler
IT for Learning Enhancement	Moira Monteith
The Virtual Classroom	Starr Roxanne Hiltz
Computers for Educational Administrators	Greg Kearsley

Visit www.intellectbooks.com